Music as Discourse

OXFORD STUDIES IN MUSIC THEORY

Series Editor Rick Cohn

Music as Discourse

Semiotic Adventures in Romantic Music

KOFI AGAWU

OXFORD
UNIVERSITY PRESS

2009

OXFORD
UNIVERSITY PRESS

Oxford University Press, Inc., publishes works that further
Oxford University's objective of excellence
in research, scholarship, and education.

Oxford   New York
Auckland   Cape Town   Dar es Salaam   Hong Kong   Karachi
Kuala Lumpur   Madrid   Melbourne   Mexico City   Nairobi
New Delhi   Shanghai   Taipei   Toronto

With offices in
Argentina   Austria   Brazil   Chile   Czech Republic   France   Greece
Guatemala   Hungary   Italy   Japan   Poland   Portugal   Singapore
South Korea   Switzerland   Thailand   Turkey   Ukraine   Vietnam

Copyright © 2009 by Oxford University Press, Inc.

Published by Oxford University Press, Inc.
198 Madison Avenue, New York, New York 10016

www.oup.com

Oxford is a registered trademark of Oxford University Press

Library of Congress Cataloging-in-Publication Data
Agawu, V. Kofi (Victor Kofi)
Music as discourse / Kofi Agawu.
    p.   cm.
Includes bibliographical references and index.
ISBN 978-0-19-537024-9
1. Musical analysis.   2. Music—Philosophy and aesthetics.   I. Title.
MT6.A286 2008
781.1'7—dc22   2007052831

9   8   7   6   5   4   3   2   1

Printed in the United States of America
on acid-free paper

PREFACE

Acknowledgments

I am grateful to Dániel Péter Biró for comments on a draft of this book, Christopher Matthay for corrections and numerous helpful suggestions, Guillermo Brachetta for preparing the music examples, and Suzanne Ryan for advice on content and organization. It goes without saying that I alone am responsible for what is printed here.

Some of this material has been seen in other contexts. The comparison between music and language in chapter 1 is drawn from my article "The Challenge of Semiotics," which is included in the collection *Rethinking Music*, edited by Nicholas Cook and Mark Everist (Oxford University Press, 1999). The analysis of Beethoven's op. 18, no. 3, in chapter 5 appears in expanded form in *Communication in Eighteenth-Century Music*, edited by Danuta Mirka and myself (Cambridge University Press, 2008). The analysis of the slow movement of Mozart's Piano Sonata in A Minor, K. 310, originated in a paper presented to a plenary session at the Society for Music Theory's 2006 annual meeting in Los Angeles. And some of the material in chapter 4, "Bridges to Free Composition," began life as a keynote address delivered to the International Conference on 19th-Century Music in Manchester, England, in 2005. I'm grateful for this opportunity to recontextualize these writings and talks.

A Note to the Student

This book is aimed at advanced undergraduates and beginning graduate students who are interested in the practice of music analysis. A basic background in harmony and counterpoint is assumed. While it is not designed as a conventional textbook (complete with a didactic exposition of received knowledge, canonical examples, and graded exercises), this book is nevertheless meant to elicit reciprocal acts of analysis. You might, for example, examine the pattern of closure in one of Mendelssohn's "Songs without Words," the high-point scheme in Wagner or Bartók, periodicity in a slow movement by Mahler or in songs by Schubert or Schumann, the paradigmatic structure of a Chopin prelude or a string quartet movement by Beethoven, the narrative impulse in a tone poem by Liszt, or even antinarrative tendency in Stravinsky. For such exercises, you will find several leads in this book. In place of models to be emulated directly or mechanically, I offer suggestions and (deliberately) partial readings designed to stimulate your own fantasies.

Reading a book on music analysis is not exactly like reading a novel. You will need access to several scores and parallel recordings and a keyboard to try out certain imagined patterns. For the shorter analyses in part I (chapters 3 and 5), you will need, among others, scores of Schubert's "Im Dorfe" from *Die Winterreise*, Schumann's "Ich grolle nicht" from *Dichterliebe*, the C-major Prelude from Book 1 of J. S. Bach's *The Well-Tempered Clavier*, the slow movement of Mozart's Piano Sonata in A minor K. 310, Brahms' song "Die Mainacht," and the first movement of Beethoven's String Quartet in D major, op. 18, no. 3. For the longer analyses in part II (chapters 6 through 9), you will need scores of Liszt's *Orpheus*; Brahms' First Symphony (second movement); his Intermezzo in E Minor, op. 119, no. 2; Mahler's Ninth Symphony (first movement); Beethoven's String Quartet op. 130 (first movement); and Stravinsky's *Symphonies of Wind Instruments* (1920, though my analysis will use the 1947 version). Because the analyses constantly refer to places in the score, it would be almost pointless to attempt to read these chapters without the relevant scores at hand.

CONTENTS

Music as Discourse

Introduction

This book is an exercise in music analysis. I explore the nature of musical mean-ing from within the disciplinary perspective of music theory and propose a view of music as discourse. I do not claim to offer a new theory of meaning; rather, drawing on a handful of existing analytical theories and adding some insights of my own, I seek to illuminate core aspects of a small group of well-known compo-sitions chosen from the vast repertoires produced in nineteenth- and early twen-tieth-century Western Europe. Beethoven, Schubert, Mendelssohn, Schumann, Liszt, Brahms, Mahler, Strauss, Bartók, and Stravinsky—household names for afi-cionados of European classical music—are among the composers whose works I discuss; theoretically, I draw on Schenker, Ratner, Adorno, and the general field of musical semiotics. My perspective is resolutely that of the listener, not a "mere" listener but one for whom acts of composing and performing, be they real or imag-ined, necessarily inform engaged listening. I'd like to think that my ultimate com-mitments are to the compositions themselves rather than to theories about them, but the distinction is fragile and should not be made dogmatically or piously. The book is aimed at those who are fascinated by the inner workings of music and enjoy taking individual compositions apart and speculating on how (or, occasion-ally, whether) they cohere.[1]

Does music have meaning? This question has been debated ever since music became a subject of discourse. Aestheticians, philosophers, historians, semioti-cians, and sociologists of music have had their say; in our own day, musicolo-gists of a certain persuasion have been exercised by it. Some think that musical meaning is intrinsic while others argue for extrinsic meanings. Some believe that music is autonomous or relatively autonomous while others insist on permanent

---

1. In the terms of an ancient classification scheme, the discipline represented in this book is *musica theorica* (theoretical speculation) as distinct from *musica poetica* (composition) or *musica practica* (performance). These spheres are only notionally distinct, however; in analytical practice, they over-lap and inform each other in significant and productive ways. See Manfred Bukofzer, *Music in the Baroque Era, from Monteverdi to Bach* (New York: Norton, 1947), 370–371.

social or historical traces on all musical products. Some are surprised to find that the associations they prefer to make while listening to masterworks—associations that seem self-evident to them—are not necessarily shared by others: heroism or aggressiveness in Beethoven, domination in Wagner, ambivalence in Tchaikovsky, or femininity and worldliness in Schubert. No doubt, these debates will continue into the future. And this is as it should be, for as long as music is made, as long as it retains its essence as a performed art, its significance is unlikely to ever crystallize into a stable set of meanings that can be frozen, packaged, and preserved for later generations. Indeed, it would be a profoundly sad occasion if our ideologies became aligned in such a way that they produced identical narratives about musical works. One mark of the endurance of strong works of art is that they make possible a diversity of responses—a diversity regulated by a few shared (social or institutional) values.

Meanings are contingent. They emerge at the site of performance and are constituted critically by historically informed individuals in specific cultural situations. Basic questions about music's ontology have never received definitive answers. What music is, what and how it means, what meaning is, and why we are interested in musical meaning in the first place: these questions are not meant to be answered definitively nor with a commanding transhistorical attribution but posed periodically to keep us alert and honest. Then there are those considerations that arise when history, culture, and convention inflect the search for meaning—whether a work embodies a late style, conveys subjectivity, or reproduces the dynamics of the society in which the composer lived. While interpretation can be framed dialogically to ensure that original meanings and subsequent accretions are neither ignored nor left uninterrogated, the final authority for any interpretation rests on present understanding. Today's listener rules.

The issues raised by musical meaning are complex and best approached within carefully circumscribed contexts. For although no one doubts that music making is or can be meaningful and satisfying, or that the resultant processes and products have significance for those involved, be they composers, performers, or listeners, the nonverbal essence of music has proved resistant to facile domestication within a verbal economy. My own curiosity about the subject stems in part from an early interest in the confluence of composition, performance, and analysis and from a sociological circumstance: but for a handful of exceptions, card-carrying music theorists have been generally reticent about confronting the subject of musical meaning.[2] This does not mean that ideas of meaning do not surface in their work from time to time, nor that, in producing voice-leading graphs, metric reductions, paradigmatic charts, set-class taxonomies, and Tonnetz

2. Significant exceptions include Nicholas Cook, *Analysing Musical Multimedia* (Oxford: Oxford University Press, 2001); Cook, "Review Essay: Putting the Meaning Back into Music; or, Semiotics Revisited," *Music Theory Spectrum* 18 (1996): 106–123; Robert Hatten, *Musical Meaning in Beethoven: Markedness, Correlation, and Interpretation* (Bloomington: Indiana University Press, 1994); Michael L. Klein, *Intertextuality in Western Art Music* (Bloomington: Indiana University Press, 2005); and the collection of essays in *Approaches to Meaning in Music*, ed. Byron Almen and Edward Pearsall (Bloomington: Indiana University Press, 2006).

trajectories, they are unaware of questions of meaning. On the contrary, all analysts, including those who reduce the musical phenomenon to numbers or abstract symbols, normally rely on a certain constellation of views about meaning in order to perform a close reading. Whether it is the analytical essays gathered in Schenker's *Tonwille*, the disquisitions on structure produced by David Lewin in *Musical Form and Transformation*, the insights into form, periodicity, and topical structure offered by Ratner in *The Beethoven String Quartets: Compositional Strategies and Rhetoric*, or the demonstrations of rhythmic life by Fred Lerdahl and Ray Jackendoff in *A Generative Theory of Tonal Music*, a fully recoverable theory of meaning exists in each work. Among the factors that might have forced such views to remain implicit rather than explicit are crass scholarly conventions and prejudices about soft and hard analysis. Indeed, analysts of a certain generation (and/or institutional provenance) were especially anxious to let it be known that the object of their research was the music itself; unlike music historians and as a matter of principle, they preferred to steer clear of the extraneous and the extramusical.

Since about 1990—which is to say, not so very long ago—it has become unwise, probably for ideological rather than intellectual reasons, for workers in the American academy to retain confidence in the reality of the notion of "the music itself," or to posit a categorical distinction between text and context, between the musical and the extramusical. This problematizing of such binary oppositions was the singular achievement of a larger poststructuralist enterprise whose slate-clearing impulses left a few traces on the discourse of musicology. Arguments against formalism sought to counter the presumed ontology of music theory's objects by insisting that compositions were necessarily marked by a social trace. These arguments would have been more effective if, instead of demanding articles from music theorists affirming faith in entities larger than "the music itself," they had focused on the enabling structures of theoretical work and uncovered theories of meaning that, because they were hidden and implicit, retained considerable motivating power without having to be openly acknowledged. Certainly, the antiformalist strategy that delights in specifying the meanings of compositions has achieved little more than the introduction of a new formalism. The music itself apparently remains a treasured concept even when it is being vigorously attacked.

But what if we conceive of analysis as a mode of performance, or as a mode of composing, not as an unveiling of resident truths, not as an exercise in decoding? What if we think of the truth of a musical work as emerging from doing, from engaging with musical materiality, and not as a summary narrative that is produced after the doing? What if we think of analysis as a means to an unspecified end, a flexibly conceived end that may range from making relatively trivial observations about style and history to the less trivial pleasure of inhabiting the composition's space for prolonged periods and engaging in diverse ways with its elements?

This view of analysis as performance and composition is implicit in the framing of an influential definition of analysis put forward by Ian Bent and Anthony Pople: analysis is "that branch of the study of music that takes the music itself as its starting point rather than external factors."[3] The operative phrase here is not the polemical "the music itself" but "starting point." To proclaim this other contingency is to promote an open-ended view of analysis; it is to encourage rigorous speculation about musical meaning that takes certain core features as its point of departure and that terminates on a path toward an enriched perspective.[4]

However elusive they may be, music's meanings are unlikely to be accessible to those who refuse to engage with the musical code or those who deal with only the most general and superficial aspects of that code. Defining a musical code comprehensively presents its own challenges, but there is by now a body of systematic and historical data to facilitate such a task. The theories of Schenker, for example—to choose one body of texts that is indispensable for work on tonal music—make possible a range of explorations of everything from the imaginative expansion of simple counterpoint in works by Bach, Beethoven, and Schubert through aesthetic speculation about value and ideology in composers of different national provenance to the place of diminution in twentieth-century composers like Richard Strauss, Mahler, and Stravinsky. Adhering to the code would ensure, for example, that harmony is not ignored in the construction of a theory of meaning for Chopin and Wagner, that melody is given due attention in Mendelssohn analysis, and that the rhythmic narratives of Brahms or Stravinsky are duly acknowledged. And in examining these aspects of the code, one is wise to seek the sharpest, most sensitive, and most sophisticated tools. Analysis may bear a complex relationship to technology, but to ignore technological advancement in analytic representation is to subscribe to a form of irrationality, even a form of mysticism, perhaps.

The defensive and at the same time aggressive tone in that last remark is forced upon me by a strange circumstance. Despite the fact that music theory is one of the oldest of humanistic disciplines, and despite the enviably precise vocabulary with which the elements of music have been described and categorized, their essences captured, recent attacks on formalism have sought to belittle this commanding legacy with the claim that theorists do not deal with music's meaning and significance. This extraordinary claim is surprisingly deaf to the numerous meanings enshrined in theory's technical processes and language. True, the meanings of a motivic parallelism, or a middleground arpeggiation, or a modulation to a tritone-related key are not always discussed in affective or expressive terms, but this does not mean that the economy of relations from which they stem is pure, or based solely on abstract, logical relations, or lacking semantic or affective residue. Since the acquisition of such technical language still provides the basic elements of literacy for today's academic musician, there is work to be done in making explicit what has remained implicit and in seeking to extend theory's domain without undermining its commitment to the music itself. In short, it is not clear how a theory of musical meaning that engages the musical language can be anything other than a study of the musical code.

---

3. Ian Bent and Anthony Pople, "Analysis," *The New Grove Dictionary of Music and Musicians*, 2nd ed., ed. Stanley Sadie (London: Macmillan, 2001).
4. For an elaboration of this view of analysis, see Agawu, "How We Got Out of Analysis and How to Get Back In Again," *Music Analysis* 23 (2004): 267–286.

Engagement with the code is akin to acts of performance. Critical performance in turn entails a speculative but rational reconstruction of the musical work. The analyses in this book are guided by this credo insofar as they seek—not always directly or in a linear manner because, alas, the musical environment is full of distractions and temptations—to return readers to the works themselves, not, I hope, by offering clever propositional meanings but by encouraging readers to explore their own meanings through a hypothesizing of certain reconstructive or generative processes. Paths to understanding, not final-state meanings, are what are given priority. This stance confers a radical contingency on my analyses; even in their nascent stages, they make room for alternative modes of proceeding. Proceeding with this sort of flexibility—as opposed to the strictness that ostensibly informs theory-based analysis—is bound to elicit suspicion that a certain amount of rigor has been sacrificed. Those willing to understand analyses as performances might sense rigor differently—in the mode of speculation and in the styles of questioning, not in the mechanical accumulation of data or the tautological assembly of relations.

I have called this a study of "music as discourse," but what does the phrase mean? A fuller sense of the term *discourse* will emerge in the course of particular analyses, but it is necessary, even while conceding its polysemic reach, to emphasize three senses in which I use the phrase. First and most obviously, a musical work is conceived as a sequence of events. (A musical work typically belongs to a repertoire that is constrained historically and stylistically and that subtends its own performing conventions.) An event may be a gesture, an idea, a motive, a progression, or, more neutrally, a building block, phrase, segment, or unit, including the "intonational units" introduced by Boris Asafyev.[5] Events are generally assumed to unfold in orderly fashion. To understand a Beethoven sonata or a Liszt tone poem as discourse, therefore, is to understand it as constituted by a set of events which succeed and relate to each other, the whole making a meaningful impression on the listener. This first sense of *discourse* is familiar enough and is routinely invoked in courses on "form and analysis" and by advocates of musical rhetoric.[6]

A second, related sense of musical discourse takes its bearings from an analogy with verbal discourse. Just as linguists distinguish levels of analysis, taking the sentence as the unit for linguistic analysis, and a succession of sentences as the domain for discourse analysis, so we can think about music in terms of a succession of "sentences," themselves accretions of those smaller meaningful utterances we called events. Musical discourse, in this sense, embraces the larger hierarchical level that encompasses these sentences. Musicians typically speak of "periodicity," the sense of a period being determined by the nature and weight of the punctuation at its end. A succession of periods constitutes the form of a composition. Form in music embraces not only standard forms like fugue, rondo, minuet and trio, and

5. See "The Theory of Intonation," in Raymond Monelle, *Linguistics and Semiotics in Music* (Chur, Switzerland: Harwood, 1992), 274–303.
6. See Mark Evan Bonds, *Wordless Discourse: Musical Form and the Metaphor of the Oration* (Cambridge, MA: Harvard University Press, 1991); Elaine R. Sisman, *Haydn and the Classical Variation* (Cambridge, MA: Harvard University Press, 1993); and Patrick McCreless, "Music and Rhetoric," in *The Cambridge History of Western Music Theory*, ed. Thomas Christensen (Cambridge: Cambridge University Press, 2002), 847–879.

sonata, but a more elusive quality in which the elements of a piece—events and periods—are heard working together and evincing a distinctive profile.

Theories of form abound. From the compositional or pedagogical theories of Koch, Czerny, and Schoenberg through the aesthetic and analytical approaches of Schenker, Tovey, Caplin, Rothstein, and Hepokoski and Darcy, scholars have sought to distribute the reality of musical compositions into various categories, explaining adherence as well as anomaly in reference to constructed norms, some based on the symbolic value of an individual work (like the *Eroica* Symphony),[7] others based on statistics of usage. Yet one cannot help feeling that every time we consign a work to a category such as "sonata form," we lie. For reasons that will emerge in the course of this book, I will pay less attention to such standard forms than to the events or groups of events that comprise them. Is there a difference between the two approaches? Yes, and a significant one at that. Placing the emphasis on events promotes a processual and phenomenological view of the work; it recognizes moment-by-moment succession but worries not at all about an overall or resultant profile that can be named and held up as an archetype. Without denying the historical significance of archetypes or outer forms (such as ABA' schemata) or their practical value for teachers of courses in music appreciation, I will argue that, from a listener's point of view, such forms are often overdetermined, inscribed too rigidly; as such, they often block access to the rich experience of musical meaning. The complex and often contradictory tendencies of musical materials are undervalued when we consign them to boxes marked "first theme," "second theme," and "recapitulation." The ability to distribute the elements of a Brahms symphony into sonata form categories is an ability of doubtful utility or relevance, and it is a profound shame that musicology has devoted pages upon pages to erecting these schemes as important mediators of musical meaning. At best, they possess low-level value; at worst, they are distractions.[8]

Discourse thus embraces events ordered in a coherent fashion, which may operate in turn in a larger-than-the-sentence domain. There is a third sense of the term that has emerged in recent years, inspired in part by poststructuralist thinking. This is discourse as disciplinary talk, including the philosophical and linguistic props that enable the very formulations we make about our objects of study. Discourse about music in this sense encompasses the things one says about a specific composition, as Nattiez's *Music and Discourse* makes clear.[9] In this third sense, discourse entails acts of metacriticism. The musical composition comments on itself at the same time that it is being constituted in the discourse of the analyst. Both the work's internal commentary (represented as acts of inscription attributable

---

7. See Scott Burnham, *Beethoven Hero* (Princeton, NJ: Princeton University Press, 1995).
8. According to Jankélévitch, sonata form "is a something conceived, and not at all something heard, not time subjectively experienced." *Music and the Ineffable,* trans. Carolyn Abbate (Princeton, NJ: Princeton University Press, 2003), 17. Julian Horton notes that "any study defining sonata practice in relation to a norm must confront the problem that there is no single work which could necessarily be described as normative. The idea exists only as an abstraction." "Review of *Bruckner Studies,* ed. Paul Hawkshaw and Timothy L. Jackson," *Music Analysis* 18 (1999): 161.
9. Jean-Jacques Nattiez, *Music and Discourse: Toward a Semiology of Music,* trans. Carolyn Abbate (Princeton, NJ: Princeton University Press, 1990).

to the composer) and the analyst's external commentary feed into an analysis of discourse. The internal commentary is built on observations about processes of repetition and variation, while the external confronts the very props of insight formation. One sign of this metacritical awareness should be evident in the refusal to take for granted any of the enabling constructs of our analyses. To analyze in this sense is necessarily to reflect simultaneously upon the process of analysis.[10]

I use the phrase "semiotic adventures" in the subtitle in order to signal this book's conceptual debt to certain basic concepts borrowed from musical semiotics. Semiotics is a plural and irreducibly interdisciplinary field, and it provides, in my view, the most felicitous framework (among contemporary competing analytical frameworks) for rendering music as structure and style. Writings by Nattiez, Dougherty, Tarasti, Lidov, Hatten, Dunsby, Grabócz, Spitzer, Monelle, and others exemplify what is possible without limiting the domain of the possible. I should add quickly, however, that my aim is not to address an interdisciplinary readership but to speak within the narrower discourses of music analysis, discourses that emanate from the normal, everyday activities of teachers and students of undergraduate courses in music theory and analysis.

What, then, are the central concerns of the book's nine chapters? I have arranged the material in two broad parts. The first, dubbed "Theory," seeks to orient the reader to perspectives that might facilitate an appreciation of the practical nature of music as discourse. The second, "Analyses," presents case studies encompassing works by composers from Beethoven to Stravinsky. Specifically, chapter 1, "Music as Language," places music directly next to language in order to point to similarities and differences in sociology, ontology, psychology, structure, reception, and metalanguage. The metaphor of music as language is old—very old—and although its meaning has changed from age to age, and despite the many limitations that have been pointed out by numerous writers, it remains, in my view, a useful foil for music analysis. Indeed, a greater awareness of music's "linguistic" nature may improve some of the technical analyses that music theorists offer. The aim here, then, is to revisit an old and familiar issue and offer a series of generalized claims that might stimulate classroom discussion of the nature of musical language.

Chapters 2 and 3, "Criteria for Analysis I and II," also retain a broad perspective in isolating certain key features of Romantic music, but instead of addressing the system of music as such, I turn to selected compositional features that embrace elements of style as well as structure. Few would disagree with Charles Rosen that "it is disquieting when an analysis, no matter how cogent, minimizes the most salient features of a work. This is a failure of critical decorum."[11] These two chapters (which belong together as a pair but are separated for practical reasons) are precisely an attempt *not* to minimize such features. But salience is a contested category. Salience is not given, not naturally occurring; it is constructed. Which is

---

10. For other invocations of music as discourse, see David Lidov, *Is Language a Music? Writings on Musical Form and Signification* (Bloomington: Indiana University Press, 2005), 10–12, 70–77, 138–144; and Michael Spitzer, *Metaphor and Musical Thought* (Chicago: University of Chicago Press, 2004), 107–125. *Discourse* is, of course, a widely used term in the literature on musical semiotics.

11. Charles Rosen, *The Classical Style: Haydn, Mozart, Beethoven* (New York: Norton, 1972), 3.

why musical features that strike one listener as salient are judged to be peripheral by another. I recall once listening to a recording of Schubert's *Winterreise* with an admired teacher when he asked me what I thought was the most salient moment in the beginning of "Der greise Kopf" ("The hoary head") (example I.1). I pointed to the high A-flat in the third bar, the high point of the opening phrase, noting that it was loud and dissonant, marked a turning point in the melodic contour, and was therefore rhetorically significant. He, on the other hand, heard something less obvious: the change of harmony at the beginning of bar 11, the moment at which the unyielding C pedal that had been in effect from the very first sound of the song finally drops by a half-step. This surprised me initially, but I later came to admire the qualitative difference between his construction of this particular salience and mine. His took in the harmonic stream within the larger syntactical dimension; mine was a statistical, "surface" event. The construction of salience in tonal music is especially challenging because tonal expression relies as much on what is sounded as on what is not sounded. The stated and the implied are equally functional. Inexperienced or downright insensitive analysts who confine their interpretations to what is directly observable in scores often draw their patterns of salience from what is stated rather than what is implied; the result is a dull, impoverished, or untrue analysis.

Example I.1. Schubert, "Der greise Kopf," from *Winterreise*, bars 1–16.

The challenge, then, is to explain the basis of such construction. Out of a potentially large set of criteria, I have isolated six to guide the analyses in chapters 2 and 3: topics or *topoi*; beginnings, middles, and endings; high points and the dynamic curve; periodicity, discontinuity, and parentheses; three modes of enunciation, namely, speech mode, song mode, and dance mode; and the narrative thread. I believe that these criteria capture salient features of the Romantic repertoire and can therefore convey aspects of their truth content. Some of these categories obviously overlap, but no two are identical. Together, they provide listeners with a mechanism for organizing their intuitions about Romantic music. The resulting analyses can in turn engender further speculation about meaning.

Because they capture immediate aspects of structure, the criteria for analysis studied in chapters 2 and 3 may seem superficial to some. Schenkerians, for example, construe salience with rigorous attention to an enabling voice-leading context. Fruitful meanings are produced when compositions are heard in terms of underlying forces or in terms of idealized voices that motivate real voices, hidden forces that control manifest ones. For Schenkerians, inquiry into tonal meaning is more productive when it is framed dialectically, when a foreground is seen to take its bearings from a background, when surface and subsurface are understood as locked in a necessary relationship to one another. An analysis that is not informed by this foundational dialecticism is flawed because it produces only flat, one-dimensional, or unmotivated observations.

In chapter 4, "Bridges to Free Composition," I explore this way of thinking using one of Schenker's central metaphors in *Kontrapunkt* (1910–1922) as point of entry. Compositions are analyzed in terms of harmonic and contrapuntal prototypes. A work is thus understood as a layered structure, while the conceptual journey from background to foreground is figured as one of increasing concretization of musical content. The idea that bridges link strict counterpoint to free composition is implicit in Schenker's comprehensive exposition of contrapuntal principles in *Kontrapunkt*, but the precise nature of the bridges is discussed in somewhat muted terms. In particular, the stylistic resources that would allow a systematic inferring of a particular foreground from a generalized background are not spelled out. One is left with the suspicion that such bridges are makeshift constructions that cannot adequately convey the heterogeneity of foreground discourses.

None of this is meant to undermine the central demonstration in chapter 4 of the musical advantages of thinking in terms of deep structures or prototypes or fictional texts or subsurface constructs.[12] Familiarity with prototypes and the techniques of manipulating them enables the analyst to improvise structures that resemble the works being analyzed. But this improvisation is confined to the realm of harmony and voice leading. No doubt, harmony and voice leading are essential elements of the work, but they do not represent all of the elements. The breaks, fissures, and aporia that result from trying to approach a particular foreground with a less particular subsurface structure suggest that it may not always be possible to generate free composition from strict counterpoint. Only by renouncing its

---

12. For an authoritative study of prototypes in composition, see Matthew Brown, *Explaining Tonality: Schenkerian Theory and Beyond* (Rochester, NY: University of Rochester Press, 2006).

notional purity and incorporating such things as motivic content, topical profile, periodicity, and rhythm can strict counterpoint be brought into effective alliance with free composition.

Chapters 2 and 3, on one hand, and 4, on the other, would therefore seem to argue conflicting positions: whereas chapters 2 and 3 acknowledge the value of constructing a first-level salience (based on stylistic features that are heard more or less immediately), chapter 4 claims a more sophisticated relational approach by peering into the subsurface. Chapter 5, "Paradigmatic Analysis," adds to these competing views a semiological approach that attempts to wipe the slate clean in minimizing, but never completely eliminating, the amount of (musical) baggage that the analyst brings to the task. The approach takes repetition, the most indigenous of all musical attributes, as a guide to the selection of a composition's meaningful units and speculates on the narrative path cut by the succession of repeating units. The paradigmatic analyst in effect adopts a studiedly naïve stance in dispensing with the numerous a priori considerations that have come to burden a repertoire like that of the Romantic period. Pretense succeeds only in a limited way, however, but enough to draw attention to some of the factors we take for granted when we analyze music and to impel a more direct encounter with musical form.

With these five chapters, the main theoretical exposition is over. Next follow a number of case studies designed partly to exemplify the network of ideas exposed in the theoretical chapters, partly to push beyond their frontiers, and partly to engage in dialogue with other analytical approaches. First comes a study of the narrative thread in Liszt's symphonic poem *Orpheus* (chapter 6), followed by a study of phrase discourse in two works by Brahms: the second movement of his First Symphony and the Intermezzo for Piano, op. 119, no. 2 (chapter 7). The last case studies are of narratives of continuity and discontinuity in the first movement of Mahler's Ninth (chapter 8) and in the first movement of Beethoven's String Quartet, op. 130, juxtaposed with Stravinsky's *Symphonies of Wind Instruments* (chapter 9). The inclusion of Stravinsky—and an austere work from 1920 at that—may seem strange at first, but I hope to show continuities with the Romantic tradition without discounting the obvious discontinuities.

An analyst's fondest hope is that something he or she says sends the reader/listener back to a particular composition or to a particular moment within it. Our theoretical scaffoldings are useless abstractions if they do not achieve something like this; they may be good theory but lousy analysis. Indeed, "music was not made to be talked about," according to Jankélévitch.[13] Talking, however, can help to reinforce the point that talking is unnecessary, while at the same time reinforcing the belief that music was made to be (re)made—repeatedly, sometimes. Analysis, in turn, leads us through inquiry back to the site of remaking. Therefore, I retain some hope in the possibility that the analytical fantasies gathered here will inspire some readers to reach for the works again; to see if their previous hearings have been altered, enhanced, or challenged in any way; and, if they have, to seek to incorporate some of these insights into subsequent hearings. If this happens, my purpose will have been achieved.

---

13. Jankélévitch, *Music and the Ineffable*, 79.

PART I

Theory

CHAPTER One

Music as Language

The Idea of Music and Language

Music's contexts are many, probably infinite. Music resembles myth, animates religious ritual, and facilitates movement and dance. It is an agent in music drama and plays a catalytic if not constitutive role in film and other forms of visual narrative. Music frequently transgresses borders and seems uniquely placed among the arts to do so. Perhaps the most basic of these associations, however, is that between music and natural language. And this is because whereas language is already a common factor in myth, ritual, drama, and film, its incorporation into music takes place in particular ways and under special circumstances; it forms a second-order semiological system, according to Roland Barthes.[1] Exploring the affinities between music and this particular "other" may thus prove instructive. This chapter reviews some of the most basic of these affinities as background to my later discussion of musical meaning.

The idea that music and language are closely affiliated possesses considerable historical and geocultural depth. John Neubauer reminds us that the ancient Greeks, for example, designated music and language by a single term, *musiké*. Plato advocated a "word-dominated music" over a "mathematical music," and Saint Augustine challenged that particular prioritization while enunciating the benefits of well-chosen words for the music that accompanies worship.[2] In the seventeenth and eighteenth centuries, links between music and rhetoric were frequently acknowledged and occasionally theorized, musical rhetoric being "the most concerted effort in history to apply verbal principles to music."[3] And the ascendancy of pure instrumental or absolute music in the later eighteenth century

---

1. Roland Barthes, *Mythologies*, trans. Annette Lavers (New York: Hill and Wang, 1972), 115.
2. John Neubauer, *The Emancipation of Music from Language: Departure from Mimesis in Eighteenth-Century Aesthetics* (New Haven, CT: Yale University Press, 1986), 22–23.
3. Neubauer, *The Emancipation of Music from Language*, 40.

through the nineteenth century alongside a huge supplemental increase in word-dominated (or at least word-inflected) genres like operas, tone poems, and lieder, plus a variety of compositional experiments with language as sound, material, and sense in the works of a number of twentieth-century composers (Stravinsky, Berio, and Lansky)—all of these provide further indication of the close rapport between music and language.

The prevalence of language models for analysis of European music is the central concern of a 1980 article by Harold Powers, in which he cites the then recent work of Fred Lerdahl and Ray Jackendoff as an exemplary attempt to model a grammar of tonal music.[4] Reviewing antecedents for such efforts, Powers mentions two medieval sources, the anonymous ninth-century *Musica Enchiriadis* and the treatise of Johannes, circa 1100; he also mentions various discussions of musical grammar in German theory (Dressler 1563; Burmeister 1606; Mattheson 1737, 1739; Koch 1787; Reicha 1818; Riemann 1903) and David Lidov's 1975 study of segmentation, *On Musical Phrase*.[5] On a metalinguistic level, Powers shows how musical analysis has borrowed from semantics (as in Deryck Cooke's *The Language of Music*, 1959), phonology (as in theories of South Indian classical music), the making of propositional statements (as in Charles Boilès' semiological study of Tepehua "thought songs"), and, perhaps most significantly, grammar and syntax (as in recent semiological applications by Ruwet, Nattiez, and Lidov). In the quarter century since Powers's magisterial article appeared, research into semiology, which typically indexes the "linguisticity" of music, has grown by leaps and bounds, extending into areas of musical semantics, phonology, and pragmatics; embracing traditional studies that do not claim a semiotic orientation; and expanding the repertorial base to include various non-Western musics. All of this research tacitly affirms the pertinence of linguistic analogies for music.[6]

The decentering of previously canonical repertoires is one of the more dramatic outcomes of recent efforts to understand the relations between music and language. The resulting geocultural depth is readily seen in ethnomusicological work, which, because it is tasked with inventing other world cultures and traditions, disinherits some of the more obnoxious priorities enshrined in the discourse about Western (musical) culture. Powers's own article, for example, unusual and impressive in its movement across Western and non-Western repertoires—a throwback to the comparative musicology of Marius Schneider, Robert Lach, and Erich von Hornbostel—includes a discussion of improvisation and the mechanics of text underlay in South Asian music. A year earlier, Judith Becker and Alton Becker had constructed a strict grammar for Javanese *srepegan*, a grammar that was later revisited by David Hughes.[7] The literature on African music, too, includes several studies of the intriguing phenomenon of speech tone and its relationship

---

4. Harold Powers, "Language Models and Music Analysis," *Ethnomusicology* 24 (1980): 1–60.
5. Powers, "Language Models," 48–54.
6. See Raymond Monelle's *Linguistics and Semiotics in Music* for a valuable introduction to the field.
7. Judith Becker and Alton Becker, "A Grammar of the Musical Genre Srepegan," *Journal of Music Theory* 24 (1979): 1–43; and David W. Hughes, "Deep Structure and Surface Structure in Javanese Music: A Grammar of Gendhing Lampah," *Ethnomusicology* 32 (1988): 23–74.

to melody. There are studies of talking drums, including ways in which drums and other speech surrogates reproduce the tonal and accentual elements of spoken language. And perhaps most basic and universal are studies of song, a genre in which words and music coexist, sometimes vying for prominence, mutually transforming each other, complementing each other, and often leaving a conceptually or phenomenally dissonant residue. The practices associated with lamentation, for example, explore techniques and territories of vocalization, from the syllabic through the melismatic to the use of vocables as articulatory vehicles. And by including various "icons of crying" (Greg Urban's phrase), laments (or dirges or wails) open up other dimensions of expressive behavior beyond—but organically linked to—music and language.[8]

There is further evidence, albeit of an informal sort, of the music-language association. In aesthetic and evaluative discourses responding to performing and composing, one sometimes encounters phrases like "It doesn't speak to me" or "S/he is not saying anything."[9] Metaphors of translation are also prominent. We imagine music translated into visual symbols or images, or into words, language, or literary expression. In the nineteenth century, the common practice of paraphrasing existing works suggested transformative rendition (saying something differently), such as is evident in Liszt's or Paganini's paraphrases of music by Beethoven and Schubert. Ornamentation, likewise, involves the imaginative recasting of existing ideas, a process that resonates with certain oratorical functions. John Spitzer studied Jean Rousseau's 1687 viol treatise and concluded, "Rousseau's grammar of ornamentation corresponds in many respects to the so-called 'morphophonemic component' of Chomskian grammars."[10] Even the genre of theme and variations, whose normative protocol prescribes a conscious commentary on an existing theme, may be understood within the critical economy of explanation, criticism, and metacommentary. Finally, improvisation or composing in the moment presupposes competence in the "speaking" of a musical language. Powers likens one sense of improvisation to "an extempore oratorical discourse" while Lidov notes that musical improvisation "may be closest to spontaneous speech function."[11]

This highly abbreviated mapping—the fuller story may be read in, among other places, articles by Powers (1980) and Feld and Fox (1994, which includes a magnificent bibliography), and books by Neubauer (1986) and Monelle (1992)—should be enough to indicate that the music-language alliance is unavoidable as a creative challenge (composition), as a framework for reception (listening), and as a mechanism for understanding (analysis). Observe a certain asymmetry in the relationship,

---

8. Steven Feld and Aaron Fox, "Music and Language," *Annual Review of Anthropology* 23 (1994): 25–53.

9. See Ingrid Monson, *Saying Something: Jazz Improvisation and Interaction* (Chicago: University of Chicago Press, 1996), 73–96, for a discussion of "Music, Language and Cultural Styles: Improvisation as Conversation."

10. John Spitzer, "Grammar of Improvised Ornamentation: Jean Rousseau's Viol Treatise of 1687," *Journal of Music Theory* 33(2) (1989): 305.

11. Powers, "Language Models," 42; Lidov, *On Musical Phrase* (Montreal: Groupe de recherches en sémiologie musicale, Music Faculty, University of Montreal, 1975), 9, quoted in Powers, "Language Models," 42.

however. Measured in terms of the critical work that either term does, language looms larger than music. Indeed, in the twentieth century, language, broadly construed, came to assume a position of unprecedented privilege (according to poststructuralist accounts) among the discourses of the human sciences. Salutary reminders by Carolyn Abbate that the poststructuralist privileging of language needs to be tempered when music is the object of analysis,[12] and by anthropologist Johannes Fabian that the aural mode needs to be elevated against the predominant visual mode if we are not to forgo certain insights that come from contemplating sound,[13] have so far not succeeded in stemming the ascendancy of verbal domination. As Roland Barthes implies, to think and talk about music is—necessarily, it would appear—"inevitably to fall back on the individuation of a language."[14]

Why should the music-as-language metaphor matter to music analysts? Quite simply because, to put it somewhat paradoxically, language and music are as alike as they are unlike. No two systems—semiotic or expressive—set against one another are as thoroughly imbricated in each other's practices and yet remain ultimately separate and distinct. More important, the role of language as a metalanguage for music remains essential and is in no way undermined by the development of symbologies such as Schenker's graphic analysis or Hans Keller's notated—and therefore performable—functional analyses. The most imaginative music analysts are not those who treat language as a transparent window onto a given musical reality but those who, whether explicitly or implicitly, reflect on language's limitations even as they use it to convey insights about music. Language's persistence and domination at the conceptual level is therefore never a mere given in music analysis, demanding that music surrender, so to speak; on the contrary, it encourages acts of critical resistance which, whatever their outcome, speak to the condition of music as an art of tone.

A few of these efforts at resistance are worth recalling. Adorno, looking beyond material to aesthetic value, truth content, and psychological depth, has this to say:

> Music resembles language in the sense that it is a temporal sequence of articulated sounds which are more than just sounds. They say something, often something human. The better the music, the more forcefully they say it. The succession of sounds is like logic: it can be right or wrong. But what has been said cannot be detached from the music. Music creates no semiotic system.[15]

Thus, the "sequence of articulated sounds" has a meaning; it "*say[s]* something," something in the "human" dimension. What is said carries greater or lesser degrees

12. Carolyn Abbate, *Unsung Voices: Opera and Musical Narrative in the Nineteenth Century* (Princeton, NJ: Princeton University Press, 1991), 3–29.
13. Johannes Fabian, *Out of Our Minds: Reason and Madness in the Exploration of Central Africa* (Berkeley: University of California Press, 2000).
14. Roland Barthes, *Elements of Semiology*, trans. Annette Lavers and Colin Smith (New York: Hill and Wang, 1967), 10.
15. Theodor Adorno, "Music and Language: A Fragment," in *Quasi una Fantasia: Essays on Modern Music*, trans. Rodney Livingstone (London: Verso, 1992), 1.

of persuasiveness. Above all, what is said remains permanently imbricated in the musical system.

Acknowledging "the connection with linguistics" in the construction of their generative theory of tonal music, Fred Lerdahl and Ray Jackendoff describe as "largely futile" the search for "superficial analogies between music and language." They stress the importance of looking within purely musical structure for modes of organization, but it appears that a linguistic stance is not ultimately eliminable; indeed, their own theorizing about tonal structure has been helped by "the theoretical framework and methodology of linguistics":

> Pointing out superficial analogies between music and language, with or without the help of generative grammar, is an old and largely futile game. One should not approach music with any preconceptions that the substance of music theory will look at all like linguistic theory. For example, whatever music may "mean," it is in no sense comparable to linguistic meaning; there are no musical phenomena comparable to sense and reference in language, or to such semantic judgments as synonymy, analyticity, and entailment. Likewise there are no substantive parallels between elements of musical structure and such syntactic categories as noun, verb, adjective, preposition, and verb phrase. Finally, one should not be misled by the fact that both music and language deal with sound structure. There are no musical counterparts of such phonological parameters as voicing, nasality, tongue height, and lip rounding.
>
> The fundamental concepts of musical structure must instead involve such factors as rhythmic and pitch organization, dynamic and timbral differentiation, and motivic-thematic processes. These factors and their interactions form intricate structures quite different from, but no less complex than, those of linguistic structure. Any deep parallels that might exist can be discussed meaningfully only after a music theory…has been developed independently. If we have adopted some of the theoretical framework and methodology of linguistics, it is because this approach has suggested a fruitful way of thinking about music itself. If substantive parallels between language and music emerge…this is an unexpected bonus but not necessarily a desideratum.[16]

This string of negatives probably overstates an essential point; some will argue that it errs in denying the possibilities set in motion by an impossible alliance. But the work of music theory in which this statement appears is concerned with what is specifiable, not with what occupies interstices. It comes as no surprise, then, that the tenor of this statement notwithstanding, the authors later invoke a most valuable distinction between well-formedness and preference in order to register one aspect of the music-language alliance. Criteria of well-formedness, which play an essential role in linguistic grammar, are less crucial in musical grammar than preference rules. This is another way of stacking the musical deck in favor of the aesthetic. To put it simply: music is less about right and wrong—although, as Adorno says, these are important—than about liking something more or less.

Jean Molino links music, language, and religion in arguing their resistance to definition and in recognizing their symbolic residue:

---

16. Fred Lerdahl and Ray Jackendoff, *A Generative Theory of Tonal Music* (Cambridge, MA: MIT Press, 1983), 5–6.

> The phenomenon of music, like that of language or that of religion, cannot be defined or described correctly unless we take account of its threefold mode of existence—as an arbitrarily isolated object, as something produced and as something perceived. It is on these three dimensions that the specificity of the symbolic largely rests.[17]

These and numerous other claims form the basis of literally thousands of assertions about music as language. On one hand, they betray an interest in isomorphisms or formal parallelisms between the two systems; on the other, they point to areas of inexactness, to the complexities and paradoxes that emerge at the site of their cohabitation. They testify to the continuing vitality and utility of the music and language metaphor, while reminding us that only in carefully circumscribed contexts, rather than at a gross level, is it fruitful to continue to entertain the prospect of a deep linkage.

Accordingly, I plead the reader's indulgence in setting forth a set of simple propositions that might form the basis of debate or discussion in a music theory class. Culled from diverse sources and originally formulated to guide a discussion of the challenge of musical semiotics, they speak to aspects of the phenomenon that have been touched upon by Powers, Adorno, Lerdahl and Jackendoff, and Molino. I have attempted to mold them into capsule, generalizable form without, I hope, oversimplifying the phenomena they depict.[18] (By "music" in the specific context of the discussion that follows, I refer to a literature, to compositions of the common practice era which form the object of analytical attention in this book. While a wider purview of the term is conceivable, and not just in the domain of European music, it seems prudent to confine the reach of these claims in order to avoid confusion.)

Ten Propositions about Language and Music

The ten propositions that follow speak, first, to the place of music and language in human society, to the issue of competence, and to the diversity of linguistic and musical products (proposition 1). Proposition 2 addresses communicative capacity. Propositions 3, 4, 5, 6, and 7 comment on material differences, while 8 and 9 treat issues of meaning. The last proposition (10) takes note of the metalinguistic dimension.

1. Music, language, and (possibly) religion occur in all known human societies. Setting aside for now evidence that nonhumans sometimes engage in these activities, we can state that in all known societies, humans make music, communicate through spoken language, and maintain prescribed sets of beliefs and practices. There are, of course, languages in which the word *music* is not found, but the

---

17. Jean Molino, "Musical Fact and the Semiology of Music," trans. J. A. Underwood, *Music Analysis* 9(2) (1990): 114.
18. Agawu, "The Challenge of Semiotics," in *Rethinking Music*, ed. Nicholas Cook and Mark Everist (Oxford: Oxford University Press, 1999), 138–160.

presence in such societies of a species of rhythmic and tonal behavior that we may characterize as music making is rarely in serious contention. Music, in short, is "necessary to us."[19]

There are, however, striking and sometimes irreconcilable differences in the materials, media, modes of production and consumption, and significance of music. Indeed, there appear to be greater differences among the world's musics than among its languages. Nicolas Ruwet says that "all human languages are apparently of the same order of complexity, but that is not the case for all musical systems."[20] And Powers comments that "the 'linguisticity' of languages is the same from language to language, but the 'linguisticity' of musics is not the same from music to music."[21] David Lidov "see[s] no variation among languages so extreme as those among musical styles."[22] It appears that music is more radically constructed, more artificial, and depends more crucially on context for validation and meaning. So whereas the phrase "natural language" seems appropriate, "natural music" requires some elaboration. While linguistic competence is more or less easily assessed, assessing normal musical competence is a rather more elusive enterprise. Speaking a mother tongue does not appear to have a perfect correlative in musical practice—is it the ability to improvise competently within a given style, to harmonize a hymn tune or folk melody in a "native" idiom, to add to the repertoire of natural songs when given a text or a situation that brings on a text, to complete a composition whose second half is withheld, or to predict the nature and size of a gesture in a particular moment in a particular composition? Is it, in other words, a creative or compositional ability, a discriminatory or perceptual ability, or a performative capability? So, beyond their mutual occurrence in human society as conventional and symbolic media, the practices associated with language and music signal significant differences.[23]

2. Unlike language, which is both a medium of communication ("ordinary language") and a vehicle for artistic expression ("poetic language"), musical language exists primarily in the poetic realm, although it can be used for "purely" communicative purposes. "Please pass the marmalade" uttered at the breakfast table has a direct communicative purpose. It is a form of ordinary language that

19. Gayle A. Henrotte, "Music as Language: A Semiotic Paradigm?" in *Semiotics 1984*, ed. John Deely (Lanham, MD: University Press of America, 1985), 163–170.

20. Nicolas Ruwet, "Théorie et méthodes dans les etudes musicales: Quelques remarques rétrospectives et préliminaires," *Music en jeu* 17 (1975): 19, quoted in Powers, "Language Models," 38.

21. Powers, "Language Models," 38. Perhaps "the same" is too strong and liable to be undermined by new anthropological findings. See, for example, Daniel L. Everett, "Cultural Constraints on Grammar and Cognition in Piraha: Another Look at the Design Features of Human Language," *Current Anthropology* 46 (2005): 621–646.

22. Lidov, *Is Language a Music?* 4.

23. The place of music and language in human evolution has been suggestively explored in a number of publications by Ian Cross. See, for example, "Music and Biocultural Evolution," in *The Cultural Study of Music: A Critical Introduction*, ed. Martin Clayton, Trevor Herbert, and Richard Middleton (New York: Routledge, 2003), 19–30. Also of interest is Paul Richards's adaptation of some of Cross's ideas in "The Emotions at War: Atrocity as Piacular Rite in Sierra Leone," in *Public Emotions*, ed. Perri 6, Susannah Radstone, Corrine Squire and Amal Treacher (London: Palgrave Macmillan, 2006), 62–84.

would normally elicit an action from one's companion at the table. "Let me not to the marriage of true minds admit impediments," by contrast, departs from the ordinary realm and enters another in which language is self-consciously ordered to draw attention to itself. This is poetic language. Whereas ordinary language is unmarked, poetic language is marked. Like all such binary distinctions, however, that between ordinary and poetic is not always firm. There are levels of ordinariness in language use; certain ostensibly linguistic formulations pass into the realm of the poetic by opportunistic acts of framing (as in the poetry of William Carlos Williams) while the poetic may inflect what one says in everyday parlance (the Ewe greet each other daily by asking, "Are you well with life?"). So although the distinction is not categorical, it is nevertheless useful at low levels of characterization.

The situation is more ambiguous in music, for despite the sporadic evidence that music may function as an "ordinary" medium of communication—as in the "talking drums" of West and Central Africa, or in the thought-songs recorded by Charles Boilès among the Tepehua of Mexico—music's discursive communicative capacity is inferior to that of language. In a magisterial survey of the music-language phenomenon, Steve Feld and Aaron Fox refer to the "informational redundancy of musical structures," thus echoing observations made by aestheticians like Leonard Meyer and others.[24] And several writers, conscious of the apparently asemantic nature of musical art, speak only with hesitation about music's communicative capability. It appears that the predominantly aesthetic function of music compares only with certain heightened or designated uses of language.

Music's ordinary language is thus available only as a speculative projection. One might think, for example, of an overt transition in, say, a Haydn sonata, which in the moment suggests a shifting of gears, a lifting of the action onto a different plane, an intrusion of craft, an exposure of seams—that perhaps such transitions index a level of ordinary usage in music. They command attention as mobile rather than presentational moments. They are means to other, presumably more poetic, ends. But one must not underestimate the extent to which a poetic impetus infuses the transition function. The work of a transition may be the moment in which music comes into its own, needing to express a credible and indigenously musical function. Such a moment may be suffused with poetry. Attending to a functional imperative does not take the composer out of his contemplative realm.

A similar attempt to hear ordinariness and poetry in certain operatic functions conveys the complexity of the application. Secco recitative in conventional understanding facilitates the quick delivery of words, thus speeding up the dramatic action, while aria slows things down and enables the beauty of music—which is inseparable from the beauty of voice—to come to the fore. Recitative may thus be said to perform the function of ordinary language while aria does the work of poetic language. This alignment is already complicated. The ordinary would seem to be musically dispensable but dramatically necessary, while the poetic is not dispensable in either sense. This is another way of restating the musical basis of the genre.

---

24. Feld and Fox, "Music and Language," 27.

Think, also, of functional music in opera. Think of the moment toward the end of act 2 of Puccini's *Tosca* when Scarpia, in return for a carnal favor, consents to give Tosca safe conduct so that she and Cavaradossi can leave the country. While Scarpia sits at his desk writing the note, the musical narrative must continue. Puccini provides functional, time-killing music, music which serves as a form of ordinary language in contrast to the more elevated utterances sung by Tosca and Scarpia both before and after this moment. Opera, after all, is music drama; the foundation of operatic discourse is music, so the functional aspect of this moment can never eclipse its contemplative dimension. The music that serves as time-killing music is highly charged, beautiful, and burdened with significance. It is as poetic—if not more so, given its isolation—as any music in *Tosca*. So while Puccini may be heard "speaking" (or singing, or communicating) in ordinary language, his utterance is fully poetic. The fact that music is not a system of communication should not discourage us from exploring the messages that music sometimes (intermittently) communicates. It is precisely in the tension between the aesthetic and communicative functions that music analysis finds an essential challenge to its purpose, its reason for being.[25]

3. Unlike language, music exists only in performance (actual, idealized, imagined, remembered). The claim that language as social expression is ever conceivable outside of the context of performance may appear counterintuitive at first. When I greet you, or say a prayer in the mosque, or take an oath, am I not performing a text? And when I read a poem or novel to myself, am I not similarly engaged in a performance, albeit a silent one? The system of language and the system of music exist in a synchronous state, harboring potential relationships, relationships waiting to be released in actual verbal or musical compositions. As soon as they are concretized in specific compositions, they inevitably enshrine directions for performance. However, partly because of language's communicative functions—as contrasted with music's aesthetic function—partly because it is possible to make true or false propositional statements in language, and partly because of its domination of our conceptual apparatus, language appears to display a wider range of articulatory possibility than does music, from performed or heightened to marked, ordinary, or unmarked.

Music, by contrast, is more restricted in its social tendency, more marked when it is rendered, and possibly silent when it is not being performed or remembered. "A musical work does not exist except in the time of its playing," writes Jankélévitch.[26] It is true that some musicians have music on the brain all the time, and it is also true that some trained musicians can hear notated music in their heads—although this hearing is surely a hearing of something imagined, itself possible only against a background of a prior (remembered) hearing if not of the particular composition then of other compositions. It appears that the constraints placed on

25. I have elsewhere used this same example to undermine the distinction, sometimes drawn by ethnomusicologists writing about African music, between functional music and contemplative music. See Agawu, *Representing African Music: Postcolonial Notes, Queries, Positions* (New York: Routledge, 2003), 98–107.

26. Jankélévitch, *Music and the Ineffable*, 70.

music making are always severe, presumably because the ontological modes of verbal behavior are more diffuse. The difference in performability between music and language is finally relative, however, not absolute.

4. Like language (in its manifestation as speech), music is organized into temporally bounded or acoustically closed texts. Whether they be oral texts (like greetings, oaths, prayers) or written texts (poems, novels, speeches, letters), verbal texts share with musical texts a comparable internal mode of existence. Certain otherwise pertinent questions about the identity of a musical work are, at this level, rendered irrelevant by the undeniable fact that a text, work, or composition has, in principle, a beginning, a middle, and an ending. At this level of material and sonic specificity, the beginning-middle-ending scheme represents only the order in which events unfold, not the more qualitative measure of the function of those parts. The work of interpretation demands, however, that once we move beyond this material level, compositions be reconfigured as open texts, conceptually boundless fields, texts whose necessary but in a sense mundane temporal boundaries are not necessarily coterminous with their "sense" boundaries.[27]

5. A musical composition, like a verbal composition, is organized into discrete units or segments. Music is, in this sense, segmentable. Understanding a temporal phenomenon is only possible if the whole, however imagined or conceptualized, is grasped in terms of its constituent parts, units, or segments. Many writings in music theory, especially the great seventeenth- and eighteenth-century treatises on rhetoric and music (Burmeister, Bernhard, Mattheson) are either premised upon or develop an explicit view of segments. And many later theories, be they prescriptive and compositional (Koch and Czerny) or descriptive and synthetic (Tovey and Schenker), lay great store by building blocks, minimal units, basic elements, motives, phrases, periods—in short, constitutive segments. In thus accounting for or prescribing the discourse of a composition, theorists rely on a conception of segmentation as an index of musical sense or meaning. Now, the issue of music's physical segmentability is less interesting than what might be called its "cultural" or "psychological" segmentability. The former is a quantitative or objective measure, the latter a heavily mediated qualitative or subjective one. Culturally conditioned segmentation draws on historical and cultural data in a variety of formal and informal discourses to determine a work's significant sense units and their mode of succession. The nature of the units often betrays allegiance to some metalanguage or other, as when we speak of musical logic, developing variation, mixture, or octatonic collection.

6. Although segmentable, the musical composition is more continuous in its real-time unfolding than is a verbal composition. The articulatory vehicles of verbal and musical composition differ, the former marked by virtual or physical rests and silences, the latter by real or imagined continuities. The issue of continuity is only partly acoustical. More important are the psychological and semantic sources of continuity. Lacking an apparent semantic dimension that can activate certain

27. On open texts, see Umberto Eco, "The Poetics of the Open Work," in Eco, *The Role of the Reader: Explorations in the Semiotics of Texts* (Bloomington: Indiana University Press, 1979), 47–66. For an incisive discussion, see Nattiez, *Music and Discourse*, 69–101.

intertextual resonances, the tonal composition pursues an essentially linear course. Linearity is not dispensable in any attempt to construct the ontology of a poem. But a sung poem exhibits a physical continuity that exceeds that of the unsung poem, whose sense of linearity is as much psychological as it is physical. The linear in this verbal medium appears less urgent from a temporal point of view than its comparable dimension in a musical composition. Edward T. Cone once characterized this as a case of the musical mind "chained to the vehicle of the moving sound."[28] But music's linearity also has its psychological or conceptual dimension, as when composers create the illusion of continuity across formal boundaries, or by means of voice-leading paths in both long and short ranges, or through a hierarchy of dependent closes. The tonal organism in this view emerges as a creature with a high degree of interdependence among its parts. An extreme or idealized formulation of this condition would be that the listener is enveloped in a present discourse, enchained by the tonal process, and allowed virtually no real-time space to develop an intertextual hearing, being compelled simply to follow a train of thought from its inception to its completion. Think of the opening movement of Beethoven's Fifth in contrast, say, to the first movement of Bruckner's Seventh or the first movement of Mahler's Fifth, where the sculpting of musical time allows the listener some breathing space, so to speak.

7. Music exists in two interdependent planes, the plane of succession ("melody") and the plane of simultaneity ("harmony"). Language lacks the plane of simultaneity. Without denying the existence of performed drama in which some form of simultaneous doing occurs, or speech acts rooted in dialogue or polyphony, one can nevertheless stress the apparent uniqueness of the phenomenon of harmony in music. Harmony is not restricted to the simultaneous soundings in a Bach chorale or a Bruckner adagio. It includes unaccompanied song, monodies with an implicit contrapuntal dimension, a dimension populated by active but unsounded voices producing a stream of sonorities that encapsulate the music's narrative. A tenuous analogy for what musicians call *compound melody* (or "bi-linear" melody in Leonard Meyer's term)[29] may be gleaned from Saussure's insight that meaning is difference. Each speech act thus subtends a normative background comprising a sequence of competing lexical items that have been purposefully excised from the reigning foreground. This paradigm shares with harmony or sonority a notion of simultaneous sounding, and just as musical harmonies are associated on the basis of likeness and compatibility and can be further associated within a linguistic-type paradigm on the basis of functional equivalence, so the elements of a linguistic paradigm are morphologically, functionally, or semantically associated. Literary invocations of "polyphony," "counterpoint," and "harmony" are metaphors, at best, and, sometimes, strained analogies.

8. While words have a more or less fixed lexical meaning, music's units—whatever they are—do not. Unlike verbal composition, therefore, musical composition

28. Edward T. Cone, "Words into Music," in *Sound and Poetry*, ed. Northrop Frye (New York: Columbia University Press, 1957), 9.
29. Leonard B. Meyer, *Explaining Music: Essays and Explorations* (Chicago: University of Chicago Press, 1973), 141.

cannot be translated. To deny music a semantic essence comparable to language is not to claim that semantic meanings cannot be imposed on a nonsignifying musical structure. And while language, too, is not always continuously semantic, as evident in poetry in which the semantic potential of words is muted in favor of their sheer sonic qualities, there remains a categorical difference between a system in which the word "kettle" harbors a core reference (a signified, an interpretant, even an infinite chain of interpretants) and one whose "vocabulary," itself already contested and elusive, remains diffuse, amorphous, and devoid of a priori meaning. In *The Language of Music*, Deryck Cooke makes the case that certain recurring tonal patterns (intervals and mainly diatonic scale patterns) are invested with verbally retrievable meaning or emotions.[30] For example, major thirds and sixths express pleasure, minor thirds grief, minor sixths pain. A sequence of intervals yields a "musical vocabulary" similarly invested with a cumulative emotional profile. Thus, the ascending $\hat{1}$–($\hat{2}$)–$\hat{3}$–($\hat{4}$)–$\hat{5}$ in major is said to express "an outgoing, active, assertive emotion of joy," whereas the pattern $\hat{1}$–($\hat{2}$)–$\hat{3}$–($\hat{2}$)–$\hat{1}$ in minor may express "brooding, an obsession with gloomy feelings, a trapped fear, or a sense of inescapable doom, especially when it is repeated over and over."[31] Although the specific examples that Cooke adduces to illustrate his theory are suggestive and persuasive—which is to say that one can bring oneself to hear music through these filters—the presumed invariance at the core of these emotional associations remains a controversial issue. Context is crucial here, and some evidence from either contemporaneous theory or reception history might have enhanced Cooke's argument. And while one could argue that understanding language is also crucially dependent on context and convention, the relative morphological stability of words and associated word meanings marks a crucial difference from the more precarious morphology of musical vocabulary.

The metaphor of translation has remained active in discourse about music despite the more or less general agreement that music is ultimately untranslatable. Whereas a news item or novel or poem can be more or less rendered equivalently in English, Yoruba, French, Russian, Swahili, or German, music cannot be translated from the medium of sound into that of words. Nor can it be translated from one stylistic milieu into another, although it can be modified to reflect the preoccupation of different eras and communities. For example, when Hans von Bülow published an edition of C. P. E. Bach's *Sechs Klavier-Sonaten* in 1862, he justified the added dynamics, the thicker accompaniment texture, the added inner voices, the composed-over gaps and pauses by invoking the metaphor of translation:

> The editor was no less convinced of the need for selection than of the necessity for "arranging" these sonatas. This should be understood as meaning neither more nor less than a translation from the keyboard language of the 18th-century to that of the nineteenth—from the clavichordistic to the pianofortistic, if I may use such inelegant terms.[32]

---

30. Cooke, *The Language of Music* (Oxford: Oxford University Press, 1959).
31. Cooke, *The Language of Music*, 115, 140.
32. Hans von Bülow, Preface to C. P. E. Bach, *Sechs Klavier Sonaten* (Leipzig: Peters, 1862), 3.

Interstylistic translation of this sort represents an honest creative response to music of the past, a way of expressing the continuing relevance of past creativity to present audiences not by piously seeking to recreate an authentic sound—which action is in any case mired in huge logical and ethical contradictions—but by openly acknowledging the pastness of the past and seeking an understanding that reflects or preserves present dispositions and sensibilities. Yet editorial practices such as those that Bülow followed have been discredited by contemporary musicology—another sign that musicology is frequently out of sync with musical practice. Where Hans von Bülow sought to "translate" C. P. E. Bach's music from its source language (the North German mid-eighteenth-century musical idiom) to a receptor or target language (the cosmopolitan nineteenth-century pianistic language), recent musicology has insisted on recovering Bach pure and whole. The new orthodoxy is to refuse to translate. What is overlooked in such a position, however, is that even the most faithfully "authentic" approach to editing and performing is already a translation, a rendition. The question then is not whether to translate but whether, having done so, you acknowledge that what you have done is to substitute a (presumably better) translation for an existing one.[33]

Translation remains a fertile metaphor for musical discourse as long as its limitations are kept in mind. Gayle Henrotte's claim that "musical styles are not translatable, but the impulses that produce music are"[34] discourages activity of the sort in which Hans von Bülow was engaged and recommends a more elusive search for creative impulses which presumably can be expressed in a metalanguage common to several creative arts. Émile Benveniste posits a "principle of non-redundancy between semiotic systems," seeking thereby to show that "two semiotic systems of different types cannot be mutually interchangeable." This "nonconvertibility of systems with different bases" affirms the impossibility of finally translating music without denying the existence of morphological or expressive resemblances between systems.[35]

9. Musical and linguistic meaning (or reference) may be extrinsic or intrinsic.[36] In music, intrinsic meaning predominates over extrinsic meaning, whereas in language it is the other way around. This is another way of stating the absence of lexical meaning for music and music's resistance to translation, or its problematizing of translation. Extrinsic and intrinsic are convenient but highly problematic terms for distinguishing one mode of musical signification from another. A Wagnerian leitmotif; a word painting in Monteverdi, Lassus, or Handel; the depiction of a narrative in a Liszt or Strauss tone poem; and the expression of verbal images in the accompaniment to a Schubert song—these are all examples of extrinsic or iconic reference. A leitmotif, for example, bears the weight of an assigned reference.

33. The incorporative practices associated with jazz improvisation, as heard in performances by Louis Armstrong, Art Tatum, Bud Powell, and Charlie Parker, among numerous others, can be usefully figured in terms of translation. For a discussion of "improvisation as conversation," see Monson, *Saying Something*, 73–96.

34. Henrotte, "Music as Language," 169.

35. Émile Benveniste, "The Semiology of Language," in *Semiotics: An Introductory Reader*, ed. Robert E. Innis (London: Hutchinson, 1986), 235.

36. Nattiez, *Music and Discourse*, 111–127.

In painting words, the composer finds—often invents—an iconic sign for a non-musical reality. Relying upon these "musical-verbal dictionaries,"[37] composers and listeners constrain musical elements in specified ways in order to hear them as one thing or another. While such prescription does not eliminate alternative meanings for the listener, it has a way of reducing the potential multiplicity of meanings and directing the willing listener to the relevant image, narrative, or idea. Extrinsic meaning therefore depends on layers of conventional signification.

Intrinsic meaning, too, depends on an awareness of convention, but because we often take for granted our awareness of conventions, we tend to think of intrinsic meanings as internally directed and of immediate significance. A dominant-seventh chord indexing an immediate or postponed tonic, a rising melodic gap filled by a complementary stepwise descent, an opening ritornello promising a contrasting solo, or an inaugural chromatic pitch bearing the full potential of later enharmonic reinterpretation—these are examples of intrinsic meaning, meaning that is apparently grasped without recourse to external, nonmusical, knowledge.

The extrinsic-intrinsic dichotomy is ultimately false, however, for not only do intrinsic meanings rely on certain conventional constructs, but their status as "intrinsic" is continually transformed in the very moment that we apprehend their signifying work. It requires external knowledge—or, at least, conventional knowledge—to expect a dominant-seventh to move to the tonic; it could just as readily move to the submediant; also, depending on its position and the local voice-leading situation, its behavior may be modified accordingly. Although some theories claim nature as the origin of some of their central constructs—such as the major triad or the notion of consonance—not until there has been cultural intervention is the natural made meaningful. The extrinsic-intrinsic dichotomy, then, enshrines an opposition that is only apparent, not real. Indeed, oppositions like this are common throughout the literature, including subjective-objective, semantic-syntactic, extramusical-(intra)musical, extroversive-introversive, extrageneric-congeneric, exosemantic-endosemantic, expression-structure, and hermeneutics-analysis. As points of departure for the exploration of musical meaning, as tools for developing provisional taxonomies, such dichotomies may be helpful in distributing the basic features of a given composition. But beyond this initial stage of the analysis, they must be used cautiously, for the crucial issue is not whether a given composition has meaning extrinsically or intrinsically but in what sense one or the other term applies.

10. Whereas language interprets itself, music cannot interpret itself. Language is the interpreting system of music.[38] If musical units have no fixed meanings, if the semantic element in music is "merely intermittent,"[39] if it is not possible to make a propositional statement in music, and if music is ultimately untranslatable, then music cannot interpret itself. There are, to be sure, intertextual resonances in music that might be described in terms of interpretive actions. For example, a variation set displays different, sometimes progressively elaborate and affectively

37. Powers, "Language Models," 2.
38. Benveniste, "The Semiology of Language," 235.
39. Carl Dahlhaus, "Fragments of a Musical Hermeneutics," trans. Karen Painter, *Current Musicology* 50 (1991): 5–20.

contrasted reworkings of an initial theme—acts of interpretation that help us to "understand" the theme, appreciate its latent possibilities, and admire the composerly intellectual effort. But insofar as the variation set exists as a composition, all of its internal commentaries are absorbed by that larger generic identity. They do not rise to the level of separate critical acts even though they may display critical tendencies. It is only when such acts are read by the analyst within a discourse explicitly designated as analytical or critical that they assume that function. We would not ordinarily describe a subsequent variation as an "analysis" of the theme, or even as an interpretation of it, even though it probes the theme, as if "discovering its essence."[40] The level of the work and the level of discourse about the work are normally kept categorically separate.

The closest we come to music interpreting itself is in Schenker's unique method of conveying analytical insights. His graphic notation adapts musical notation to the representation of musical structure, thereby hoping to minimize the gap between the music and the analysis. In *Free Composition*, for example, Schenker declares—provocatively, perhaps—that his graphs are "part of the actual composition."[41] But proof that the graphs only eliminate some words but not the concepts that constrain the graph as a whole lies in the fact that since each element in Schenker's symbology denotes a specific technical procedure (stemmed open notes, slurs, S signs, etc.), the graph is in principle translatable into prose. The exercise would be cumbersome, but it is in principle possible in a way that a translation of the *Eroica* Symphony—as distinct from a translation of its scoric representation—is impossible. Indeed, the difficulty of banishing words entirely from the Schenkerian enterprise arises in part because, in spite of the undoubted elegance and economy of graphic notation, the complementary aspects of sense, expression, and meaning that must elevate an analysis toward its truth content are held in abeyance, awaiting the verbal supplement. Forays into such aspects of musical significance depend crucially on the metaphorical suggestiveness and imprecision of words, not on the relative fixity of stemmed and unstemmed note heads. It is not, therefore, that an expressive dimension is missing from Schenker's graphs but rather that articulating the meaning of a composition depends upon an apparently ineliminable verbal supplement.[42]

Preliminary Analytical Adventures

It is time now to turn from the broader world of language-music affinities to a narrower, more focused one of (purely) musical attributes in order to take up questions of musical meaning. Two passages from piano sonatas by Schubert and Mozart will start us off here. Both may be considered complete in principle in

40. Rosen, *The Classical Style*, 437.
41. Heinrich Schenker, *Free Composition*, trans. Ernst Oster (New York: Longman, 1979), xxiii.
42. See also Hans Keller's functional musical analyses, which attempt to minimize the role of words in music analysis. An introduction to Keller's work may be found in "Hans Keller (1919–1985): A Memorial Symposium," ed. Christopher Wintle, *Music Analysis* 5 (1986): 343–440.

order to simplify aspects of the analysis. The choice of instrumental (or untexted) music should require no further justification at this point, except to say that if musical analysis is obliged to deal with musical problems, then dispensing—if only temporarily—with the influence of words, drama, or dance may be advantageous. The purpose of the analysis is to pinpoint a few salient features of each composition and to suggest some of the meanings to which they give rise. It will be obvious, I trust, that although no attempt is made to "apply" the principles enshrined in the ten propositions discussed earlier, the following observations about structure are largely consistent with the ontology of music implicit in the propositions.[43]

Schubert, Sonata in C Minor, D. 958, Adagio, bars 1–18

Where does the motion begin in this beautiful adagio? Where does it end? How does it get there? As a first—naïve—response to these questions, we might say that the motion begins with the sounding of the tonic in bar 1 and ends when the same chord with the same disposition of voices is sounded on the downbeat of bar 18. The material identity of the two moments is, however, offset by their temporal nonidentity. The first sounding is given (without contestation); it is a gift. The latter sounding is achieved; it is a product of labor. Where bar 1 initiates the context in which the opening chord will be eventually understood, bar 18 is the outcome of a drawn-out discourse that unfolds gradually, incorporates parenthetical moves, reaches a point of intensity, and then concludes. Thus, the two framing moments feel different. The beginning has only the past—a past constituted by silence and memory—with which to contend; the end represents an attained goal, a sonority born of struggle and desire.

What kind of ending is this cadence in bars 17–18? If we have been following the course of the work from the beginning, we may wonder about the designation of bar 18 as the point at which the motion ends. Didn't bars 13–14 do the same thing? Not only that, but don't bars 15–18, taken as a whole, repeat—albeit with registral and slight textural alteration—bars 11–14? So we have two contiguous, nearly identical 4-bar units. If the first achieved closure—that is, brought the phrase to a satisfying conclusion—then the second may be said to reiterate and thus reinforce what was previously asserted. In one sense, then, bars 15–18 "say the same thing" as 11–14.

Can we then get out a pair of classroom scissors and dispense with the last 4 bars? Are they redundant from a syntactic point of view? To pose these questions

---

43. In this and subsequent analyses, I treat music as text or as a textual field, that is, as something woven by the composer and represented in a score. Reading the score as text is not a hermetic activity, however; it entails tapping into a huge and necessary supplement made possible by, but not represented directly in, the score. Regular reference to the score should thus be understood as a pragmatic move designed to ensure that my readers and I are on the same material page. Naturally, the score does not exhaust the dimensions of a work's textuality or, for that matter, its ontology. The charge that one is engaged in "scorism" because one uses the score as a point of reference makes sense only if the role of the supplement is overlooked. On scorism, see Monelle, *The Sense of Music: Semiotic Essays* (Princeton, NJ: Princeton University Press, 2000), 3.

Example 1.1. Schubert, Piano Sonata in C Minor, D. 958, Adagio, bars 1–18.

is to broach the subject of repetition as a constructive force. If bars 11–14 serve a structural function by closing off the period, bars 15–18 serve a rhetorical one by echoing the previous cadence. The answer to the question "Where does the motion end?" then would be bar 14, not bar 18, as postulated earlier. Bars 15–18 function as a rhetorical supplement, that is, they are dispensable from a structural point of view but not from a phenomenal point of view. But "structure" and "rhetoric" are slippery terms, especially when used in the criticism of an art form that depends foundationally on repetition. There is no structure without rhetoric; rhetoric does not merely adorn—it defines.

We should hesitate, therefore, to qualify repetition as "mere." In Schubert, nothing is ever *merely* repeated. Consider another example of repetition, this time on a very local level: the repeated Cs in the melody in bar 3. These are harmonized in such a way as to produce a surge of energy in the approach to the half-cadence in bar 4. When we hear them again in bar 11, their number has increased to four, the first three harmonized as before, the fourth rendered with a charge similar to the second in order to enhance its motion to the subdominant, itself tonicized in bars 11–12. The destinations of the repeated Cs in bars 3 and 11 are thus different. We will hear bars 11–12 again as 15–16, now in a higher register and in a thicker texture. Are these high Cs merely an echo of what we heard earlier in bars 11–12? We know better than to use "mere."

The kinds of interpretive issues raised by the repeated Cs bring us to what may well be the core aspect of this composition, namely, its tonal life. For many musicians, meaning in this Schubert work is intimately tied to the tonal tendencies in each phrase, and the sense of each phrase is, in turn, conveyed by the degree of closure it exhibits. The first of these punctuation marks occurs in bars 3–4, where the half-cadence pronounces the first 4 bars unfinished, incomplete, open—a promissory note. The status of the dominant chord in bar 4 is elevated in bars 7–8 through tonicization. By acquiring its own dominant in bars 6–7, the dominant on the downbeat of bar 8 displays an egotistical tendency, as Schenker would say, demanding recognition for itself rather than as a mere accessory to the reigning tonic. But this moment in the sun is short-lived as D-natural is replaced by D-flat in bar 8 to transform the E-flat major chord into a dominant-seventh of A-flat. The join between bars 8 and 9 is smoothed over, and in no time we are back where we started: bar 9 is the "same" as bar 1. Notice how the bass progression by fifths in 5–8 (C–F–B♭–E♭) offers us a heightened view of the tonicized dominant in bar 8. Thus, what was "said" at the conclusion of bars 1–4 is intensified in the course of bars 5–8.

At 9, the motion begins again. By this act of beginning again, Schubert lets us understand that the destination of the next 8 bars will be different, that whereas the two previous 4-bar phrases (1–4 and 5–8) remained open, closure is now a definite possibility. But for the registrally elevated lower voices, all is as before from the downbeat of bar 9 through the third eighth-note of bar 11, after which point Schubert slips into the subdominant (bar 12, downbeat), extending the chord through its own minor subdominant. This is not a destination we would have inferred from the beginning of the piece, and the manner of its attainment tells us that the D-flat major chord is on its way somewhere, that it is not a goal but a station. Schubert confirms the transitory nature of bar 12 by composing past it into the cadence at bars 13–14. In retrospect, we might hear the pause on the subdominant in 12 as a pause on the predominant sonority within a larger cadential group, IV–V7–I across bars 12–14. That the motion would end eventually in a satisfying close we took for granted from the beginning; but with what imagination and play this would be accomplished, we could not have predicted. With the cadence in 13–14, the composition reaches an end, a definitive end, perhaps. Alas, Schubert is not done yet. He opens up a new, upper register, repeats the progression of bars 11–12, leading to the predominant at 15–16, abandons that register, and returns to the lower register in order to close, using the cadence figure from 13–14 in 17–18 to mark the end of the "composition" as a whole.[44]

With this first pass through the composition under the guide of its cadences, we have begun to broach the nature of Schubert's tonal imagination and the nature of musical meaning. There is more to the tonal life than the sense conveyed by cadences, however. The golden rule for exploring tonal meaning is to be mindful of the origin and destination of every event, to understand that no moment stands in isolation. Tonal composing is premised on an always-connected ideology that governs the community of tones. This is not to deny that some connections can be interpreted in terms of contextual discontinuities; it is only to claim a premise of

---

44. The play with register hinted at here is brought to a spectacular finish at the end of the movement.

connectedness. A chosen event comes from somewhere and leads elsewhere. Within this broader goal-directedness, an engaging network of motions unfolds at more local levels. Structural entities are elaborated, decorated, or extended in time. Some events emerge as hierarchically superior within individual prolongational contexts.

Subsequent chapters in this book will explore the nature of tonal meaning, but we can make a second start on the terrain of Schubert's sonata by observing the process by which structural entities are elaborated. Example 1.2 rewrites Schubert's 18-bar composition as a series of 11 building blocks or units.[45] Each expresses a tonal-contrapuntal motion; therefore, each is akin to an item of vocabulary. My presentation of each fragment begins with its putative structural underpinning and then hypothesizes a series of transformations that set Schubert's surface into relief. In this way, tonal meaning is understood in reference to tonal composition, not external association. The best way to appreciate example 1.2 is to play through it at the piano and observe what Schubert does with simple processes like extension of a chord (units 1, 6), voice exchange (units 2, 7), half-cadence (unit 3), full cadence (units 5, 9, and 11), progression from tonic to subdominant (on its way to a cadential dominant; units 8, 10), and circle-of-fifths progression (unit 4).

With these speculative derivations, we can claim to have accounted in one way or another for all of the local harmonic and voice-leading motions in the composition. Here is a summary:[46]

Bars $1–2^1$ = extension of tonic, I–I6
Bars $2^1–3^1$ = extension of tonic by voice exchange
Bars $3^1–4$ = progression from I–V
Bars 5–8 = cadence in V
Bars $8–9^1$ = V7–I progression
Bars $9–10^1$ = bars $1–2^1$
Bars $10^1–11^1$ = bars $2^1–3^1$
Bars $11^1–12$ = progression from I–IV, on its way to V (double meaning)
Bars 13–14 = cadence in I
Bars 15–16 = bars 11–12
Bars 17–18 = bars 13–14

Understanding these ways of proceeding forms the basis of tonal understanding. The analyst imagines Schubert's decision-making process from the point of view of the finished work. There is no recourse to biography or other external information

---

45. Here and in subsequent examples, the units of a composition are numbered using a simple ordinal scheme: 1, 2, 3, etc. The main advantage of this practice is the neutrality it confers on the succession of units. This is part of a larger strategy to escape the overdetermination of a more conventional apparatus. For an important (but by no means isolated) precedent, see Derrick Puffett, "Bruckner's Way: The Adagio of the Ninth Symphony," *Music Analysis* 18 (1999): 5–100. Puffett's units are designated as "periods," and there are 33 of them in this movement. He also cites an earlier instance of "period analysis" in Hugo Leichtentritt's *Musical Form* (Cambridge, MA: Harvard University Press, 1951; orig. 1911).

46. Superscripts are used to locate a specific beat within the bar. Thus, 2^1 denotes beat 1 of bar 2, 2^2 is beat 2 of bar 2, and so on.

Example 1.2. Origins of units in Schubert, Piano Sonata in C Minor, D. 958, Adagio, bars 1–18.

at this level of the analysis, only an understanding of the possibilities of manipulating the language.

When we first noted the different registral placement of the nearly identical material in bars 11–12 and 15–16, we retreated from assigning structural function to registral differentiation. Register as a dependent dimension is not thought to have a syntax. But without contesting this theoretical "fact," we can see from the ways in which Schubert manipulates register during the return of the opening (example 1.3) that speaking in terms of a *registral discourse* may not be hyperbolic. It is the destination of the tonal narrative in association with register that is of interest here.

Example 1.3. Schubert, Piano Sonata in C Minor, D. 958, Adagio, bars 102–115.

Bars 102–105 are the equivalent of 9–13. There is an important change of mode from A-flat major to A-flat minor, which in turn affects the destination of the phrase, C major. Then C, as V (bar 105), leads to a repeat of the local I–IV–I progression (compare 105 and 106), a "correction," really, of the previous 2 bars, the point being to bring things in line with the events of the exposition. But the succession C–Db is apparently part of an emerging chromatic ascent to D (bar 107). From here, it is possible to get to A major and to play the cadential phrase there (bar 108). But Schubert, realizing the wrongness of A major, withholds the final resolution (bar 109) and returns to where he should have been. There is something fantasy-like about these last 14 bars of the movement. Schubert seems to forget himself for a moment—or to pretend to forget himself. The effect is a momentary derailment of the tonal process, a heightening of tension, an assertion of authorial presence rather than control. Tonal process and register eventually find their ultimate goals, however. All is well that ends well.

Mozart, Piano Sonata in D Major, K. 576, first movement, bars 1–8

The syntactical meaning of this sprightly 8-bar period is secured by the perfect cadence in bars 7–8, a V–I progression with a 9–8 and 4–3 double suspension over I. This final cadence answers directly the half-cadence "posed" in bars 3–4 by the progression ii6–v6/4–5/3. When juxtaposed, the two cadences carry the respective senses of question and answer, open utterance followed by closed one. Indeed, from the beginning of the composition, we have been offered a dualistic gesture as rhetorical figure and premise. The unison hunt-style figure that suggested trumpets or horns (bars 1–2) is answered by the more delicate figures of bars 3–4, perhaps a hint at the *Empfindsamer* style. Similarly, the sequential repetition of bars 1–2 as 5–6 poses another "question" that is answered immediately by the equivalent of bars 3–4, namely, bars 7–8. In terms of textural design, then, the period is symmetrical: 4 + 4 subdivided into (2 + 2) + (2 + 2). Phrase division of this sort is part of the unmarked or ordinary syntax of the classical style. From this point of view, the period is regular and unproblematic.

Example 1.4. Mozart, Piano Sonata in D Major, K. 576, first movement, bars 1–8.

Beneath this trim, balanced, indeed classical exterior, however, there lurk a number of meaningful tensions that grow out of the closing tendencies of Mozart's materials. Three such tensions may be identified. The first resides in the play of register. In the initial 2 + 2 pairing, the second pair answers the first in a higher but contiguous register. The effect of registral change is readily felt if we rewrite the 4-bar phrase within a single register (example 1.5). Although it preserves the question-and-answer pattern together with topical and textural contrasts, this hypothetical version mutes the sense of a new plane of activity in bars 3–4. The second 4-bar phrase rehearses the registral patterning in the first, so we hear the contrast of register as an emerging contextual norm. The norm, in other words, enshrines a residual registral dissonance: the question posed at "home," the answer delivered away from "home." When aligned with the syntactically normative, repeated I–V harmonic progression, an interdimensional dissonance results.

Example 1.5. Registral modification of bars 3–4 in Mozart, Piano Sonata in D Major, K. 576, first movement.

But this is only the most superficial of animating tensions, indeed one that might be dismissed entirely by those who regard register as a secondary rather than primary parameter. (According to Leonard Meyer, primary parameters in the common practice era are harmony, melody, and rhythm, while dynamics, register, and timbre are secondary.)[47] Register apparently resists a syntactical reading. Consider, though, a second source of tension, namely, the events in bar 7. Had Mozart continued the phrase mechanically, he would have written something like what is shown in example 1.6, thereby preserving the rhythmic profile of bars 3–4. But he eschews a mechanical answer in favor of a little display of invention via his variation technique.[48] The charming figure in bar 7 seems literally to escape from the phrase and to run toward a little infinity; it suggests an improvisation, an utterance with an otherworldly aura. This heightened sense is set into relief by the decidedly ordinary cadential chords in bars 7–8, which remind us of where we are in the formal process. The cadence is unmarked, dutifully executed in fulfillment of a syntactic obligation; it is part of Mozart's ordinary language.

Example 1.6. Normalized version of bar 7 compared with Mozart's version.

The effect of bar 7, then, is to undermine the 4 + 4 division. Bar 7 is in a sense marked, and it may be heard in retrospect as the turning point of the period, the climax. It provides the final and most dramatic reinforcement of the absence of the tonic since bar 3. It confers the shape of a dynamic curve on the period as a whole. Indeed, its occurrence roughly three-quarters of the way through may encourage us to hear a process of gradual intensification culminating in bar 7 and the dissolution of tension at the cadence in 8.

We must not exaggerate the organicism of these 8 bars, however. Two-bar segments remain alive; indeed, the little figures that Mozart uses convey a series of poses or stances in an almost cartoon-like presentation. The temporal manner is one of succession, not a composing through time in the manner of the Schubert composition we discussed earlier. There is, according to this view, only the most minimal sense of continuity across the span of the period—a necessary minimum that counters an inactive discontinuity. There are other compositions in which Mozart effects a deeply organicist manner (think of the opening movement of the G Minor Symphony, or the slow movement of the String Quintet in C Major, K. 515), but here the abundance of ideas complicates the temporal landscape.

---

47. Leonard Meyer, "Exploiting Limits: Creation, Archetypes and Style Change," *Daedalus* (1980): 177–205.
48. See Roman Ivanovitch, "Mozart and the Environment of Variation" (Ph.D. diss., Yale University, 2004), for an engaging study of Mozart's variation technique.

Cross-referencing seems as significant as driving to a cadence. To speak implicitly of discontinuity between, say, bars 1–2 and 3–4 may seem exaggerated, but it would be an interpretive deficit to discount resistance to continuity by acknowledging only our privileged lines and voice-leading paths.

There is yet another source of tension, one that takes us into the realm of tonal tendency. Bar 5, too, is marked rather than unmarked. This is not the consequent we would normally expect to the 4-bar antecedent. Since bars 1–4 began on I and finished on V, bars 5–8 might begin on V and return to I, or begin on I and return to it via V. To begin on ii, as Mozart does here, is to create a sense of a different—perhaps more extended—temporal and tonal trajectory. It is as if we were beginning a sequential motion in 4-bar units, one that would presumably result in a 12-bar period. Thus, the initiating A–D motion (bar 1, including upbeat) is followed by B–E (bar 5, including upbeat), and would presumably continue as C♯–F♯; eventually, of course, the pattern will have to be broken. The promise of a sequence is not fulfilled, however. Mozart turns the phrase inward and releases an ordinary functional cadence in bars 7–8. The effect of bars 5–6, then, is to reorient the overall harmonic trajectory. The clear I–V progression that shapes bars 1–4 is answered by an expanded ii–V–I cadence in bars 5–8, with the ii occupying three-quarters of the complementary phrase. It is as if the motion were begun and suspended at V (bars 1–4) and then resumed and brought to completion in the complementary ii–V–I progression (bars 5–8). To subsume this quite palpable drama under a simple I–V–I global progression, as Felix Salzer's Schenkerian reading does,[49] would be canonically correct, of course, but it would fail to convey the sharply etched shapes that give Mozart's composition its distinct rhetorical character and meaning.

More could be said about these two compositions by Schubert and Mozart, but what has been said should suffice in this introductory context. I hope that the chapter has, first, provided a general orientation to the differences between music and language, and second, through these preliminary analytical ventures, indicated some of the issues raised in an analysis of musical meaning. Some readers may sense a gap—a phenomenological gap, perhaps—between the more general discussion of music as language and the specific analytical discussion that followed. This is partly a question of metalanguage. The language of music analysis often incorporates nomenclature different from ordinary language, and this, in turn, is motivated in part by the need to refer to specific portions of the musical text, the object of attention. The score, however, is not a simple and stable object but a nexus of possibilities. Analytical language carries a host of assumptions about the analyst's conception of musical language—how notes connect, how tonal meanings are implied, how a sense of ending is executed, and so on. The point to be emphasized here is that the search for meaning and truth content in any composition is not productive without some engagement with the musical material and its technical structure. It should be clear, too, that probing the technical structure of a composition is a potentially never-ending process. The answers obtained from

49. Felix Salzer, *Structural Hearing: Tonal Coherence in Music*, vol. 2 (New York: Dover, 1952), 95.

such an exercise are provisional, never final. Ideally, such answers should engender other, more complex questions, the process continuing ad infinitum. Final-state declarations about the meaning of this or that composition should be approached with the greatest care so as not to flatten, cheapen, or undercomplicate what the work of art makes possible. Readers may wish to keep this ideal in mind while reading the analyses in subsequent chapters, where the imperatives of theory-building sometimes enjoin us to curtail exploration in order to frame the (necessarily provisional) outcomes for critical assessment.

CHAPTER Two

Criteria for Analysis I

If music is like language but not identical to it, how might we formulate a description of its material content and modes of organization that captures its essence as an art of tone within circumscribed historical and stylistic contexts? The purpose of this chapter and the next is to provide a framework for answering this question. To this end, I have devised six rubrics for distributing the reality of Romantic music: topics or *topoi*; beginnings, middles, and endings; high points; periodicity (including discontinuity and parentheses); three modes of enunciation, namely, speech mode, song mode, and dance mode; and narrative. The first three are discussed in this chapter, the other three in chapter 3. Together, they facilitate an exploration of the immediately perceptible dimensions of Romantic compositions. Not every criterion is pertinent to every analytical situation, nor are the six categories nonoverlapping. But for each compositional situation, one, two, or some combination of the six can help to convey salient aspects of expression and structure. It is best, then, to think of the criteria variously as enabling mechanisms, as schemes for organizing intuited insights, and as points of departure for further exploration. Romantic repertoires are of course vast and diverse, but to claim that "there is no consistent principle of structure that governs Romantic music" may be to undervalue a number of recurring strategies.[1] We need to find ways to manage and characterize heterogeneity, not to contain, mute, or erase it. We need, in short, to establish some *conditions of possibility* by which individual students can pursue in greater analytical detail the effervescent, evanescent, and ultimately plural signification of Romantic music.

Topics

Setting out the compositional and stylistic premises of music in the classic era, Leonard Ratner draws attention to its mimetic qualities:

---

1. Leonard G. Ratner, *Music: The Listener's Art*, 2nd ed. (New York: McGraw-Hill, 1966), 314.

From its contacts with worship, poetry, drama, entertainment, dance, ceremony, the military, the hunt, and the life of the lower classes, music in the early 18th century developed a thesaurus of characteristic figures, which formed a rich legacy for classic composers. Some of these figures were associated with various feelings and affections; others had a picturesque flavor. They are designated here as topics—subjects for musical discourse.[2]

Ratner's topics include dances like minuet, contredanse, and gavotte, as well as styles like hunt, singing, fantasia, and Sturm und Drang. Although the universe of eighteenth-century topics is yet to be formulated definitively as a fixed, closed category with an attendant set of explicit discovery procedures, many of Ratner's core topics and his ways of reading individual compositions have served in recent years to enliven interpretations of music by Mozart, Haydn, Beethoven, and their contemporaries. The concept of topic provides us with a (speculative) tool for the imaginative description of texture, affective stance, and social sediment in classic music.[3]

A comparable exercise of establishing the compositional and stylistic premises of Romantic music, although challenging in view of the greater heterogeneity of compositional ideals in the latter repertoire, would nonetheless confirm the historical persistence of *topoi*. Chorales, marches, horn calls, and various figures of sighing, weeping, or lamenting saturate music of this era. There is, then, a level of continuity between eighteenth- and nineteenth-century styles that would undermine historical narratives posited on the existence of a categorical distinction between them. It would be equally problematic, however, to assert a straightforward historical continuity in the way topics are used. On one hand, the largely public-oriented and conventional topics of the eighteenth century often exhibit a similar orientation in the nineteenth century. For example, the communal ethos or sense of unanimity inscribed in a topic like *march* remains largely invariant. The slow movement of Beethoven's *Eroica* Symphony; Mendelssohn's *Song without Words* in E minor, op. 62, no. 3; the little march with which the protagonist of Schumann's "Help me sisters," from *Frauenliebe und Leben, no.* 6, projects the joy of a coming wedding; Liszt's *Rákozcy* March; the Pilgrims' march from Berlioz's *Harold in Italy*; and the determined opening movement of Mahler's Sixth Symphony—all are united by a mode of utterance that is irreducibly social and communal, a mode opposed to aloneness. On the other hand, the ascendancy in the nineteenth century of figures born of a private realm, figures that bear the marks

2. Leonard G. Ratner, *Classic Music: Expression, Form, and Style* (New York: Schirmer, 1980), 9.

3. On topics in classic music, see Ratner, *Classic Music*; Wye Jamison Allanbrook, *Rhythmic Gesture in Mozart: Le nozze di Figaro and Don Giovanni* (Chicago: University of Chicago Press, 1983); Agawu, *Playing with Signs: A Semiotic Interpretation of Classic Music* (Princeton, NJ: Princeton University Press, 1991); Elaine Sisman, *Mozart: The "Jupiter" Symphony* (Cambridge: Cambridge University Press, 1993); Hatten, *Musical Meaning in Beethoven*; Monelle, *The Sense of Music*; Raymond Monelle, *The Musical Topic: Hunt, Military and Pastoral* (Bloomington: Indiana University Press, 2006); and William E. Caplin, "On the Relation of Musical *Topoi* to Formal Function," *Eighteenth-Century Music* 2 (2005): 113–124.

of individual composerly idiolects, speaks to a new context for topic. If topics are commonplaces incorporated into musical discourses and recognizable by members of an interpretive community rather than secret codes to be manipulated privately, then the transition into the Romantic period may be understood not as a replacement but as the incorporation of classic protocol into a still more variegated set of Romantic discourses.

In order to analyze a work from the point of view of its topical content, one needs access to a prior universe made up of commonplaces of style known to composers and their audiences. Topics are recognized on the basis of prior acquaintance. But recognition is an art, and there is simply no mechanical way of "discovering" topics in a given work. Topics are therefore also constructions, not naturally occurring objects. Without deep familiarity with contemporaneous as well as historically sanctioned styles, it is simply not possible to know what the categories are nor to be able to deploy them imaginatively in analysis.

Few students of classical music today grew up dancing minuets, bourrées, and gavottes, marching to janissary music, or hearing fanfares played on hunting horns. Only a few are skilled at paraphrasing existing compositions, improvising keyboard preludes, or setting poetry to music in a consistent personal idiom, not in preparation for professional life as a composer but to enhance a general musical education. In other words, thorough grounding in the sonic residue of late eighteenth- and nineteenth-century styles, which constitutes a prerequisite for effective topical analysis, is not something that can be taken for granted. Lacking this background, we need to construct a universe of topics from scratch.

For the more extensively researched classic repertoire, a universe of topic is already implicit in the writings of Ratner, Allanbrook, Hatten, and Monelle. I list 61 of the more common topics here without elaboration simply to orient readers to the worlds of affect, style, and technique that they set in motion. Some are everyday terms used by musicologists; others are less familiar terms drawn from various eighteenth-century sources. All occur in various compositions—some well known, others obscure.

The Universe of Topic for Classic Music

1. Alberti bass
2. alla breve
3. alla zoppa
4. allemande
5. amoroso style
6. aria style
7. arioso
8. bound style or stile legato
9. bourrée
10. brilliant style
11. buffa style
12. cadenza
13. chaconne bass
14. chorale
15. commedia dell'arte
16. concerto style
17. contredanse
18. ecclesiastical style
19. *Empfindsamer* style
20. *Empfindsamkeit* (sensibility)
21. fanfare
22. fantasia style
23. French overture style
24. fugal style
25. fugato
26. galant style
27. gavotte
28. gigue
29. high style
30. horn call
31. hunt style
32. hunting fanfare
33. Italian style
34. *Ländler*
35. learned style
36. *Lebewohl* (horn figure)
37. low style
38. march

39. middle style	48. polonaise	55. singing style
40. military figures	49. popular style	56. strict style
41. minuet	50. recitative (simple,	57. Sturm und
42. murky bass	accompanied,	Drang (storm
43. musette	obligé)	and stress)
44. ombra style	51. romanza	58. tragic style
45. passepied	52. sarabande	59. Trommelbass
46. pastorale	53. siciliano	60. Turkish music
47. pathetic style	54. singing allegro	61. waltz

How is this universe domesticated within a given work? Because there exist, by now, several considered demonstrations of topical analysis, we can pass over the eighteenth-century portions of this discussion rapidly by simply mentioning the topical content of four canonical movements by Mozart. The first movement of the Piano Sonata in F Major, K. 332, includes aria style, singing style, Alberti bass, learned style, minuet, horn duet, horn fifths, Sturm und Drang, fanfare, amoroso style, bound style, and brilliant style. The first movement of the Piano Sonata in D Major, K. 284, incorporates (references to) concerto style, murky bass, singing style, Trommelbass, brilliant style, march, recitative obligé style, fanfare, and bound style. The first movement of the *Jupiter* Symphony, K. 551, includes fanfare, march, singing style, Sturm und Drang, contredanse, and learned style. And the introduction to the *Prague* Symphony, K. 504, includes (allusions to) French overture, *Empfindsamkeit*, singing style, learned style, fanfare, and ombra. Where and how these topics are used and their effect on overall expression and structure are the subjects of detailed studies by Allanbrook, Ratner, Sisman, Silbiger, and myself.[4]

Topical analysis begins with identification. Compositional manipulations of rhythm, texture, and technique suggest certain topical or stylistic affiliations, and the analyst reaches into his or her stock (or universe of topics) assembled from prior acquaintance with a range of works in order to establish correlations. Identification is followed by interpretation. Topics may enable an account of the form or inner dynamic of a work, its expressive stance, or even its structure. The use of identical or similar topics within or between works may provide insight into a work's strategy or larger aspects of style. And the shapes of individual topics

---

4. For a fuller discussion of topics in K. 332, see Wye J. Allanbrook, "Two Threads through the Labyrinth," in *Convention in Eighteenth- and Nineteenth-Century Music: Essays in Honor of Leonard G. Ratner*, ed. Wye J. Allanbrook, Janet M. Levy, and William P. Mahrt (Stuyvesant, NY: Pendragon, 1992), 125–171; and Alexander Silbiger, "'Il chitarrino le suonerò': Commedia dell'arte in Mozart's Piano Sonata K. 332" (paper presented at the annual meeting of the Mozart Society of America, Kansas City, November 5, 1999). On K. 284, see Leonard G. Ratner, "Topical Content in Mozart's Keyboard Sonatas," *Early Music* 19(4) (1991): 615–619; on K. 551, see Sisman, *Mozart: The "Jupiter" Symphony*; and on K. 504, see Ratner, *Classic Music*, 27–28 and 105–107; Agawu, *Playing with Signs*, 17–25; and Sisman, "Genre, Gesture and Meaning in Mozart's 'Prague' Symphony," in *Mozart Studies*, vol. 2, ed. Cliff Eisen (Oxford: Oxford University Press, 1997), 27–84.

may enhance appreciation of the sonic quality of a given work and the nature of a composer's rhetoric.

Constructing a comparable universe for Romantic music would fill more pages than we have at our disposal. Fortunately, the material for constructing such a universe may be gleaned from a number of books and articles. Ratner's book on Romantic music, although not deeply invested in notions of topic, draws attention to those aspects of compositions that signify in the manner of topics even while stressing the role of sheer sound, periodicity, texture, and harmony in this repertoire.[5] In two related books, Raymond Monelle has given due consideration to ideas of topic. The first, *The Sense of Music*, supplements a critical account of Ratner's theory with a set of semiotic analyses of music by Bach, Mahler, Tchaikovsky, and others. The second, *The Musical Topic: Hunt, Military and Pastoral*, explores the musical and cultural contexts of three musical topics through a broad historical landscape. Monelle's interest in the latter book is not in reading individual compositions for possible topical traces (although he provides a fascinating description of "hunts in instrumental music" by Mendelssohn, Schumann, Paganini, Franck, and Bruckner),[6] but in assembling a kaleidoscope of contexts for topics. While *The Sense of Music* constitutes a more or less traditional (but highly suggestive) music-analytical exercise—complete with the theoretical self-consciousness that became evident in musical studies during the 1990s—*The Musical Topic* moves in the direction of the larger humanistic enterprise known as cultural studies, emphasizing an array of intertextual resonances. There are, however, writers who remain committed to close readings of musical works informed by topic. One such writer is Robert Hatten, whose *Interpreting Musical Gestures, Topics, and Tropes: Mozart, Beethoven, Schubert* extends the interpretive and reflective exercise begun in his earlier book, *Musical Meaning in Beethoven: Markedness, Correlation and Interpretation*, and supplements it with a new theory of gesture.[7]

Most pertinent is a valuable article by Janice Dickensheets in which she cites examples from a broad range of composers, among them Carl Maria von Weber, Chopin, Schubert, Berlioz, Mendelssohn, Smetana, Grieg, Heinrich Herz, Saint-Saëns, Liszt, Verdi, Brahms, Mahler, and Tchaikovsky. She notes the persistence into the nineteenth century of some of Ratner's topics, including the musical types minuet, gigue, siciliano, and march, and the musical styles military, hunt, pastoral, and fantasia; the emergence of new styles and dialects; and the contextual inflection of old topics to give them new meanings. Her lexicon includes the following, each of which is illustrated with reference to a specific compositional manifestation:[8]

5. Ratner, *Romantic Music: Sound and Syntax* (New York: Schirmer, 1992).
6. Monelle, *The Musical Topic*, 85–94.
7. Robert Hatten, *Interpreting Musical Gestures, Topics, and Tropes: Mozart, Beethoven, Schubert* (Bloomington: Indiana University Press, 2004).
8. Janice Dickensheets, "Nineteenth-Century Topical Analysis: A Lexicon of Romantic *Topoi*," *Pendragon Review* 2(1) (2003): 5–19.

1. archaizing styles	9. demonic style	*Kriegslied*, and
2. aria style	10. fairy music	*Winterlied*)
3. bardic style	11. folk style	17. pastoral style
4. bolero	12. gypsy music	18. singing style
5. Biedermeier style	13. heroic style	19. Spanish style
6. Chinoiserie	14. Indianist style	20. style hongrois
7. chivalric style	15. Italian style	21. stile appassionata
8. declamatory	16. lied style or song	22. tempest style
style (recitative	style (includ-	23. virtuosic style
style)	ing lullaby,	24. waltz (*Ländler*)

In studies of the music of Liszt, Márta Grabócz postulates 16 topical classes called "classemes" (after Greimas) that might serve as a basis for interpretation.[9] Classemes resemble what Asafyev calls "intonations" and are defined as "units having exact meanings, having crystallized and accumulated in the course of the history of music." For the music of Liszt, Grabócz proposes the following constituents for a universe of topic:

1. appassionato,	10. recitativo	and lamentoso
agitato	11. lamenting, elegiac	(lagrimoso)
2. march	12. citations	15. the pathetic, which
3. heroic	13. the grandioso,	is the exalted form
4. scherzo	triumfando (going	of bel canto
5. pastoral	back to the heroic	16. the pantheistic,
6. religioso	theme)	an amplified
7. folkloric	14. the lugubrious	variant of either
8. bel canto, singing	type deriving at	the pastoral theme
9. bel canto, declama-	the same time	or of the religious
tory	from appassionato	type

Grabócz's interest is not merely in identifying classemes but in interpreting them. This leads her to develop a series of categories for distributing the quality and associations of themes and gestures in Liszt. Elementary signifying units are semes, classemes, or isotopies, and these three types of building block make possible a reading of Liszt's music as a form of narrative.[10]

---

9. Márta Grabócz, "Semiological Terminology in Musical Analysis," in *Musical Semiotics in Growth*, ed. Eero Tarasti (Bloomington: Indiana University Press, 1996), 195–218. See also her *Morphologie des oeuvres pour piano de Liszt: Influence du programme sur l'évolution des formes instrumentales*, 2nd ed. (Paris: Kimé, 1996). Before Grabócz, Keith Thomas Johns studied the use of *topoi* to express the program in Liszt's tone poems. See Johns, *The Symphonic Poems of Franz Liszt* (Stuyvesant, NY: Pendragon, 1996).

10. A similar narrative impulse is evident in the succession of "different stylistic characters" that Jim Samson hears in Chopin's Fourth Ballade (Samson, "Extended Forms: Ballades, Scherzos and Fantasies," in *The Cambridge Companion to Chopin*, ed. Samson [Cambridge: Cambridge University

In the music of Mahler, the essential utterance is heterogeneous at the core, and although not all aspects of such heterogeneity can be given a topical designation, many can. The following are some of the topics regularly employed by Mahler:[11]

1. nature theme	7. march (including	13. bell motif
2. fanfare	funeral march)	14. *Totentanz*
3. horn call	8. arioso	15. lament
4. bird call	9. aria	16. *Ländler*
5. chorale	10. minuet	17. march
6. pastorale	11. recitative	18. folk song
	12. scherzo	

Conventional topics do not, however, exhaust the sources of expressivity in Mahler. Counterpoint, for example, is sometimes figured as a topic by being disposed in a manner that suggests enclosure within quotation marks. Use of a form like sonata, too, may suggest a new awareness that takes the utterance out of a first-level efficacious or natural use to a second-level quotational or marked use. Finally, there is an entire network of quotation (including self-quotation and the simulation of quoting) and allusion that brings into view varying levels and intensities of dialogue with earlier composers: J. S. Bach, Beethoven, Schumann, Brahms, and Wagner, among others. The size of the enterprise notwithstanding, it is hard to imagine any worthwhile analysis of meaning in Mahler that can dispense entirely with the notion of topic.

Among the things that the foundational hybridity of Mahler's music made possible for later composers was an increasingly normative blurring of boundaries in material and conceptual realms. Approaching the pluralistic world of twentieth-century music, it might be thought at first that topics as conventional signs operating in an economy in which contracts exist between composers and their audiences would cease to play a central role. This supposition arises partly because the modernist revolution of the century's early decades aimed in part to be seen as severing connections with recent musical pasts (but not all musical pasts). But aesthetic ideology, whether stated explicitly by practitioners or constructed after the fact by critics, rarely coincides with the complex traces produced by the musical work itself. While the presumed erasure of certain aspects of convention may indeed be superficially observed in certain "musicologically sanctioned"

Press, 1992], 115), and in Liszt's use of symbols in his Transcendental Études (see Samson, *Virtuosity and the Musical Work: The Transcendental Studies of Liszt* [Cambridge: Cambridge University Press, 2007], 175–197). In an unpublished study of Paganini's violin concertos, Patrick Wood highlights a sharply profiled expressive genre which progresses from a march topic to an opposing lyrical topic (such as the singing style) as the frame of the exposition of the first movement. See Wood, "Paganini's Classical Violin concerti" (unpublished seminar paper, Princeton University, 2008).

11. Among commentators on Mahler's music, something approaching the notion of *topos* appears most explicitly in the writings of Constantin Floros. See, for example, his *Gustav Mahler: The Symphonies*, trans. Vernon Wicker (Portland, OR: Amadeus, 1993).

compositions like the *Rite of Spring, Pierrot Lunaire, Salome,* or Webern's Five Pieces for String Quartet, op. 5, resistance to the past is, paradoxically, a way of registering belief in its potency, ultimately of displaying that past even while denying it. A topical approach supports such counternarratives.

The universe of topic has thus undergone a range of transformations from the eighteenth through the nineteenth and twentieth centuries and into the twenty-first. To put these developments in a nutshell: in the eighteenth century, topics were figured as stylized conventions and were generally invoked without pathos by individual composers, the intention being always to speak a language whose vocabulary was essentially public without sacrificing any sort of will to originality. In the nineteenth century, these impulses were retained, but the burgeoning of expressive possibilities brought other kinds of topic into view. Alongside the easily recognized conventional codes were others that approximated natural shapes (such as the dynamic curve or high-point scheme that we will discuss shortly) and some that were used consistently within a single composer's oeuvre or idiolect (Schumann's numerous ciphers and the Florestan, Eusebius, and Raro personifications are cases in point). Twentieth-century topical practice became, in part, a repository of eighteenth- and nineteenth-century usages even as the universe was expanded to include the products of various strategic denials. Thus, certain rhetorical gestures associated with Romantic music took on a "historical" or topical role in twentieth-century music, while the dynamic curve, which we will discuss under the rubric "high point," was, despite its quintessentially Romantic association, also found in a variety of twentieth-century repertoires, including electronic music.[12] Musics associated with specific groups (Jewish, gypsy) retained their vitality for quotation and allusion, while newer musical developments—such as the African-American traditions of blues, gospel, funk, jazz, and rap—provided material for topical exploration and exploitation by composers.

In an unpublished construction of a topical universe for twentieth-century music, Danuta Mirka divides topics into three groups. The first (group A) embraces eighteenth-century dances, the second (group B) lists musics associated with various ethnicities, and the third (group C) is a diverse collection of styles:

Group A
1. menuet
2. gavotte
3. bourrée
4. sarabande
5. gigue
6. pavane
7. passepied
8. tarantella

9. tango
10. waltz

Group B
11. Jewish music
12. Czech music
13. Polish music
14. Hungarian music

15. Gypsy music
16. Russian music
17. Spanish music
18. Latin-American music (Brazilian, Argentinean, Mexican,)
19. "Oriental" music (Chinese,

12. See Patrick McCreless, "Anatomy of a Gesture: From Davidovsky to Chopin and Back," in *Approaches to Musical Meaning*, ed. Byron Almen and Edward Pearsall (Bloomington: Indiana University Press, 2006), 11–40, for a study of this phenomenon.

Japanese,	23. Russian orthodox	32. circus music
Indian)	church style	33. barrel organ
20. North American	24. learned style	34. lullaby
country music	25. chaconne	35. children's song
	26. recitativo	36. fanfare
Group C	27. singing style	37. military march
21. Gregorian	28. barcarole	38. funeral march
chant	29. Negro spirituals	39. pastoral style
22. chorale	30. jazz	40. elegy
	31. cafe music	41. machine music

The music of Bartók and Stravinsky lends itself well to topical analysis. In a study of Bartók's orchestral works, Márta Grabócz has identified 10 recurring topics:[13]

1. the ideal or the quest for the ideal, expressed through the learned style
2. the grotesque, signaled by a combination of rhythmic practices (mechanical, the waltz), instrumental association (clarinet), and the octatonic collection
3. the image of the hopeless and gesticulating hero, expressed in dissonant, bitonal contexts with repeated fourths and fifths
4. nature (calm, friendly, or radiant), signaled by the acoustic scale
5. nature (hostile, menacing), conveyed by minor harmonies and the chromatic scale
6. nocturnal nature, expressed by string timbre, march-like melody, enchanting sonorities
7. elegy, expressed in a static or passive atmosphere
8. perpetuum mobile, manifest in ostinato or motoric movement
9. popular dance, song in a peasant style
10. metamorphosis, restricted to certain moments in the form and characterized by the transcendence or transubstantiation of the last appearance of a musical idea that has been present in varied form since the beginning

In Stravinsky's music, an essentialized parasitical tendency often originates in a play with, or appropriation of, established topics. At the root of the aesthetic lies a desire to creatively violate commonplaces or figures burdened with historical or conventional meaning. In their important study *Apollonian Clockwork: On Stravinsky*, Louis Andriessen and Elmer Schönberger unveil many of the composer's subtexts, thus bringing into aural view the foils and intertexts that form an essential part of the composer's work. *Apollonian Clockwork* is as much a study of topic as of anything else. To choose just one example that readers can readily recall: "L'histoire du soldat," composed in 1918, is a veritable catalog of topical references.

---

13. Márta Grabócz, "'Topos et dramaturgie': Analyse des signifiés et de la strategie dans deux movements symphoniques de B. Bartok [*sic*]," *Degrés* 109–110 (2002): j1–j18. The article includes a summary of the secondary literature on Bartók that alludes to or deals directly with topics, even where authors do not use the term.

To facilitate the narrating of the soldier's tale, Stravinsky draws on four central topical classes. The first, march, is presented in different guises or expressive registers (soldier's march, royal march, and the devil's triumphal march) without ever losing its intrinsic directionality. The second is dance, of which tango, waltz, and ragtime serve as conventional exemplars alongside a devil's dance. The third is pastorale, complete with airs performed by a stream. The fourth is chorale, manifest in two sizes, a little chorale that lasts only 8 bars and the grand chorale, which goes on for some 29 bars, interspersed with the soldier's narration. Within these bigger topical umbrellas, little topics are invoked: fanfares, drones reminiscent of musette, and the "Dies Irae" chant. The play element that guides the disposition of these materials is equally important, of course, especially as a window onto a discourse of repetition. But recognizing the *Soldier's March* as a veritable parade of historical styles is already a step in the right direction.[14]

To hear Romantic and post-Romantic music topically, then, is to hear it as a repository of historically situated conventional styles that make possible a number of dialogues. The examples mentioned here—by Mozart, Beethoven, Schumann, Liszt, Mahler, and Stravinsky—are only an indication of what is a vast and complex universe. Identifying topics, however, is only the first stage of analysis; interpretation must follow. Interpretation can be confined to meanings set in motion within a piece or include those that are made possible in intertextual space. The analyst might assess the work done by individual topics in a composition and, if s/he so desires, fashion a narrative that reflects their disposition. In some contexts, a plot will emerge for the individual composition; in others, topics will be absorbed into a larger expressive genre[15] or indeed a commanding structural trajectory; in still others, fragments will retain their identities on the deepest levels, refusing absorption into or colonization by an archetypal, unified plan. In practice, identifying topics can produce relatively stable results; interpreting topics, by contrast, often turns up diverse plots. Whereas identification entails a discovery of familiar or relatively objective configurations, interpretation is the exercise of an imaginative will—a fantasy fueled by the analyst's capacity for speculation. There are no firm archetypes upon which to hang an interpretation of the plots arising from topical succession. The results of identification differ from composition to composition. A topical analysis confirms the uniqueness of a given composition while also making possible a comparison of material content that might enable an assessment of affinity among groups of compositions.[16]

---

14. Debussy's Prelude for Piano, "Minstrels," makes a fascinating case study in topical expression. Within its basic scherzo-like manner, it manages to incorporate diverse allusions to other musical styles. One should perhaps distinguish between topical use and the kinds of deliberate quotation or allusion studied by Christopher Reynolds in *Motives for Allusion: Context and Content in Nineteenth-Century Music* (Cambridge, MA: Harvard University Press, 2003); and David Metzer in *Quotation and Cultural Meaning in Twentieth-Century Music* (Cambridge: Cambridge University Press, 2003). Among twentieth-century composers whose music strongly invites topical treatment, Kurt Weill ranks high.

15. Hatten, *Musical Meaning in Beethoven*, 67–90.

16. For a recent assessment of topic theory, see Nicholas Peter McKay, "On Topics Today," *Zeitschrift der Gesellschaft für Musiktheorie* 4 (2007). http://www.gmth.de/zeitschrift/artikel/0124/0124.html. Accessed August 12, 2008.

Beginnings, Middles, Endings

Aristotelian poetics bequeathed an enduring representation of the structure of any expressive, temporally bound utterance: it has a beginning, a middle, and an ending. This formal model or paradigm has an immediate, intuitive appeal. In poetry as well as in music, composers and listeners/readers regularly attend to the manipulation of or play with beginnings, middles, and endings. And throughout the history of thought about music, ideas relating to these functions exist. Mattheson described the shape of a musical oratory in terms that recognize these functions,[17] Koch developed a compositional theory of form featuring appendixes and suffixes,[18] and Schenker located a "definitive close of a composition" in the moment in which î appears over I.[19] More recently, Dahlhaus has put forward a tripartite structure consisting of an initial phase, evolution, and epilogue.[20] My own earlier study of classic music postulated a beginning-middle-ending paradigm,[21] while William Caplin's influential theory of formal functions recast ideas pertaining to beginnings, middles, and endings. Thus the formal unit or theme type known as *sentence* consists of a *presentation phrase* in which a basic idea is stated and repeated (beginning), followed by a *continuation phrase* featuring fragmentation, harmonic acceleration, liquidation, and sequential repetition (middle) and a *cadential idea* (ending). Similarly, the fundamental harmonic progressions that define the classic style are said to belong to one of three categories: prolongational, cadential, and sequential. Sequential processes are most characteristic of continuation phases or middles, cadences mark endings (including endings of beginnings as well as endings of endings), while the stasis of prolongation may initiate the structure, prolong it at its middle, or close it.[22]

And yet, but for a handful of attempts, the beginning-middle-ending model has remained implicit in music-theoretical work; it has not come to occupy as central a place in current analytical thinking as it might. There are two reasons for this. One is that the model seems so obvious and banal (Craig Ayrey's word)[23] that it is not immediately clear how the analyst can explore its ramifications in a rigorous fashion. But only if one understands beginnings, middles, and endings solely as temporal locations rather than as complex *functions* with conventional and logical attributes that operate at different levels of structure would the model seem banal. A second, more significant reason has to do with the unavoidable

---

17. Johann Mattheson, *Der vollkommene Capellmeister*, trans. Ernest Harriss (Ann Arbor, MI: UMI Research Press, 1981; orig. 1739).

18. Heinrich Christoph Koch, *Versuch einer Anleitung zur Composition*, vols. 2 and 3 (Leipzig: Böhme, 1787 and 1793).

19. Schenker, *Free Composition*, 129.

20. Carl Dahlhaus, *Between Romanticism and Modernism*, trans. Mary Whittall (Berkeley: University of California Press, 1980), 64.

21. Agawu, *Playing with Signs*, 51–79.

22. William E. Caplin, *Classical Form: A Theory of Formal Functions for the Instrumental Music of Haydn, Mozart and Beethoven* (Oxford: Oxford University Press, 2000), 3–5 and 24.

23. Craig Ayrey, "Review of *Playing with Signs*," *Times Higher Education Supplement* 3 (May 1991), 7.

fact that, as a set of qualities, beginnings, middles, and endings are not located in a single musical dimension but cut across various dimensions. In other words, interpreting a moment as a beginning or an ending invariably involves a reading of a combination of rhythmic, melodic, and harmonic factors as they operate in specific contexts. In an institutional climate in which analysts tend to work within dimensions as specialists, theories that demand an interdimensional approach from the beginning seem to pose special challenges. These difficulties are, however, not insurmountable, and it will be part of my purpose here to suggest ways in which attending to beginnings, middles, and endings can enrich our perception of Romantic music.

For many listeners, the impression of form is mediated by beginning, middle, and ending functions. Tchaikovsky's First Piano Concerto opens with a powerful beginning gesture that, according to Edward T. Cone, dwarfs the rest of what follows—a disproportionately elaborate opening gesture that sets the introduction off as "an overdeveloped frame that fails to integrate itself with the rest of the movement."[24] Some openings, by contrast, proceed as if they were in the middle of a process previously begun; such openings presuppose a beginning even while replacing it with a middle. Charles Rosen cites the long dominant pedal that opens Schumann's Fantasy in C Major for Piano, op. 17, as an example of a beginning in medias res.[25] And an ending like that of the finale of Beethoven's Fifth, with its plentiful reiteration of the tonic chord, breeds excess; strategically, it employs a technique that might be figured as rhetorically infantile to ensure that no listener misses the fact of ending. Ending here is, however, not merely a necessary part of the structure; it becomes a subject for discussion as well—a meta-ending, if you like.[26]

As soon as we begin to cite individual works, many readers will, I believe, find that they have a rich and complex set of associations with beginnings, middles, and endings. Indeed, some of the metaphors employed by critics underscore the importance of these functions. Lewis Rowell has surveyed a variety of beginning strategies in music and described them in terms of birth, emergence, origins, primal cries, and growth.[27] Endings, similarly, have elicited metaphors associated with rest and finality, with loss and completion, with consummation and transfiguration, with the cessation of motion and the end of life, and ultimately with death and dying. "No more," we might say at the end of *Tristan and Isolde*.

How might we redefine the beginning-middle-ending model for internal analytic purposes? How might we formulate its technical processes to enable exploration of Romantic music? Every bound temporal process displays a beginning-middle-ending structure. The model works at two distinct levels. First is the pure material or acoustical level. Here, beginning is understood ontologically as that which inaugurates the set of constituent events, ending as that which demarcates

24. Cone, *Musical Form and Musical Performance* (New York: Norton, 1968) 22.
25. Rosen, *The Classical Style*, 452–453.
26. Donald Francis Tovey comments on the appropriateness of this ending in *A Musician Talks, vol. 2: Musical Textures* (Oxford: Oxford University Press, 1941), 64.
27. Lewis Rowell, "The Creation of Audible Time," in *The Study of Time*, vol. 4, ed. J. T. Fraser, N. Lawrence, and D. Park (New York: Springer, 1981), 198–210.

the completion of the structure, and middle as the necessary link between beginning and ending. At this level, the analyst is concerned primarily with sound and succession, with the physical location of events.

There is a second, more qualitative level at which events (no longer mere sounds) are understood as displaying tendencies associated with beginnings, middles, and endings. These functions are based in part on convention and in part on logic. A beginning in this understanding is an event (or set of events) that enacts the normative function of beginning. It is not necessarily what one hears at the beginning (although it frequently is that) but what defines a structure qualitatively as a beginning. A middle is an event (or set of events) that prolongs the space between the end of the beginning and the beginning of the ending. It refuses the constructive profiles of initiation and peroration and embraces delay and deferral as core rhetorical strategies. Finally, an ending is an event (or set of events) that performs the functions associated with closing off the structure. Typically, a cadence or cadential gesture serves this purpose. An ending is not necessarily the last thing we hear in a composition; it may occur well before the last thing we hear and be followed by rhetorical confirmation. The task of an ending is to provide a decisive completion of structural processes associated with the beginning and middle.

The first level of understanding, then, embodies the actual, material unfolding of the work and interprets the beginning-middle-ending model as a set of place marks; this is a locational or ordinal function. The second speaks to structural function within the unfolding. Distinguishing between location and function has important implications for analysis. In particular, it directs the listener to some of the creative ways in which composers play upon listeners' expectations. For example, a locational opening, although chronologically prior, may display functions associated with a middle (as in off-tonic beginnings, or works that open with auxiliary cadences) or an ending (as in works that begin with cadences or with a $\hat{3}$–$\hat{2}$–$\hat{1}$ or $\hat{5}$–$\hat{4}$–$\hat{3}$–$\hat{2}$–$\hat{1}$ melodic progression). Location and function would thus be nonaligned, creating a dissonance between the dimensions. Similarly, in a locational ending, the reiterative tendencies that index stability and closure may be replaced by an openness that refuses the drive to cadence, thus creating a sense of middle, perhaps an equivocal ending. Creative play of this kind is known in connection with classic music, whose trim procedures and firmly etched conventions have the great advantage of sharpening our perception of any creative departures that a composer might introduce. It is also frequently enacted by Romantic composers within their individual and peculiar idiolects.

Although all three locations are necessary in defining a structure, associated functions may or may not align with the locations. It is also possible—functionally speaking—to lose one element of the model by, for example, deploying a locational ending without a sense of ending. It would seem, in fact, that beginnings and endings, because they in principle extend in time and thus function as potential colonizers of the space we call middle, are the more critical rhetorical elements of the model. In certain contexts, it is possible to redefine Aristotle's model with no reference to middles: a beginning ends where the ending begins. It is possible also to show that, in their material expression, beginnings and endings frequently draw on similar strategies. The stability or well-formedness needed to create a point of reference at the beginning of a musical journey shares the material forms—but not necessarily the rhetorical presentation—of a comparable stability that is needed to ground a dynamic and evolving structure at its end. It is also possible that endings, because they close off the structure, subtend an indispensable function. From this point of view, if we had to choose only one of the three functions, it would be ending. In any case, several of these functional permutations will have to be worked out in individual analyses.

It is not hard to imagine the kinds of technical processes that might be associated with beginnings, middles, and endings. Techniques associated with each of a work's dimensions—harmony, melody, rhythm, texture—could be defined normatively and then adapted to individual contexts. With regard to harmony, for example, we might say that a beginning expresses a prolonged I–V–(I) motion. (I have placed the closing I in parenthesis to suggest that it may or may not occur, or that, when it does, its hierarchic weight may be significantly less than that of the initiating I.) But since the beginning is a component within a larger, continuous structure, the I–V–(I) progression is often nested in a larger I–V progression to confer prospect and potential, to ensure its ongoing quality. A middle in harmonic terms is the literal absence of the tonic. This often entails a prolongation of V. Since such prolonged dominants often point forward to a moment of resolution, the middle is better understood in terms of absence and promise: absence of the stable tonic and presence of a dependent dominant that indexes a subsequent tonic. An ending in harmonic terms is an expanded cadence, the complement of the beginning. If the larger gesture of beginning is represented as I–V, then the reciprocal ending gesture is V–I. The ending fulfills the harmonic obligation exposed in the beginning, but not under deterministic pressure. As with the beginning and ending of the beginning, or of the middle, the location of the beginning and ending functions of the ending may or may not be straightforward. In some genres, endings are signaled by a clearly marked thematic or tonal return or by a great deal of fanfare. In others, we sense the ending only in retrospect; no grand activity marks the moment of death.

Similar attributions can be given for other musical dimensions. In doing so, we should remember that, if composition is figured essentially as a mode of play, what we call norms and conventions are functional both in enactment and in violation. On the thematic front, for example, we might postulate the imperatives of clear statement or definition at the beginning, fragmentation in the middle, and a restoration of statement at the ending, together with epigonic gestures or effects of reminiscence. In terms of phrase, we might postulate a similar plot: clarity (in the establishment of premises) followed by less clarity (in the creative manipulation of those premises) yields, finally, to a simulated clarity at the end. In addition to such "structural" procedures, we will need to take into account individual composerly routines in the choreographing of beginnings and endings. Beethoven's marked trajectories, Schubert's way with extensive parentheses and deferred closure, Mendelssohn's delicately balanced proportions, and the lyrical inflection of moments announcing home-going in Brahms—these are attitudes that might be fruitfully explored under the aegis of a beginning-middle-ending scheme. We have space here for only one composer.

As an example of the kinds of insights that might emerge from regarding a Romantic work as a succession of beginnings, middles, and endings on different levels, I turn to Mendelssohn's *Song without Words* in D major, op. 85, no. 4 (reproduced in its entirety as example 2.1). The choice of Mendelssohn is not accidental, for one of the widely admired features of his music is its lucidity. In the collection

Example 2.1. Mendelssohn, *Song without Words* in D major, op. 85, no. 4.

(continued)

Example 2.1. continued

of songs without words, each individual "song" typically has one central idea that is delivered with a precise, superbly modulated, and well-etched profile. The compositional idea is often affectingly delivered. And one reason for the composer's uncanny success in this area is an unparalleled understanding of the potentials of beginning, middle, and ending in miniatures. I suggest that the reader play through this song at the piano before reading the following analytical comments.

We might as well begin with the ending. Suppose we locate a sense of home-going beginning in the second half of bar 26. Why there? Because the rising minor seventh in the melody is the first intervallic event of such magnitude in the composition; it represents a marked, superlative moment. If we follow the course of the melody leading up to that moment, we hear a physical rise in contour (starting on F-sharp in 24) combined with an expansion of intervals as we approach the high G in bar 26. Specifically, starting from the last three eighth-notes in bar 25, we hear, in succession, a rising fourth (A–D), a rising sixth (G–E), and finally a rising seventh

(A–G). Then, too, this moment is roughly two-thirds of the way through the song, is underlined by an implicative 6/5 harmony that seeks resolution, and represents the culmination of a crescendo that has been building in the preceding 2 bars. The moment may be figured by analogy to an exclamation, an expected exclamation perhaps. It also marks a turning point, the most decisive turning point in the form. Its superlative quality is not known only in retrospect. From the beginning, Mendelssohn, here as in other songs without words, crafts a listener-friendly message in the form of a series of complementary gestures. Melody leads (that is, functions as a *Hauptstimme*); harmony supports, underlines, and enhances the progress of the melody; and the phrase structure regulates the temporal process while remaining faithful in alignment. The accumulation of these dimensional behaviors prepares bar 26. Although full confirmation of the significance of this moment will come only in retrospect, the balance between the prospective and retrospective, here as elsewhere in Mendelssohn, is striking. Luminous, direct, natural, and perhaps unproblematic (as we might say today), op. 85, no. 4 exemplifies carefully controlled temporal profiling.

Ultimately, the sense of ending that we are constructing cannot be understood with respect to a single moment, for that moment is itself a product of a number of preparatory processes. Consider bar 20 as the beginning of the ending. Why bar 20? Because the beautiful opening melody from bar 2 returns at this point after some extraneous, intervening material (bars 12–19). For a work of these modest dimensions, such a large-scale return readily suggests a reciprocal sense of closure within a tripartite formal gesture.

If we continue to move back in the piece, we can interpret the passage beginning in bar 12 as contrast to, as well as intensification of, the preceding 11 bars. Note the quasi-sequential process that begins with the upbeat to bar 12. Phrase-wise, the music proceeds at first in 2-bar units (11^4–13^3, 13^4–15^3; these and subsequent designations of phrase boundaries in this paragraph all include an eighth-note prefix), then continues in 1-bar units in the manner of a stretto (15^4–16^3 and 16^4–17^3), and finally concludes with 2 relatively neutral bars—"neutral" in the sense of declining a clear and repeated phrase articulation—of transition back to the opening theme (17^4–19^3).[28] The moment of thematic return on the downbeat of bar 20 is supported not by tonic harmony as in bar 2 but by the previously tonicized mediant, thus conferring a more fluid quality on the moment and slightly disguising the sense of return. The entire passage of bars 12–19 features rhetorically heightened activity that ceases with the thematic return in bar 20. If, in contrast to the earlier hearing, the passage from bar 20 to the end is heard as initiating a closing section at the largest level of the form, then bars 12–19 may be heard as a functional middle.

Finally, we can interpret the opening 11 bars as establishing the song's premises, including its material and procedures. A 1-bar introduction is followed by a 4-bar phrase (bars 2–5). Then, as if repeating (bar 6), the phrase is modified (bar 7) and led through B minor to a new tonal destination, F-sharp minor (bars 8–9^3).

---

28. Bars 17^4–18^2 begin in the manner of the previous 1-bar units but modify their end in order to lead elsewhere.

In what would normally be a confirmatory gesture (bars 9^4–11^3), F-sharp minor is replaced by the more conventional dominant, A major. This is a deliberate shifting of gears, as if to say, "This is really where we want to be."

If we now return to our initial proposition to hear bar 26^3 as the beginning of the end, we must still reckon with the fact that this moment is still some way from the ending. How does Mendelssohn sustain the compositional dynamic between bars 26 and 37? By creating a web of events, all of them promoting the larger agenda of closure. The indispensable technique is none other than repetition, which Mendelssohn uses in exact and varied forms. Let us follow the main events from bar 26 on. After the high point on G at bar 26^3, a preliminary attempt to close is made in bars 28^3–29^1. But the cadence is evaded: melodically, we hear not $\hat{3}$–$\hat{2}$–$\hat{1}$ but $\hat{3}$–$\hat{2}$–$\hat{5}$ (F♯–E–A not F♯–E–D), the $\hat{1}$ sounding in an inner voice so that the less conclusive melodic $\hat{5}$ can initiate a second attempt at closure. The local harmony at 28^3–29^1 is not V6/4-5/3-I (with the second and third chords in root position) but the more mobile V6/4–V4/2–I6.[29] Part of Mendelssohn's strategy here is to embed the more obvious gestures of closure within a larger descending-bass pattern that will lend a sense of continuity to the closing moment. This line starts with bass A on the third beat of 28, passes through G (also in 28) then falls through F-sharp, F-natural, and E before reaching a mobile D on the downbeat of 30, making room for an intervening A at 29^4. A similarly directed bass line preceded this one and served to prepare the high point of bar 26. We can trace it from the third beat of bar 23: D–C♯–B (bar 23), A♯–A♮–G–F♯ (bar 24), then, transferred up the octave, E–D–C♯–B (bar 25), and finally A (downbeat of 26), the whole spanning an octave and a half.

Unlike the attempt at closure in bars 28–29, the one in bars 31–32 reaches its destination. A conventional $\hat{3}$–$\hat{2}$–$\hat{1}$ over a V–I offers what was previously denied. Many listeners will hear the downbeat of bar 32 as a defining moment, a longed-for moment, perhaps, and, in this context, the place where various narrative strands meet. Schenker would call this the "definitive close of the composition";[30] it marks the completion of the work's subsurface structural activity. Syntactic closure is achieved. We might as well go home at this point.

But syntactic closure is only one aspect—albeit an important one—of the full closing act. There is also a complementary dimension that would secure the rhetorical sense of the close, for although we have attained $\hat{1}$ over I, we need to savor D for a while, to repose in it, to dissolve the many tensions accumulated in the course of the song. This other dimension of closure can be described in different ways: as rhetorical, as gestural, or even as phenomenal. In this song without words, Mendelssohn writes a codetta-like segment (bars 32–end) to meet this need. These last 6 bars are a tonic prolongation. We sense dying embers, a sense of tranquility, the serenity of homecoming, even an afterglow. We may also hear in them a sense of reminiscence, for the sense that death is approaching can be an invitation to

29. Here and elsewhere, I follow Schenkerian practice in understanding cadential 6/4s as dominant-functioning chords featuring a double suspension to the adjacent root-position dominant chord. Hence the symbol V6/4–5/3.
30. Schenker, *Free Composition*, 129.

relive the past in compressed form. It is as if key moments in the form are made to flash before our very eyes, not markedly as quotations, but gently and subtly, as if in a mist, as if from a distance. One of the prominent elements in this ending is a simple neighbor-note motive, ABA or $\hat{5}$–$\hat{6}$–$\hat{5}$, which was adumbrated in the very first bar of the song, where B served as the only non-chord tone within the tonic expression. Subsequently, the notes B and A were associated in various contexts. Then, in bars 32–33, the ABA figure, now sounding almost like a wail, presses the melodic tone A into our memories. The V6/5 harmony in the second half of bars 32 and 33 may also remind us of the high point in bar 26. Then, too, we experience a touchingly direct $\hat{5}$–$\hat{4}$–$\hat{3}$–$\hat{2}$–$\hat{1}$ descent across bars 33–35. This collection of scale degrees was introverted in bars 2^1–3^3, sung in V but without $\hat{4}$ in bars 10–11, introverted again in bars 20^1–21^3, embedded in bars 28–29, heard with $\hat{5}$ playing only an ornamental role in bars 31–32, before appearing in its most direct and pristine form in bars 32^4–35^3. Even the dotted-note anacrusis at bar 32^4 has some precedent in bars 11–12, where it energized the first major contrasting section in the song. And the extension of the right hand into the highest register of the piece in the penultimate bar recalls salient moments of intensification around bars 16 and 17 and of the high point in bar 26 and its echo in 29. These registral extensions afford us a view of another world. Overall, then, the last 6 bars of Mendelssohn's song make possible a series of narratives about the compositional dynamic, among which narratives of closure are perhaps most significant.

We began this analysis of Mendelssohn's op. 85, no. 4, by locating the beginning of the ending in bar 26; we then worked our way backward from it. But what if we begin at the beginning and follow the course of events to the end? Obviously, the two accounts will not be wholly different, but the accumulation of expectations will receive greater emphasis. As an indication of these revised priorities and so as to fill in some of the detail excluded from the discussion so far, let us comment (again) on the first half of the song (bars 1–19). Bar 1 functions as a gestural prelude to the beginning proper; it familiarizes us with the sound and figuration of the tonic, while also coming to melodic rest on the pitch A as potential head tone. The narrative proper begins in bar 2 with a 4-bar melody. We are led eventually to the end of the beginning in bar 11, where the dominant is tonicized. Mendelssohn's procedure here (as also frequently happens in Brahms, for example, in the song "Wie Melodien zieht es mir," op. 105) is to begin with a head theme or motif and lead it to different tonal destinations. In the first 4-bar segment (bars 2–5), the harmonic outline is a straightforward I–V. A second 4-bar segment begins in bar 6, passes through the submediant in 7–8, and closes in the mediant in bar 9. But, as mentioned before, the emphatic upbeat to bar 10, complete with a Vii–6/5 of V (thinking in terms of A major), has the effect of correcting this "wrong" destination. If one is looking to locate the end of the beginning, one might assign it to the emphatic cadence on the dominant in bar 11. Yet, the end of the beginning and the beginning of the middle are often indistinguishable. The exploratory potential signaled by A-sharp in bar 7, the first nondiatonic pitch in the song, confers a gradual sense of middle on bars 7–11. This sense is intensified in a more conventional way beginning with the upbeat to bar 12. From here until bar 20, the music moves in five waves of increasing intensity that confirm the instability associated with a middle. Example 2.2 summarizes the five waves. As can be seen, the melodic profile is a gradual ascent to A, reached in wave 4. Wave 3 is interrupted in almost stretto fashion by wave 4. Wave 5 begins as a further intensification of waves 3 and 4 but declines the invitation to exceed the high point on A reached in wave 4, preferring G-sharp (a half step lower than the previous A) as it effects a return from what, in retrospect, we understand as the point of greatest intensity. Wave 5 also adopts the contour of waves 1 and 2, thus gaining a local reprise or symmetrical function. It emerges that the tonicized mediant in bar 9 was premature; the mature mediant occurs in bars 19–20.

Example 2.2. Five waves of action across bars 12–20 in Mendelssohn, *Song without Words* in D major, op. 85, no. 4.

Stepping back from the detail of Mendelssohn's op. 85, no. 4, we see that the beginning-middle-ending model allows us to pass through a Romantic composition by weighing its events relationally and thus apprehending its discourse. The model recognizes event sequences and tracks the tendency of the musical material. In this sense, it has the potential to enrich our understanding of what musicians normally refer to as *form*—a complex, summary quality that reflects the particular constellation of elements within a composition. There is no mechanical way to apply a beginning-middle-ending model; every interpretation is based on a reading of musical detail. Interpretations may shift depending on where a beginning is located, what one takes to be a sign of ending, and so on. And while the general features of these functions have been summarized and in part exemplified in the Mendelssohn analysis, the fact that they are born of convention means that some aspects of the functions may have escaped our notice. Still, attention to musical rhetoric as conveyed in harmony, melody, phrase structure, and rhythm can prove enlightening.

The beginning-middle-ending model may seem banal, theoretically coarse, or simply unsophisticated; it may lack the predictive power of analytical theories that are more methodologically explicit. Yet, there is, it seems to me, some wisdom in resisting the overdetermined prescriptions of standard forms. This model substitutes a set of direct functions that can enable an individual analyst to get inside a composition and listen for closing tendencies. Musicology has for a long time propagated standard forms (sonata, rondo, ternary, and a host of others) not because they have been shown to mediate our listening in any fundamental way, but because they can be diagrammed, given a two-dimensional visual appearance, and thus easily be represented on screens and blackboards and in books, articles, and term papers. A user of the beginning-middle-ending model, by contrast, understands the a priori functions of a sonata "exposition" as mere designation; a proper analysis would inspect the work afresh for the complex of functions—many of them of contradictory tendency—that define the activity within, say, the exposition space. To say that a dialogue is invariably set up between the normative functions in a sonata form and the procedures on the ground, so to speak, is an improvement, but even this formulation may overvalue the conventional sense of normative functions. Analysis must deal with the true nature of the material and recognize the signifying potential of a work's building blocks—in short, respond to the internal logic of the work, not the designated logic associated with external convention. Reorienting thinking and hearing in this way may make us freshly aware of the complex dynamism of musical material and enhance our appreciation of music as discourse.

High Points

A special place should be reserved for high points or climaxes as embodiments of an aspect of syntax and rhetoric in Romantic musical discourse. A high point is a superlative moment. It may be a moment of greatest intensity, a point of extreme tension, or the site of a decisive release of tension. It usually marks a turning point in the form (as we saw in bar 26 of example 2.1). Psychologically, a single high point typically dominates a single composition, but given the fact that a larger whole is often constituted by smaller parts, each of which might have its own intensity curve, the global high point may be understood as a product of successive local high points. Because of its marked character, the high point may last a moment, but it may also be represented as an extended moment—a plateau or region.

No one performing any of the diverse Romantic repertoires can claim innocence of high points. They abound in opera arias; as high notes, they are sites of display, channels for the foregrounding of the very act of performing. As such, they are thrilling to audiences, whose consumption of these arias may owe not a little to the anticipated pleasure of experiencing these moments in different voices, so to speak. The lied singer encounters them frequently, too, often in a more intimate setting in which they are negotiated with nuance. In orchestral music, high points often provide some of the most memorable experiences for listeners, serving as points of focus or demarcation, places to indulge sheer visceral pleasure. Indeed, the phenomenon is so basic, and yet so little studied by music theorists, that one is inclined to think either that it resists explanation or that it raises no particularly challenging theoretical issues. Perhaps high points are superficial, effects of the foreground to be set aside as soon as the search for deeper-level processes begins.[31]

Since the analytical criteria we are developing in this chapter are aimed mostly at an illumination of the foreground, it is appropriate to draw our attention to the notion of points of culmination. High points convey one aspect of the dynamic profile of a composition. Their pertinence may vary from work to work or from context to context. They may illuminate the expressive dimension or the form of a work. Seen in the context of the five other analytical criteria, high points take on an auxiliary or gluing function insofar as they can be folded into the other processes. Do certain topics facilitate the attainment of climax? Where in the course of a beginning-middle-ending structure does the high point occur? How does the high-point scheme interact with the implicit circularity of periodic organization? Are particular modes of enunciation especially appropriate at high points? How is a particular compositional narrative shaped by its succession of high points?

The simplest and most direct form of a high-point scheme is the dynamic curve. This curve, which embodies a variety of dimensional processes, rises gradually from a relatively low point, reaches a high point about two-thirds of the way through the structure, then subsides rapidly thereafter. The scheme is amply represented in organic life and psychological processes. Its proportions convey the sense that the attainment of the high point should come later, not immediately. Parameters that define this basic shape differ from work to work. The most direct embodiment is melody, and this is because the melodic impulse is often the fundamental motivating impulse in Romantic expression. Melodic high points are often literal high points; they may be unique within a work or, if they recur, be marked in ways that differentiate them from other occurrences. Harmony, too, is a critical conveyor of points of intensity. For example, an arresting harmony like a diminished-seventh chord may embody the high point. Sometimes, a large-scale distant harmony (such as a tritonal key relation, as we will see in the *Tristan* Prelude) serves to convey a sense of extremity within a normative departure-return trajectory.

More immediately palpable is the behavior of quantifiable parameters like texture and dynamics. A high point may coincide with the piling on of instrumental layers, or it may be the loudest moment in its context. Leonard Meyer has postulated the increasing importance in nineteenth-century music of so-called secondary parameters (texture, dynamics, orchestration) over primary parameters (melody, harmony, rhythm). His idea is that secondary parameters challenged primary ones for functional priority in the course of the nineteenth century. There

---

31. The most comprehensive early study of high points is George Muns, "Climax in Music" (Ph.D. diss., University of North Carolina, 1955). Leonard Meyer's "Exploiting Limits" introduces an important distinction between statistical climaxes and syntactical ones. See also Agawu, "Structural Highpoints in Schumann's *Dichterliebe*," *Music Analysis* 3(2) (1984): 159–180. Most important among more recent studies is Zohar Eitan's *Highpoints: A Study of Melodic Peaks* (Philadelphia: University of Pennsylvania Press, 1997), which may be read in conjunction with David Huron's review in *Music Perception* 16(2) (1999): 257–264.

are many examples to support this theory, but there are counterexamples as well. It would seem that the nineteenth century evinces a plural set of practices. Some high points are syntactical while others are statistical.[32]

The basic model of the dynamic curve may, of course, be subject to variation. A high point may occur earlier rather than later in the form. It may appear with relatively little preparation and perhaps be followed by prolonged decline. It may be known more in retrospect than in prospect; that is, while some high points are clearly the culmination of explicit preparatory processes, others pass into consciousness only after the fact. These creative manipulations bespeak a simultaneous interest in natural shapes and the artifice of artistic transformation.

Let us follow the achievement of high points in some well-known moments. In Schubert's glorious "An die Musik," the high point occurs toward the end of the first strophe on a high F-sharp (*Welt*) in bar 16. The strophe itself is nearly 20 bars long, so the high point occurs closer to its end, not in the middle or at the beginning. How does Schubert construct this moment as a turning point? The structural means are simple, and the timing of their disposition is impeccable. From the beginning, Schubert maintains a relatively consistent distinction among three types of pitch configuration: arpeggio, stepwise diatonic, and chromatic. If we think of these as modes of utterance, we see that they work in tandem to create the high point in bar 16. First, the pianist offers the singer an arpeggiated figuration (*lh*, bars 1–2). She accepts (bars 3–4) but only for a limited period; the imperatives of musical closure favor stepwise melodic motion (bars 5–6). The pianist repeats his triadic offer (*lh*, bars 6–7) and, while the singer responds, continues in stepwise mode (*lh*, bars 8–9). Meanwhile, the singer's response incorporates the single largest melodic leap in the entire song (descending minor-seventh in bars 7–8). But this change of direction is merely the product of an octave transference; if we rewrite Schubert's melody in these bars (7–9) within a single octave, we see that the diatonic stepwise mode is what regulates this second utterance. Now, the pianist presses forward in chromatic mode (*lh*, bars 10–11). This is not the first time that chromatic elements have been used by the pianist (G♯–A in *lh* bars 4–5 and A–A♯–B in *lh* bar 8), but the utterance in bar 10 is more decisive and carries an aura of intensification. Here, at the start of the singer's third vocal phrase (bar 11), she does not respond directly to what is offered by the pianist but is led by the momentum of her own previous utterances. The mixture of arpeggiated and stepwise motion regulates this phrase. Then, in the final sweep of the phrase (bar 14), the pianist gives full rein to the chromatic mode, yielding only to an implicit triad at the conclusion of the phrase (A–D in *lh* bars 18–19). The singer's articulation of the high point takes the form of an extended stepwise diatonic rise from A to F-sharp (bars 14^4–16^3). Observe, however, the gap that Schubert introduces in the approach to the climactic pitch: D–F♯, not E–F♯. The rhetorical effect of this gap of a third is underlined by the local harmonic situation: a secondary dominant in 6/5 position

---

32. Meyer, "Exploiting Limits." See also his later volume *Style and Music: Theory, History, and Ideology* (Philadelphia: University of Pennsylvania Press, 1989).

Example 2.3. Schubert, "An die Musik."

supports the high F-sharp in bar 16. Then comes release in a configuration that mixes stepwise with triadic motion (bars 17–19). Note that the high point in bar 16 is not the only occurrence of that particular F-sharp in the song. We heard it three bars earlier (bar 13), but without accentual or harmonic markedness.

Indeed, pitch-class F-sharp functions throughout as an anchor, a turning point, a marker of boundaries, and, eventually, a high point.

Attending to the high point, then, means attending to the form as a whole. One reason that this particular criterion for analysis has not caught on in American theoretical circles is that the constituent parameters cannot be specified in advance. Rather, the analyst must attend to the sounding forms within each individual context. To do this is, I believe, to take in more of the music than what emerges from a mode of analysis that is confined, say, to voice leading or hypermetric processes. It is to gain access to the peculiar contours of the foreground not as autonomous structure but as a parametrically entangled, emergent set of qualities.

Example 2.4. Chopin, Prelude, op. 28, no. 1.

The rhetorical shape of the first of Chopin's preludes, op. 28, is perfection itself (example 2.4). An 8-bar antecedent closes in a half-cadence. (The fact that the harmony in bar 8 is a dominant-seventh rather than a dominant inflects but does not erase the sense of a half-cadence.) Then, Chopin begins a repetition of those 8 bars. After the fourth, he intensifies the procedure. Melody now incorporates chromaticism, enlists the cooperation of the bass (parallel movement between bass and treble), adopts a stretto mode so as to intensify the sense of urgency in the moment, and eventually culminates in a high point on D–C (bar 21)—the highest melodic pitch in the prelude. From there, things are gradually brought to a close. The melody returns from on high and approaches $\hat{1}$—teasingly at first, eventually attaining rest in bar 29. The entire passage after the high point features a diminuendo, and the last 10 bars sit on a tonic pedal, C. The expression is archetypically Romantic: the means are clear but subtle, the rhetoric self-evident but never banal, the effect touching, and there is no unmotivated lingering. To finish, Chopin reminds us that there is more to come. The attainment of $\hat{1}$ in bar 29 did not do it; a terminal $\hat{3}$ (bar 34) leaves things suspended, adding a touch of poetry to the ending.

It seems likely that the high point in bar 21 shapes the experience of many players and listeners. Bar 21 is a turning point. The intensifying stretto effect is abandoned here; the consistently rising chromatic melody, doubled an octave below (bars 16–20), is overcome by a diatonic moment (bar 21); and the complementary melodic descent from the high point is entirely diatonic. The only vestige of chromaticism is in the region of the high point (bar 22). The rest is white notes.

Chopin takes time to close. This is no routine deployment of conventional syntax to close off a structure. The motifs $\hat{5}$–$\hat{6}$ and $\hat{3}$–$\hat{2}$ which provided the essential melodic opposition in bars 1–3 and 5–7, respectively, are briefly restored (bars 25–26 and 27–28) in a gesture laden with reminiscence. We reminisce as the end nears. When the longed-for $\hat{1}$ finally appears in bar 29, it is cuddled by a fourfold 6/4–5/3 double suspension (bars 29–32).

Chopin's op. 28 collection as a whole is a rich site for the study of high points. In no. 3 in G major, for example, the beginning of the end is marked not by a tensional high point but by a turn to the subdominant (bars 16–19), a reorientation of the harmonic trajectory. The deeply expressive, minor-mode no. 4 is made up of two large phrases, an antecedent (bars 1–12) and its consequent (bars 13–25). The high point occurs in the middle of the consequent (bars 16–17), complete with Chopin's stretto marking, forte dynamic, and momentary contact with a low-lying B—the lowest note in the piece so far, to be superseded only in the final bar by an E. In no. 6 in B minor, the point of furthest remove is the Neapolitan region in bars 12–14, positioned about halfway through the work. This relatively early turning point is followed by an especially prolonged period of closure (bars 15–26). The little A Major Prelude, no. 7, marks its high point by a secondary dominant to the supertonic (bar 12). Delivered in two symmetrical phrases (bars 1–8 and 9–16), the high point forms part of the precadential material leading to the final cadence. In no. 9 in E major, an enharmonic reinterpretation of the mediant harmony (A-flat in bar 8) conveys the sense of a high point. In no. 13 in F-sharp major, an E-natural functioning as a flattened-seventh of the tonic chord (bar 29) signifies home-going and serves as a critical turning point in the form. And in the dramatic Prelude no. 22

in G Minor, a modified repeat of the opening, bass-led period (bars 1–8, 9–16) is followed by a still more intense phrase promising closure (bars 17–24) and its immediate repetition (bars 25–32). Finally, the cadential gesture of bars 31–32 is repeated as 33–34 and overlapped with what appears to be another statement of the opening theme. The bass gets stuck in bars 36–38, however, and it needs the (divine) intervention of an inverted augmented sixth chord in bar 40 to usher in the final cadence. Chopin's trajectory here is one of increasing intensity until a colossal or even catastrophic event (bar 39) arrests the motion and closes the structure.[33]

In the Prelude to *Tristan and Isolde*, successive waves of motion culminate in bar 83 with a chord containing the notes A-flat, E-flat, C-flat, and F. This moment marks the decisive turning point in the prelude. What follows is a return to the opening, a recapitulation of sorts that completes the larger tripartite shape. Volumes of commentary attest to the fact that this famous work can support a variety of analytical agendas. Our concern here is with the simplest and most direct apprehension of the overall shape of the prelude. With bar 83 as anchor, we can understand the preparatory tendencies manifest in the preceding 82 bars as well as the complementary function of the succeeding 28 bars. Just as Schubert's "An die Musik" and Chopin's C Major Prelude, op. 28, no. 1, rose to a melodic high point and resolved from there, so, on a grander scale, Wagner's prelude rises in waves to a high point and resolves from there.

The means are direct and ancient. Bar 83 is the loudest moment in the prelude. The progress of the dynamics conspires to convey that fact. This bar is also one of the densest. Earlier points, like bars 55 and 74, prepared this one, but the superlative effect here derives from its terminal position. After the explosion in bar 83, nothing comparable happens in the prelude, whereas with the previous moments of intensification, there was always the promise of more. Psychologically, bar 83 denies the possibility of a greater moment of intensity.

These features are on the surface of the surface and are immediately noticeable. But there are others. The chord in bar 83 is known to us from the very first chord in the prelude, the Tristan chord itself (example 2.5). However one interprets it, its function as a (relative) dissonance within the opening 3-bar phrase is uncontested. Of course, from a certain point of view, every one of the resulting sonorities in bars 2–3 is a dissonance, but there is also a sense that the closing dominant-seventh (bar 3) provides a measure of resolution, albeit a local and provisional one. In other words, the Tristan chord marks a point of high tension which is resolved—at least in part—by the dominant-seventh chord. It is true, as Boretz and others have reminded us, that the Tristan chord and the dominant-seventh are equivalent within the systems of relation that assert inversional and transpositional equivalence.[34] But even if we devised a narrative that has the

---

33. For more on closure in the Chopin preludes, see Agawu, "Concepts of Closure and Chopin's op. 28," *Music Theory Spectrum* 9 (1987): 1–17.

34. "It now emerges," writes Benjamin Boretz, "that the notoriously 'ambiguous' Tristan chord, so elusive or anomalous in most tonal explications of the piece, and the familiar 'dominant seventh,' so crucial to these same tonal explications, are here just exact, balanced, simple inverses of one another, with very little local evidence to support their consideration as anything but equivalents in this sense." See Boretz, "Metavariations, Part 4: Analytic Fallout," *Perspectives of New Music* 11 (1973): 162.

Tristan chord progressing to another version of itself in bars 2–3, the actual path of the progression would be understood in terms of an expressive trajectory that confers a sense of lesser tension on an element by virtue of its terminal position.

Example 2.5. Wagner, Prelude to *Tristan and Isolde*, bars 1–3.

The high point in bar 83 therefore reproduces a sound that has been part of the vocabulary of the work from the beginning. In its local context, however, the chord has a precise harmonic function: it is a half-diminished-seventh chord on the supertonic in the local key of E-flat minor. The main key of the prelude is A minor (with an intervening major inflection and excursions to other keys). E-flat minor is at a significant distance from A. Heard in terms of the prescribed distances that regulate a construct such as the circle of fifths, E-flat, prepared mainly by its dominant, B-flat, is the point of greatest harmonic remove from A. The prelude's high point is thus, among other processes noted earlier, a product of subsurface activity that exploits the conventional property of harmonic distance.[35]

Such coincidence between expressive and structural domains is the exception rather than the rule when it comes to the articulation of high points. Subsurface activity, confined by an explicit system of theoretical relations, has to be domesticated in particular ways in order to do expressive work. Often the "rhythm" of the system of relations has little or nothing to do with the work's unfolding rhythm, even at a macro level. Systems are based on atemporal logical relations, while works unfold temporally in simulation of organic life. And this circumstance may encourage some listeners to doubt the pertinence of the coincidence we have just identified in the *Tristan* Prelude, whereby the Tristan chord and the dominant-seventh chord are held to be equivalent. Another way of putting this is to say that structural procedures are up for expressive grabs. One who wishes to argue a difference between bar 2 and bar 83 will point to differences of notation and destination; one who wishes to argue a sameness will invoke enharmonic synonymity. To admit this openness in interpretation is not to suggest any kind of hopelessness in the analytical endeavor.

---

35. For a complementary view of the *Tristan* Prelude, see Robert P. Morgan's demonstration that the formal process consists of repeating units and processes of variation (a semiological reading, in effect): "Circular Form in the Tristan Prelude," *Journal of the American Musicological Society* 53 (2000): 69–103.

It is rather to deny the self-evidence of any of the alliances we draw between systemic rhythm and real-time rhythm and to remind us that it is the plots we bring to the analytical table that determine what relations we observe to be significant in a work. I believe that analysts have ignored the inherent rhythms of theoretical constructs and have sought opportunistic parallels—quick marriages of convenience, we might call them—with the more palpable organic rhythms of the expressive surface. In the worst cases, this amounts to a lie, to claims that the apparent rhythms exposed within a system of atemporal logic can be transposed directly into a temporal realm. No, it would be more truthful to retain the separate enabling spheres of these features. And if by chance they coincide, as in bar 83 of the *Tristan* Prelude, then we should treat the moment as a one-time occurrence.[36]

Probably the most memorable moment in the first movement of Mahler's unfinished Tenth Symphony is the high point sounded in bars 204–206 and again in 208. Even without looking at the score, one knows from hearing the movement that a superlative moment has been prepared by a series of waves of action. The climactic chord is constituted as a stack of thirds, the moment is loud (marked *ff*) and dense, and there is no gesture of comparable rhetorical weight anywhere else in the movement. Both prospectively and retrospectively, the high point is well marked. Looking at the score reveals a number of supplementary details. The high point is a 10-note chord sitting on a low C-sharp (example 2.6). The movement itself is in F-sharp major, with significant portions in B-flat. Within the immediate environment of the high point, we

Example 2.6. Ten-note chord in Mahler, Tenth Symphony, first movement, bar 204.

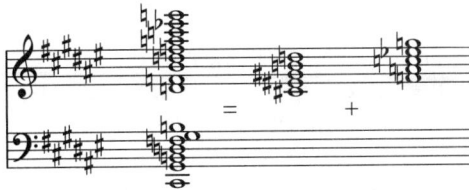

36. David Lewin broaches this topic in the course of a discussion of two competing Schenkerian readings of the familiar Christmas hymn "Joy to the World," set to a tune by Handel, in "Music Theory, Phenomenology, and Modes of Perception," in Lewin, *Studies in Music with Text* (Oxford: Oxford University Press, 2006), 85–88. One reading renders the tune as an $\hat{8}$ line (*Joy* to the world), the other as a $\hat{5}$ line (Joy to the *world*). Although Lewin recognizes that "the Schenkerian reading does not claim that the 'world' is 'more important' than 'joy,'" he nevertheless proceeds to explore the metaphorical prospects for either reading. But since the *Kopfton* as imagined and postulated by Schenker belongs to a sequence of idealized voices, not necessarily a flesh-and-blood occurrence, its salience at the foreground (by means of accentual or durational prominence, for example) is *not* a defining feature. Thus, to seek to interpret idealized voices hermeneutically is to seek to transfer values across a systemic border. In our terms, it is to confuse the "rhythm" of the system with the actual rhythm of the work.

hear first an A-flat minor chord (bar 194), then the 10-note chord on C-sharp (204), whose resolution is delayed until the second half of bar 220. If we read the A-flat minor chord enharmonically as G-sharp minor, we might hear the entire passage as a ii–"V"–I cadence writ large. This conventional underpinning occurs elsewhere in Mahler (see, for example, the excerpt from *Das Lied von der Erde* analyzed later in this book in example 4.34) and reinforces the grounding of his musical language in the harmonic norms of the eighteenth century. But the composing out of this progression incorporates numerous modifications that ultimately take the sound out of an eighteenth-century environment and place it squarely within a late nineteenth- or early twentieth-century material realm.

From the point of view of harmonic syntax, the 10-note chord functions as a dominant on account of its C-sharp grounding. Above it are two dominant-ninth chords, one a minor ninth, the other a major ninth, on C-sharp and F-natural, respectively. In other words, the 10-note chord combines the dominant-ninths of the keys of F-sharp and B-flat. Since these are the two principal keys of the movement, the combination of their expanded dominants at this moment would be a logical compositional move. Perceiving the separate dominants presents its own challenges, of course, but the conceptual explanation probably presents no comparable difficulties. As in the *Tristan* Prelude, a combination of structural and expressive features marks this high point for consciousness.

The aftermath of the high point in the Mahler movement is worth noting because of the way closure—which typically follows the high point—is executed (bars 213–end). The charged dominant-functioning chord on C-sharp has set up an expectation for resolution, which could have come as early as bar 214, allowing for the 4-bar lead-in (209–212) to the thematic return in 213. Mahler maintains the C-sharp pedal for the first phase of this return (213–216). With the tempo and thematic change at 217, the pitch C-sharp persists, but is now incorporated in very local V–I progressions. It is not until the end of bar 220 that the proper resolution occurs in the form of an authentic cadence featuring 3̂ in the top voice. This understated close cannot, it seems, provide the rhetorical weight needed to counter the effect of the gigantic 10-note dominant, so a network of closing gestures, some of them harmonic (bars 229–230), others more melodic (bars 240–243), is dispersed throughout the closing bars of the movement. Cadential gestures, reminiscences in the form of fragments, and strategically incomplete melodic utterances transfigure Mahler's ending. (This movement, incidentally, was the most complete in draft form of all of the movements of the unfinished Tenth.)[37]

Talk of high points, then, dovetails into talk of closure, for it would seem that the logical thing after the attainment of a high point is to engineer a close. And this reinforces the point made earlier that, although the six criteria being developed in this chapter and in chapter 3 have been chosen in order to focus attention on specific features and mechanisms, they are not wholly autonomous.

---

37. For further discussion, see Agawu, "Tonal Strategy in the First Movement of Mahler's Tenth Symphony," *19th-Century Music* 9(2) (1986): 222–233.

Indeed, in a fuller analysis of this movement, we might go back to the viola melody that opens the work, trace its subsequent appearances, and note how at high points the pitches D and A are given special attention. Then, it will come as no surprise that in the neighborhood of the 10-note chord, the same pitches are highlighted close together (A-natural on the downbeat of 203, D-natural in 209).

Within an essentially Romantic language, where premium is often placed on effect and immediacy, the logic of moment-by-moment succession sometimes offers a better explanation than such syntactical procedures as the combining of two dominant-ninths at the high point of the movement, or even the exploitation of tritonal distance from the tonic in the *Tristan* Prelude. Without denying the coherence of their individual approaches to composition, we might nevertheless distinguish between composing as a way of *speaking* within a relatively stable conventional language and composing by the use of a *system*. Around the time that Mahler was working on his Tenth Symphony (1910–1911), other composers were embracing composing by system, and their doing so was something that some later critics would consider a historical inevitability. While adherence to system does not in principle preclude the speaking of language—for Saussure, language *was* system—there is a significant difference in rhetoric between composing by system and composing by making utterances in a natural or pseudo-natural language.

The construction of the high point in the first movement of Bartók's *Music for Strings, Percussion and Celesta* embodies the dual pressures of system and language in composition and will serve as a convenient final illustration of the notion of high point. Bartók's means are as direct as anything the nineteenth century had to offer. From a central pitch, A, two contrapuntal lines trace opposing paths by fifths, culminating in E-flat, the high point of the movement. Then, the procedure is reversed until the lines converge on the starting A (see example 2.7 for a display of successive head tones and example 2.8 for the closing bars of the movement, which summarize the larger A–E♭–A progression). All of the available fifths in these trajectories are utilized except C-sharp/D-flat between the A-flat of bar 58 and the F-sharp of bar 65. Proportionally, the ascending portion of the movement extends across roughly two-thirds of its overall span, while the descent is rapid, covering the remaining third. Reinforcing this pitch-based process are two other dimensional processes. Registrally, the entries of the main subject diverge from the A below middle C; when the two lines reach E-flat in bar 56, they are at a point of maximum registral distance. Even more immediately palpable is the sequence of dynamics. Bartók uses a graded system starting at *pp* (bar 1), reaching *fff* at the E-flat climax (bar 56), and returning to a point below *ppp* (bar 88). It would seem that the dynamics were deployed as a set, so that whatever was missing in ascent is restored in descent. The dynamic *ppp*, for example, occurs at the end of the descent portion but not in the ascent, *mf* occurs in the descent but not in the ascent, and *ff* occurs in the ascent but not in the descent. The net effect is of traveling the entire dynamic range from the quietest to the loudest.

Example 2.7. Pitch-structural elements in Bartók, *Music for Strings, Percussion and Celesta*, first movement.

Example 2.8. Closing bars of Bartók, *Music for Strings, Percussion and Celesta*, first movement.

How does the listener experience this particular confluence of dimensional processes? For some listeners, dynamics and textural density are primary influences on their hearing. These ostensibly secondary, quantifiable parameters make an immediate impact, requiring no interpretation within syntactical systems. Indeed, for such listeners, the high point would be unaltered if the pitches were rearranged (within the confines of this particular idiolect); it is enough to follow the course of the statistical parameters and to experience the palpable rise in intensity to a high point and the fall from there. But what about the matter of tonal distance? Bartók's diverging fifths originate in a precompositional matrix. Although tonality in the sense of a composed-out triad is not the motivating force here, there are pitch-classes of priority defined by various forms of emphasis and assertion. And as much as one would like to think that the A–E♭–A progression is a deep structure, comparable perhaps to a I–V–I progression, the disposition of pitch-classes A and E-flat, not to mention their intervening associates, does not necessarily enable a dependent tonal hearing. It would be premature, therefore, to draw a connection between the *Tristan* Prelude and the first movement of the *Music for Strings*, even though the A–E♭–A framing is present in both. In the *Tristan* Prelude, the semantics of tonality allow us to postulate hierarchies readily; moreover, the prolongation of A through its dominant is given such emphasis that its dominance is uncontested. But Bartók's fifths seem to live for the moment and to discourage hierarchic interpretation. And so the A–E♭ tritone has no a priori status within the compositional grammar as a consonance or a dissonance. Indeed, in Lendvai's axis system, pitch-classes A and E-flat belong to the same (tonic) axis, so that departure from one and arrival on the other is figured not as a progression from a center to an opposing other center, possibly a substitute dominant, but as a progression within a single functional domain, the tonic.[38]

38. Erno Lendvai, *Bela Bartók: An Analysis of His Music* (London: Kahn & Averill, 1971).

In any case, we must not draw too categorical a distinction between hearing Romantic music as language and hearing post-Romantic music as system or even antisystem. Tempting as it is to interpret one as natural and the other as artificial, or one as "intuitionist," the other as "constructivist," we might consider the more likely reality to involve a blurring of boundaries, an interpenetration of the two modes. Any such comparisons have to be validated analytically. In the brief examples that we have seen, the hierarchic subsumption of scale steps in Wagner and Mahler contrasts with the contextual centricity of Bartók. But Bartók, too, employs some of the same secondary parameters used by earlier composers.

The high point, then, is a central feature of Romantic foregrounds and belongs in any taxonomy of criteria for analysis. Context is everything in analysis, so one should always look to it for clarification of ambiguous situations. As a quality, the high point embodies a sense of the supreme, extreme, exaggerated, and superlative, and these qualities are often distributed across several of a work's dimensions. My comments on passages from Schubert, Chopin, Mahler, Wagner, and Bartók will, I hope, have confirmed the view that some attention to these ostensibly surface features might enhance our appreciation of the particularities of Romantic music.

CHAPTER Three

Criteria for Analysis II

Periodicity

A *period* is a regulating framework for organizing musical content. Every large-scale musical utterance needs to be broken down into smaller chunks in order to assure communication and comprehensibility. Like sentences, phrases, or paragraphs in verbal composition, periods serve as midlevel building blocks, markers of a composition's sense units. Does the subject speak in short or long sentences? How does the succession of periods define an overall form or "structural rhythm" for the work? Are periodic rhythms interchangeable or are they fixed?

The enduring tradition of *Formenlehre* has devised elaborate sets of terms, concepts, and modes of symbolic representation for the description of this vital aspect of music. Some offer general theories of formal organization, some illuminate specific historical styles, some prescribe actions for composition, while others offer models for analytic description. Taxonomies abound in theoretical and analytical writings by Burmeister, Koch, A. B. Marx, Riemann, Schoenberg, Tovey, Ratner, Rosen, Rothstein, Caplin, and Hepokoski and Darcy—to mention only a dozen names. The very large number of writings on this topic suggests that, for many scholars, form as a specifically temporal or periodic experience lies at the core of musical understanding and enjoyment.

A rapid overview of some of the terms and concepts employed by a few leading theorists to describe the temporal aspects of musical structure will provide an indication of the range of techniques and effects that originate in notions of periodicity. According to Ratner, periodicity "represents the tendency ... to move toward goals, toward points of punctuation.... [A] passage is not sensed as being a period until some sort of conclusive cadence is reached.... The length of a period cannot be prescribed." Among the terms he employs are motion, points of arrival, symmetry (including disturbances of symmetry), sentence structure, period extensions, and internal digressions.[1] Like Ratner, William Rothstein draws on

1. Ratner, *Classic Music*, 33.

contemporaneous and more recent theories in his study of eighteenth- and nine-teenth-century phrase rhythm. His terms include phrase (including fore-phrase and after-phrase), phrase rhythm, phrase linkage, phrase expansion, prefix, suffix, parenthetical insertion, hypermeasure, lead-in, elongated upbeat, and successive downbeats.[2] Caplin's theory of form draws on various kinds of cadence (aban-doned, authentic, elided, evaded); cadential progression; concluding, initiating, and medial functions; period; interpolation; and sentence.[3] And Christopher Hasty's vocabulary is chosen to capture the temporal aspects of musical experi-ence and to distinguish diverse temporalities: motion, projective process, deferral, now, instant, timelessness, and denial.[4]

Every listener to Romantic music possesses an intuitive understanding of peri-odicity. When we hear a Chopin prelude, a Liszt song, a Brahms intermezzo, a Bruckner motet, or a Verdi aria, we are aware of its ebbs and flows, its high and low points, its moments of repose and dynamism. We routinely sense that a thought has been concluded here, that a process begun earlier has been abandoned, or that an event of a certain gravity is about to take place. Listeners who also move (silently) to music and dancers who respond physically are alert to regularities and irregularities in phrasing and groupings beyond the beat level. Schubert proceeds in measured groupings throughout the C Major Quintet, but disrupts the period-icity from time to time, deploying unison passages to move the discourse self-con-sciously from one state of lyric poetry to another. Schumann's Piano Quintet, op. 44, does not disappoint when it comes to 4-bar phrases, but we are aware, too, of the speech mode that intrudes here and there and projects an alternative periodic-ity; sometimes, we sense a cranking of gears—as if to break an ongoing periodicity in order to introduce a new one. And in Mendelssohn's Violin Concerto, the man-ner of delivery is controlled by 4-bar units. This partly facilitates exchange between (the more restricted) orchestral discourse, on the one hand, and (the freer) soloist's narrative, on the other. It also contributes to the more or less immediate compre-hensibility of the "message" in a genre whose unabashed suasive intent generally leaves few aspects of outer form to the connoisseur's imagination.

The most important consideration for analysis is the *sense of periodicity*, by which I mean the tendency of the sonic material to imply continuation and to attain a degree of closure. To get at this quality, I will ask the same three ques-tions that were introduced at the end of chapter 1: Where does the motion begin? Where does it end? How does it get there? These questions are meant to help chan-nel our intuitions about the shape of the compositional dynamic and to guide the construction of periodicity.

One final, general point needs to be made before we begin the analyses. Although the large literature dealing with form, rhythm, and periodicity in tonal music has made available a wealth of insights, one aspect of the literature sug-gests that we might think a little differently. Too many studies of Romantic music

2. William Rothstein, *Phrase Rhythm in Tonal Music* (New York: Schirmer, 1989).
3. Caplin, *Classical Form.*
4. Christopher Hasty, *Meter as Rhythm* (New York: Oxford University Press, 1997).

have adopted an overdetermined approach to the analysis of form. Lured by the conventions of phrase-structural organization, they have blurred the possible distinction between periodicity as a practical mechanism for composition and periodicity as a resultant presence that guides a listener's listening. Without denying the pertinence of convention, I want to retain this distinction—which may be largely a matter of emphasis—in order to suggest that the act of listening may take a direct, less mediated form, based at best on an appreciation of key moments of punctuation, not necessarily on an in-time awareness of the succession of precise phrase groupings. For the listener, the occurrence of a punctuation mark signals the partial or full completion of an idea or process and the imminent beginning of something new. Punctuations may be regular or irregular, but even in the most regular contexts, there is often more to the sense of periodicity than what is conferred by grouping. The analytical emphasis, then, should not be on antecedents and consequents, well-defined or malformed sentences, or sonata formations and deformations, although these can be helpful in the initial stages of analysis. The emphasis, rather, should be on the *sense* behind the musical gestures, the tendency of the material to remain open or closed, or its predilection to refuse either tendency and remain suspended between them.

Mahler, Fourth Symphony, 3rd movement, bars 1–61

Marked *poco adagio*, the first part of this intense and beautiful movement unfolds with a deliberateness that obscures a sense of regular periodicity (example 3.1 provides a piano score for the following analysis, but readers may wish to keep the orchestral score in view since instrumentation is referred to here and there). Yet, there are moments of clear articulation, exaggerated moments, points of return— all of which make it possible to segment the work. How is the sense of periodicity enacted across these 61 bars?

Since melody (or, sometimes, two simultaneously unfolding melodies) leads the action, following the course of the melody can serve as a reliable mechanism for understanding how the musical utterance is regulated. We begin in the tenor range with a warm cello sound accompanied by pizzicato string basses. Emerging without haste, the song meanders a little, heightens its expression, and then pauses at a half-cadence (bar 16). The melodic thought has not been concluded, we understand, but it's another singer's turn to lead. At bar 17, cellos go under, singing the same song, while second violins take the lead with something apparently new. Because we have heard the cello melody before, we know that the new melody is an addition, a countermelody in the manner of a countersubject; it represents the piling up of polyphonic layers. This second breath, too, reaches a moment of intensification (bars 22–24), heightened not only by the higher register, but by increased rhythmic activity, the incorporation of Mahler's favorite appoggiaturas, and, perhaps, most significant, a merging of the violin and cello voices in such a way that the vocal utterance that started off in bar 17 as two voices becomes one and the same by bar 24. So, even though second violins and cello are not in unison, the musical line defines the latter's role as subsidiary.

The stepwise melody played by second violins starting in the second half of bar 23 leads so directly to the new beginning initiated in bar 25 that one is inclined to hear an elision of phrases. Bar 24, analogous to bar 16 in one hearing, suggests a

Example 3.1. Mahler, Symphony no. 4, third movement, bars 1–61.

(continued)

Example 3.1. continued.

comma, a half-cadence, a preliminary point of repose figured as temporary. In bar 16, Mahler seemed to say, "I'm not done yet"; in bar 24, he says the same thing. On the other hand, the melodic continuity between 24 and 25, including the implicit $\hat{7}$–$\hat{8}$ motion over V, inclines the ear to hear an authentic cadence across the 2 bars. These kinds of ambiguity are basic to the periodic experience. They are perhaps one reason that the study of this vital aspect of Romantic music has so far not lent itself to standardization.

Consider another aspect of the two periods we have heard so far, bars 1–16 and 17–24/25. Both end incompletely and as such convey the sense of a work in progress. But the second is half as long as the first—a feature that may surprise listeners who are not looking at the score or marking time with their feet. And the fact that the second period intensifies the expression suggests that the entire 24-measure passage is a single utterance, beginning low (so to speak) and reaching a rhetorically heightened moment in 23–24. Sorting out these trajectories is a challenge in itself and depends crucially on where we as listening subjects are temporally located.

Bar 25 marks another beginning, the third since the movement began. The opening cello song is now given to first and second violins playing two octaves and one octave, respectively, above the initial cello register. At the same time, the countermelody from bars 17ff. is here entrusted to the oboe. Double basses and cellos meanwhile play the pizzicato bass to which we have become accustomed since the beginning. This third period engenders a strong cadential feeling from its fifth bar

(bar 29) onward. Mahler pulls all the usual stops available to the Romantic composer—a high register that we know to be unsustainable, a rounding-up circle-of-fifths harmonic progression (E–A–D–[and, eventually]G), chromatic inflection, and perhaps most significant, arrival on a dominant-functioning 6/4 chord in bar 31, an archetypal sign of impending closure. The sense of dominant will extend through bars 31 to 36, conferring on the entire 25–36 phrase a concluding function. In colloquial terms, it is as if we began the movement singing a song that we did not finish (1–16), repeated it in an intensified version without attaining closure (17–24), and then sang it in an even more intensified version, reaching a longed-for cadence on this third attempt (25–37). These qualities of intensification and repetition reside in the domain of periodicity; we might even say that they embrace the whole of the music.

Bar 37 marks the onset of yet another beginning in the movement—the fourth, in the larger scheme of things. The by-now-familiar pizzicato bass (that Schubert played on the piano to accompany his singer in "Wo ist Sylvia?") is heard, and it recalls the three previous beginnings at 1, 17, and 25, only now doubled an octave lower. The uppermost melody is now tinged with a sense of resignation, dwarfed in its ambitions by the melodic achievements of the previous period. By now, we are beginning to sense a circularity in the overall process. Perhaps the formal mode here is one of variation. This fourth period, however, is soon led to a decisive cadence in bars 44–45, and the attainment of the cadence is confirmed by a conventional I–IV–V–I progression, complete with a tonicization of IV (bars 46–47). The fact that the music beginning in bar 37 showed no ambitions initially and then moved to enact a broad and decisive cadence confers on this fourth period a sense of closing, a codetta-like function, perhaps. After the cadence in bars 36–37, we might have sensed a new, strong beginning. But the simulated strength was short-lived, and the cumulative pressure of closure held sway, hence the big cadence in bars 44–45.

The relative strength of the cadence in bars 44–45 sets the character of the joins between phrases into relief. Every time we locate a musical process as beginning in a certain measure, we are in danger of lying, or at least of undercomplicating a complex situation. Attending to periodicity and the tendency of the material is a useful way of reminding ourselves of how fluid are phrase boundaries and how limited are conventional means of analytic representation. Consider the succession in bars 16–17. The approach to bar 16 tells the listener that we are about to make a half-cadence. Indeed, Mahler writes an apostrophe into the score at this point, registering the separateness of the moment and the musical thought that it concludes. There is therefore, strictly speaking, no cadential (V–I) progression between bars 16 and 17. Moreover, bar 17 is marked by other signs of beginning (entrance of a new melody, return of the old melody slightly decorated) thus encouraging us to hear 16 as concluding a process—albeit an incomplete one. The join at bars 24–25, too, is illusory. Here, too, we should, strictly speaking, not imagine an authentic cadence because the approach to 24 effects the manner of a conclusion of an incomplete thought, a conclusion prepared by a passionate melodic outburst. What complicates this second join is the rather deliberate physical movement led by the dueting voices, second violin and cello. In a more nuanced representation, we might say that the 24–25 join conveys a greater dependency than the 16–17 join, but that neither join approximates a proper cadence.

The third main join in the movement is at 36–37. Here, the sense of cadence is harder to ignore. I mentioned the big dominant arrival in 31, which harmonic degree is extended through 36, finding resolution at the beginning of 37. Thus, while bars 1–16 and 17–24 each end with a half-cadence, bars 25–37 conclude with a full cadence. Notice, however, that the join in 36–37 is undermined by the return of our pizzicato bass, by now a recognizable signifier of beginnings. We might thus speak of a phrase elision, whereby 37 doubles as the end of the previous phrase and the beginning of another.

From bar 37 on, the business of closing is given especial prominence. If the cadence in bars 36–37 is authentic but perhaps weakly articulated because of the phrase elision, the next cadence in bars 44–45 is a stronger authentic cadence. The melodic tendency in bars 43–44 sets up a strong desire for $\hat{1}$, whereas that in 36–37, passing as it does from $\hat{5}$ through $\hat{4}$ to $\hat{3}$, forgoes the desire for $\hat{1}$. In addition, the precadential subdominant chord in bar 43 strengthens the sense of cadence in bars 44–45. Working against this, however, is the new melody sung by bassoons and violas beginning in bar 45, which Mahler took over from an earlier symphony. Again, the elision weakens the cadence and promotes continuity, but not to the same extent as happened in bars 36–37. The intertextual gesture also underlines the discontinuity between bars 44 and 45.

The next punctuation is the authentic cadence at bars 50–51. Some listeners will hear the pizzicato bass notes—reinforced, this time, by harp—not only as a sign of beginning, as we have come to expect, but, more important, as a sign of ending—the poetic effect that Brahms, among other composers, uses to signal ultimate home-going. Since the close in 50–51 comes only 7 bars after the one in 44–45, our sense that we are in the region of a global close is strengthened. Indeed, from bar 51 onward, the musical utterance gives priority to elements of closure. Launching this last closing attempt are bars 51–54. Then, bars 55–56 make a first attempt at closure, complete with an archetypal $\hat{3}$–$\hat{2}$ melodic progression harmonized conventionally as I–V7 (V7 is literally expressed by V4/2 but the underlying sense is of V7). A second attempt is made in 57–58, also progressing from I–V. The third attempt in 59–61 remains trapped on I. It is then stripped of its contents, reduced to a single pitch class, B, which in turn serves as $\hat{5}$ in the E-minor section that follows in bar 62.

With the benefit of hindsight, we may summarize the segments or units that articulate a feeling of periodicity as follows:

1–16	16 bars	51–54	4 bars
17–24	8 bars	55–56	2 bars
25–37	13 bars	57–58	2 bars
37–45	9 bars	59–61	3 bars
45–51	7 bars		

That some segments are relatively short (2, 3, or 4 bars) while others are long (8, 9, 13, or 16 bars) may lead some readers to suspect that there has been a confusion of levels in this reckoning of periodicity. But the heterogeneity in segment length is a critical attribute of the idea of periodicity being developed here. Periods must be understood not as fixed or recurring durational units but as constellations that promote a feeling of closing. If it takes 16 bars to articulate a sense of completion, we will speak of a 16-bar period. If, on the other hand, it takes only 2 bars to convey the same sense, we will speak of a 2-bar period. Periodicity in this understanding is similar to the function of periods in prose composition; it is intimately tied to the tendency of the musical material. It is not necessarily based on an external regulating scheme. Of course, such schemes may coincide with the shapes produced by the inner form, but they need not do so and often do not. The listener who attends to the specific labor of closing undertaken by individual segments of a work attends to more of the overall sense of the music than the listener who defers to the almost automatic impulse of a regulating phrase-structural scheme.

Finally, it is evident that talk of periodicity is implicitly talk of some of the other features that I am developing in this and the previous chapter. The idea of beginnings, middles, and endings is germane to the experience of periodicity. Similarly, high points mark turning points within the form and are likely to convey the periodic sense of a work.

Schubert, "Im Dorfe"

Periodicity in song is a complex, emergent quality. The amalgamation of words and music expands the constituent parameters of a work. The poem comes with its own periods, its own sense units, and when words are set to music, they develop different or additional periodic articulations based on their incorporation into a musical genre. And if it is to remain coherent within the constraints of its own language, the music must be subject to certain rules of well-formedness. It must, in other words, work at the dual levels of *langue* and *parole*, that is, conform simultaneously to the synchronic state of early nineteenth-century tonal language and to the peculiarities, mannerisms, and strategies of the composer.

The harmonic trajectory of Schubert's "Im Dorfe" from his *Winterreise* cycle exemplifies such well-formedness. An atmospheric night song, "Im Dorfe" exemplifies a mode of periodicity based on the statement and elaboration of a simple, closed harmonic progression. I will have more to say about harmonic models and processes of generation in coming chapters. Here, I simply want to show how simple transformations of an ordinary progression confer a certain periodicity on the song.[5]

---

5. I'm restricting my comments here to the periodicity of harmonic succession. A full musico-poetic analysis is not part of my aim here. For a helpful orientation to some of the principal features of "Im Dorfe," see John Reed, *The Schubert Song Companion* (Manchester: Manchester University Press, 1985), 453; and Arnold Feil, "Two Analyses ['Im Dorfe' from *Winterreise* and Moment Musical in F Minor, op. 94, no. 3 (D. 780)]," in *Schubert: Critical and Analytical Studies*, ed. Walter Frisch (Lincoln: University of Nebraska Press, 1986), 104–116.

Example 3.2 shows the nine periods of "Im Dorfe" in the form of chorale-like harmonic summaries. Ordered chronologically, the periods are as follows:

Period 1	bars 1–8	Period 6	bars 26–28
Period 2	bars 8–19	Period 7	bars 29–31
Period 3	bars 20–21	Period 8	bars 31–40
Period 4	bars 22–23	Period 9	bars 40–49
Period 5	bars 23–25		

Ordered conceptually (as in example 3.2), the order of periods is as follows: 1, 2, 8, and 9; 6 and 7; 3 and 4; and 5. The conceptual ordering proceeds from the most normative expression of the basic model (1) through two expansions (periods 2, 8, and 9) and two truncations (periods 6 and 7) to three expressions of the model away from home in the subdominant key: periods 3, 4, and 5 (where 5 represents a slight expansion of 3 and 4).

The top line of example 3.2 shows the model as a simple cadential progression, I–ii6/5–V–I. By adding passing notes in the outer voices and delaying the arrival on the dominant by means of a dominant-functioning 6/4 chord, we arrive at Schubert's harmony for period 1 (bars 1–8). The next period, 2 (bars 8–19), is also a closed unit and begins exactly as the previous one. From its fifth bar onward, how-ever, the dominant is expanded by intervening 6/4s and by incorporating mixture toward the end of the period (16–17). Bars 8–19 are thus an expansion of 1–8.

The bars 18 and 19 stand outside a periodic framework. The rumbling in the bass in bar 18 asks us to wait for Schubert's next move and to begin to get ourselves out from under the constraints of the first two periods. And the complementary note D intoned in the treble in bar 19 is a ray of light; it prepares us for a change of affect brought on by a key change (to G major, IV) and a change of rhythmic pacing. The protagonist's stance is altered: things slow down somewhat, and we experience a sense of distance.

The periods in the middle section of "Im Dorfe" are notably shorter. First comes period 3, a 2-bar prolongation of G (bars 20–21; see the model in example 3.2). This is repeated in bars 22–23 as period 4. Next comes another 2-bar period, 5 (bars 24–25), this one based on a cadential progression that incorporates a root movement by fifth in the bass. An internal sequence may encourage us to hear this 2-bar period as comprising two 1-bar units, but the overall prolongation of G elevates the 2-bar grouping to prominence. Finally, an appendix (bar 26) reaches D as V of G, which is in turn extended by means of a right-hand decorated arpeg-giation, leading to 2 bars of V7 in the key of D (bars 29–30) in preparation for the return of the A section. If the harmonic model for bars 26–31 is a repeated V–I progression, then bars 26–28 may be heard expressing the progression over a pedal (period 6) while bars 29–31 (period 7) show a root-position dominant-sev-enth prefixed by a chromatic upper neighbor-note in the bass, again overlapping with the return. In sum, the middle section is broken up into five little periods (periods 3, 4, 5, 6, and 7) on the basis of local harmonic articulation.

With the return in bar 31 (figuratively prepared since bar 29), we also return to the harmonic model of the opening of the song. The basic model again guides

Example 3.2. Periodic structure of Schubert's "Im Dorfe," from *Winterreise*.

bars 31–40 (period 8). Expansion of this model begins in bar 36, where the 6/4 is minor rather than major, which then opens up the area around B-flat. B-flat later supports an augmented-sixth chord that prepares the elaborate hymn-like cadence of bars 38–40. (The similarity between the chorale texture of Schubert's music in these bars and the chorale texture employed in the demonstration of our harmonic models may provide some justification—if such were needed—for the exercise represented in example 3.2.) This model is now repeated as period 9 in bars 40–49, with bars 46–49 functioning simply as an extension of tonic. In short, the A' section consists of two longer periods, 8 and 9.

If the sense units of Schubert's "Im Dorfe" as described here are persuasive, we can appreciate one aspect of Schubert's craft. In responding to the mimetic and declamatory opportunities presented by a verbal text, he retains a secure harmonic vision distributed into nine periods of varying length. Longer periods occur in the outer sections while shorter ones occur in the more fragmented middle section. The periodicity story is, of course, only one of several that might be told about the song, but the strength of Schubert's harmonic articulation may encourage us to privilege this domain in constructing a more comprehensive account of the song's overall dynamic.

Schumann, "Ich grolle nicht"

Like Schubert's "Im Dorfe," this song from Schumann's *Dichterliebe* cycle has a periodic form that is complexly distributed. That Schumann's instincts in setting Heine's text were strongly musical is conveyed by the liberties he took with the poem—repeating certain words as well as the phrase "Ich grolle nicht" almost as a refrain.[6] There are reasons, therefore, to hear the song in terms of a dominating musical impulse without denying the value of the insights that emerge from regarding the conjunction of word and tone.

The outer form of the song suggests two main parts, reflecting Heine's stanzaic division. The first is bars 1–18, the second bars 18–36. We might thus speak of two large periods, the first incomplete, the second complete. But this first reading of periodic form hides the high-point structure of the song. As most listeners know and remember, a high A (added, incidentally, by Schumann late in the compositional process) on the word *Herzen* in bar 27 forms the climax of the song. From there, the melody descends gradually to the tonic, as one would expect after such a point of great intensity. If we go back and now look at the occurrences of the key word *Herz* in the song, we notice that the trajectory mapped by its recurrence across the song is a rising one. There is thus a sense in which "Ich grolle nicht" comes across as a single, indivisible whole, comprising a single period that begins at the beginning and ends at the end, and follows a sweeping, commanding trajectory.

There is a third way of conceiving the periodicity of this song and that is to note a recurring bass pattern that confers a kind of ground bass feel. We can follow this process of composition and recomposition easily from the course of the bass line as set out in example 3.3. The song is divided into six periods, each of them closed, although—and not unexpectedly—adjacent periods overlap with one another, the last half-note of one becoming the first of its successor. The first

---

6. See Cone, "Words into Music," for a discussion of Schumann's emendations.

4 bars comprise period 1, and this may also be taken as the model for harmonic motion in the song. Beginning on the tonic, period 1 outlines the subdominant area, incorporates mixture at the beginning of bar 3 (by means of the note A-flat), and then closes with a perfect cadence. The second period is twice as long (bars 4–12), but it covers the same ground, so to speak. That is, the bass line descends by step, filling in the gaps left in the model (period 1). And the bass approaches the final tonic also by step, including a chromatic step. Bars 4–12 are therefore a recomposition of 1–4.

Example 3.3. Periodic structure of Schumann's "Ich grolle nicht," from *Dichterliebe*.

The next period, period 3, occupies bars 12–19, overlapping with periods on either side. Here, the I–IV6 motion from the beginning of period 1 is expanded by the incorporation of the dominant of vi, so that instead of I–IV6, we have I–V/vi–vi. And the close of the period, bars 16–19, uses the same bass progression as that at the end of the previous period (9–12; the notes are G–A–A♯–B–C). Given these affinities, we can say that this third period is a recomposition of the second, itself an expansion and reconfiguring of the first. Note that periods 2 and 3 are of roughly the same length in bars, while period 1, the model, is about half their length. In other words, periods 2 and 3 are (temporally) closer than 2 and 1 or, for that matter, 3 and 1. Again, the feeling of periodicity is conveyed by punctuation (including its absence), not by phrase length in bars.

Period 4 is identical to period 1. Period 5 begins and continues in the manner of period 2 but closes with a decisive cadence in bars 28–30. This is exactly the same cadence that concluded periods 1 and 4. Thus, the idea that period 5 recomposes period 4 is enhanced. Thematically speaking, period 5 is a recomposition of period 2, but it incorporates the cadence pattern of periods 1 and 4. Since period 2 is itself already a recomposition of period 1, the status of period 5 as a member of the basic paradigmatic harmonic model is guaranteed. Finally, period 6 closes off the song with a straightforward cadential progression. We may, if we choose, divide this last period into two overlapping smaller periods of 3 and 5 bars, respectively (bars 30–32 and 32–36), and thus extend the overall period count to seven. I have chosen not to recognize a separate period here because bars 32–36 are so obviously an extension of the tonic chord reached in 32 that, without denying their harmonic progress, I would emphasize the overriding sense of the plateau announced by the arrival on tonic in bar 32.

This view of periodicity in "Ich grolle nicht" suggests a circular rather than linear trajectory. The ground bass that is announced in the first 4 bars appears five more times in different but recognizable guises. I will have more to say about this dimension of circularity in tonal-harmonic process when I discuss the paradigmatic method in chapter 5, but it is worth stressing the sense in which circularity runs counter to the more linear views of periodicity delivered by the two earlier vistas. The first view, which emphasized two periods, also claimed a certain stasis by implicitly arguing that stanza 2 is the same as stanza 1. However, the two stanzas are so long (18 bars) that, without denying the obvious parallels between them, the stanzaic rhythm may be not be heard immediately since only two instances are given. The second view ignores the stanzas and hears one broad, sweeping trajectory. This view reads the form of the song as a dynamic curve with a relatively low beginning, rising to a high point, and then ending at a dynamic higher than that of the beginning. The third view makes explicit the circular element contained in the stanzaic reading. Here, though, the stanzas are significantly shorter and, in a way, more readily perceptible. The arrivals on C that mark the beginning of each cycle are also marked musically. Although it would be possible to exhort the listener to incorporate all three perspectives on periodicity, this would represent a rather facile invocation of pluralism. Listeners normally make choices, following this trajectory and not another, so it is not immediately clear how one can listen simultaneously in these three ways. One can listen *for* each of these ways, or perhaps move in and out of them even within a single audition, but that is already a different kind of behavior from "normal" listening.

The example of "Ich grolle nicht" is a clear indication of an enduring tension between linear and circular tendencies in the Romantic expression of periodicity. It helps to complicate our view of Romantic music even at this basic, grammatical level by bringing the regularity of phrase sense into confrontation with the irregularity of periodicity. It also suggests that the narrative curve is composed of both forward-pointing linear tendencies and backward-pointing circular ones. To think more generally of tonal music in these ways conveys, I believe, a richer view of structure.

Stravinsky, *The Rake's Progress, act 1, scene 3, Anne's aria, "Quietly, night"*

When the intrinsic tendencies of dominant- and diminished-seventh sonorities no longer form the basis of a composer's idiolect, periodicity has to be sought in other realms. Sometimes, it is conferred in retrospect rather than in prospect, the musical procedures having dispensed with a baggage of desire carried by tonal impulse; sometimes, it is given entirely in the melody. And sometimes, the periodic space is left as a blank slate for listeners to inscribe their own patterns of periodicity.

Anne's aria in act 1, scene 3, of Stravinsky's *Rake's Progress* illustrates some of these transformations. Unlike the tendency described in Schubert, Schumann, and Mahler, the constructive force of harmony in Stravinsky provides triadic (or bi-triadic) articulation and emphasis without necessarily generating longer-term expectations. To say that Anne's aria is "in B minor" is to say, in the first instance, that the triad of B minor (inflected by the diminished fifth, B–F♮) frames the aria and sounds again in the course of it. The self-consciously accompanimental manner of the orchestra defers the burden of periodic articulation to Anne. At the largest level (the bars in example 3.4 are reckoned from 1 to 35, corresponding to rehearsal numbers 183–189 in Stravinsky's score), her utterances may be gathered into two large waves (bars 1–20 and 21–35), corresponding to Auden's and Kallman's verses. We may speak in a preliminary way of strophic song (as we did in the earlier discussion of Schumann's "Ich grolle nicht").

Example 3.4. Stravinsky, The *Rake's Progress*, act 1, Anne's aria, "Quietly, night."

How are the two strophes enacted? We begin with a 1-bar orchestral vamp, then Anne sings her phrases in 2-bar segments. The phrase "Although I weep" bears the climactic moment. Stravinsky allows Anne a rest before intoning the F-sharp in bar 12 to begin this intensified expression. Twice she sings the phrase, ending, first, with a question mark (bar 15) and, on the second try, with a period (bar 18). The second try continues the verbal phrase to the end, "Although I weep, it knows of loneliness." The close on B minor in bar 18 recalls the opening and, in the more recent context, answers directly to the "dominant" of bar 15. Anne also manages to incorporate a tiny but significant $\hat{3}$–$\hat{2}$–$\hat{1}$ melodic motion on the second and third syllables of "loneliness." Woodwinds immediately echo the second of Anne's climactic phrases in part as remembrance and in part as a practical interlude (or time out for the singer) between two strophes.

The listener's ability to form a synoptic impression of this first period (bars 1–20) is made challenging by the additive phrase construction. There is no underlying periodic framework except that which is conveyed by the pulsation. But pulsation is only the potential for periodicity, not periodicity itself. It is Anne's two climactic phrases that gather the strands together and compel a feeling of closure. Here, it is difficult to predict the size of individual periods. We simply have to wait for Stravinsky to say what he wants to say and how.

"Guide me, O moon" begins the second strophe to the melody of "Quietly, night." For 4 bars, strophe 2 proceeds as an exact repetition of strophe 1, but at the words "And warmly be the same," Stravinsky takes up the material of the climactic phrase "Although I weep." The effect is of compression: the preparatory processes in bars 5^2–12^1 are cut out, bringing the climactic phrase in early. The reason for this premature entrance in bar 24 is that the climactic region is about to be expanded. Anne now intensifies her expression by affecting a coloratura manner on her way to the high point of the aria, the note B-natural lasting a full bar and a half (bars 30–31) and extended further by means of a fermata. This duration is entirely without precedent in the aria. Indeed, the string of superlatives that mark this moment—including the withdrawal of the orchestra at the end of the note so that the timbre of Anne's voice does not compete with any other timbre—is such that little can or need be "said" in the aftermath of the high point. Anne simply speaks her last line ("A colder moon upon a colder heart") in a jagged, recitative-like melody that spans two octaves from the high B of the climax to the B adjacent to middle C. The orchestra comments perfunctorily, without commitment.

Two aspects of the periodicity of Anne's aria may be highlighted here. First, the apparent two-stanza division that enabled us to speak of two large periods is, as previously noted, somewhat limited. The second period (starting in bar 21) is not merely a repeat of the first, although it begins like it and goes over some of its ground; it is rather a continuation and intensification of it. We might speak legitimately here, too, of a Romantic narrative curve beginning at a modest level, rising to a climax, and then rapidly drawing to a close. A second aspect concerns the modes of utterance employed by Anne. These modes reflect greater or lesser fidelity to the sound of sung language. If we locate three moments in the vocal trajectory, we see that Anne begins in speech mode or perhaps arioso mode (bars 2–3), reaches song mode at "Although I weep," and then exceeds song mode at the words "It cannot, cannot be thou art." The latter is an extravagant vocal gesture that, while singable, begins to approximate instrumental melody. This moment of transcendence is followed by withdrawal into speech mode—a strictly syllabic, "unmelodic" rendering of "A colder moon upon a colder heart," finishing with a literal, speech-like muttering of "a colder heart" on four B-naturals with durations that approximate intoned speech. In sum, Anne begins in speech mode, reaches song mode, then a heightened form of song mode, before collapsing into speech mode. Again, according to this account of modes of utterance, the periodic sense cuts across the aria as a whole, forming one large, indivisible gesture.

Bartók, Improvisations for Piano, *op. 20, no. 1*

To complete this discussion of periodicity, I turn to a work of Bartók's from 1920 for another view of structuring time (example 3.5). Crossing over into a post-Romantic idiom will set into relief both continuities and discontinuities in the construction of periodicity.

Example 3.5. Bartók, *Improvisations for Piano*, op. 20, no. 1.

(attacca)

Bartók uses a Hungarian folk song that he had collected in 1907 as the basis for this written-down improvisation. The compositional conception, therefore, is from song to instrumental music. The idea in the First Improvisation—as indeed in several of the others—is to preserve the folk source, not to transform it. The melody is 4 bars long, and Bartók presents it three times in direct succession and then appends a 4-bar codetta. The first presentation borrows the opening major-second dyad from the melody (F–Eb) and uses it at two different pitch levels to accompany the song. The pitch material of the accompaniment, although sparse, is wholly derived from the melody itself. In terms of periodicity, these first 4 bars retain the intrinsic periodicity of the melody itself. One aspect of that periodicity is evident in the rhythmic pattern: bars 1–3 have the same pattern while bar 4 relinquishes the dotted note and the following eighth-note. In the tonal realm, bar 1 presents an idea, bar 2 questions that idea by reversing the direction of the utterance, bar 3 fuses elements of bars 1 and 2 in the manner of a compromise as well as a turning point, and bar 4 confers closure by incorporating the subtonic (B-flat). These 4 bars promote such a strong sense of coherence and completeness that they may be said to leave little room for further expectations; they carry no implications and produce no desires. Whatever follows simply follows; it is not necessitated by what preceded it.

The second statement of the melody (bars 5–8) replaces the dyads of the first statement with triads. Triadic succession, though, is organum-like or, perhaps, Debussy-like, insofar as the triads move in parallel with no obvious functional purpose. In other words, the melody merely reproduces itself in triadic vein. Thus, the trajectory of the original melody remains the determinant of the periodic sense of these second 4 bars. By merely duplicating the melody, this second 4-bar period is figured as simpler and more consonant than the first; it incorporates no contrapuntal motion. As before, no internal expectations are generated by the triadic rendition of the Hungarian folk song. Formal expectations will, however, begin to emerge from the juxtaposition of two statements of the folk song. We may well suspect that we will be hearing it in different environments.

The third statement (bars 9–12) turns out to be the most elaborate. Beginning each of the first 3 bars with a D-minor triad, the second half uses what may well come across as nontonal sonorities.[7] The melody, now doubled, is placed where it should be, namely, in the upper register (this contrasts with the first two appearances of the folk song). This third occurrence marks the expressive high point of the improvisation, not only because Bartók marks it *espressivo* but because of the thicker texture, the more intense harmonies, the more salient projection of the melody, and the full realization of a melody-accompaniment relationship.

This climactic region (bars 9–12) is also—and more obviously—known in retrospect. The last 4 bars of the improvisation do not begin by stating the folk melody as before. Rather, the first of them (bar 13) echoes the last bar of the folk melody in a middle—that is to say, unmarked—register; then the next three present an intervallically augmented version of the same last bar, modifying the pitches but retaining the contour. The harmony supporting this melodic manipulation in the last 4 bars is perhaps the most telling in conveying a sense of closure. A succession of descending triads on E-flat minor, D minor, and D-flat minor seems destined for a concluding C major, but this last is strategically withheld and represented by a lone C, middle C. Bars 13–16 may be heard as a recomposition of

---

7. Paul Wilson finds instances of pitch-class sets 4–18 and 5–16 in this 4-bar period, thus acknowledging the nontriadic nature of the sonorities. See Wilson, "Concepts of Prolongation and Bartók's opus 20," *Music Theory Spectrum* 6 (1984): 81.

bar 8—one difference being that the missing steps are filled in—and, more broadly, as a reference to the entire second statement of the folk melody in bars 5–8.

The feel of periodicity in this improvisation is somewhat more complex. Self-contained are the first three 4-bar phrases, so they may be understood from a harmonic, melodic, and phrase-structural point of view as autonomous, as small worlds in succession. The last 4-bar phrase carries a closing burden: it embodies a conventional gesture of closure—echo what you have heard, slow things down, and let every listener know that the end is nigh. Indeed, to call it a 4-bar phrase is to mislead slightly because there are no internal or syntactical necessities to articulate the 4-bar-ness. The number 4 depicts a default grouping, not a genuine syntactical unit. (The recomposition in example 3.6 compresses Bartók's 4 bars to 2, but their periodic effect is not really different from the original.) By eschewing the dependencies of common-practice harmony, without however dispensing with gestures of intensification and closure, the compositional palette in this work becomes diversified. This is not to say that common-practice repertoires are lacking this potential autonomization of parameters. It is rather to draw attention to their more obvious constructive role in Bartók's language.

Example 3.6. Recomposed ending of Bartók, *Improvisations for Piano*, op. 20, no. 1.

The foregoing discussion of periodicity should by now have made clear that periodicity is a complex, broadly distributed quality that does not lie in one parameter. It is an emergent, summarizing feel that enables us to say that something begun earlier is now over or about to be concluded. Talk of periodicity therefore necessarily involves us in talk about some of the other criteria for analysis that I have been developing in chapter 2 and the present chapter. Like form, the notion of periodicity embraces the whole of music. Focusing on punctuation and closure and their attendant techniques helps to draw attention to this larger, emergent quality. To complete this introduction to notions of periodicity, I must discuss two related techniques that are frequently encountered in Romantic music: discontinuity and the use of parentheses.

Discontinuity and Parentheses

The lure of organicism as an organizational principle may have blinded us to certain aspects of Romantic music, one of which is the discontinuity principle. Romanticism and organicism, yoked together like toe and toenail, emphasize interdependency, mutual growth, and the naturalness of connection. According to the conventional account, Beethoven led in the early 1800s, followed by Liszt, Brahms, and Wagner. By contrast, some of the radical discontinuities that listeners hear in twentieth-century compositions by Varèse, Webern, Stravinsky, and Stockhausen seem so much more real that they dwarf any sense that music of the previous century might manifest any but the most cursory instances of discontinuity. And yet many of us listening to Romantic opera, symphony, ballet, or program music frequently experience moments when one thing does not necessarily lead to another, when a process is interrupted or a thought abandoned, when a new compositional idea seems to come from nowhere—in short, instances of succession as distinct from progression. Some of these moments feature what we might call *strong* forms of discontinuity; others are instances of *weak* forms of discontinuity. Some are apparent, belonging only to a given level of conceptualization; others are real and more deep-rooted, valid at all relevant structural levels. Between these two extremes lie a host of intermediate steps. The prospect that events that follow each other may or may not be continuous with each other sheds light on an aspect of a composition's formal drama and rhetoric.

As always, the discontinuity principle has to be understood in context, for one person's continuity may be another's discontinuity. Unlike their counterparts working with twentieth-century materials (such as Jonathan Kramer, Arnold Whittall, and Christopher Hasty), music theorists working with Romantic repertoires have so far not invested considerably in accounts of discontinuity.[8] Their methods all too often produce connections and continuities; explanations aim at promoting cohesion rather than breaks, fissures, or incoherence. Indeed, some may argue that aiming at demonstrating an absence of connection may be perverse. The analyst has simply not tried hard enough—or is inadequately equipped—to uncover sources of connection. And with this commitment to their methods rather than to the peculiarities of a given work of art, analysts undervalue what may sometimes be a central principle of structure.

It should be noted that music critics who are not normally constrained by a theory-based framework for validating observations about a musical work are more likely to entertain ideas of discontinuity in Romantic music. In a discussion of the *Todtenfeier* movement of Mahler's Second Symphony, for example,

---

8. But see Hatten's *Interpreting Musical Gestures, Topics, and Tropes*, 267–286.

Carolyn Abbate describes the onset of the so-called *Gesang* theme as an "interruption . . . a radically different musical gesture." For her, this moment marks "a deep sonic break"; indeed, "cracks fissure the music at the entry of the 'Gesang.'"[9] These characterizations ring true at an immediate level. This otherworldly moment is clearly marked and maximally contrasted with what comes before. Difference embodies discontinuity. Note, however, that this characterization works in part because it refuses technical designation. If, instead of responding to the aura of the moment, we seek to understand, say, the motivic logic or the nature of succession in the realms of harmony, voice leading, or even texture, the moment will seem less radically discontinuous and more equivocal. For one thing, in the bars preceding the onset of the *Gesang* theme, a triplet figure introduced in the bass continues past the ostensible break and confers an element of motivic continuity. Attending to the voice leading in the bass, too, leads one to a conjunct descent, C–Cb–B♮, the ostensible crack occurring on C-flat. On the other hand, texture and timbre are different, as are dynamics and the overall affect. Thus, while the action in the primary parameters presents a case for continuity, the action in the secondary parameters presents a case for discontinuity. Recognizing such conflicting tendencies by crediting the potential for individual parameters to embody continuity or discontinuity may help to establish a more secure set of rules for analysis. My task here, however, is a more modest one: to cite and describe a few instances of discontinuity as an invitation to students to reflect on its explanatory potential.

Looking back at the classical style as point of reference, we can readily recall moments in which discontinuity works on certain levels of structure. A good example is the first movement of Mozart's D Major Sonata, K. 284, which I mentioned in the previous chapter on account of its active topical surface. A change of figure occurs every 2 bars or so, and listeners drawn to this aspect of Mozart are more likely to infer difference, contrast, and discontinuity than smooth continuity. Indeed, as many topical analyses reveal and as was implied in discussions of character in the eighteenth century, the dramatic surface of classic music sometimes features a rapid succession of frames. There is temporal succession, but not progression. Things follow each other, but they are not continuous with each other.

Think also of the legendary contrasts, fissures, and discontinuities often heard in the late music of Beethoven. In the "Heiliger Dankgesang" of op. 132, for example, a slow hymn in the Lydian mode alternates with a Baroque-style dance in 3/8, setting up discontinuity as the premise and procedure for the movement. The very first page of the first movement of the same quartet is even more marked by items of textural discontinuity. An alla breve texture in learned style enveloped in an aura of fantasy is followed—interrupted, some would say—by an outburst in the form of a cadenza, then a sighing march tune in the cello, then a bit of the sensitive

9. Abbate, *Unsung Voices*, 150–151. See Agawu, "Does Music Theory Need Musicology?" *Current Musicology* 53 (1993): 89–98, for the context of the remarks that follow. A discussion of discontinuity in Beethoven can also be found in Lawrence Kramer, *Music as Cultural Practice* (Berkeley: University of California Press, 1990), 190–203 and in Barbara Barry, "In Beethoven's Clockshop: Discontinuity in the Opus 18 Quartets," *Musical Quarterly* 88 (2005): 320–337.

or *Empfindsamer* style, then a cadenza again, now complete with a conventional 6/4 chord preparation, and so on. At this level of structure, these gestures succeed each other in discontinuous fashion.[10]

Insofar as a normative modus operandi exists for Romantic music, it is less invested in the sharply profiled and rapid shifts of texture like those that I have just cited from Mozart's K. 284/i and Beethoven's op. 132/i and iii. The shifting of gears is a common enough occurrence, but the material images thus set into relief do not always carry the sharply stylized or conventional stances associated with classic music. Rather, they embody affective transformation, and this transformation is often enacted before our very eyes/ears, not served up as prefabricated action units with cosmopolitan mimetic values. Mendelssohn's Violin Concerto exemplifies this mode of Romantic discourse. A compositional voice emanating from within pauses to reflect and recall, seeming now and again to forget something, abandoning a line of argument, then forging its way forward with great introspective confidence, paying only lip service to the trappings of external obligation. The protagonist's manner (and by "protagonist," I do not mean the solo violin but the leading voice that carries the line of narrative from beginning to end) is not that of a librarian shuffling cards, or of a child ordering pebbles on the beach, but of a guru speaking with the dual authority of oracular knowledge and affected mysticism.

Think, too, of opera, of the numerous discontinuous musical effects that seem practically unavoidable. Plot, of course, is in principle continuous, or more readily invites attributions of continuity. Discontinuity is thus buffered. But although music and plot are imbricated within each other's domains, their individual sets of capacities are not thereby erased. In one moment during the second act of Wagner's *Tannhäuser*, Tannhäuser interrupts Wolfram with a hymn of praise to Venus. This is the fourth and, as it happens, the last time he sings this song, so there is an immediate context for establishing long-range musical connections. But the local situation (example 3.7) involves a juxtaposition that produces a striking discontinuity. In this moment of tonal drama, two keys, Wolfram's E-flat major and Tannhäuser's E major, lying on opposite sides of the tonal spectrum, are brought into direct confrontation. Wolfram's is the interrupted voice, Tannhäuser's the interrupting one, and it is the latter that gains temporary priority. Wolfram's world will ultimately triumph in the opera's key scheme.

Similar effects figured as interruptions, visits from other worlds, shiftings of dramatic gears, etc., are common in opera. They suggest that discontinuity is not merely a rhetorical option for individual composers; indeed, the musical utterance specifically, and the musical utterance more generally, may be intrinsically discontinuous. If so, analytical labor is better spent exploring the dynamics of discontinuity than in confirming the tautologies of continuity.

One final aspect of periodicity, which is related to discontinuity, is *parenthesis*. Musical parentheses are enclosures within musical sentences. In a strict sense,

---

10. For a fuller discussion of topics in op. 132/i, see Agawu, *Playing with Signs*, 110–126. For a study that tracks the onsets and endings of topics in the same movement, see Carol Krumhansl, "Topic in Music: An Empirical Study of Memorability, Openness, and Emotion in Mozart's String Quintet in C Major and Beethoven's String Quartet in A Minor," *Music Perception* 16 (1998): 119–132.

Example 3.7. E-flat/E-natural conflict in Wagner, *Tannhäuser*, act 2.

they are syntactically dispensable. Both the opening and closing of a parenthesis enact a discontinuity with the events that precede and follow, respectively. In the harmonic realm, for example, a parenthesis may introduce a delay in the approach to a goal or enable a prolongation or even a sustaining extension for the sake of play; it may facilitate the achievement of temporal balance or be used in response to a dramatic need contributed by text. In the formal realm, a parenthesis may introduce an aside, an insert, a by-the-way remark. Parentheses in verbal composition have a different significance from parentheses in musical composition. In a verbal text, where grammar and syntax are more or less firmly established, the status of a parenthetical insertion as a dispensable entity within a well-formed grammatical situation is easy to grasp. In a musical situation, however, although we may speak of musical grammar and forms of punctuation, an imagined excision of the material contained in a so-called parenthesis often seems to deprive the passage in question of something essential, something basic. What is left seems hardly worthwhile; the remaining music is devoid of interest; it seems banal. This suggests that musical parentheses are essential rather than inessential. A grammar of music that does not recognize the essential nature of that which seems inessential is likely to be impoverished.

Consider a simple chordal example. In the white-note progression shown in example 3.8, we can distinguish between structural chords and prolonging chords. The sense of the underlying syntax—the progression's harmonic meaning—can be conveyed using the structural chords as framework. In that sense, the intervening chords may be said to be parenthetical insofar as the structure still makes sense without them. And yet the prolongational means are so organically attached to the structural pillars that the "deparenthesized" progression, while able to convey something of the big picture by displaying the structural origins of the original passage, seems to sacrifice rather a lot. Indeed, what is sacrificed in this musical context may be more than what is sacrificed in an analogous linguistic situation. Once again, we note an important difference between musical meaning and linguistic meaning. If there is no meaningful musical structure apart from its prolongational means, then parentheses should be understood as indispensable.[11]

Example 3.8. Harmonic progression incorporating two parentheses.

The work of parentheses may be readily observed in the shaping of musical forms, but the transforming effect of erasing the contents of a parenthesis—even as a thought experiment—is a sign that making a firm distinction between events that lie inside and those that lie outside a given parenthesis is phenomenologically problematic. In the large opening movement of Beethoven's F Major String Quartet, op. 59, no. 1, the development contains a huge insertion that Ratner has characterized as a parenthesis. Occupying bars 152–222 within the larger span 98–241, the parenthesis constitutes 42.36% of the development section. According to Ratner, the smaller form has an integrity of its own in the shape of a fantasia-like prelude (bars 152–184) followed by a fugato (bars 185–210) and finally an epilogue or postlude (211–222), also in fantasia style. He calls this a parenthesis because the development section can be imagined as coherent from a structural point of view without bars 152–222, a few adjustments at beginning and ending notwithstanding. But the resulting coherence carries a sizable phenomenal deficit. All of the secondary relationships and intertextual resonances made possible by the parenthesis disappear, and we are left with an almost naked syntactic structure, one with minimum temporal content and none of the gestural qualities necessitated by an exposition conceived on the grandest possible scale.

The third movement of this same quartet—a movement that is also in sonata form—contains a parenthesis in the latter part of the development section, bars 70–80. The exposition occupies bars 1–45 and ends in the dominant minor, C minor, from an F minor tonic. The development begins in A-flat major (bar 46), passes through D-flat/C-sharp (bars 50ff.) to D minor (bar 57), and eventually reaches the dominant of F minor in bar 67. But after 3 bars of waiting on the dominant in anticipation of a return to tonic, the music veers off into a different key, D-flat major (bar 70). This is the beginning of the parenthesis, which will be closed in bar 80, where the dominant of F minor returns to prepare the cadence onto F

11. In some generative theories of tonal structure, the idea of parenthesis is implicit in the assignment of hierarchical values to various members of a musical progression. Thus, the left or right branches in a tree diagram distinguish controlling elements from controlled elements, making it possible to describe some as essential to the structure and others as dispensable. See Alan Keiler, "The Syntax of Prolongation: Part 1," *In Theory Only* 3 (1977): 3–27; and Lerdahl and Jackendoff, *A Generative Theory of Tonal Music.*

minor for an actual recapitulation (bar 84). The parenthetical passage is the only sustained major-mode passage in the movement. Its expressive manner is intense. I hear a foreshadowing of a passage from one of Richard Strauss's *Four Last Songs*, "September," in bars 72–75 of the Beethoven. Locally, the parenthetical material continues the process of textural intensification begun earlier in the movement. If the achievement of tonal goals is accorded priority, then interpreting bars 70–80 as a parenthesis is defensible. But the material inside the parenthesis is dispensable only in this limited sense.

Periodicity, then, embraces the whole of music. As a quality, it is distributed across several dimensions. I have talked about cadences and cadential action, closure, high points, discontinuity, and parenthesis. The overarching quality is closure, including its enabling recessional processes. A theory of musical meaning is essentially a theory of closure.

Modes of Enunciation: Speech Mode, Song Mode, Dance Mode

Conventional musicological knowledge normally distinguishes between aria and recitative in vocal genres like opera and cantata. From the late eighteenth century on, for example, aria approaches the song end of the continuum while recitative signals the speech end. Aria is closer to music while recitative is closer to language. Their temporal feels are similarly different: aria is on the slower end while recitative is on the fast end. As modes of enunciation, aria is more reticent than recitative when it comes to dispensing words. As a medium for the delivery of data or information, recitative has priority; aria is relatively inefficient.

Between these two normative poles are a number of complications. Arias come in a wide variety of forms. Arioso, for example, lies midway between aria and recitative. An aria may incorporate the modality of a recitative sporadically or occasionally. Accompanied recitative, or *recitative obligé*, begins to shed its speech-like mode and to incorporate song-like movement. And there are cases in which the two modes, while normatively different, interpenetrate in ways that are not readily distinguishable.

If we understand instrumental music as taking some of its bearings from vocal music, we can postulate three modes of enunciation that seem to function regularly in Romantic music: speech mode, song mode, and dance mode. Historically, the dance mode represents a sedimentation of corporeality in music, as we find regularly in a variety of dance-based compositions by Schubert, Chopin, Brahms, and Dvořák.[12] The song mode is the native and most natural mode of enunciation for the Romantic composer; it is the mode in which he sings, in which something approaching a purely musical being is enacted. Schumann, Mendelssohn, Bruckner, Rossini, Donizetti, and Verdi exploit this mode most imaginatively,

---

12. On corporeality in music, with an emphasis on Chopin, see Eero Tarasti, *Signs of Music: A Guide to Musical Semiotics* (Berlin: de Gruyter, 2002), 117–154.

although it remains the unmarked mode for all Romantic composers. And the speech mode, although hierarchically differentiated from the song mode, also possesses near-native status for composers; given the deep but ultimately problematic affinities between natural language and music (discussed in chapter 1) and given the qualitative intensification of word dependency in nineteenth-century instrumental practice, it is not surprising to find composers exploring and exploiting the speech mode of enunciation to set the others into relief.

How are these three modes manifested in actual composition? In speech mode, the instrument speaks, as if in recitative. The manner of articulation is syllabic, and resulting periodicities are often asymmetrical. Song and dance modes inhabit the same general corner of our conceptual continuum. Song mode is less syllabic and more melismatic. Periodicity is based on a cyclical regularity that may be broken from time to time for expressive effect. And, unlike speech mode, which is not obligated to produce well-formed melody, the song mode puts melody on display and calls attention to the singing voice, be it an oboe, English horn, violin, flute, or piano. Song mode departs from the "telling" characteristic of speech. The impulse to inform or deliver a conceptually recoverable message is overtaken by an impulse to affect, to elicit a smile brought on by a beautiful turn of phrase. Accordingly, where speech mode may be said to exhibit a normative past tense, song mode is resolutely wedded to the present. While the dance mode often includes song, its most marked feature is a sharply profiled rhythmic and metric sense. The invitation to dance—to dance imaginatively—is issued immediately by instrumental music in dance mode. This mode is thus deeply invested in the conventional and the communal. Since dance is normally a form of communal expression, the stimulus to dance must be recognizable without excessive mediation. This also means that a new dance has to be stabilized over a period of time and given a seal of social approval. A new song, by contrast, has an easier path to social acceptance.

As always with simplified models like this, the domains of the three modes are not categorically separate. I have already mentioned the close affinity between song mode and dance mode. A work whose principal affect is located within the song mode may incorporate elements of speech. Indeed, the mixture of modes is an important strategy for composers of concertos, where the rhetorical ambitions of a leading voice may cause it to shift from one mode to another in the manner of a narration.

Examples of the three modes abound, but given our modest purposes in this and the previous chapter—namely, to set forth with minimum embroidery certain basic criteria for analysis—we will mention only a few salient examples and contexts. Late Beethoven is especially rich in its exploitation of speech, song, and dance modes. Scherzos, for example, are normative sites for playing in dance mode. A good example is the scherzo movement of the Quartet in B-flat Major, op. 130. Dance and song go hand in hand from the beginning. They have different trajectories, however. Once the dance rhythm has been established, it maintains an essential posture; we can join in whenever we like. Song mode, on the other hand, refuses a flat trajectory. The degree of "songfulness" may be intensified (as in bars 9ff.) or rendered normatively. Of particular interest in this movement, however, is Beethoven's speculative treatment of the dance. While the enabling material is typically disposed in a nonteleological manner—except at very local levels—Beethoven interrupts the progress of dance with a passage in speech mode (bars 48–63, quoted in example 3.9). The fast-slower rhythmic articulation in the form of quarter-notes followed by dotted half-notes unsettles the earlier periodicity, and the ensuing call-and-response between first violin and the ensemble as a whole brings a strong responsorial manner redolent of verbal exchange. Perhaps most important, the bare octaves approximate the monophony of speech, avoiding for a moment a normative harmonic texture. With the speech mode comes a foregrounding of music's ordinary language, which differs from the normal register of poetic language. Compositional labor is laid bare, and the listener is invited to observe directly the means by which the music moves forward; the

Example 3.9. The speech mode in Beethoven, String Quartet in B-flat Major, op. 130, third movement, bars 48–63.

listener's persona merges with the composer's for a brief moment. Finally, in bar 64, Beethoven reactivates the dance and song modes by shutting the window that allowed us a peek into his workshop and reengages the listener as dancer for the remainder of the movement.

Similarly striking is the invocation of speech mode in the transition from the fourth to the fifth movements of the Quartet in A Minor, op. 132. The fourth movement, marked "alla Marcia," begins as a 24-bar march in two-reprise form. Marching affects the communality of dance mode. Immediately following is an invocation of speech mode in the form of a declamatory song, complete with tremolo effects in the lower strings supporting the first violin. This emergence of a protagonist with a clear message contrasts with the less stratified stance of the preceding march. In this mode of recitative, meter and periodicity are neutralized, as if to neutralize the effect of the march, which, although written in four, succumbs to groupings in three that therefore complicate the metrical situation. (The coming finale will be in an unequivocal three.) The rhetorical effect of this instantiation of speech mode is to ask the listener to wait—wait for a future telling. But the gesture is fake, a simulation; there is nothing to be told, no secrets to be unveiled, only the joy of playing and dancing that will take place in the finale. These games never fail to delight.

Robert Schumann is one composer in whose music the speech and song modes of enunciation play a central role. Numerous passages in the favorite Piano Quintet tell of a telling, stepping outside the automatic periodicity built on 4-bar phrases to draw attention to the music itself, thus activating the speech mode. The D Minor Symphony, too, features moments of speech whose effect is made more poignant by the orchestral medium. His songs and song cycles are rich sources of this interplay; indeed, they are very usefully approached with a grid based on the interaction between speech and song modes. In *Dichterliebe*, for example, song 4 unfolds in the interstice between speech mode and song mode, a kind of declamatory or arioso style; song 9 is in dance mode; song 11 in song mode; and song 13 in speech mode. The postlude to the cycle as a whole begins in song mode by recalling the postlude to song 12 (composers typically recall song, not speech). As it prepares to close, the speech mode intrudes (bars 59–60). Then, some effort has to go into reclaiming the song mode, and it is in this mode that the cycle reaches its final destination. (We will return to this remarkable postlude in connection with the discussion of narrative below.)

When the poet speaks at the close of the *Kinderszenen* collection ("Der Dichter spricht"), he enlists the participation of a community, perhaps a protestant one. A chorale, beginning as if in medias res and inflected by tonal ambivalence, starts things off (bars 1–8). This is song, sung by the congregation. Then, the poet steps forward with an introspective meditation on the head of the chorale (bars 9–12). He hesitates, stops, and starts. This improvisatory manner moves us out of the earlier song mode toward a speech mode. The height of the poet's expression (bar 12, second half) is reached by means of recitative—speech mode in its most authentic state. Here, we are transported to another world. Our community is now far behind. We hold our breaths for the next word that the poet will utter. Speech, not song, makes this possible. Then, as if waking from a dream, the poet joins the congregation in beginning the chorale again (bar 18). In song mode, we are led gradually but securely to a place of rest. The cadence in G major at the end has been long awaited and long desired. Its attainment spells release for the body of singers.

None of these modes is written into Schumann's score. They are speculative projections based on affinities between the composition's specific textures and conventional ones. The sequence I have derived—song mode, speech mode, heightened speech mode (recitative), and finally song mode—seeks to capture the composer's way of proceeding. Of course, the modes are not discrete or discontinuous; rather, they shade into each other in accordance with the poet's modulated utterances.

Chopin, too, often interrupts a normative song mode with passages in speech mode. The Nocturne in B Major, op. 32, no. 1, proceeds in song mode from the beginning, until a cadenza-like flourish in bar 60 prepares a grand cadence in bar 61. The resolution is deceptive, however (bar 62), and this opens the door to a recitative-like passage in which speech is answered in the manner of choral affirmation. In these dying moments of the nocturne, speech mode makes it possible to enact a dramatic effect.

The three modes of enunciation introduced here are in reality three moments in a larger continuum. As material modes, they provide a framework for registering shifts in temporality in a musical work. In song, where words bear meaning and also serve as practical vehicles for acts of singing, it is sometimes possible to justify a reading of one mode as speech, another as song, and a third as dance by appealing to textual meaning and by invoking a putative intentionality on the part of the composer. In nonprogrammatic instrumental music, by contrast, no such corroborative framework exists; therefore, hearing the modes remains a speculative exercise—but this says nothing about their credibility or the kinds of insight they can deliver.

Narrative

The idea that music has the capacity to narrate or to embody a narrative, or that we can impose a narrative account on the collective events of a musical composition, speaks not only to an intrinsic aspect of temporal structuring but to a basic human need to understand succession coherently. Verbal and musical compositions invite interpretation of any demarcated temporal succession as automatically endowed with narrative potential. Beyond this basic level, music's capacity to craft a narrative is constantly being undermined by an equally active desire—a natural one, indeed—to refuse narration. Accordingly, the most fruitful discussions of musical narrative are ones that accept the imperatives of an aporia, of a foundational impossibility that allows us to seek to understand narrative in terms of nonnarration. When Adorno says of a work of Mahler's that it "narrates without being narrative,"[13] he conveys, on the one hand, the irresistible urge to make sense

13. Theodor Adorno, *Mahler: A Musical Physiognomy*, trans. Edmund Jephcott (Chicago: University of Chicago Press, 1992), 76.

of a temporal sequence by recounting it, and, on the other hand, the difficulty of locating an empirical narrating voice, guiding line, or thread. Similarly, when Carl Dahlhaus explains that music narrates only intermittently—akin, in our terms, to the intrusion of speech mode in a discourse in song or dance mode—he reminds us of the difficulty of postulating a consistent and unitary narrative voice across the span of a composition.[14] Using different metalanguages, Carolyn Abbate, Jean-Jacques Nattiez, Anthony Newcomb, Vera Micznik, Eero Tarasti, Márta Grabócz, Fred Maus, and Lawrence Kramer have likewise demonstrated that it is at once impossible to totally resist the temptation to attribute narrative qualities to a musical composition and, at the same time, challenging to demonstrate narrative's musical manifestation in a form that overcomes the imprecision of metaphorical language.[15]

Ideas of narrative are always already implicit in traditional music analysis. When an analyst asks, "What is going on in this passage?" or "What happens next?" or "Is there a precedent for this event?" the assumption is often that musical events are organized hierarchically and that the processes identified as predominant exhibit some kind of narrative coherence either on an immediate level or in a deferred sense. The actual musical dimensions in which such narratives are manifest vary from work to work. A favorite dimension is the thematic or motivic process, where an initial motive, figured as a sound term, is repeated again and again, guiding the listener from moment to moment, thus embodying the work's "narrative." Another ready analogy lies in tonal process, specifically in the idea of departure and return. If I begin my "speech" in C major and then move to G major, I have moved away from home and created a tension that demands resolution. The process of moving from one tonal area to another depends on the logic of narrative. If I continue my tonal narrative by postponing the moment of return, I enhance the feeling of narrative by setting up an expectation for return and resolution. The listener must wait to be led to an appropriate destination, as if following the plot of a novel. And when I return to C major, the sense of arrival, the sense that a temporal trajectory has been completed, the sense that a promise has been fulfilled—this is akin to the experience of narration.

On the deficit side, however, is the fact that, because of the high degree of redundancy in tonal music, because of the abundant repetition which we as listeners enjoy and bathe in, a representation of narration in, say, the first movement of Beethoven's Fifth Symphony, comes off as impoverished and uninspiring insofar as it is compelled, within certain dimensions, to assert the "same thing" throughout the movement. The famous four-note motif (understood as rhythmic pattern as

14. Dahlhaus, "Fragments of a Musical Hermeneutics."

15. See Fred Everett Maus, "Narratology, Narrativity," in *The New Grove Dictionary of Music and Musicians*, 2d ed. (London: Macmillan, 2001) for a straightforward introduction to the field of musical narratology. Students interested in pursuing narrative further will wish to eventually study works by the authors mentioned in the text. For an exemplary, holistic study, see Karol Berger, "The Form of Chopin's Ballade, op. 23," *19th-Century Music* 20 (1996): 46–71. A rewarding recent study is Matthew McDonald, "Silent Narration? Elements of Narrative in Ives' *The Unanswered Question*," *19th-Century Music* 27 (2004): 263–286.

well as intervallic configuration with the potential to do various kinds of harmonic work) dominates the surface of the movement through repetition and transformation—a charged, constant presence. From a documentary or informational perspective, such sameness does not allow us to craft a varied discourse about what might be going on; the motif denotes a kind of stasis. But the prospect that what, for many listeners, is a charged and exciting movement can be accurately described as "static" is problematic. Which is why some musicians prefer to dispense with such ostensibly superficial analogies between verbal and musical narrative and to confront music's ostensible redundancy head on, celebrating music's refusal to move (as distinct from simulating motion), to narrate (as distinct from inviting accounts of narration), or to inform (as distinct from being assigned that role in certain contexts). Under this view, Beethoven plays imaginatively with tones, and so the analyst's task is to explicate these acts of the imagination. Musical rules formed from habit, precedent, and convention serve as the scaffolding for such an investigation, not a documentary or narrative impulse.

A related obstacle to reading music as narrative—this one readily exemplified in the sonata-form protocol—is the fact that a large portion of a movement may be given over to "narrating" something that has already been narrated. The linear impulse that subtends verbal narrating generally dispenses with such large-scale recapitulation, moving things forward toward a goal in response to the reader's desire to know. But in musical narrative, such retelling, although it varies in manner and extent, is generally unavoidable, in part because the stance of music is very much geared to the present, to the phenomenal moment, not to an unspecified future or to a past of doubtful relevance (which is not to say that future and past are extrinsic to music's ontology).

In Liszt's tone poems, the program or extramusical plot provides a framework for interpreting musical events in terms of narrative. Since we know that the composer sought to give musical life to a given story, we are encouraged to hear the music through this enabling narrative. Sometimes, the relationship is close or iconic, as horses gallop, lovers sing passionately to each other, and Orpheus strikes his lyre. In other contexts, the relationship may be obscure, as when a generalized musical effect is appropriated (by the analyst) for a particular textual expression. Interpreting tone poems and other texted work is an invitation to arrange marriages of convenience. Music is made to bear the weight of an assigned verbal narrative. Persuasion, not proof, is the goal here.

A single example from Schumann will have to suffice in indicating the dimensions of musical narrativity and incorporating the modes of enunciation discussed previously. Example 3.10 reproduces the final page of Schumann's *Dichterliebe* cycle. The protagonist has now buried his loved one and his songs in the ocean, abandoned the domain of vocal singing, and deferred the final rites of resolution and closure to the pianist. It is well to remember the number of characters that create the sense of narrative in this cycle: singer and pianist (sometimes individually as singer and accompanist, sometimes dually as self-accompanying singer), poet (Heine), composer (Schumann), poet/composer (Heine/Schumann), and finally the protagonist and his loved one as principal actors in the plot. Each of these characters can and does inflect the sense of narrative.

Example 3.10. Song mode and speech mode at the close of Schumann's *Dichterliebe.*

At the start of example 3.10, the job of unveiling the ultimate destination of the last song (and, for that matter, the cycle) is entrusted to the pianist. The singer dropped off on a predominant sonority, leaving the pianist to carry the thought through a dominant-seventh and on to a tonic for conventional resolution. The join between bars 52 and 53 admits of elements of both narrative continuity and discontinuity. A $\hat{5}$–$\hat{1}$ progression in the bass provides a strong sense of an authentic cadence, but it lacks the cooperation of the upper parts, for the V7 is initially held over at the start of 53 and then dissipated. Harmonic resolution is therefore only partial, not complete. At the same time, a song—a certain song, we might say after the first few melodic notes—is recalled, starting in bar 53. Climbing slowly and dripping with accompanying arpeggios, this melody takes us back to an earlier moment in the cycle, to the close of song 12, where it was heard a minor third lower in the key of B-flat major. Here, in the postlude to song 16, the initial 2-bar gesture (bars 53–54) sets the tone for the rhythm of speech. Bars 53–54 are repeated in bars 55–56 with tiny but telling variations, and then we move onward toward closure with a strong and implicative 6/4 chord in bar 57. We expect resolution on the downbeat of bar 59, but here too, Schumann suspends the dominant from the previous bar over the tonic, resolving it only partially (partially because he adds a flattened-seventh to the tonic sonority in bar 60). At this moment, the poet goes into speech mode for 2 bars, as if commenting on the song recalled since bar 53 and as if promising resolution. Then, in bar 61, the pianist begins to reclaim the abandoned or interrupted song mode and to seek ultimate resolution. First is a 1-bar gesture (bar 61), which is repeated (bar 62), and then repeated and extended, leading finally to a cadence (bars 63–65). The cadence is then repeated two more times, the last decorated with a 4/3 suspension, as if holding on and deferring proper closure until the last possible moment. Certainly, by the time we hear this threefold cadential reiteration, we are back in song mode, and it is in this mode that the protagonist bids us farewell. The lucidity of Schumann's rhetoric in this postlude tempts us to advance a narrative interpretation like the following: first, retrieve a lost song (itself marked by effort and aspiration by virtue of its rising, hopeful contour), repeat it, and then signal your desire to close; but defer full closure by letting the poet speak in his favorite speech mode; finally, regain—not without a little struggle—the song mode, incorporating an expansion of register and a faster rate of harmonic motion; these agents of peroration will then bring things to an end.[16]

Conclusion

Chapter 2 and the present chapter have introduced six criteria for the analysis of Romantic music: topics; beginnings, middles, and endings; high points; periodicity (including discontinuity and parentheses); modes of enunciation (speech mode, song mode, dance mode); and narrative. The specific aspects of this repertoire that the criteria seek to model are, I believe, familiar to most musicians. So,

16. For an imaginative, thorough, and incisive account of this postlude, see Beate Julia Perrey, *Schumann's Dichterliebe and Early Romantic Poetics: Fragmentation of Desire* (Cambridge: Cambridge University Press, 2003), 208–255.

although they are given different degrees of emphasis within individual analytical systems, and although there are still features that have not been discussed yet (as indeed will become obvious in the following two chapters), I believe that these six, pursued with commitment, have the potential to illuminate aspects of meaning in the Romantic repertoire. Readers are invited to plug in their favorite pieces and see what comes out.

Is it possible to put the concerns of our criteria together into a single, comprehensive model? And if so, what would the ideological underpinning of such a gesture be? The criteria offered here seek an account of music as meaningful discourse, as language with its own peculiarities. They are not mutually exclusive, as we have seen, but necessarily overlapping; some may even lead to the same end, as is easily imagined when one student focuses on periodicity, another on the high-point scheme, and a third on narrative. A certain amount of redundancy would therefore result from treating the criteria as primitives in an axiomatic or generative system. Nor are they meant to replace the processes by which musicians develop intuitions about a piece of music through performance and composition; on the contrary, they may function at a metalinguistic level to channel description and analysis formed from a more intuitive engagement.

Does this imply that the more perspectives one has at one's disposal, the better? If putting it all together were a statistical claim, then the more perspectives that one could bring to bear on a work, the better the analysis. But this kind of control is not my concern here. Making a good analysis is not about piling on perspectives in an effort to outdo one's competitors; it has rather to do with producing good and interesting insights that other musicians can incorporate into their own subsequent encounters with a work. The institutional burdens—marked during the heyday of structuralist methods in the 1980s—of having to deal with wholes rather than parts and of publicizing only those insights that could be given a "theoretical" underpinning may have delayed the development of certain kinds of analytical insight. If, therefore—and respectfully—I decline the invitation to try and put it all together here, I hope nonetheless that the partial and provisional nature of these outcomes will not detract from the reader/listener enjoying such moments of illumination as there may have been.

CHAPTER Four

Bridges to Free Composition

Tonal Tendency

Let us begin with the assumption that a closed harmonic progression constitutes the norm of coherent and meaningful tonal order. Example 4.1 exemplifies such a progression. Hearing it initially not as an abstraction but as a real and immediate progression allows us to identify a number of tendencies fundamental to tonal behavior and crucial to the development of a poetics of tonal procedure.

Example 4.1. Closed harmonic progression.

The progression is characterized by a sense of departure (from sonority 1) and return (through 2 to 3), which may be glossed as motion from one (relatively) stable point to another (more stable point). Departure generates tension and arouses expectations, while return provides resolution and fulfillment of expectations. The progression as a whole is continuous and continually meaningful. Elements are utterly dependent on each other for their meaning. In the progression 2–3, for example, 3 is meaningful in relation to 2; indeed 2–3 constitutes an idiomatic expression, a unit of harmonic syntax. The strong interdependency between the two chords is further enhanced if 2 acquires an internal tritone (B–F), as shown in example 4.2. It would not be hyperbolic to speak in this case of a sense of inevitability in the 2–3 progression because the desire for resolution is so strongly felt. Indeed, 2 finds its fulfillment in 3.

Example 4.2. Same progression with intensified middle element.

The possibility of detaching the 2–3 segment suggests that 1 and 3, previously regarded as identical, are different from another point of view. As the first sounding element, 1 is given; it is a gift, we might say. Sonority 3, on the other hand, as the last sounding element, is achieved through a powerful set of linear tendencies mediated by 2—a product of labor, we might say. Sonority 1 thus has a different kind of significance from 3. The two share an identity in difference; that is, chordal sameness contrasts with phenomenological difference.

Succession carries implications for meaning. The 1–2 progression is a space-opening gesture, providing the first indication of the potential for disrupting a postulated order. The sounding of 2 marks a departure from 1 even while setting 1 into relief as point of reference, an origin to be remembered; 2 in turn sets up an expectation that this initial departure (from 1 to 2) will be rationalized later on—perhaps immediately, perhaps after a delay.

Finally, the melody's journey from $\hat{3}$ through $\hat{2}$ to $\hat{1}$ in this particular harmonization reinforces the sense that sonorities 1 (with $\hat{3}$ in the top voice) and 3 (with $\hat{1}$ in the top voice), although both instances of the same harmonic class (I), are in different states of rest, the latter being in a more complete state than the former. The latter is bounded by $\hat{1}$ and I in treble and bass, respectively, while the former is bounded by $\hat{3}$ and I, thus carrying a potential for $\hat{3}$ to move toward a goal. The closing leap in the bass from G down to C further carries an archetypal sense of finality; indeed, V–I in this disposition is unmatched in syntactical strength as agent of closure. No other bass progression within the tonal universe is comparably privileged.

In short, examples 4.1 and 4.2 show that tonal tendency is the product of tonal dependency, that meaning is context while context is meaning, that succession generates expectations, and that the disposition of voices and lines signifies, as does intervallic motion. I dwell on these elementary properties to remind us of the meaningfulness of tonal motion in and of itself. Chord succession, chord progression, linear motion, identity, and difference—all of these contribute to our understanding of this "music." We have not identified a composer, instrumental medium, work, date, or style; there is no text, program, or genre. Yet we can all agree, I think, that example 4.1 is coherent and that it satisfies the conditions for establishing good tonal order in a modest way. To the extent that these meanings arise from intrinsic tonal behavior, we may speak of purely tonal meanings and oppose these in principle to extratonal meanings. This, at least, is the conventional understanding that underpins the ostensibly problematic opposition between "purely musical" and "extramusical." Of course, there is always a conventional aspect to the assignment of meanings, so to claim purity for one meaning is not to deny the mediation of conventional usage. Nevertheless, within the cultural constraints of the repertoires studied in this book, it is acceptable, I believe, to identify these sorts of meanings and to oppose them to those that arise from music's engagement with other semiotic systems. If, as I have already indicated in chapter 1, the dichotomy between intrinsic and extrinsic meanings in music turns out to be ultimately untenable, it can nevertheless provide insight at preliminary levels of analysis.

We have studied example 4.1 in its immediate acoustic particularity, but its highly compressed, white-note framework is more usefully conceptualized as an idealization, a background to more expansive foregrounds, a token for numerous potential types. In an actual composition, a phrase, period, section, or indeed an entire work may subtend the kind of structure represented in example 4.1. Schenker recognized the synonymity, noting that such structures lack "the thousandfold variety of presuppositions that inhere in the small configurations replacing the cantus firmus."[1] In studying the "small configurations" produced by dimensional actions and interdimensional interactions, we are thrown into the concrete world of living musical works; yet, the cantus firmus, here generalized to denote an archetypal essence or a minimally elaborated subsurface construct endowed with procreative or generative power, is never conceptually dispensable.

How does one proceed from a restricted, albeit well-formed, background such as example 4.1 to a full-fledged, living foreground? How can a white-note progression lacking periodic, motivic, phrase-structural, rhythmic, or hypermetrical content provide the conditions of possibility for an actual flesh-and-blood composition? Schenker used the striking metaphor of *bridges to free composition*[2] to support his contention that "free composition is essentially a continuation of strict counterpoint."[3] I have titled this chapter thus with the purpose of showing that the idea that a continuous bridge links the world of strict counterpoint to that of free composition is at once deeply suggestive and at the same time hugely problematic. By recognizing and defining a series of voice-leading models as scaffolding for tonal composition, Schenker provided us with the single most potent tool for understanding and imaginatively reconstructing a tonal composition. However, by declining to specify the full range of historically specific stylistic resources that enable the generation of a given composition from a generalized background to a unique foreground, or by consigning such tasks to a less urgent category in the hierarchy of theoretical concerns, he evaded one of the challenging issues in understanding musical style. Granted, training in strict counterpoint was for Schenker

1. Schenker, *Der Tonwille: Pamphlets in Witness of the Immutable Laws of Music*, vol. 1, ed. William Drabkin, trans. Ian Bent et al. (Oxford: Oxford University Press, 2004), 66, 13.

2. Heinrich Schenker, *Counterpoint: A Translation of Kontrapunkt*, trans. John Rothgeb and Jürgen Thym (New York: Schirmer, 1987), 175.

3. Schenker, *Der Tonwille*, 21.

not a method of composition but a way of training the ear, so in one sense it is beside the point what (superficial) stylistic forms a particular structural procedure takes. An 8–5–8–5–8–5 intervallic pattern between treble and bass, an extensive prolongation of the dominant via the flattened-sixth, or a delay in the arrival of a melody's structural 1̂—all of these can assume myriad stylistic forms, depending on whether they occur in music by Corelli, Handel, or Bach; Beethoven or Mozart; Brahms, Wagner, Mahler, or Richard Strauss. Understanding music as discourse, however, demands engagement with the temporal, rhythmic, and motivic aspects of a work—with aspects of topical signification; high-point articulation; periodicity; beginnings, middles, and endings; modes of enunciation; and narrative discussed in the previous chapters. We might say then that the Schenkerian vision needs to be *supplemented*—not transformed from within or without, not replaced—by other analytical proceedings.

But is such supplementation possible? Is it productive? Beyond commonsense values inherent in a more-is-better philosophy, it is not at all clear in what sense a Schenkerian vision can or needs to be supplemented. If, following Derrida, we think of a strong supplement as a potential replacement, something that can conceivably take the place of the object, not something that adds a few decorative attributions, then adding observations about, say, motivic process to a Schenkerian graph of a Beethoven piano sonata, or constructing a hermeneutic account of Haydn's "Chaos" from *The Creation* by incorporating contemporaneous ideas about chaos from literature and visual art, or fleshing out the poetic associations of Heine's "Ihr Bild" in compensation for Schenker's modest explication of the song within the context of a voice-leading interpretation amount to supplementarity only in a weak sense. The question of whether supplementarity is productive is an ideological as well as an institutional one. If one feels better by restoring Heine's words to Schenker's graph of the second song from Schumann's *Dichterliebe*, there can be no objection in principle; at the same time, the claim that the restoration of the words completes Schenker's analysis is unintelligible. The "problem" with a Schenkerian approach is not that Schenker overlooks certain musical features (as if it is ever possible not to overlook certain features in any analysis), but that the vision is notionally complete within the terms laid out by the theory, thus leaving little room for the facile addition of other observations. Think, for example, of the analysis of the C Major Prelude from book 1 of the *Well-Tempered Clavier* in *Five Graphic Musical Analyses*. Of course, the prospect of a "complete" analysis is not a problem at all; indeed, it is the very reason to celebrate the musical and explanatory power of his approach to analysis.

This is only the beginning of a discussion of Schenkerian supplementarity and the interesting conceptual and ideological issues raised by the notional completeness of different analytical systems. But further discussion will have to be saved for another occasion, for it is time to turn to the main business of this chapter, namely, to revisit Schenker's idea of the relation between strict counterpoint and free composition and to provide a range of illustrations of the relationship between the two drawn from a variety of stylistic contexts. There are two possible gains from this exercise. First, the approach provides what I believe is one of the most satisfying hands-on approaches to tonal analysis. If we are to understand musical meaning and the nature of music as discourse, then a practical, speculative exploration of the conceptual origins of musical configurations can prove useful. Second, the ability to abstract a simpler structure from a more complex surface will be called upon both in the paradigmatic analyses of the next chapter and throughout the case studies in the following chapters. Although musical semiology has so far not drawn extensively upon Schenker's insights,[4] I hope to show that the paradigmatic approach is already implicit in Schenker's theory and that, by substituting models or modules of tonal action for motives, one can develop a well-formed paradigmatic analysis that may in turn enable the exploration of musical meaning in harmonically rich repertoires.

A final preliminary word: in presenting the examples in this chapter, I wish to emphasize a *generative* approach over a reductive one. I wish, in other words, to encourage students to work from the abstract level to the concrete, from a prototype to a piece-specific manifestation, from a background to a foreground. Rather than thinking in terms of rules for striking out embellishments in a composition in order to arrive at a background, it will be more productive to think in the reverse: how to enrich a bare musical outline in order to arrive at a full-fledged surface. Of course, one does not know which background to work from unless one already knows the foreground for which one is aiming, so the generative and reductive approaches entail each other by definition. From a strictly pedagogical point of view, however, the generative approach offers certain advantages. Searching for imaginative and stylistically appropriate ways of, for example, bringing a I–V–I progression to life à la Schubert, Brahms, or Mahler is, in my view, significantly more rewarding than merely discovering such a progression in the composer's work. A generative approach compels empathy with the imagined compositional process; in the best of cases, it brings genuine insight into how a particular composition works.

Strict Counterpoint and Free Composition

Between 1910 and 1921—that is to say, while working on his treatise *Kontrapunkt*—Schenker made a firm distinction between *strict counterpoint* and *free composition*. This was a necessary and convenient dichotomy, for it allowed him

---

4. There are exceptions, of course. Already in 1981, Jonathan Dunsby and John Stopford announced a program for a Schenkerian semiotics that would take up questions of musical meaning directly. See Dunsby and Stopford, "The Case for a Schenkerian Semiotic," *Music Theory Spectrum* 3 (1981): 49–53. More recently, Naomi Cumming has drawn on Schenker in developing a theory of musical subjectivity. See her *The Sonic Self: Musical Subjectivity and Signification* (Bloomington: Indiana University Press, 2000). See also David Lidov's discussion of "segmental hierarchies" in *Is Language a Music?* 104–121. And there are other names (e.g., Alan Keiler, William Dougherty) that could be added to this list. Nevertheless, it would be hard to support the contention—judging from the writings of leading semioticians like Nattiez, Monelle, Tarasti, and Hatten—that a Schenkerian approach is central to the current configuration of the field of musical semiotics.

to separate the study of (Fuxian) species counterpoint from the study of the music itself. But although convenient in concept, the dichotomy proved to be hard to sustain at a practical level. Schenker, no doubt in possession of a huge supplement of information pertaining to free composition, drew regularly on this supplement in making his analyses, but he did not always make explicit the source of this other knowledge. Instead, he held fast to the more immediate theoretical challenge.

Strict counterpoint is a closed world, a world built on rules and prescriptions designed to train students in the art of voice leading and therefore to prepare them for better understanding of the music of the masters. In strict counterpoint, there are, in principle, no *Stufen*; there is no harmonic motivation, no framework for making big plans or thinking in large trajectories. All we have are consonances and dissonances, voice leading, and specific linear and vertical dispositions of intervals. There is no repetition, no motivic life, no dance—only idealized voices following very local impulses and caring little for phraseology, outer form, or the referential potency of tonal material. Free composition, by contrast, deals with the actual work of art; it is open and promiscuous and admits all sorts of forces and licenses. Unlike strict counterpoint, it relies on scale steps, possesses genuine harmonic content, incorporates repetition at many levels, and perpetuates diversity at the foreground. The essential nature of strict counterpoint is its strictness, that of free composition its freedom.[5] This is why "counterpoint must somehow be thoroughly separated from composition if the ideal and practical verities of both are to be fully developed."[6] Indeed, according to Schenker, the "original and fundamental error" made by previous theorists of counterpoint—including Bellerman and Richter and even Fux, Albrechtsberger, and others—is the "absolute and invariable identification of counterpoint and theory of composition." We must never forget that "a huge chasm gapes between the exercises of counterpoint and the demands of true composition."[7]

So much for the fanfare announcing the separation between strict counterpoint and free composition. If we now ask what the connection between the two might be, distinctions become less categorical, their formulations more qualified and poetic. "Free composition is essentially a continuation of strict counterpoint," writes Schenker in *Tonwille*.[8] The phrase "essentially a continuation" implies that these are separate but related or relatable domains. In *Kontrapunkt*, Schenker says that, "despite its so extensively altered appearances, free composition is mysteriously bound…as though by an umbilical cord, to strict counterpoint."[9] Thus, at a practical or analytical level, the dividing line between them is porous, perhaps nonexistent. Their separation is a matter of principle.

Schenker used the suggestive metaphor *bridges to free composition* to suggest a relationship between subsurface and surface, between background and foreground, and ultimately between strict counterpoint and free composition. The discussion of

5. Schenker, *Counterpoint*, book 1, 55.
6. Schenker, *Counterpoint*, book 1, 10.
7. Schenker, *Counterpoint*, book 1, 9.
8. Schenker, *Der Tonwille*, 21.
9. Schenker, *Counterpoint*, book 2, 270.

bridges is implicit throughout *Kontrapunkt*, but only modestly explicit. Do these bridges exist? What forms do they take? How secure are they?

Strictly speaking, there are no bridges from strict counterpoint to free composition.[10] If bridges exist, they do so in a very restricted sense. From a generative point of view, not every feature of free composition can be generated from an arhythmic contrapuntal background. Schenker would not disagree with this observation, but he would respond by saying that everything *essential* about free composition can be so generated. There are many issues to untangle in this complex and controversial claim, issues ranging from what a composition is, through which parameters have what properties, to what is essential and what is dispensable. As always with debates framed within a binary axis, aligning oneself with the existence or nonexistence of bridges is ultimately not as valuable as simply being aware of what each position enables, affirms, hides, or denies.

In what follows, I present a number of relatively brief passages from various composers to show the relationship between strict counterpoint and free composition. Strict counterpoint is here generalized to encompass subsurface, sometimes chorale-like structures, and I have done this in part to keep a harmonic motivation present at all relevant levels of the analysis. As a practical step, I recommend that the reader first play through examples 4.3 to 4.36 at a piano and then return to read my commentary. For readers who associate Schenker's successes with the published comprehensive analyses of works like Mozart's G Minor Symphony, K. 550; Beethoven's *Eroica* Symphony; or J. S. Bach's Prelude no. 1 from book 1 of the *Well-Tempered Clavier*—all decked out on several levels (nominally three) and burdened with an extraordinary amount of detail in the realms of motive and voice leading—my own concentration here on fragments will seem grossly incomplete. Confining demonstration to this local level is deliberate, however, for it enables the analyst to reconstruct a composition through improvisation by focusing on those simple modules of tonal utterance that serve as building blocks or constructional units.

We begin with three examples (4.3, 4.4, and 4.5) taken from Schenker's *Kontrapunkt*. Please note that I have reversed Schenker's order of presentation by proceeding from background to foreground; I have also used letters (*a, b, c,* etc.) to indicate structural levels.

In example 4.3, at level *a* is a simple ii6–V–I progression shown in treble and bass—familiar enough, ordinary enough, conventional enough, one of the basic utterances of the tonal system. (This level, by the way, is not part of Schenker's demonstration, but I have included it to suggest a harmonic motivation.) Enrich it as shown at *b* with the resources of early eighteenth-century rhythmic practice— passing notes, anticipations, suspensions, arpeggiations, and neighbor-notes—and we are well on our way to Handel's elaborated sixteenth-note version at *c*. If we think of level *a* as origin or background, level *b* as development or middleground, and level *c* as present or foreground, we gain a view of what Schenker calls "the

---

10. See also Eytan Agmon, "The Bridges That Never Were: Schenker on the Contrapuntal Origin of the Triad and the Seventh Chord," *Music Theory Online* 3 (1997).

spatial depth of a musical work."[11] According to him, *c* "stands for" *b*—and we might add that *b* in turn stands for *a*. The beauty of this example of free composition lies in the fact that "the figuration [at level *c*] writes within itself several strands of voice leading in the most artistic way."[12] The derivational process makes explicit one aspect of that artistry.

Example 4.3. Handel, *Suites de pieces*, 2nd collection, no. 1, Air with Variations, var. 1 (cited in Schenker, *Counterpoint*, 59).

While all of this sounds logical, there has been a gap in the analysis. How did we get from level *b* to level *c*? Obviously, we did this by knowing the design of level *c* in advance and inflecting the derivational process in level *b* to lead to it. But how do we know what stylistic resources to use so that *c* comes out sounding like Handel and not Couperin or Rameau? How did we invent the design of the musical surface?

Schenker does not dwell on these sorts of questions; indeed, he seems to discourage us from dwelling on these aspects of the foreground. We are enjoined, instead, to grasp the coherence that is made possible by the background. But if the possibilities for activating the progression shown at level *a* are not spelled out, if they are consigned to the category of unspecified supplement, and if the analyst of Handel's suite is not already in possession of knowledge of a whole bunch of allemandes from the early eighteenth century, how is it possible to generate a specific surface from a familiar and common background? Without, I hope, overstating the point, I suggest that the journey from strict counterpoint (level *a*) to free composition (level *c*) makes an illicit or—better—a mysterious leap as it approaches its destination. I draw attention to this enticing mystery not to suggest a shortcoming but to illustrate one consequence of this particular setting of theoretical limits.

11. Schenker, *Free Composition*, 3.
12. Schenker, *Counterpoint*, book 1, 59.

In the 2 bars from Bach's C-sharp Minor Prelude from book 1 of the *Well-Tempered Clavier* in example 4.4, we hear a familiar progression in which the bass moves by descending fifths while the upper voices enrich the progression with 7–6 suspensions. This model of counterpoint ostensibly enables Bach's free composition (level *b*). But here, too, there are no rules that would enable us to generate the specific dance-like material that is Bach's actual music.

Example 4.4. J. S. Bach, Well-Tempered Clavier, book 1, Prelude in C-sharp Minor, bars 26–28 (cited in Schenker, Counterpoint, 337).

Level *a* of example 4.5 looks at first like a second species exercise, although its incorporation of mixture (G-flat) takes it out of the realm of strict Fuxian species. Whereas the demonstrations in the two previous examples "approximate . . . form[s] of strict counterpoint," thus placing the emphasis on a generative impulse, this

Example 4.5. Brahms, Handel Variations, op. 24, var. 23 (cited in Schenker, *Counterpoint*, 192).

passage from Brahms is "reduced to a clear two-voice counterpoint"; the emphasis rests on a reductive impulse. Schenker points out that the "real connection between strict counterpoint and free composition can in general be discovered only in reductions similar to [example 4.5]."[13] In other words, in the case of certain complex textures, the contrapuntal underpinning may lie further in the background, requiring the analyst to postulate additional levels of explanatory reduction. (Constructing the additional levels could be a valuable student exercise in the case of example 4.5.) Whether the degree of reducibility is reflected in a larger historical-chronological narrative or whether it conveys qualitative differences among compositions are issues left open by Schenker.

The mode of thinking enshrined in examples 4.3, 4.4, and 4.5 of hearing complex textures through simpler structures makes possible several valuable projects, some of them historical, others systematic. We might envisage, for example, a history of musical composition based strictly on musical technique. This project was already implicit in Felix Salzer's 1952 book, *Structural Hearing*, but it has yet to engender many follow-up studies.[14] Imagine a version of the history of composition based on the function of a particular diminution, such as the passing note, including leaping passing notes; or imagine a history of musical technique based on neighbor-note configurations, or arpeggiations. Granted, these are not exactly the sexiest research topics to which students are drawn nowadays, but they have the potential to illuminate the internal dynamics of individual compositions and to set into relief different composers' manners. Without attempting to be comprehensive, I can nevertheless hint at the kinds of insights that might accrue from such an approach by looking at a few examples of a single diminution: the neighbor-note.

Neighbor-Notes as Expansion of Content

Although neighbor-notes occupy a lower rung of the diminutional ladder than do passing notes, they have served as a useful technique "for the expansion of content" in a variety of Romantic contexts.[15] The big *N* in examples 4.6 to 4.12 identifies the neighboring action.

In example 4.6, the opening of Schubert's C Major Quintet, the tonic chord is prolonged—before our very eyes and ears—by neighbor-note motion, not diatonic neighbors from the subdominant or supertonic harmonies, but neighbors incorporating two chromatic pitches. While a labeling of the chord in bars 3–4 as a common-tone diminished-seventh chord is harmless enough insofar as it recognizes its quality, fuller understanding comes from grasping the leading of voices to and from that sonority.

13. Schenker, *Counterpoint*, book 1, 200.
14. See Salzer, *Structural Hearing*, for a history of musical technique. See also Arnold Whittall, *Musical Composition in the Twentieth Century* (Oxford: Oxford University Press, 2000).
15. Schenker, *Free Composition*, 71.

Example 4.6. Schubert, String Quintet in C Major, first movement, bars 1–6.

In example 4.7, an example from Schubert cited by Schenker,[16] neighbor-note harmony in the first bar, echoed up the octave in the second, serves to enrich the first-inversion E minor chord. The neighboring configuration guarantees the meaning of the progression, thus freeing the composer to incorporate strong dissonances of mimetic effect. Schubert's *Winterreise* is full of such rationalized dissonances; indeed, in this context, the effect is literally indexical.

Example 4.7. Schubert, "Frühlingstraum," from *Winterreise* (cited in Schenker, *Counterpoint*, 192).

Example 4.8 cites two similar 2-bar passages from the opening movement of Mahler's Tenth. In the first bar of each, the content of the opening tonic chord (F-sharp major) is expanded through neighbor-note motion. Note that while the bass is stationary in the first excerpt (as in the Schubert quintet cited in example 4.6), it acquires its own lower neighbor in the second.

Example 4.8. Mahler, Symphony no. 10, first movement, (a) bars 16–17, (b) bars 49–50.

Example 4.9 is from Richard Strauss's *Till Eulenspiegel*, which is cited by Schenker.[17] At level *a* is the model, while *b* shows the realization. Schenker singles

16. Schenker, *Counterpoint*, book 1, 192.
17. Schenker, *Counterpoint*, book 1, 192.

out Strauss as a composer who "could compose neighboring notes conceived even in four voices in a most masterful way"[18]—a rare compliment from a theorist who was usually railing against Strauss and his contemporaries Mahler, Reger, and Debussy.

Example 4.9. Richard Strauss, *Till Eulenspiegels lustige Streiche* (cited in Schenker, *Counterpoint*, 192).

Example 4.10, also from *Till*, is a little more complex, so I have included a speculative derivation to make explicit its origins from strict counterpoint. Start at level *a* with a simple, diatonic neighbor-note progression; alter it chromatically while adding inner voices (level *b*); then—and here comes a more radical step—displace the first element up an octave so that the entire neighbor-note

Example 4.10. Richard Strauss, *Till Eulenspiegels lustige Streiche* (level *d* cited in Schenker, *Counterpoint*, 192).

18. Schenker, *Counterpoint*, book 1, 192.

configuration unfolds across two different registers (level *c*). Level *d* shows the outcome. Note, again, that while one can connect Strauss's theme to a diatonic model as its umbilical cord, nothing in the generative process allows us to infer the specific play of motive, rhythm, and articulation in the foreground.

Staying with Strauss for a moment longer, example 4.11 summarizes the chordal motion in the first 6 bars of his beautiful *Wiegenlied*. Over a stationary bass (recall the Schubert excerpt in example 4.6 and the first of the Mahler excerpts in example 4.8), the upper voices move to and from a common-tone (neighboring) diminished-seventh chord. Two other details add to the interest here: the expansion of the neighboring chord in bar 4 by means of an accented passing note (see C# in rh), the effect of which is to enhance the dissonance value of the moment; and the similarity of melodic configuration involving the notes A–D–C#–B–A in both the accompaniment and the vocal melody, which produces a sort of motivic parallelism.

Example 4.11. Richard Strauss, *Wiegenlied*, bars 1–6.

Finally, in example 4.12, I quote two brief passages from the "Credo" of Stravinsky's *Mass*, where, in spite of the extension of ideas of consonance and dissonance, the morphology of neighbor-note formation is still evident.[19]

A history of musical technique based on the neighbor-note would not be confined to the very local levels just shown; it would encompass larger expanses of music as well. Think, for example, of the slow movement of Schubert's String Quintet, whose F minor middle section neighbors the E major outer sections; or of his "Der Lindenbaum" from *Winterreise*, where the agitated middle section prolongs C-natural as an upper chromatic neighbor to the dominant, B, intensifying our

19. See Harald Krebs, "The Unifying Function of Neighboring Motion in Stravinsky's *Sacre du Printemps*," *Indiana Theory Review* 8 (Spring 1987): 3–13; and Agawu, "Stravinsky's *Mass* and Stravinsky Analysis," *Music Theory Spectrum* 11 (1989): 139–163, for more on Stravinsky's use of neighbor-notes.

Example 4.12. Stravinsky, *Mass*, "Credo," (a) bars 1–3, (b) bars 00–00.

desire for the tonic. Or think of Debussy's prelude *Bruyères*, whose contrapuntal structure, based on the succession of centers A♭–B♭–A♭, features an expanded neighbor-note progression. Readers will have their own examples to add to the few mentioned here. A comprehensive study would be illuminating.

Generative Analysis

Returning now to the white-note progression whose tonal tendencies we mentioned earlier, let us recast its elements as a set of ideal voices, an abstract model that is subject to a variety of enactments (example 4.13). A compositional orientation allows us to imagine how this progression might be embellished or expanded in order to enhance musical content. The act of embellishing, which is affined with prolongation, is better conceptualized not as an additive process but as a divisive one. An event is prolonged by means of certain techniques. How to delay reaching

Example 4.13. Archetypal white-note progression.

that final dominant? How to enhance the phenomenal feel of an initial tonic? How to intensify desire for that cadence? This bottom-up mode of thinking casts the analyst into a composerly role and urges a discovery of the world of tonal phenomena from the inside, so to speak. Analysis, in this understanding, is not a spectator sport.

Let us join in with the most elementary of moves. The progression in example 4.14 responds to a desire to embellish sonority 2 from example 4.13. This strengthens the sonority by means of a retroactive prolongation using a lower neighbornote, the bass note F. While the essence of the prolongation is that given in example 4.13, the form given in example 4.14 acquires greater content. Similarly, example 4.15 responds to the challenge of extending the functional domain of that same middle element by arpeggiating down from the tonic to the predominant chord. This represents an embellishment of a previous embellishment. Alternatively, we may hear example 4.15 in terms of two neighbor-notes to the G, an upper (A) and a lower (F), both prefixes. But if we think in terms of the ambitions of the initial C, then it could be argued that the bass arpeggiation (C–A–F) embellishes C on its way to the dominant G. These explanations begin to seem confused, but that is precisely the point. That is, the domains of both a prospective prolongation of C (by means of a suffix) and a retroactive prolongation of G (by means of a prefix) overlap. Such is the nature of the continuity and internal dependence of the elements of tonal-functional material.

Example 4.14. Same with predominant sonority.

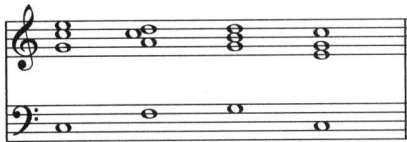

As a logical generative procedure, the process enshrined in example 4.15 may be schematized in three phases. First, we state the basic I–V–I progression. (The basic progression is an archetype or a well-formed tonal primitive that is familiar from conventional usage.) Second, we expand the middle element by introducing a predominant chord. Third, we expand the initial sonority by means of

Example 4.15. Same with alternative flowing bass line.

Alternative bass:

arpeggiation. This allows us to link up the first and second sonorities. This kind of logic can be operationalized as pedagogy and taught to students. Indeed, it is what happens in some sectors of jazz pedagogy. While it is not unheard of in the pedagogy associated with classical music, its centrality is not yet complete. Yet there is clearly an advantage to forging cooperation between student and composer, encouraging students to take responsibility as co-composers. Although such cooperation could blossom into bigger and more original acts of creativity, the modest purpose here is simply to find ways of inhabiting a composition by speculatively recreating some aspects of it.

Example 4.16 is yet another recomposition of our basic model. The steps involved may be stated as follows:

a. State the basic progression.
b. Expand the middle element by means of a predominant sonority.
c. Extend the first element by means of voice exchange between treble and bass in order to obtain a smooth, stepwise bass line.
d. Further expand the first sonority of the voice exchange by means of a neighbor-note prolongation.

Example 4.16. Prolonging the archetypal progression.

A logical procedure is not, of course, an account of compositional genesis. It is not an account of how a particular composition was made, although it could give insight into how pieces are made. Composition remains a complex and mysterious process. For some, it is a logical process; others think of it as a game; while some consider it a mode of improvisation. What our simple generative rules do is explain the harmonic-contrapuntal content of a composition as a repository of certain techniques. Although the process of generation may occasionally coincide with the compositional process, its validity does not rest on such corroboration. Indeed, unlike the compositional process, which traces an essentially biographical/diachronic/historical process, the logical procedure advances a systematic fictional explanation. Music analysis is centrally concerned with such fictional procedures. As analysts, we trade in fictions. The better the fictional narrative, the more successful is the analysis. The more musical the rules, the better is the analysis; the more musically plausible the generative bases, the better is the analysis.

Affinities with Generative Analysis: Sechter, Czerny, Ratz, and Tovey

The world of white-note progressions and neighbor-note prolongations may seem anachronistic—a twenty-first-century approach to nineteenth-century music. But although my concern in this book is not with historical precedents for the approaches taken, a brief word about what we're calling the generative process will suggest connections to traditions that seem far removed from this particular cold room.

Example 4.17 is taken from Simon Sechter's 1843 analysis of Mozart's *Jupiter* Symphony.[20] Sechter's analysis of the passage proceeds from what is given here as level *c* through *a* to *b*. Level *c*, closest to Mozart's but lacking the full orchestral dress reproduced in level *d* (excluded from Sechter's analysis), features a theme in the treble imitated canonically in the bass. Sechter writes: "If some readers find the harmony between these two voices not pure enough for their liking, they may care to think of this canonic imitation in the following way [levels *a* and *b* in example 4.17]." Level *a*, then, is an explanatory, white-note progression, revealing the harmonic basis of *c*, even while conveying the canon between the two voices. Level *b* in Sechter's view is an alternative to *c*; that is, it exists on the same structural level. Passing notes now link all of the thirds, making the lines completely stepwise. From here, it is but a short step to level *c*, where the eighth-note passing notes (in the first, third, and fifth bars in the treble and in the second, fourth, and sixth bars in the bass) are enlarged to quarter-notes.

From our point of view, we could conceivably begin with a diatonic circle-of-fifths progression (see bass notes C–F♯–B–E–A–D–G) as structural prototype. Level *a* would flow from that, although the specific design here cannot be predicted from the circle of fifths. Then *b* would fill in the blanks while *c* modifies the filling in by elevating the nonharmonic notes so that the passage sounds more dissonant, more daring.

20. Simon Sechter, "Analysis of the Finale of Mozart's Symphony no. [41] in C [K. 551 ('Jupiter')]," in *Music Analysis in the Nineteenth Century*, vol. 1: *Fugue, Form and Style*, ed. Ian D. Bent (Cambridge: Cambridge University Press, 1994), 85.

Example 4.17. Sechter's generative analysis of bars 56–62 of the finale of Mozart's Symphony in C (*Jupiter*).

Example 4.18 reproduces the first 13 bars of Czerny's "harmonic groundwork" of Beethoven's *Waldstein* Piano Sonata, op. 53. This analysis dates from 1854.[21] I have aligned piece and analytical foil in order to convey their affinities directly. The chorale-like groundwork offers a concise summary of Beethoven's more expansive, piece-specific gestures. Repetitions, certain motivic details, and registers are eliminated in order to render these 13 bars as a framework. As before, playing the framework first and then playing Beethoven's "realization" should help to convey the structural basis of the work. Czerny calls this a "scheme," claims that op. 53 was "composed in this way," and advises the student to compare his harmonic

Example 4.18. Beethoven's Piano Sonata in C Major, op. 53 (*Waldstein*), bars 1–13, with Czerny's "harmonic groundwork."

21. Carl Czerny, "Harmonic Groundwork of Beethoven's Sonata [no. 21 in C] op. 53 ('Waldstein')," quoted in *Music Analysis in the Nineteenth Century*, vol. 2, ed. Ian D. Bent (Cambridge: Cambridge University Press, 1994), 188–196.

groundwork with the original and thus learn something about "harmonic construction" and—in the context of the groundwork for the entire movement—the way in which ideas are ordered.

The progression quoted in example 4.19 is Erwin Ratz's summary of the harmonic basis of an entire composition—and a contrapuntal one at that: the first of J. S. Bach's two-part inventions.[22] As a synopsis, this progression lies sufficiently close to the surface of the composition to be appreciated by even a first-time listener. It can also serve as a horizon for appreciating the tonal tendency conveyed by Bach's sixteenth-note figures. Beginning in the tonic, the invention tonicizes V, then vi, before returning home via a circle of fifths.

Example 4.19. Ratz's harmonic summary of J. S. Bach, Two-Part Invention in C Major.

In generative terms, the models of tonal motion used by Bach include two kinds of cadence (a perfect cadence and an imperfect cadence) and a circle-of-fifths progression. If we number the sonorities in Ratz's synopsis as 1–12, we can define their functions as follows. The 11–12 sequence is a perfect cadence in the home key, 4–6 is also a perfect cadence but on vi (4 being the predominant sonority, 5 the dominant, and 6 the concluding tonic), 1–2 forms a half cadence (an open gesture), and 7–10 constitutes a circle-of-fifths progression, A–D–G–C.

The journey from the white-note level to a black-note one may be illustrated with respect to bars 15–18 of Bach's invention (example 4.20). At level *a* is the bare linear intervallic pattern of descending bass fifths in a two-voice representation. At level *b*, passing notes at the half-note level provide melodic continuity. Rhythmic interest is introduced at level *c* with the 4–3 suspensions in the second and fourth bars. And from here to Bach's music (level *d*) seems inevitable, even without us being able to predict the exact nature of the figuration.

At an even more remote level of structure lies Tovey's harmonic summary of the first movement of Schubert's C Major Quintet (example 4.21).[23] He is not concerned with the generative steps leading from this postulated background to Schubert's multifaceted surface, but with a synopsis that incorporates a hierarchy reflected in the durations of individual triads. The longer notes are the focal points, the shorter ones are "connexion links." Although Tovey elsewhere understands and employs notions akin to Schenkerian prolongation, he is not, it appears, concerned with establishing the prolongational basis of the movement as such, nor with

---

22. Erwin Ratz, *Einführung in die musikalische Formenlehre*, 3rd ed. (Vienna: Universal, 1973), 55.
23. Donald Francis Tovey, *Essays and Lectures on Music* (Oxford: Oxford University Press, 1949), 150.

exploring the prolongational potential of this progression. Still, the idea is suggestive and shares with notions of generation the same procreative potential.[24]

Example 4.20. Journey from white-note to black-note level in bars 15–18 of J. S. Bach, Invention no. 1 in C Major.

Example 4.21. Tovey's synopsis of the harmonic content of Schubert's String Quintet in C Major, first movement.

Prolonged Counterpoint

The larger enterprise in which Sechter, Czerny, Ratz, Tovey, and numerous other theorists were engaged is the speculative construction of tonal meaning drawing on the fundamental idea that understanding always entails understanding in terms of, and that those terms are themselves musical. Widespread and diffuse, these collective practices have been given different names, pursued in the context of different genres of theory making, and illustrated by different musical styles and composers. Already in this chapter, we have spoken of diminutions, prolongation,

24. In "Schenker and the Theoretical Tradition," *College Music Symposium* 18 (1978): 72–96, Robert Morgan traces aspects of Schenkerian thinking in musical treatises from the Renaissance on. Finding such traces or pointing to affinities with other theoretical traditions is not meant to mute the force of Schenker's originality.

the relationship between strict counterpoint and free composition, harmonic summaries and the expansion of musical content, and generating a complex texture from simpler premises. Can all of these analytical adventures be brought together under a single umbrella? Although it is obviously desirable to stabilize terminology in order to increase efficiency in communication, the fact, first, that the core idea of this chapter is shared by many musicians and music theorists, and second, that it can be and has been pursued from a variety of angles, is a sign of the potency of the idea. We should welcome and even celebrate this kind of plurality, not retreat from it as a sign of confusion.

For our purposes, then, the choice of a single rubric is in part an arbitrary and convenient gesture. I do so to organize the remaining analyses in this chapter, which, like previous analyses, will involve the construction of bridges from background to foreground within the limitations noted earlier. The term *prolonged counterpoint* is borrowed directly from Felix Salzer and Carl Schachter's *Counterpoint in Composition*.[25] Distinguishing between elementary counterpoint and prolonged counterpoint, they understand the latter in terms of "the development and expansion of fundamental principles," specifically, as "the significant and fascinating artistic elaboration of basic ideas of musical continuity and coherence." Salzer and Schachter devote several chapters to the direct application of species counterpoint in composition and then conclude by studying counterpoint in composition in a historical framework, going from Binchois to Scriabin.

More formally, we say that an element is *prolonged* when it extends its functional domain across a specified temporal unit. The prolonged entity controls, stands for, is the origin of, or represents other entities. (The historically rooted idea of *diminution* is relevant here.) Prolongation makes motion possible, and the prolonged entity emerges—necessarily—as the hierarchically superior member of a specific structural segment. And by *counterpoint*, we mean a musical procedure by which two (or more) interdependent lines are coordinated (within the conventions of consonance-dissonance and rhythm) in a way that produces a third, meaningful musical idea.

One important departure from Salzer and Schachter concerns the place of harmony in the generative process. Although the proto-structures we have isolated so far are well-formed from a contrapuntal point of view, they are regarded as harmonic structures as well. The harmonic impetus is regarded here as fundamental, and especially so in relation to the main repertoires studied here. To say this is to admit that we have conflated ideas of counterpoint and harmony in these analyses. Prolonged harmony/counterpoint would be a more accurate rubric, but because counterpoint always entails harmony (at least in the repertoires studied in this book), and harmony always entails counterpoint, this more literal designation would carry some redundancy.

The basic generative method involves the construction of an underlying structure as a supplement or potential replacement (Derrida's sense of "supplement")

25. Felix Salzer and Carl Schachter, *Counterpoint in Composition* (New York: Columbia University Press, 1989), xiv.

for the more fully elaborated target surface. We might speak of logically prior structures, of surface and subsurface elements, of immediate as opposed to remote structures, and of "body" as distinct from "dress." Analysis involves the reconstruction of prototypes, underlying structures, or contrapuntal origins of a given composition or passage. In some of the examples, I have been concerned to reveal the generative steps explicitly. Of course, these subsurface structures are fictional structures invented for a specific heuristic purpose, namely, to set the ruling surface into relief by giving us a speculative glimpse into its putative origins; these rational reconstructions act as a foil against which we can begin to understand the individual features of the composition. The aim of a generative analysis is not to reproduce a known method of composition (based on historical or biographical reconstruction) but to draw on fabricated structures in order to enable the analyst to make imaginative projections about a work's conditions of possibility.

Finally, let me rehearse just three of the advantages of the approach. First, by engaging in acts of summary, synopsis, or paraphrase, we are brought into close encounter with a composition; we are compelled to, as it were, speak music as a language. Second, the reduced structures will encourage a fresh conceptualization of form. (This will become clearer in the larger analyses in part 2 of this book.) How do the little (white-note) progressions, contrapuntal structures, or building blocks succeed one another? I believe that answers to this question will lead us to a more complex view of form than the jelly-mold theories canonized in any number of textbooks. Third, by comparing treatments of the same or similar contrapuntal procedures or figures across pieces, we become even more aware of the specific elements of design that distinguish one composer from another, one work from another, or even one passage from another.

The purpose of an analysis is to establish the conditions of possibility for a given composition. Although other dimensions can support such an exercise, harmony and voice leading seem to be the most important. The analytical method consists of inspecting all of the harmonic events and explaining them as instances of cadential or prolongational motion (prolongation here includes linear intervallic patterns). Cadences and prolongations are subject to varying degrees of disguise, so an essential part of the analysis is to show how a simple, diatonic model is creatively embellished by the composer. The possible models are relatively few and are postulated by the analyst for a given passage. Then follows the speculative task of demonstrating progressive variations of those models. Varying or enriching these simple models encourages the analyst to play with simple harmonic and contrapuntal procedures, procedures that are grammatically consistent with the style in question. While the analysis aims at explaining the whole composition from this perspective, it is not committed to the unique ordering of models within a particular whole. (This last point becomes an issue at a further stage of the analysis.) The whole here is succession, not progression; the whole is a composite assembled additively. Analytical labor is devoted to identifying those elements— cadences and prolongational spans—that constitute the composite. By focusing on the things that went into the compositions, the arsenal of devices, we prepare for a fuller exploration of the work as a *musical* work, not as a musical *work*. We establish what made it possible, leaving individual listeners to tell whatever story they wish to tell about the finished work. Following this method is akin to navigating the work in search of its enabling prolongations and cadences. Once these are discovered, the analytical task is fulfilled. Obviously, there will always be more to say about the work. Works endure, and as along as there are listeners and institutions, there will be additional insights about the most familiar works. But shifting attention from the work as such to its grammatical constituents may reward analysts, who are not passive consumers of scores but active musicians who wish to engage with musical works from the inside. This kind of analysis rewrites the work as a series of speculative projections; it establishes the conditions of possibility for a given work.

Strauss, "Morgen," op. 27, no. 4, bars 1–16

Example 4.22 suggests some paths to the free composition of the first 16 bars of Richard Strauss's beloved 1894 song, "Morgen." Three simple contrapuntal/harmonic techniques are sufficient to generate the passage. First is a space-opening progression, I–ii6–V, which is in effect an expanded half-cadence (bars 1–4). As the example shows, level *a* presents a two-voice model, level *b* activates this with a 7–6 suspension followed by a 4–3 configuration deriving from an accented passing tone, level *c* prolongs the initial B (3̂) by an arpeggiation (the arpeggiated chord includes an added sixth which, for stylistic reasons, may be regarded as consonant), and level *d* places the ametrical material in levels *a, b,* and *c* in a durationally expanded 4-bar phrase, incorporating a passing chromatic pitch.

The second technique is a reciprocal closing progression, an expanded perfect cadence. We hear this at the end of the excerpt (bars 13–16). Level *a* here is the bare 5–8 intervallic motion, level *b* enriches it by a cadential sixth (implying a 6/4 chord), level *c* elaborates the sixth through voice exchange, and level *d* further enriches the exchange by incorporating a chromatic passing note and melodic appoggiaturas. Finally, level *e* restores a metrical framework, prolongs the initial B (3̂) via a downward arpeggiation, and delays the arrival on the goal tone, G (1̂).

Between these two poles of beginning (bars 1–4) and ending (bars 13–16) is a middle comprising a dominant prolongation—our third technique.[26] The first phase of this prolongation is heard in bars 5–8, where the dominant is prolonged retroactively by upper and lower neighbors in the bass (E and C, supporting vi and ii6 chords), as shown at level *a*. Level *b* expands this progression by employing a secondary dominant to enhance the move to vi and incorporating an appoggiatura to ii6. Finally, level *c* incorporates this progression into Strauss's 4-bar passage.

Bars 9–12 are essentially a continuation of the dominant prolongation of bars 5–8. They are harmonically sequential, as suggested in the two-voice representation at level *a*. Level *b* enriches this progression with the usual passing notes and appoggiaturas, and level *c* restores the metrical context.

---

26. Although the literal span of the V prolongation is bars 5–15, my interest here is in the rhetoric of prolongational expression, so I will maintain reference to the 4-bar segments previously isolated.

With these procedures, we have established one set of conditions of possibility for this 16-bar period. Of course, there are alternative paths to Strauss's song. The one shown here is, I believe, consistent with what we might call the ordinary tonal language "spoken" in the time of Strauss. Note that the means are simple, even reminiscent of the eighteenth century: a half-cadence (4 bars) followed by a dominant prolongation (8 bars) leading to an elaborated full cadence (4 bars). And yet Strauss's song obviously does not sound like an eighteenth-century composition. The Straussian difference resides, among other things, in the techniques of enrichment and their timing. (I'm leaving aside more surface matters like the setting

Example 4.22. Paths to free composition in Richard Strauss's "Morgen."

(continued)

Example 4.22. continued

of the text in a kind of declamatory or speech mode, the first violin's memorable song-mode melody, the orchestration, and the willful playing with time.) By establishing some connection with tonal norms, we can, I believe, appreciate better the nature of Strauss's creativity.

Schubert, "Dass sie hier gewesen," op. 59, no. 2, bars 1–18

Example 4.23 develops a similar generative account of bars 1–18 of Schubert's song "Dass sie hier gewesen." We start at level *a* with a simple auxiliary cadence, ii6–V–I. An idiomatic progression, this guiding model comprises a predominant, dominant, tonic succession. At level *b*, the predominant is prefaced by its own dominant-functioning chord, a diminished-seventh in 6/5 position, introduced to intensify the move to the predominant. At level *c*, this same progression is enriched by neighbor-notes and passing notes and then expanded: it is disposed first incompletely (bars 1–8), then completely (bars 9–16). Schubert (or the compositional persona) in turn extends the temporal reach of the opening dissonance across 4

Example 4.23. Bridges to free composition in Schubert's "Dass sie hier gewesen," op. 59, no. 2, bars 1–18.

bars, incorporates appoggiaturas to the dissonance, and places the initial statements in a high register on the piano.

Corelli, Trio Sonata, op. 3, no. 1

Performers of Corelli's music have been struck by the recurring strategy whereby:
a cogent harmonic progression gets things off the ground; then, a chain of suspensions, a linear intervallic pattern, or an equivalent sequential pattern serves
as a means of continuation; finally, a cadence or cadential group closes things
off. We may represent this formal imperative as a tripartite scheme: idea-lines-
close; or theme-sequence-cadence; or statement-continuation-cadence. The
first area establishes the thematic idea of the movement, the second provides a
means of extending or prolonging that idea (or an aspect thereof), and the third
brings matters to a close in a conventional way. The consistency of this modus
operandi across Corelli's oeuvre makes the style easy to imitate, which is partly
why it is often included in courses in pastiche composition. It will serve here as
another illustration of the transformation of simple models into more complex
surfaces.

In a fascinating study of what he calls Corelli's "tonal models," Christopher
Wintle identifies a key element of the composer's style:

> Corelli's oeuvre is founded upon a fairly limited number of musical figures or mod-
> els, which are capable of sustaining a considerable variety of modes of presentation.
> These modes can be simply decorative, or alternatively they can have a deeper func-
> tion of transforming or prolonging these models.[27]

The chronology favored by Wintle privileges a compositional rather than an analytic or synthetic approach. He concentrates on "the workbench methods of the
composer" by isolating "models" and showing how they are composed out. These
fictional texts are meaningful units that exist in a dialectical relationship with the
segments of actual music that they model. Each is syntactically coherent but has
minimum rhetorical content. In Corelli (unlike in the Strauss and Schubert works
discussed previously), both the model and its variants may occur in the work.

The opening "Grave" movement of the Church Sonata, op. 3, no. 1 (shown in its
entirety in example 4.24), will serve as our demonstration piece. Example 4.25 displays the generating model at level *a* as a straightforward, closed progression. Following the model are a number of variants that are referable to the model. At level
b, a I6 chord substitutes for the initial root-position chord and effectively increases

27. Christopher Wintle, "Corelli's Tonal Models: The Trio Sonata op. 3, no. 1," in *Nuovissimi Studi
Corelliani: Atti del Terzo Congresso Internazionale Fusignano, 1980*, ed. S. Durante and P. Petrobelli
(Florence, Italy: Olschki, 1982), 31. Methodologically similar is William Rothstein's article "Trans-
formations of Cadential Formulae in Music by Corelli and His Successors," in *Studies from the Third
International Schenker Symposium*, ed. Allen Cadwallader (Hildersheim, Germany: Olms, 2006).

the mobility in the approach to the cadence. (Cadential groups originating from I6 are typical in this and later styles.) At level *c*, the $\hat{5}$-line of the model is reharmonized by beginning not on I but on V and approaching the tonic in the manner of an expanded cadence. The next two transformations are more far-reaching. The one at level *d*, also a cadential approach from I6 (as at level *b*), closes deceptively, substituting a vi chord for I. And the one at level *e* is a tonally open model, proceeding from I to V in the manner of an antecedent phrase that is assured of its immediately answering consequent. Overlooking slight variations in voicing and harmonization, the model in example 4.25 and its variants are sufficient to explain the entire "Grave" movement.

Example 4.24. Corelli, Church Sonata, op. 3, no. 1, "Grave."

I have divided the movement into 13 units or building blocks, some of them overlapping:

1. Bars 1–2²
2. Bars 2³–4⁴
3. Bars 5–6⁴
4. Bars 6⁴–7³
5. Bars 7⁴–8³
6. Bars 8⁴–9⁴
7. Bars 9⁴–10⁴

8. Bars 10⁴–11⁴
9. Bars 11⁴–12³
10. Bars 13–14¹
11. Bars 14²–15²
12. Bars 15²–17¹
13. Bars 17²–19⁴

Example 4.25. Generating model of Corelli's op. 3, no. 1, "Grave."

Before we look at the disposition of units in the movement, let me provide a quick illustration of the kind of transformational process found in the movement. Example 4.26 shows this for unit 2, bars 2^3–4^4. At level *a* is the model, *b* is a very slight variant (altering the bass in the first chord), and *c* introduces Corelli's favorite suspensions and cadential decoration. Finally, at *d*, we reach Corelli's music by further decorating the voices and disposing them registrally in a typical trio-sonata texture.

Let us now see how the movement as a whole is constituted by the 13 units. Example 4.27 displays this content by juxtaposing quotations from Corelli's score with abstracts of each progression (shown at the right) in an order that reflects each unit's distance from the model. The basic model (shown in example 4.25) is most clearly expressed in units 2, 12, and 13 (example 4.27). Units 6 and 7 are

Example 4.26. Bridges from the basic model to bars 2^3–4^4.

truncated versions; units 5 and 8 and 9, also truncated, are heard in the dominant (5) and the relative minor (8 and 9). Unit 11 substitutes a beginning on V for the model's I, while unit 4 closes deceptively, substituting a local vi for I (in C). These units express the basic model in the following order of conceptual complexity:

2	5
12	9
13	8
6	11
7	4

Fully 10 of the work's 13 units are variants of this basic model. What about the rest? The remaining three are based on a tonally open progression shown at level *e* of example 4.25. That model is almost identical to the basic model, except that instead of closing, it reaches only the penultimate dominant—it is interrupted, in other words. In structural-melodic terms, it unfolds a $\hat{5}$–$\hat{2}$ span, not the $\hat{5}$–$\hat{1}$ of the

Example 4.27. Generating all 13 units of Corelli's op. 3, no. 1.

(continued)

Example 4.27. continued

unit 7 ... from

unit 5 ... from

or

... from

unit 9 ... from

or

... from

(continued)

Example 4.27. continued

unit 8 ... from

6   6 6   9   8
     5 5

or

from

6   6 6   9   8
     5 5

unit 4 ... from

8 6   6   5   4 3
        5   4

or

from

8 6   6   5   4 3
        5   4

unit 11 ... from

7   5   5   6
          4

(continued)

Example 4.27. continued

basic model. This second model is heard as unit 1, that is, right at the outset of the work. It is also heard as unit 10 and finally as unit 3 (in conceptual order).

With this demonstration of the affinities and affiliations between the two models and all of the segments of Corelli's Trio Sonata, op. 3, no. 1/i, the purpose of this restricted analysis—to establish the conditions of possibility for the movement—has been served. This does not mean that there is nothing more to say about the work. Indeed, as we will see when we turn to the paradigmatic approach in the next chapter, several interesting questions and issues are raised by this kind of analysis. For example, what kind of narrative is enshrined in the piece-specific succession of units? I have largely ignored this issue, concentrating instead on conceptual order rather than chronology. But if we think back to the conceptual succession of units 2, 12, and 13, the units that lie closest to the basic model, then it is clear that the strongest expressions of that model lie near the beginning of the work and at the end. And the fact that the ending features a twofold reiteration of the model (units 12 and 13) may reinforce some of our intuitions about the function of closure.

We may also wish to pursue the matter of *dispositio* (form), stimulated in part by Laurence Dreyfus's analysis of the first of Bach's two-part inventions (whose harmonic content I summarized in example 4.19 from Ratz).[28] Dreyfus suggests that the level of *dispositio* may not be as important as that of *inventio* and *elaboratio*. If the essential compositional labor is expended on *inventio* and *elaboratio*, then the work of a transformational approach (which entails unearthing prime forms or basic, diatonic, models) is more or less done, the rest being given over to a conventional disposition of what has been worked out. Dreyfus calls his approach "mechanistic" and opposes it to the organic. Clearly, his mechanistic approach is easily affiliated with the elaboration of tonal models. One difference, however, lies in the fact that here (as elsewhere in this chapter), I work not from themes as such but from the models that underlie those themes. Dreyfus, on the other hand, bases his analysis on the specific thematic content of Bach's invention. Corelli's music, however, is not the best exemplar of a gap between model and elaboration for, as we have seen, models and their enactments are often thematically close.

J. S. Bach, Minuet II, BWV 1007

Three models are sufficient to generate Bach's polyphonic 24-bar minuet: first, a perfect cadence approached from I6; second, a circle-of-fifths progression; and third, an opening out I–V progression expressed as a descending bass line, $\hat{8}$–$\hat{7}$–$\hat{6}$–$\hat{5}$. The three are shown in examples 4.28, 4.29, and 4.30, respectively. (This might suggest to the pedagogically inclined that training students to compose and realize such models might be an effective way of getting them to appreciate what Bach does. Harmony is better taught not as chords with individual identities but as progressions within a community, not as single "words" but as idioms embedded in phrases.)

The cadence in example 4.28 shows the bass line of the approach to a perfect cadence from I6 followed by a two-voice version and an alternative three-voice version incorporating a suspended seventh above the bass in the second bar. This prepares Bach's version (bars 13–16). A version of the same cadence in minor mode is next shown, first as a simple bass line, then in a three-voice harmonization, then in an enriched version incorporating suspensions, and finally in Bach's expression (bars 22–24).

Example 4.29 shows an enrichment of a circle-of-fifths progression. This fun and pedagogically useful construct is popular with organists and keyboard players because it facilitates traversal of apparently great tonal distances in a short space. (It is hard to imagine Mozart succeeding in the genre of the piano concerto, for example, without a naturalized view of the circle of fifths; think of how much mileage he gets out of this construct in his development sections.) Example 4.29 begins with a bass line, then there is a harmonized version, then an enriched version featuring greater melodic movement and suspensions, and finally Bach's music (bars 9–12). The same construct is invoked elsewhere in the composition, but this time the circle is broken. As shown further in example 4.29, there is, first, the bass line,

28. Laurence Dreyfus, *Bach and the Patterns of Invention* (Cambridge, MA: Harvard University Press, 1996), 1–32.

then a two-voice version, then a version enriched with passing notes but missing two steps of the model (E♭–A), and finally Bach's music (17–22).

The third pattern used by Bach is a bass pattern proceeding from I to V in stepwise $\hat{8}$–$\hat{7}$–$\hat{6}$–$\hat{5}$ motion. The first two lines of example 4.30 display the pattern in

Example 4.28. Approach to perfect cadence from I6 as model.

Perfect cadence approached from I_6

6   6 or 6
                         5

becomes

or

or (in Bach's hands)

13

Perfect cadence approached from I_6

becomes

or

expressed by Bach as

22

thirds and tenths, respectively. Then, the "straight" tenths of line 2 are enlivened by a pair of 7–6 suspensions in the middle 2 bars (line 3). From here, it is but a short step to Bach's first 4 bars, which include a 4–3 suspension in the fourth bar (line 4). The 4-bar passage is repeated immediately (line 5).

These three patterns are, of course, ordinary patterns in eighteenth-century music. The $\hat{8}$–$\hat{7}$–$\hat{6}$–$\hat{5}$ bass pattern, familiar to many from Bach's *Goldberg Variations*, reaches back into the seventeenth century, during which it functioned as an emblem of lament.[29] It was also subject to various forms of enrichment,

Example 4.29. Circle of fifths as model.

A circle-of-fifths progression

may be expressed as

or as

and by Bach as

9

A circle-of-fifths progression

may be rendered as

or in decorated form (and without the boxed notes) as

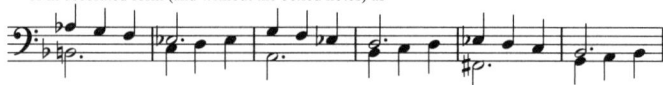

and by Bach as

17

29. Ellen Rosand, "The Descending Tetrachord: An Emblem of Lament," *Musical Quarterly* 65 (1979): 346–359.

including the incorporation of chromatic steps. It functions here as a beginning, an opening out. Bach claims this space, this trajectory, not by inventing a new bass pattern, but by expressing the familiar within a refreshed framework. For example, he treats the medium of solo cello as both melodic and harmonic, and thus incorporates within a compound melodic texture both conjunct and disjunct lines. Apparent disjunction on the musical surface is rationalized by the deeper-lying harmonic/voice-leading patterns revealed here. Bach's ingenious designs owe not a little to the security of his harmonic thinking. In bars 1–4, for example, the first and third notes of the G–F–E♭–D bass motion appear as eighth-notes in metrically weak positions, but this in no way alters the harmonic meaning of the phrase. Similarly, the B-natural at the beginning of bar 17 resolves to a C an octave higher in the middle of the next bar, but the registral

Example 4.30. The 8̂–7̂–6̂–5̂ bass pattern as model.

discontinuity and the nonisomorphism in design are mediated by an underlying harmonic continuity.

The analyst's task, then, is to identify these models, many of them commonplaces of the style, and hypothesize their compositional origins through a speculative play with their elements. Again, the matter of final chronology—how these three models are ordered in this particular piece—is, at this stage of the analysis, less important than simply identifying the model. If we think of Bach as improviser, then part of our task is to understand the language of improvisation, and this in turn consists in identifying tricks, licks, clichés, and conventional moves. How these are ordered on a specific occasion may not ultimately matter to those who view compositions as frozen improvisations, and to those who often allow themselves to imagine alternatives to what Bach does here or there. On the other hand, those who are fixated on scores, who cling to the absolute identity of a composition, who interpret its ontology literally and strictly, and who refuse the idea of open texts will find the compositional approach unsatisfactory or intimidating. Indeed, emphasis on the formulaic places Bach in some great company: that of African dirge and epic singers who similarly depend on clichés and, inevitably, of jazz musicians like Art Tatum and Charlie Parker.

A few preliminary comments about style need to be entered here. Obviously, Corelli and Bach utilize similarly simple models in the two compositions at which we have looked. For example, both invest in the cadential approach from I6. Yet there is a distinct difference between the Corelli sound and the Bach sound. How might we specify this? One source of difference lies in the distance between model and composition. Simply put, in Corelli, the models lie relatively close to the surface; sometimes, they constitute that surface, while at other times they can be modified by the merest of touches—an embellishment here and there—to produce that surface. In Bach, the relationship between model (as a historical object) and composition is more varied. Some models are highly disguised while a few are hardly hidden. The more disguised ones evince a contrapuntal depth that is not normally found in Corelli. Bach's music is therefore heterogeneous in the way that it negotiates the surface-depth dialectic, whereas Corelli's is relatively homogeneous. It is possible that this distinction lies behind conventional perceptions of Bach as the greater of the two composers.

Bach, Prelude in C Major, Well-Tempered Clavier, *book 1*

Unlike the polyphonic minuet for solo cello that we have just discussed, which invites the listener to complete the (harmonic) texture by realizing implied voices, this keyboard prelude leaves nothing to the textural imagination. The consistent texture reinforces the constant harmony, indeed throws the harmonic course into relief so that the listener can almost bracket the texture and concentrate on the flow of harmony and voice leading. Like the minuet, however, the prelude draws on familiar models or idioms together with their procedures of embellishment. Bach knew and utilized these elements of vocabulary and syntax as part of his ordinary language. The two most relevant techniques found in this prelude involve, first, enriching an archetypal I–V–I or I–V progression (using neighboring and passing motion, including chromaticism) and, second, deploying a circle-of-fifths progression to create trajectories of tonal action.

Proceeding in the spirit of building bridges to free composition, I invite the reader to compare the material assembled in example 4.31 to the relevant passages in Bach's prelude, and then to imagine embarking on a similar exploration of other preludes. (Numbers between staves refer to the bar numbers in Bach's music.) There are four groups of models. Begin with the closed models found in bars 1–4, 32–35, 15–19, and 7–11 (group 1). These model most of the material in Bach's composition. Then, continue with a model that closes but whose opening is now transformed: bars 12–15 and 5–7 (group 2). Next, play though the open I–V model as expressed in bars 19–24 (group 3). Finally, play through the open V model, which features a voice exchange over a dominant pedal in bars 24–27 and chromatic enrichment in bars 27–31 (group 4).

In short, Bach here employs a range of familiar progressions, sometimes directly and sometimes in embellished forms, alongside a repertoire of embellishments featuring neighbor-notes and passing notes. Stated so clinically, this conclusion is bound to sound less than inspiring. If, however, the aim of our analysis is to convey what makes a work possible, then the best response to the foregoing demonstration would be the kind of silent nodding in agreement that inspires the analyst to reach for the next prelude, and the next one, to see if s/he, too, can hypothesize a series of paths from background to foreground, from model to realization. Analysis here terminates in doing, not in generating a narrative about what the prelude means. One can easily imagine a harpsichordist experimenting with the kinds of progressions posited here.

This achronological approach should not lead to a discounting of how Bach's prelude comes across as a single, unified composition. As Joel Lester has shown, this and several of the early preludes in book 1 of the *Well-Tempered Clavier* proceed from a tonic area—sometimes over a pedal—through a prolonged dominant (often expressed as a pedal) to a concluding tonic pedal, often with an intervening descending bass.[30] But this larger I–V–I progression is all but inevitable for Bach. Uncovering it cannot therefore be the principal aim of the analyst. Rather, uncovering those tendencies that work against or in spite of it directs attention to conflict, which, in turn, helps to convey the richness of the work. Those who feel threatened by this kind of approach are of course at liberty to seek reassurance from their much-cherished formal archetypes, which proceed from beginning to end and attain a resultant unity. But those for whom analysis is most productive when it elicits reciprocal acts of doing may find the emphasis on unordered fragments and imaginative ways of recomposition to be stimulating.

---

30. Joel Lester, "J. S. Bach Teaches Us How to Compose: Four Pattern Preludes of the *Well-Tempered Clavier,*" *College Music Symposium* 38 (1998): 33–46.

Example 4.31. Generating J. S. Bach's Prelude in C *Major, Well-Tempered Clavier,* book 1.

(continued)

Chopin, Prelude in C Major, op. 28, no. 1

We mentioned this prelude in connection with the rhetoric of closure (Example 2.4). Here, our concern is to establish bridges from an underlying background to Chopin's free composition. Example 4.32 sets these out using Forte and Gilbert's rhythmic reduction of Chopin's music as point of reference in the bottom-most system.[31]

Example 4.31. continued

Group 2

(continued)

31. Allen Forte and Steven Gilbert, *Introduction to Schenkerian Analysis* (New York: Norton, 1982), 191–192.

Example 4.31. continued

Group 3

The prelude may be understood in reference to six tonal progressions, all of which are displayed in example 4.32 and referred to as moods. Model 1 (which also counts as unit 3 because of the repetition of bars 1–4 as 9–12) is an extension of the tonic chord through a neighboring 6/5 (level *a*) and a melodic arpeggiation (level *b*) to produce bars 1–4 and 9–12 (level *c*). Model 2 is an opening out I–V progression (level *a*). This progression is first enriched by a predominant chord (level *b*), and further by the addition of a melodic appoggiatura and a chromatic passing note in the bass (level *c*). Then, a rising arpeggio leads to ˆ3 (level *d*), bringing us close to Chopin's music (level *e*). Model 4 is a succession of rising sixths spanning an octave. The bare sixths are shown at level *a*, followed at *b* by their specific melodic order and the specific inner voices of the sixths (mostly 6/3s, but including a couple of 6/4s and one 6/5), and then Chopin's music (level *c*). Model 5 is an expanded cadential progression, a five-line departing from I6 (level *a*), enriched by chromatic passing notes and an appoggiatura (level *b*), which gives rise to Chopin's music (level *c*). Model 6 is a closed, I–V–I progression (level *a*), which is then expressed over a tonic pedal and incorporates neighbor-notes (level *b*), preparing Chopin's music (level *c*).

Example 4.31. continued

Group 4

Voice exchange model

expressed by Bach as

revoiced as

enriched by Bach as

It should be immediately obvious that the six models, while idiomatically different, are structurally related. Indeed, models 1, 3, 4, 5, and 6 express the same kind of harmonic sense. Only model 2 differs in its harmonic gesture. From this perspective, the prelude goes over the same harmonic ground five out of six times. And yet, the dynamic trajectory of the prelude does not suggest circularity; indeed, the melodic line is shaped linearly in the form of a dynamic curve. Both features are "in" the prelude, suggesting that its form enshrines contradictory tendencies. We will see other examples of the interplay between the circular and the linear in the next chapter.

Mahler, Das Lied von der Erde, *"Der Abschied," bars 81–95*

The guiding model for this brief excerpt from *Das Lied* (example 4.33) is the same basic ii–V–I progression we encountered in Schubert's "Dass sie hier gewesen." Shown at level *a* in example 4.34, the progression is end-oriented in the sense that only at the passage's conclusion does clarity emerge. While Schubert's interpretation

Example 4.32. Bridges to free composition in Chopin, Prelude in C Major, op. 28, no. 1.

(continued)

Example 4.32. continued

of the model allows the listener to predict an outcome (both immediately and in the long term) at every moment, Mahler's inscription erases some of the larger predictive tendency enshrined in the progression while intensifying other, more local aspects. Of the three functional chords, the predictive capability of ii is the most limited; only in retrospect are we able to interpret ii as a predominant chord. The V chord, on the other hand, is highly charged at certain moments (especially in bars 86 and 92), so it is possible to hear its potential destination as I/I or vi or ♭VI. And the closing I/i moment attains temporary stability as the resolution of the previous V, but this stability is quickly dissipated as the movement moves on to other tonal and thematic goals.

A possible bridge from the guiding model to Mahler's music is indicated at level *b* of example 4.34. The white notes in the bass—D, G, G, and C—are of course the roots of our ii–V–I/i progression. The enrichment in the upper voices, however,

Example 4.33. Mahler, *Das Lied von der Erde*, "Der Abschied," bars 81–97.

disguises the progression in more complex ways than we have seen so far, calling for a more deliberate explication. Example 4.35 offers a detailed voice-leading graph that will enable us to examine in a bit more detail the contrapuntal means with which Mahler sustains the guiding progression.[32]

Example 4.34. Bridges to free composition in Mahler, *Das Lied von der Erde,* "Der Abschied," bars 81–95.

Example 4.35. Voice leading in "Der Abschied," bars 81–97.

32. For further discussion of techniques of prolonged counterpoint in Mahler, see John Williamson, "Dissonance and Middleground Prolongation in Mahler's Later Music," in *Mahler Studies,* ed. Stephen Hefling (Cambridge: Cambridge University Press, 1997), 248–270; and Agawu, "Prolonged Counterpoint in Mahler," also in *Mahler Studies,* 217–247.

Prolongation of ii (bars 82–83)

Example 4.36 makes explicit the possible compositional or contrapuntal origins of these 2 bars. First, a complete neighbor-note progression, then an incomplete one, then a simple passing motion within the chord, and finally a delay in the resolution of the neighbor-note such that the inner voice progression precedes it. We may call this a 4–3 suspension over D, with inner voice motion from the fifth to the third of the chord.

This kind of explanation may seem unduly cumbersome for a passage that was, as far as we know, composed quite instinctively. But instinct is trained, and training often entails exposure to convention. So the point of this didactic exercise is to establish the conventional well-formedness of the passage as a horizon against which we can appreciate Mahler's peculiar rhetoric—his preferences, which are sometimes drawn from ossified harmonic traditions. The background at level *a* in example 4.34 reminds us of the link to the eighteenth century, the middleground at level *b* shows a modern or late Romantic approach to enriching that background, while Mahler's music (example 4.33) confirms the uniqueness or stylistic particularity of this early twentieth-century work.

Prolongation of V, bars 84–92.

Mahler's means may be hypothesized in four stages (refer to example 4.34, level *b*, and compare it to the relevant portion of example 4.35). First, prolong V through

Example 4.36. Origins of bars 82–83.

VI to create a V–VI–V neighboring progression. Second, prolong the closing V prospectively using two chromatic neighbor-note prefixes, one lower (♯4), the other upper (♭6). (Bach uses this same device in bars 22–24 of the C Major Prelude from book 1 of the *Well-Tempered Clavier*, which we analyzed earlier.) Third, prolong the prolonging VI chord by extending it through an ascending third in parallel tenths with the treble (C/A, D/B♭, E/C). Fourth, embellish the first V in bars 84–86 by incorporating neighbor-note motion 7/3–♭7/♭3–7/3 above the bass; further embellish the terminal V in 91–92 by introducing a ♭9 (A-flat) above the bass. This note will eventually acquire enharmonic linear meaning as ♯5̂ leading through 6̂ and 7̂ to the top of the scale, 8̂.

Prolongation of I/i, bars 93–97

Melodically, the E–D progression in the high treble in bars 93–94 points to an eventual arrival on C or 1̂, but 1̂ does not literally arrive in this promised register; it is woven, instead, into the texture. The principle is of displacement between treble and bass. Note also the incorporation of the parallel minor in 95–97. A list of figured motions above the final bass tonic would include 4–♭3 on the deepest level, 9–8 (to provide melodic closure), 7–8 (also to enhance melodic closure in the face of numerous auxiliary chromatic pitches), and ♯5–6–♭7–♮7–8 (to intensify the linear approach to the final tonic).

There is probably more analytical data in the foregoing description than is strictly necessary to follow Mahler's generative path, but readers may wish to test the claims made here by reconstructing Mahler's passage along the lines set out here. Start by playing the pure ii–V–I progression, continue by generating each of the chordal areas, and finish by playing the entire passage. Hopefully, the rationality of Mahler's procedure will be evident.

As in the Schubert analysis presented earlier, however, the journey from our fictional models to the actual surface of Mahler's music finishes prematurely, one might say. The orchestration, for example, suggests that there are several more layers to be traversed before we arrive at Mahler's music from a background that is in principle neutral with respect to timbre. These imagined layers are not contrapuntal, for the process in examples 4.34 and 4.35 only displays the key contrapuntal elements. If we refer back to the piano score in example 4.33, we see that, in the prolongation of ii (bars 82–84), for example, first violins "speak" in speech mode, accompanied by tremolo murmurings reminiscent of an operatic character; meanwhile, rustic horns sing a line that might sound like a symbolic closing gesture (3̂–2̂–1̂) were it not in the wrong key. In the prolongation of V (starting in bar 84), first violins lead with expanded sighing gestures (bars 84–85) before pressing on (*etwas drängend* is Mahler's direction) by means of a melodic ascent to a high point (bars 86–87). Points of local culmination in this passage are marked by declamatory diction (bars 83 and 87). The high points in bars 88 and 90 are approached by leaps, while the biggest of them all (bars 93–94) is approached by stepwise motion. In the lead-up to the high point in bars 93–95, Mahler asks his first violins not to skimp on bow usage (*viel Bogen!* he writes in the score). The great point of culmination is underlined by glissandi in harps, first violins, and cellos (bars 93–95). A wonderfully liberating device, glissando is the ultimate dissolver. It wipes the slate clean by momentarily denying the boundaries between discrete pitches. In the process, it conveys a sense of extremity while allowing us to glimpse the contours of another world. This entire musical discourse is further marked by various competing thematic statements, some of them of merely local contrapuntal significance, others of larger intertextual import. The horns, especially, have things to say and insist on their right to do so, maintaining timbral and thematic independence. One almost feels a sense of simultaneous speaking, a network of fragmented but ultimately coordinated utterances. This, after all, is a tone poem about twilight. Parts light up, flames flicker, and we hear in the distance the sounds of dusk.

For those whose experience of this music is closer to the description given at the end of the previous paragraph, the idea of a conventional ii–V–I background might seem distant, perhaps even irrelevant, because it bypasses the immediately expressive aspects of Mahler's rhetoric. Others might hear the composer's rhetoric—those discharges of ecstasy that Donald Mitchell hears[33]—not instead of, but mediated by, the grammar reconstructed earlier. Still others will insist that the two approaches are irreconcilable. The foreground textures—the motives, timbres, and "tone"—do not mix readily with the neighbor-notes and passing formations. Have we arrived at an impasse? Can different listeners find no common ground? Can these diverse modes of insight formation be activated at once and in the course of a single audition of the work, or are we doomed always and forever to a series of partial experiences?

These are complex questions, of course, and I bring them up at the end of this exploration of bridges from strict counterpoint to free composition in order to set into relief the limits of the various demonstrations undertaken here. No one analytical approach can tell us everything there is to know about a piece of music. Every approach is ultimately partial. The question for the students who have been willing to pursue these paths from subsurface to surface is whether they are willing to accept the contingency of the insights that flow from this particular approach while secretly drawing on supplementary insights to complete their hearing.

Conclusion

We have been exploring the idea of bridges to free composition through several stylistic contexts, including Corelli, J. S. Bach, Schubert, Chopin, Mahler, and Richard Strauss. These bridges connect the structures of an actual composition

---

33. Donald Mitchell, *Gustav Mahler*, vol. 3: *Songs and Symphonies of Life and Death* (London: Faber and Faber, 1985), 344.

with a set of models or proto-structures. In Schenker's formulation, these proto-structures stem from the world of strict counterpoint. In pursuing the Schenkerian idea, however, I have incorporated harmony into the models in the belief that harmonic motivation is originary in all of the examples I have discussed. Although we retained some skepticism about whether the bridges are ultimately secure—and this because they privilege harmony and its contrapuntal expression—we agreed that the *idea* of bridges, an idea that links a complex compositional present to its reconstructed and simplified past, is a potent and indispensable tool for tonal understanding.

As always with analysis, value accrues from practice, and so I have encouraged readers to play through the examples in this chapter and observe the transformational processes. While it is possible to summarize the results of the analyses—by, for example, describing the *Ursatz*-like guiding ideas, their elaboration by use of functional predominants, the role of diminutions in bringing proto-structures to life, and the differences as well as similarities among composerly manners—it is not necessary. A more desirable outcome would be that, having played through a number of the constructions presented here, the student is stimulated to reciprocal acts of reconstruction.

Still, a few issues pertaining to the general approach and its connection to the subject of this book need to be aired. First, the generative approach, by presenting compositions as prolonged counterpoint, brings us close to speaking music as a language. That the ability to do so is most desirable for the music analyst is, to my mind, beyond dispute. In regard to practice, because the generative posture encourages active transformation, it is more productive than the reductive posture, which maintains the object status of the musical work and succumbs to instruction, to rules and regulations, and to narrow criteria of correctness. Second and related, because the generative method is not locked into certain paths—alternative bridges are conceivable—the analyst is called upon to exercise improvisatory license in speculating about compositional origins. This flexibility may not be to everyone's taste; it certainly will not be to the taste of students who take a literal view of the process. But it seems to me that whatever we can do nowadays to foster a measure of rigorous speculation in and through music is desirable. What such speculation guarantees may be no more than the kinds of edification that we associate with performing, but such benefits are a crucial supplement to word-based analytical systems, which do not always lead us to the music itself. Third, approaching tonal composition in general and the Romantic repertoire in particular in this way has the potential to illuminate the style of individual composers. We glimpsed some of this in the different ways in which diminutions are manipulated by Corelli and Bach and by Strauss and Mahler. Fourth and finally, working with notes in this way, embellishing progressions to yield others and playfully reconstructing a composer's work, is an activity that begins to acquire a hermetic feel. Although it can be aligned morphologically with other analytical systems, it refuses graceful co-optation into other systems. The fact that this is a peculiar kind of doing—and not a search for facts or for traces of the social—places the rationale in the realm of advantages that accrue from hands-on playing. There is, then, a kind of autonomy in this kind of doing that may not sit well with authorities who demand summarizable, positivistic results of analysis.

If music is a language, then speaking it (fluently) is essential to understanding its production processes. It has been my task in this chapter to provide some indication of how this might work. I will continue in this vein in the next chapter, where I take up more directly matters of repetition.

CHAPTER Five

Paradigmatic Analysis

Introduction

We began our exploration of music as discourse by noting similarities and differences between music and language (chapter 1). Six criteria were then put forward
for the analysis of Romantic music based on salient, readily understandable features; these features influence individual conceptualizations of Romantic music as
meaningful, as "language" (chapters 2 and 3). In the fourth chapter, I took a more
interested route to musical understanding by probing this music from the inside, so
to speak. I hypothesized compositional origins as simple models that lie behind or
in the background of more complex surface configurations. This exercise brought
into view the challenge of speaking music as a language. Although no attempt
was made to establish a set of overarching, stable, context-invariant meanings, the
meaningfulness of the generative activity was noted. Meaning is doing, and doing
in that case entailed the elaboration of models, proto-structures, or prototypes.

In this chapter—the last of our theoretical chapters, the remaining four being
case studies—we will explore an approach that has already been adumbrated in
previous analyses, namely, the paradigmatic approach. Whereas the search for
bridges from strict counterpoint to free composition (chapter 4) depends on the
analyst's familiarity with basic idioms of tonal composition, the paradigmatic
approach, in principle, minimizes—but by no means eliminates—dependency on
such knowledge in order to engender a less mediated view of the composition.
Thinking in terms of paradigms and syntagms essentially means thinking in terms
of repetition and succession. Under this regime, a composition is understood as a
succession of events (or units or segments) that are repeated, sometimes exactly,
other times inexactly. The associations between events and the nature of their succession guides our mode of meaning construction.

The terms *paradigm* and *syntagm* may feel unwieldy to some readers, but since
they possess some currency in certain corners of music-semiotic research—and
linguistic research—and since their connotations are readily specified, I will retain

163

them in this context too. A *paradigm* denotes a class of equivalent—and therefore interchangeable—objects. A *syntagm* denotes a chain, a succession of objects forming a linear sequence. For example, the harmonic progression I–ii6–V–I constitutes a musical syntagm. Each member of the progression represents a class of chords, and members of a class may substitute for one another. Instead of ii6, for example, I may prefer IV or ii6/5, the assumption being that all three chords are equivalent (in harmonic-functional terms and, presumably, also morphologically); therefore, from a syntactic point of view, substituting one chord for another member of its class does not alter the meaning of the progression. (One should, however, not underestimate the impact in effect, affect, and "semantic" meaning that such substitution engenders.)

Stated so simply, one can readily conclude that theorists and analysts have long worked with implicit notions of paradigm and syntagm, even while applying different terminology. We have been semioticians all along! For example, the aspect of Hugo Riemann's harmonic theory that understands harmonic function in terms of three foundational chordal classes—a tonic function, a dominant function, and a subdominant function—fosters a paradigmatic approach to analysis. Or think of Roland Jackson's essay on the Prelude to *Tristan and Isolde*, which includes a summary of the prelude's leitmotivic content (see example 5.1). The six categories listed across the top of the chart—grief and desire, glance, love philter, death, magic casket, and deliverance-by-death—name thematic classes, while the inclusive bar numbers listed in each column identify the spread of individual leitmotivs. Thus, "glance" occurs in five passages spanning the prelude, while "grief and desire" occurs at the beginning, at the climax, and at the end. The occurrences of each leitmotivic class are directly and materially related, not based on an abstraction. While Jackson does not describe this as a paradigmatic analysis, it is one for all intents and purposes.[1]

Example 5.1. Jackson's analysis of leitmotivic content in the *Tristan* Prelude.

Grief and Desire	Glance	Love Philtre	Death	Magic Casket	Deliverance-by-Death
1 — 17	17 — 24	25 — 28	28 — 32		
	32 — 36			36 — 44 *A	
		45 — 48	48 — 54		
	55 — 63				63 — 74 (& Desire *F)
	74 — 83 (T chd.)				
83 — 89 (& Glance)				89 — 94 *F	
	94 — 100				
101 — 106					

1. Roland Jackson, "*Leitmotive* and Form in the *Tristan* Prelude," *Music Review* 36 (1975): 42–53.

Example 5.2. Cone's analysis of "stratification" in *Symphony of Psalms*, first movement.

Another example may be cited from Edward T. Cone's analysis of the first movement of Stravinsky's *Symphony of Psalms* (example 5.2). Cone isolates recurring blocks of material and sets them out in the form of strata. This process of stratification, well supported by what is known of Stravinsky's working methods, enables the analyst to capture difference, affinity, continuity, and discontinuity among the work's blocks of material. Unlike Johnson's leitmotifs, Cone's paradigms are presented linearly rather than vertically. Thus, stratum A in Cone's diagram, which consists of the recurring E minor "Psalms chord," is displayed horizontally as one of four paradigmatic classes (labeled A, X, B, and C, respectively). Cone explains and justifies the basic criteria for his interpretation. Without entering into the details, we can see at a glance the workings of a paradigmatic impulse.

The connotations of paradigm and syntagm are numerous, and not all writers take special care to differentiate them. Paradigm is affiliated with model, exemplar, archetype, template, typical instance, precedent, and so on, while syntagm is affiliated with ordering, disposing, placing things together, arranging things in sequence, combining units, and linearity.[2] My own intent here is not to narrow the semantic field down to a specific technical usage, but to retain a broad sense of both terms in order to convey the considerable extent to which traditional music analysis, by investing in notions of repetition and the association between repeated units, has always drawn implicitly on the descriptive domains of paradigm and syntagm.

In the practice of twentieth-century music analysis, the paradigmatic method is associated with musical semiologists and has been set out didactically in various writings by Ruwet, Lidov, Nattiez, Dunsby, Monelle, and Ayrey, among others.[3] Its most noted applications—as a method—have been to repertoires the premises of

---

2. See *Oxford English Dictionary*, 3rd ed. (Oxford: Oxford University Press, 2007).

3. For a helpful orientation to the field of musical semiotics up to the early 1990s, see Monelle, *Linguistics and Semiotics in Music*. Among more recent writings in English, the following two volumes provide some indication of the range of activity in the field: *Musical Semiotics in Growth*, ed. Eero Tarasti (Bloomington: Indiana University Press, 1996); and *Musical Semiotics Revisited*, ed. Eero Tarasti (Helsinki: International Semiotics Institute, 2003).

whose languages have not been fully stabilized. Ruwet, for example, based one of his demonstrations on medieval monodies, while Nattiez chose solo flute pieces by Debussy and Varèse for extensive exegesis. Craig Ayrey and Marcel Guerstin have pursued the Debussy repertoire further—a sign, perhaps, that this particular language or idiolect presents peculiar analytical challenges, being neither straightforwardly tonal (like the chromatically enriched languages of Brahms, Mahler, or Wolf) nor decidedly atonal (like Webern). A handful of attempts aside,[4] the paradigmatic method has *not* been applied extensively to eighteenth- and nineteenth-century music. The reason, presumably, is that these collective repertoires come freighted with so much conventional meaning that analysis that ignores such freight—even as a foil—would seem impoverished from the start.

By privileging repetition and its associations, the paradigmatic method fosters a less knowing stance in analysis; it encourages us to adopt a strategic naïveté and to downplay—without pretending to be able to eliminate entirely—some of the a priori concerns that one normally brings to the task. The questions immediately arise: which concerns should we pretend to forget, which understandings should we (temporarily) unlearn, and of which features should we feign ignorance? Answers to these questions are to some extent a matter of choice and context and may involve the basic parameters of tonal music: rhythm, timbre, melodic shape, form, and harmonic succession. In seeking to promote an understanding of music as discourse, I am especially interested in dispensing—temporarily—with aspects of conventional *form*. I want to place at a distance notions such as sonata form, rondo form, binary and ternary forms, and reckon instead—or at least initially—with the traces left by the work of repetition. It is true that different analysts use different signifiers to establish a work's fidelity to a particular formal template, and so the pertinence of the category *form* will vary from one analytical context to the next. Nevertheless, by denying an a priori privilege to such conventional shapes, the analyst may well hear (familiar) works freshly. For, despite repeated claims that musical forms are not fixed but flexible, that they are not molds into which material is poured but shapes resulting from the tendency of the material (Tovey and Rosen often make these points), many students still treat sonata and rondo forms as prescribed, as possessing certain distinctive features that must be unearthed in analysis. When such features are found, the work is regarded as normal; if the expected features are not there, or if they are somewhat disguised, a deformation is said to have occurred.[5] A

---

4. See, for example, Patrick McCreless, "Syntagmatics and Paradigmatics: Some Implications for the Analysis of Chromaticism in Tonal Music," *Music Theory Spectrum* 13 (1991): 147–178; and Craig Ayrey, "Universe of Particulars: Subotnik, Deconstruction, and Chopin," *Music Analysis* 17 (1998): 339–381.

5. I use the word "deformation" advisedly. See the comprehensive new "sonata theory" by James Hepokoski and Warren Darcy, *Elements of Sonata Theory: Norms, Types, and Deformations in the Late-Eighteenth-Century Sonata* (Oxford: Oxford University Press, 2006). For a good critique, see Julian Horton, "Bruckner's Symphonies and Sonata Deformation Theory," *Journal of the Society for Musicology in Ireland* 1 (2005–2006): 5–17.

paradigmatic view of form is less concerned with establishing conformity to an existing template than with telling what happens in an individual context. Of course, we need both mediated and unmediated perspectives to make the fullest sense of a work, but since the former has been accorded more privilege by analysts and musicologists, emphasis on the latter may serve a useful counterbalancing purpose.

Finally, a word about method: a paradigmatic analysis typically gathers the signifying units of a work into groups, columns, or paradigms and arranges each according to an explicit criterion. The number and content of the paradigms and their mode of succession in turn serve as a basis for interpreting musical meaning. By privileging repetition, the paradigmatic approach ensures that the outcome of an analytical proceeding remains intuitively in tune with what most musicians agree is the essence of tonal behavior. At the same time, paradigmatic charts make possible the telling of a number of stories about individual compositions. Some stories may corroborate conventional narratives; others may contradict them. For example, the paradigmatic approach often unveils circularity in the formal process, and this suggests a kind of counterstructure to the more conventional linear narrative. The interplay between circular and linear tendencies serves to complicate our view of the nature of musical form and musical discourse.

There are other gains from following a paradigmatic approach. By attending to the unfolding of contextually defined events, the analyst reconstructs a set of items of musical vocabulary that shows how a composer "speaks." Then also, gathering events into paradigms supports interpretation of a work as both a *logical form* and a *chronological form*. Conventional analysis of tonal structure (as expressed, for example, in Schenker's voice-leading graphs) has often privileged the chronological manifestation of form; a paradigmatic approach compels us to reckon with atemporal logical form as well. If we ask, for example, where the simplest and most complex forms of a given unit occur—at the beginning of a work, in its middle, or at the end?—we find that often the simple-to-complex ordering that defines logical form does not necessarily map onto chronological ordering in the syntagmatic chain. This kind of dissonance between domains is far more widespread and fundamental than has so far been recognized.[6] In short, by drawing on insights from the vertical as well as horizontal dimensions, from both x and y axes, so to speak, and from temporal as well as atemporal orderings of material, paradigmatic analysis provides a rich network of vistas from which to view tonal process and, through that, to infer musical meaning.

---

6. For an early recognition, see Richard Cohn and Douglas Dempster, "Hierarchical Unity, Plural Unities: Toward a Reconciliation," in *Disciplining Music: Musicology and Its Canons*, ed. Catherine Bergeron and Philip Bohlman (Chicago: University of Chicago Press, 1992), 156–181; see also Eugene Narmour, *The Analysis and Cognition of Basic Melodic Structures: The Implication-Realization Model* (Chicago: University of Chicago Press, 1990).

The Paradigmatic Method in Outline: "God Save the King"

By way of a quick introduction (for those not familiar with this method) or review (for those already familiar with it), let me summarize a paradigmatic analysis that I have developed elsewhere of bars 1–6 of "God Save the King."[7] I will pretend that this is the work in its entirety. Example 5.3 shows the tune in F major and in 3/4 meter. The aim of the analysis is to discover repeated patterns, construct associations among them, and thereby account for the piece as a network of repetition. Repetitions of what? This is the first of several qualitative questions that the analyst must answer. In general, the so-called primary parameters of tonal music (rhythm, melody, and harmony) may serve as guides to determining relevant repetitions. For each parameter, we need to establish a mode of succession in order to determine its units. We then explore equivalence among units on the basis of explicit criteria. Associations may be based on identical pitch but different rhythms, different pitch but identical rhythms, pitch-class rather than pitch identity, and so on. We may also associate units that are diminutionally equivalent, others with identical functional-harmonic content, and still others whose rhythmic patterns map onto each other durationally, periodically, or hypermetrically. These factors may also be combined. There are, in other words, numerous possibilities, and it is up to the analyst to determine those that are pertinent in a given context on historical, stylistic, or systematic grounds. Framing a paradigmatic analysis thus calls on the usual exercise of judgment, discrimination, and subjectivity that other analytical methods do. It is the degree of explicitness required by this approach, however, that sets it apart.

Example 5.3. The tune of "God Save the King."

Turning now to "God Save the King," let us begin by using literal pitch identity as a criterion in associating its elements. Example 5.4 sets out the result graphically. The 16 attack points are then summarized in a paradigmatic chart to the right of the graphic presentation. What kinds of insight does this proceeding make possible?

As unpromising as patterns of literal pitch retention might seem, this exercise is nevertheless valuable because it displays the work's strategy in terms of entities that are repeated, including when, how often, and the rate at which new events appear. (Critics who refuse to get their feet wet because they find an analytical premise intuitively unsatisfying often miss out on certain valuable insights that

7. See Agawu, "The Challenge of Musical Semiotics," 138–160. My own analysis was preceded by that of Jonathan Dunsby and Arnold Whittall in *Music Analysis in Theory and Practice* (London: Faber, 1988), 223–225. See also the analysis of "pattern and grammar" by David Lidov in his *Elements of Semiotics* (New York: St. Martin's, 1999), 163–170.

Example 5.4. Paradigmatic structure of "God Save the King" based on pitch identity.

Summary				
1				
2	3	4		
5	6		7	
			8	9
			10	
		11		
12	13			
14		15		
16				

Totals	6	4	2	3	1

emerge later; until you have worked through the analytical proceeding, you don't really know what it can accomplish.) The horizontal succession 2–3–4, for example, describes the longest chain of "new" events in the work. This occurs close to the beginning of the work. The vertical succession 1–2–5 (first column) shows the predominance of the opening pitch in these opening measures. Strategically, it is as if we return to the opening pitch to launch a set of departures. First, 1 is presented, then 2–3–4 follow, and finally 5–6–7 complete this phase of the strategy, where the initial members of each group (1, 2, and 5) are equivalent. (This interpretation is based strictly on the recurrences of the pitch F and not on its function nor the structure of the phrase.) A similar strategy links the group of units 1–7 to 12–16. In the latter, units 12–13 lead off, followed by 14–15, and concluded by 16, where—again—the initiating 12, 14, and 16 are identical.

A similar concentration may be heard in the 7–10 succession, although here the contiguity (7, 8, and 10 are identical) is broken by the intervention of 9, the only "event" in the entire work that is never replicated. It is the pitch B-flat, the highest literal pitch in the work, and appears close to the midpoint. (Coming up with speculative, ad hoc, or rhetorical explanations for situations like this is not difficult: one could say that because B-flat is the high point of the work, duplicating it would make a poor aesthetic effect; it would reduce the impact of a superlative and unique moment.)

The summary chart in example 5.4 conveys aspects of the work's overall strategy. There are five columns of paradigms consisting of six, four, two, three, then one event(s), respectively. (If, given the restricted context of "God Save the King," we let a pitch stand analogously for an event, that is, a procedure that involves musical action, then we can be less anxious about calling a pitch an event.) This confirms our intuition that material presented at or near the beginning of the work dominates the subsequent action. We note also that the succession 12–14–16 (belonging to the first column) conveys a sense of recapitulation, a return to the earlier 1–2–5 segment. As a global linear strategy, the work departs from one group of units (1–6), goes to another group (7–11), and returns to the first (12–16). Note, more broadly, that paradigms one, two, and three occupy the outer segments of the work, while four and five are contained.

Are these connections hearable? Do we hear pitches digitally, registering every F-natural that passes by, and associating them? These questions are both relevant and not relevant. They are relevant because most analysis appeals on some level to audibility, so that an analysis whose findings have no corroboration in listeners' experience is often held as suspect. On the other hand, these questions are irrelevant if the aim is to display a certain empirical reality or to display a first-level content, not to report an individual listener's hearing. Clearly, not every listener will note the recurrence of the pitch F-natural throughout the piece. But many will hear departure and return and be alert to the sense of rest that comes with the long-held F at the end, a pitch that they may well remember from the beginning and for which a deep desire will have been implanted once the work reached the turning point on B-flat. The strength of a paradigmatic analysis, then, is that it makes explicit a set of possibilities for interpretation. Some of these possibilities may coincide with one's hearing, some may contradict it, while some may engender a fresh approach to hearing.

Sophisticated listeners and music theorists will complain that the analysis in example 5.4 does not touch the heart of the musical language. Identity formation in tonal music, they will say, is based on relational rather than absolute values. Whether the music approaches an F from the G above it or from the E below it is far more relevant to the musical experience than noting the occurrences of F. Tonal music in this view is supremely relational, and any analysis that ignores this foundational relationality cannot have anything worthwhile to communicate. Let us respond by embracing the idea of relation and pattern in the next stage of our paradigmatic analysis.

Example 5.5 constructs an alternative distribution of content, taking the first bar as a guide and segmenting the work at this larger level—not, as before, into single notes called events, but into groups of notes coinciding with notated bars. Example 5.5 thus incorporates contour (itself an index of minimal action) as a criterion. Units 1 and 3 rise by step, while units 4 and 5 descend through a third. Since these 4 bars account for two-thirds of the work, it is not indefensible to let these features guide a segmentation. Again, we can develop our narratives of both paradigm and syntagm on this basis. As example 5.5 suggests, we begin with a pattern, follow it with a contrasting one, return to the first (only now at a higher pitch level), continue with a new pattern, repeat this down a step, and conclude with a final stationary unit. The contiguity of units 4–5 opposes the interruption of units 1–3 by 2 and leads us to imagine that, in the drive toward closure, saying things again and again helps to convey the coming end.

Example 5.5. Paradigmatic structure of "God Save the King" based on melodic contour.

Example 5.6. Paradigmatic structure of "God Save the King" based on rhythmic patterns.

Listeners for whom rhythmic coherence considered apart from pitch behavior is more dominant in this work will prefer a slightly different segmentation, the one given in example 5.6. Here, the three paradigms are determined by a rhythmic equivalence whereby units 1, 3, and 5 belong together; 2 and 4 also belong together;

while 6 stands alone. In this perspective, we are immediately struck by the alternation of values, a procedural duality that we might say defines the work's syntagmatic strategy. Whatever one's commitments are to the proper way of hearing this composition, it is obvious from comparing and aligning examples 5.5 and 5.6 that, while they share certain features—such as the uniqueness of the concluding F, which, incidentally, example 5.4 denies—they also emphasize different features. Placing one's intuitions in a larger economy of paradigmatic analyses may perform several critical functions for listeners. It may serve to reassure them of their way of hearing, challenge that way by pointing to other possibilities, or show how remote is their way from those revealed in paradigmatic analyses. This exercise may also sharpen our awareness of the role of agency in listening by contextualizing the paths we choose to follow when listening to a particular work. We may or may not hear—or choose to hear—in the same general ways, but we can understand better what we choose or choose not to choose while engaged in the complex activity we call listening.

So far, we have relied on the implicit tonal-harmonic orientation of "God Save the King" to determine our construction of patterns. But what if we try to analyze the work in full harmonic dress, as shown in example 5.7? When, some years ago, David Lidov presented an analysis of a Bach chorale ("O Jesulein süss") to illustrate the paradigmatic method, he labeled the chords using figured bass and roman numerals and then, discounting modulation, constructed a paradigmatic scheme according to which the harmonic progressions fell into three paradigms.[8] The question of whether that particular chorale represented something of an exception in terms of its harmonic organization was not definitively answered by Lidov. Although a certain amount of invariance usually occurs between phrases of a chorale, the issue of what is norm and what is exception requires a larger comparative sample. For our purposes, a meaningful harmonic analysis must proceed with idioms of harmonic usage, not with individual chords. Proceeding in this belief means taking note of harmonic gesture. The harmonic gesture at the largest level of "God Save the King" (example 5.7) begins with a 2-bar open phrase (I–V in bars 1–2) followed by a 4-bar closed phrase (I–V–I in bars 3–end), the latter closing deceptively at first (in bar 4) before proceeding to a satisfying authentic close (bars 5–6). Obviously, the initial I–V progression is contained within the following I–V–I progression, and while it is theoretically possible to detach that I–V from the subsequent I–V–I succession in order to see an internal parallelism between the two harmonic phrases, the more palpable motivation is of an incomplete process brought to completion, the latter unsuccessful at first attempt, and then successful at the second. The identities of tonic and dominant chords are, in a sense, less pertinent than the hierarchy of closings that they engender, for it is this hierarchy that conveys the meaning of the work as a harmonic stream. Reading the harmonized "God Save the King" in terms of these dynamic forces downplays the role of repetition and so produces less compelling results from a paradigmatic point of view.

---

8. David Lidov, "Nattiez's Semiotics of Music," *Canadian Journal of Research in Semiotics* 5 (1977): 40. Dunsby cites this same analysis in "A Hitch Hiker's Guide to Semiotic Music Analysis," *Music Analysis* 1 (1982): 237–238.

Example 5.7. Simple harmonization of "God Save the King."

Example 5.8. Chromatically enriched harmonization of "God Save the King."

None of this is to suggest that the realm of the harmonic is resistant to paradigmatic structuring, for as we saw in the generative exercises in chapter 4, the existence of differentially composed harmonic idioms makes possible analyses that are alert to repetition. The point that seems to be emerging here, however, is that the forces that constrain harmonic expression are often so linearly charged that they seem to undermine the "vertical thinking"—the intertexts—normally conveyed in paradigmatic analysis. But let us see how the harmonic perspective of example 5.7 can be intensified by use of chromaticism and various auxiliary notes without erasing the basic harmonic substructure. Example 5.8, based loosely on Brahms' manner, is a reharmonization of "God Save the King." For all intents and purposes, example 5.8 is a version of example 5.7: the tune is decorated here and there in 5.8, and the structural harmonies are more or less the same. The two versions therefore belong to the same paradigmatic class in the same way that variations on a theme belong in principle to a single paradigmatic class. A middleground comparison of the two harmonized versions reinforces that identity, but what a contrast at the foreground level. Between various chord substitutions and auxiliary interpolations, this new version (example 5.8) seems to depart in significant ways from the previous one. It is in connection with situations like this that the paradigmatic approach to tonal music begins to meet some difficulty. The fact that a literal surface must be understood in terms of underlying motivations means that analysis based on internal relations without recourse to prior (or outside) texts will likely miss an important structural and expressive dimension. One cannot, in other words, approach the kind of musical expression contained in example 5.8 with the naïveté of the empiricist because what is heard is always already embedded in what is functional but unsounded. We will confront this challenge in the coming analyses of Mozart and Beethoven, where some reliance on conventional idioms will be invoked in order to render the surface accessible. Analysis must find a way, even at this fundamental level, to redefine the object of analysis in a way that makes this background accessible.

Returning to the unharmonized version of "God Save the King" (example 5.3), we might explore still other ways of interpreting it as a bundle of repetitions. For example, a listener struck by the interval of a descending minor third between bars 1 and 2 might take this as an indication of potential structural importance. The gap is between the notes G and E, the two adjacencies to the tonic, F; in other words, the gap encompasses the gateways to the tonic. It is also unique in the piece insofar as all other movement is stepwise. As a gap, it demands in principle to be filled, and this is precisely what happens in the penultimate bar with the G–F–E succession. But we have encountered these notes before, specifically in bar 2, immediately after the gap was announced, where the fill proceeds in the opposite direction, E–F–G. In sum, a descending gap (between bars 1 and 2) is followed by an ascending fill (bar 2) and complemented by a descending fill (bar 5).

In this light, other relations become apparent. We hear bars 4 and 5 in close relation because, although rhythmically different, bar 5 is a sequence of bar 4 down a step. We can thus relate bar 4, a descending major third, to the minor third processes mentioned previously. And, if we look beyond the immediate level, we see that, taking the first (metrically accented) beats only of bars 4, 5, and 6, we have a descending A–G–F progression, the same one that we heard on a more local level within bar 4. The larger progression in bars 4–6 therefore has nested within it a smaller version of its structural self. We might hear a similar expanded progression across bars 1–3, this time in ascending order: F at the beginning of bar 1, G at the end of bar 2, and A at the beginning of bar 3. This mode of thinking, unlike the ones explored in example 5.4, depends on patterns and diminutions. The literalism that marked early demonstrations of the paradigmatic method by Ruwet and Nattiez was unavoidable in part because the objects of analytical attention seemed to be made from less familiar musical languages. But for a heavily freighted tonal language like that of "God Save the King," we need an expanded basis for relating phenomena.

These remarks about "God Save the King" will, I hope, have suggested possibilities for the construction of musical meaning based on criteria such as literal pitch retention, association of pitch-based and rhythm-based patterns, diatonic and chromatic harmonization, and an intervallic discourse determined by gaps and fills—or some combination of these. But the monodic context of "God Save the King" is relatively restricted, and some may wonder how we might proceed from it to a more complex musical work. Answers to this question may be found in the more methodologically oriented studies by Ruwet, Nattiez, Vacarro, and Ayrey.[9] Because my own interests here are more directly analytical, I will forgo discussion

9. Nicholas Ruwet, "Methods of Analysis in Musicology," trans. Mark Everist, *Music Analysis* 6 (1987): 11–36; Jean-Jacques Nattiez, "Varèse's 'Density 21.5': A Study in Semiological Analysis," trans. Anna Barry, *Music Analysis* 1 (1982): 243–340; Jean-Michel Vaccaro, "Proposition d'un analyse pour une polyphonie vocale dux vie siècle," *Revue de musicology* 61 (1975): 35–58; and Craig Ayrey, "Debussy's Significant Connections: Metaphor and Metonymy in Analytical Method," in *Theory, Analysis and Meaning in Music*, ed. Anthony Pople (Cambridge: Cambridge University Press, 1994), 127–151.

of abstract methodology for the concrete discussion of a handful of well-known pieces. Each analysis is carried out under the sign of a paradigmatic impulse, but I have also framed the analyses in reference to certain overarching qualities or features: discontinuity in Mozart, logical and chronological form in Chopin, the consistent use of a handful of tonal models in Beethoven, and the will to melodic variation in Brahms. It is my hope that the analyses will convey something of the interpretive potential of paradigmatic analysis.

Discontinuity in Mozart's Piano Sonata in A Minor, K. 310, second movement

While the basic method of paradigmatic analysis—determine the units of a composition, establish the bases of their association, and thus explain the unique system of the individual work—is easy enough to describe, the real value of paradigmatic analysis may well lie in its ability to illuminate compositional features and strategies sensed intuitively. My next example is a slow movement of a piano sonata by Mozart. Although its textures are more uniform than the discursive textures we typically hear in his first movements—think, for example, of the topically marked and thus apparently discontinuous first movements of K. 284 and K. 332—my intuition here is that discontinuity is an essential feature of this movement as well. This claim may seem counterintuitive at first. Yet, if we focus on the contrapuntal subsurface, we will see that a succession of tonal models or little progressions—each tastefully ornamented, sometimes elaborately, sometimes modestly—accrues an additive feel made possible by local discontinuities. We are reminded of A. B. Marx's claim, which Schenker denies, that Mozart employs "a succession of many small structures."[10] These discontinuous structures group into families, and their affiliations can be brought out in a paradigmatic analysis.

More formally, then: the purpose of the analysis is to reveal the harmonic cum contrapuntal relations that make Mozart's composition possible and to suggest that their disposition by means of a technique of aggregation is enabled in part by discontinuity. There are three steps to the method. First, responding to the usual imperative to domesticate the movement for analysis, I have followed Schenker in preparing a two-voice version of Mozart's composition (example 5.9).[11] As a second step, and in keeping with our concerns in this chapter, I scanned the movement for smaller but meaningful units (labeled 1, 2, 3…28 in example 5.9). A third and final step involved arranging these units into a paradigmatic chart (example 5.10) with three columns labeled A, B, and C. Units in each column express one of three types

---

10. A. B. Marx, *Die Lehre von der musikalischen Komposition, praktisch-theoretisch* (Leipzig: Breitkopf & Härtel, 1837–1847), quoted by Schenker in *Der Tonwille*, 66.
11. See Schenker, *Der Tonwille*, 58, figure 2. There are slight differences between my representation and Schenker's. I have kept note values in treble and bass throughout, retained Mozart's literal registers, added a continuous figured bass between the two staves, and dispensed with roman numerals.

of basic motion. The first is an open (I–V) progression, such as we have in the first 4 bars of the movement. (See unit 1 and its return as unit 19; see also units 5, 18, and 21. Unit 16 is also open since it expresses a V prolongation.) Column B represents a closed (I–V–I) progression, such as we have in bars 5–8 of the movement (unit 2), although it, too, can be modified to begin on I6, ii, or IV. Column B is by far the most populated paradigm of the three. Column C, the least populated, expresses a linear intervallic pattern (10–10–10–10) enlivened by 9–8 suspensions. It occurs only once, near the end of the so-called development section, the "point of furthest remove" (in Ratner's terminology).[12] If, as stated earlier, the purpose of the analysis is to establish the conditions of possibility for this particular movement, then once we have figured out how to improvise these three kinds of tonal expression—an open one, a closed one, and a sequential, transitional progression—using a variety of stylistic resources, the essential analytical task has been fulfilled. The rest is (harmless) interpretation according to the analyst's chosen plot.

It is possible to tell many stories about this movement on the basis of the demonstration in examples 5.9 and 5.10. For example, virtually all of the units in the first reprise except unit 1 are column B units. Because each unit is notionally complete—that is, it attains syntactic closure—the narrative of this first reprise may be characterized as a succession of equivalent states or small worlds. We might say therefore that there is something circular about this first reprise and that this circular tendency, operative on a relatively local level, counters the larger, linear dynamic conferred by the modulatory obligations of what is, after all, a sonata-form movement.

Other stories may be fashioned around parallelism of procedure. For example, the second reprise begins with two statements of unit 2 (units 13 and 14), now in the dominant. But this same unit 2 was heard at the end of the first reprise (units 11 and 12). The music after the bar line thus expands the temporal scope of the music before the bar line. Since, however, units 11 and 12 functioned as an ending (of the first reprise), while 13–14 function as a beginning (of the second reprise), their sameness at this level reminds us of the reciprocal relationship between endings and beginnings.

We might also note the uniqueness of unit 17, which marks a turning point in the movement. Heard by itself, it is a classic transitional unit; it denies both the choreographed incompletion of column A units and the closed nature of the widespread column B units. It could be argued that strategic turning points as represented by unit 17 are most effective if they are not duplicated anywhere else in the movement. This interpretation would thus encourage us to hear the movement as a whole in terms of a single trajectory that reaches a turning point in unit 17. Finally, we might note the prospect of an adumbrated recapitulation in the succession of units 18 and 19. While the microrhythmic activity on the surface of 18 forms part of the sense of culmination reached in the development, and while the onset of unit 19 is an unequivocal thematic reprise, the fact that the two units belong to the same paradigm suggests that they are versions of each other. No doubt, the thematic power of unit 19 establishes its signifying function within the form, but we might also hear unit 18 as stealing some of unit 19's thunder.

12. Leonard G. Ratner, *The Beethoven String Quartets: Compositional Strategies and Rhetoric* (Stanford, CA: Stanford Bookstore, 1995), 332.

Example 5.9. Outer voice reduction (after Schenker) of Mozart's Piano Sonata in A Minor, K. 310, second movement.

Example 5.10. Paradigmatic arrangement of units in Mozart, K. 310, second movement.

(continued)

Readers will have their own stories to tell about this movement, but I hope that the paths opened here will prove helpful for other analytical adventures. I have suggested that, if we agree that the slow movement of Mozart's K. 310 can be recast as an assembly of little progressions—mostly closed, independently meaningful expressions of harmonic-contrapuntal order—then the inner form of the movement might be characterized as a succession of autonomous or semiautonomous small worlds. Units follow one another, but they are not necessarily continuous with one another. If anything rules in this Mozart movement, it is *discontinuous succession.* Paradigmatic analysis helps to convey that quality.

Chronological versus Logical Form in Chopin's Prelude in F-sharp Major, op. 28, no. 13

The technique of elaborating a chorale-type texture served as a useful means of poetic expression in the nineteenth century. Among others, Chopin excelled at this. We can explore his manner by comparing chronological order with logical order in the F-sharp Major Prelude, op. 28 no. 13.

Example 5.10. continued

B

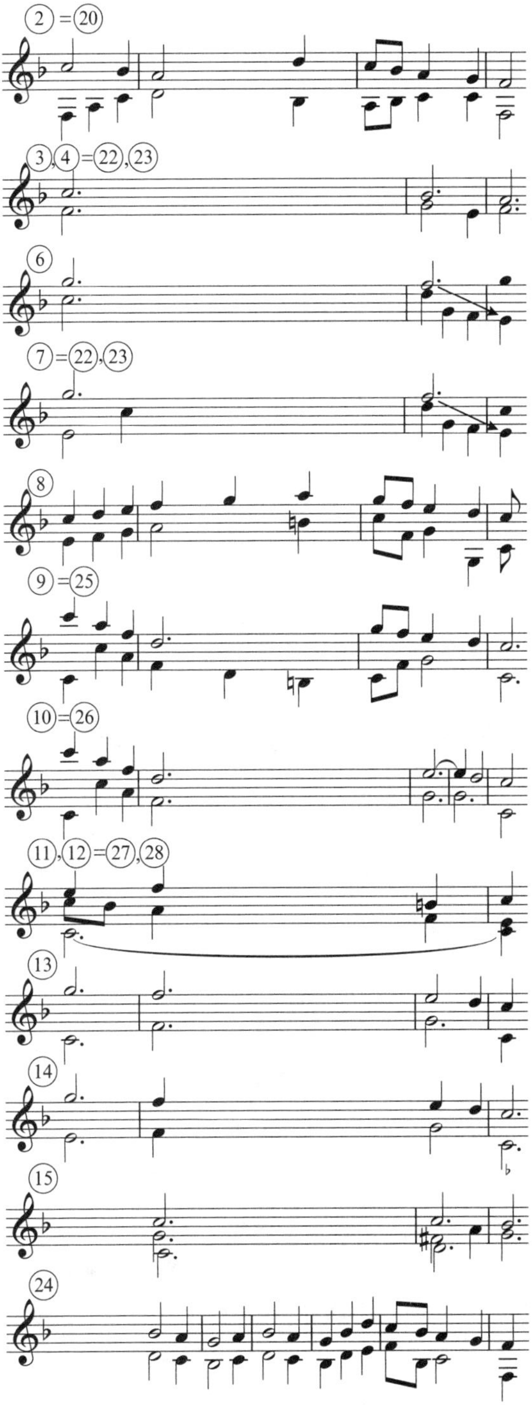

(continued)

Example 5.10. continued

C

Example 5.11. Harmonic generators of Chopin, op. 28, no. 13.

The harmonic means are radically simple, and the reader is invited to real-ize them at the piano using example 5.11 as guide. Start by playing an archetypal closed progression (1), expand it by incorporating a predominant sonority that intensifies the motion to the dominant (2), truncate the progression by withhold-ing the closing tonic while tonicizing the dominant (thus creating a desire for reso-lution; 3, 4), repeat the truncated progression in transposed form (5), and restore closure using the conventional progression previously used in 2 (6).

With these resources, we are ready to improvise Chopin's prelude as a har-monic stream (example 5.12). The prelude as a whole breathes in eight (often over-lapping) units or segments. These are summarized below (successive bar numbers are listed to convey the relative sizes of units):

Segment	Bars
1	1 2 3 4 5
2	5 6 7 8
3	9 10 11 12
4	12 13 14 15 16 17 18 19 20
5	20 21 22
6	22 23 24
7	24 25 26 27 28
8	29 30 31 32 33 34 35 36 37 38

We may call this the chronological order in which events unfold. But what if we order the segments according to a logical order? Logical order is qualitative; it is not given, but has to be postulated on the basis of certain criteria. Let us privilege the harmonic domain and allow the paradigmatic impulse to dictate such logic. We begin with closed progressions, placing the most expansive ones in front of the less expansive ones. Units 8 and 4 are the most expansive, while units 1 and 3 are less expansive. Next is a unit that attains closure but is not bounded by the tonic chord, as the previous four units are. This is unit 7. Finally, we add units that, like 7, reach closure but on other degrees of the scale. Two close on the dominant (2 and 5), and one closes on the subdominant (6). The logical order thus begins with closed, bounded units in the tonic, continues with closed unbounded units in the tonic, and finishes with closed unbounded units on other scale degrees (first dominant, then subdominant). In short, where the chronological form is 1 2 3 4 5 6 7 8, the logical form is 8 4 1 3 7 2 5 6, which, following precedent, may be written as follows:

Segment	Bars
8	29 30 31 32 33 34 35 36 37 38
4	12 13 14 15 16 17 18 19 20
1	1 2 3 4 5
3	9 10 11 12
7	24 25 26 27 28
2	5 6 7 8
5	20 21 22
6	22 23 24

Example 5.12. Chopin, Prelude in F-sharp Major, op. 28, no. 13.

(continued)

Example 5.12. continued

2

Many stories can be told about this prelude. First, if we ignore the global toni-cizations of dominant and subdominant, then all of the units in the prelude are closed. In that sense, a paradigmatic analysis shows a single paradigm. This stack-ing of the vertical dimension speaks to a certain economy of means employed by Chopin. It also suggests the same kind of aggregative tendency we isolated in Mozart—in colloquial terms, the same thing is said again and again eight times. Second, the most expansive closed progressions are placed—strategically, we'll have to say—at the end of the prelude and in the middle (units 8 and 4, respec-tively). Unit 8 provides the final culmination while unit 4 serves as a preliminary point of culmination. Third, the opening unit is in fact only a less elaborate form of units 8 and 4; this means that the prelude begins with a closed progression of mod-est dimensions, which it then repeats (3) and expands not once but twice (4 and 8). This speaks to a cumulative or organic strategy.

Again, it should be acknowledged that we can order the logic differently. For example, we might start not with the most expansive but simply with a well-formed cadence, then go to the more expansive ones. Or, we might treat the tonicizations of V and IV in primary reference to the cadences in the home key. Whatever order analysts settle on, they are obliged to explain its basis. We might also note the affinities between generative analysis (as practiced in the previous chapter) and paradigmatic analysis. The model that allows generation is in a sense a paradigm, but where the emphasis in the previous chapter was on turning something simple into something more complex, the emphasis here is seeing how these transformations articulate a larger whole.

Tonal Models in Beethoven's String Quartet in D Major, op. 18, no. 3/i

Beethoven's op. 18, no. 3, begins with two violin whole notes and continues to a cadence in bar 10 either in whole notes (the lower strings) or in diminutions of those whole notes (the first violin; example 5.13). The texture suggests alla breve style, an archaic style domesticated within the pedagogy of counterpoint. From this simple intuition, we might go on to reason that, if the first 10 bars can be represented in something like a two-voice first-species contrapuntal exercise (as shown in the reduction in example 5.13), the entire movement might respond similarly. The material displayed in examples 5.13 through 5.29 concretizes this intuition by reproducing the content of the whole movement in arrangements that demonstrate affinity among units rather than chronology. For each unit, I have written out the outer voices, added figures between the staves to register intervallic content in reference to the sounding bass, and simplified the rhythmic texture to make the analysis more manageable.

Example 5.13. Beethoven, String Quartet in D Major, op. 18, no. 3, bars 1–10, with two-voice reduction.

Although some of them may be self-evident, the criteria for dividing up the movement into meaningful units (sense units, utterances, ideas, phrases, periods) require comment. The challenge of segmentation remains at the heart of many analytical endeavors, and while it seems more acute in relation to twentieth-century works (as Christopher Hasty and others have shown),[13] it is by no means straightforward in Beethoven. Following the precedent set in the Mozart and

---

13. Christopher Hasty, "Segmentation and Process in Post-Tonal Music," *Music Theory Spectrum* 3 (1981): 54–73.

Chopin analyses, I have opted for the most basic of conventional models of tonal motion based on the I–V–I nexus as the principal criterion. Some support for this proceeding may be garnered from Adorno:

> To understand Beethoven means to understand tonality. It is fundamental to his music not only as its "material" but as its principle, its essence: his music utters the secret of tonality; the limitations set by tonality are his own—and at the same time the driving force of his productivity.[14]

Whatever else this might mean, it engenders an idea that seems tautological at first sight, but actually fuses a historical insight with a systematic one, namely, foundations as essences. The implication for Beethoven analysis is that the most fundamental modes and strategies of tonal definition constitute (part of) the essence of his music. The analytical task, then, is to discover or uncover ways in which these essences are thematized.

Based on a normative principle of departure and return, the fundamental mode of tonal definition may be glossed as a I–V–I harmonic progression and subject to a variety of modes of expression and transformation.[15] I could, for example, tonicize V, prolong it by introducing a predominant element, or prolong it even further by tonicizing the predominant. More radically, I might truncate the model by deleting part of its frame. Thus, instead of the complete I–V–I chain, I may opt for an auxiliary V–I progression, in which form it still attains closure but relinquishes the security of a beginning tonic. Or, I may prefer a I–V progression, in which form the model is understood as open and incomplete. Modifications are understood in reference to the larger, complete progression.

Stated so abstractly, these procedures sound obvious, mechanical, and uninspiring. Indeed, they belong at the most elementary level of tonal expression. And yet, without some sense of what is possible at this level, one cannot properly appreciate the ecology (or economy, or horizon) that sustains a given composition. If music is language, a language based in conventional codes, then it is trivial to have to point out that, by 1800, Beethoven the pianist, improviser, composer, student of counterpoint, and copier of other people's scores, thoroughly spoke a language enabled by what might be called the "first utterances of the tonal system": I–V–I progressions and what they make possible.

What, then, are the specific tokens of these first utterances of the tonal system, and how are they composed out in the course of the first movement of op. 18, no. 3? Example 5.14 provides a broad orientation to the movement by summarizing a segmentation of the movement into 40 sense units (left column) and indicating some of the topical references that might be inferred from the sounding surfaces

14. Theodor Adorno, *Beethoven: The Philosophy of Music*, trans. Edmund Jephcott, ed. Rolf Tiedemann (Stanford, CA: Stanford University Press, 1998), 49.

15. On tonal models as determinants of style, see Wintle, "Corelli's Tonal Models," 29–69; and Agawu, "Haydn's Tonal Models: The First Movement of the Piano Sonata in E-flat Major, Hob. XVI:52," in *Convention in Eighteenth- and Nineteenth-Century Music: Essays in Honor of Leonard G. Ratner*, ed. Wye J. Allanbrook, Janet M. Levy, and William P. Mahrt (Stuyvesant, NY: Pendragon, 1992), 3–22.

Example 5.14. Structural units and topical references in Beethoven, op. 18, no. 3/i.

Unit	Bars	Topical references
1	1–10	alla breve, galant
2	11–27	alla breve, cadenza, *messanza* figures
3	27–31	alla breve, stretto, galant
4	31–35	bourrée
5	36–39	bourrée
6	40–43	bourrée
7	43–45	bourrée
8	45–57	Sturm und Drang, brilliant style, march
9	57–67	brilliant style, fantasia, march
10	68–71	march, alla zoppa
11	72–75	march, alla zoppa
12	76–82	fanfare
13	82–90	fanfare
14	90–94	musette
15	94–103	musette
16	104–110	fantasia
17	108–116	alla breve
18	116–122	alla breve, fantasia
19	123–126	bourrée
20	127–128	bourrée
21	129–132	bourrée
22	132–134	bourrée
23	134–138	alla breve, *furioso*, Sturm und Drang
24	138–142	alla breve, *furioso*, Sturm und Drang
25	143–147	alla breve, *furioso*, Sturm und Drang
26	147–156	Sturm und Drang, *concitato* style
27	158–188	alla breve, ricercar style, march
28	188–198	brilliant style, march
29	199–202	march, alla zoppa
30	203–206	march, alla zoppa
31	207–213	fanfare
32	213–221	fanfare
33	221–225	musette
34	225–234	musette
35	235–241	fantasia
36	239–247	alla breve
37	247–250	march, alla zoppa
38	251–255	march, alla zoppa
39	255–259	alla breve, stretto, *messanza* figures
40	259–269	alla breve

Example 5.15. Paradigmatic display of all 40 units in Beethoven, op. 18, no. 3/i.

Models	1c	1b	1a	1d	2	3	
	1						Exposition
	2	3					
		4	5				
			6	8			
			7		9		
					10		
					11		
				12			
				13			
		14					
		15					
						16	
	17			18			Development
			19				
			20				
			21				
			22				
					23		
					24		
					25		
					26		
	27						Recapitulation
					28		
					29		
					30		
				31			
				32			
		33					
		34					
						35	Coda
	36						
					37	38	
	39						
	40						

(right column). Example 5.15 lists the same 40 units only now in reference to a series of tonal models and a conventional sonata-form outline. As will be immediately clear from the examples that follow, each of the 40 units belongs to one of three models, which I have labeled 1 (with subdivisions 1a, 1b, 1c, 1d), 2, and 3.

Model 1 expresses a closed I–V–I progression, while models 2 and 3 express open and closed I–V and V–I progressions, respectively. Let us explore the tonal models in detail.[16]

Model 1a, shown in abstract in example 5.16 and concretely in example 5.17, features a straightforward closed progression, I–ii6/5–V–I, perhaps the most basic of tonal progressions. Example 5.17 aligns all seven units affiliated with the model. Its first occurrence is in the tonic, D major, as unit 5 in a portion of the movement that some have labeled a bridge passage (bars 36ff.) The melodic profile of this unit— ending on scale-degree 3 rather than 1—confers on it a degree of openness appropriate for a transitional function, this despite the closed harmonic form. Conflicts like this—between harmonic tendency (closed) and melodic tendency (open)—are important sources of expressive effect in this style.

Example 5.16. Origins of model 1a units.

Other instantiations of the model are units 6 (in B minor), 19 (in B-flat major), and 21 (in G minor), all of which display the same thematic profile. Units 7 in A minor and 22 in G minor abbreviate the progression slightly, beginning on first-inversion rather than root-position chords. And unit 20 in B-flat major withholds the normative continuation of the unit after the tonic extension of the model's first 2 bars.

All seven units—5, 6, 7, 19, 20, 21, 22—belong to a single paradigmatic class. They are harmonically equivalent, tonally disparate—a factor bracketed at this level—thematically affiliated, and melodically similar. Of course, they occur at different moments in this sonata-form movement. Unit 5, for example, begins the transition to the second key, but it also is imbued with a sense of closing by virtue of its harmony. Unit 6 signals tonal departure, while unit 7 intensifies the sense of departure with a shift from the B minor of the previous unit to A minor. These units thus perform different syntagmatic functions while sharing a network of (harmonic) features. Ultimately, it is the tension between their equivalence

---

16. Alternative segmentations of the movement are, of course, possible—even desirable. My interest here, however, is in the plausibility of the units isolated, not (primarily) in the relative merits of competing segmentations. Whenever my chosen criteria seem especially fragile, however, I offer some explanation.

Example 5.17. Model 1a units.

at this level—their resistance to change, so to speak—and the nonequivalence of their temporal positioning and formal functioning that accounts for their meaning. These are purely musical meanings insofar as they emerge from the native tendencies of tones, not from associations with extramusical usage. Hanslick's "forms set in motion by sounding," Roman Jakobson's "introversive semiosis," and Lawrence Zbikowski's "dynamic processes" index roughly the same group of qualities.[17]

Model 1b also expresses a complete I–IV–V–I progression (example 5.18), but unlike 1a, includes an explicit and prominent flattened-seventh (C-natural), which effectively tonicizes the subdominant and thus intensifies the push toward the

Example 5.18. Origins of model 1b units.

Example 5.19. Model 1b units.

17. Eduard Hanslick, *Vom Musikalisch-Schönen [On the Musically Beautiful]*, trans. Martin Cooper, in *Music in European Thought 1851–1912*, ed. Bojan Buji̇́c (Cambridge: Cambridge University Press, 1988), 19; Roman Jakobson, "Language in Relation to Other Communication Systems," in Jakobson, *Selected Writings*, vol. 2 (The Hague: Mouton, 1971), 704–705, adapted in Agawu, *Playing with Signs*, 51–79; and Lawrence M. Zbikowski, "Musical Communication in the Eighteenth Century," in *Communication in Eighteenth-Century Music*, ed. Danuta Mirka and Kofi Agawu (Cambridge: Cambridge University Press, 2008).

authentic cadence. Example 5.19 shows six passages totaling 42 bars that express this model. First is unit 3, followed immediately by a registral variant, unit 4. Notice how unit 33, which recapitulates unit 14, incorporates the flattened-seventh within a walking bass pattern. The thematic profile of model 1b is more varied than that of model 1a, all of whose units belong topically to the sphere of bourrée. Here, units 3 and 4 are alla breve material (that is to say, they occupy an ecclesiastical register), whereas the others (15, 34, 14, and 33) invoke the galant style with an initial musette inflection (this signals a secular register). Note also that units 15 and 34 exceed the normative 5-bar length of the other model 1b units. This is because I have incorporated the reiterated cadential figures that emphasize the dominant key, A major, in the exposition (unit 15) and its rhyme, D major, in the recapitulation (unit 34). Again, remember that all model 1b units are harmonically equivalent but thematically differentiated.

With model 1c (whose origins are displayed in example 5.20), we come—again, as it turns out—to the central thematic material of the movement, the opening 10-bar alla breve and its subsequent appearances. Like models 1a and 1b, its units (gathered in example 5.21) might be heard as tonally closed (all except 17 and 36, which end in deceptive cadences that, however, may be understood as substitutions for authentic cadences), but its journey is a little more protracted. Moreover, the model begins with a prefix (shown in example 5.20) that does both thematic and harmonic work. Thematic work is evident in the recurrence of the rising minor seventh (sometimes in arpeggiated form) throughout the movement; harmonic work is evident in the tonicization of individual scale degrees that the seventh facilitates as part of a dominant-seventh sonority.

Example 5.20. Origins of model 1c units.

I have identified seven passages of differing lengths—ranging from 5 to 31 bars—that express model 1c. First is unit 1, the opening of the quartet, whose parallel minor version opens the development (unit 17). In a further transposition, the minor version appears in the coda (unit 36). Units 39 and 40 are the closing music of the movement; unit 39 is a truncated form of unit 1 (first five notes only), while unit 40 is inflected to convey a broad cadential feel by the incorporation of 3 bars of 6/4 harmony found in no other model 1c unit. Unit 40 also has an extra cadential tag in its last 2 bars that performs a confirmatory function comparable to that of the 5-bar cadential reiterations of model 1b units 15 and 34 (example 5.19). The two remaining units of this model, 2 and 27, are expansions of 1. Unit 2 begins in the manner of unit 1, only in a lower register, but delays the drive to the cadence by pausing on a subdominant-functioning chord for the first violin to do cadenza work. An even bigger expansion occurs in unit 27, the period that

Example 5.21. Model 1c units.

opens the recapitulation. Beginning as in unit 1, unit 27 closes deceptively after 10 bars and is then subject to a subdominant-tinged internal expansion (bars 168 to roughly 176), before attaining a broad cadence (bars 183–188). Note especially the rising bass line beginning in bar 169, which starts out diatonically (in the orbit of G major) and finishes chromatically (in the orbit of D major). This is early Beethoven at his most organic, postponing the cadence for as long as possible and expanding the phrase from the middle.

The fourth and last variant of model 1 shares with 1a, 1b, and 1c a closed harmonic progression featuring an expanded cadence (example 5.22 establishes its origins, while example 5.23 displays its six units). Model 1d, however, incorporates many more chromatic elements. Thematically, its material is in the galant sphere, not the alla breve. Notice that the relative sense of autonomy enshrined in the earlier models—the closed nature of the building block, which in turn confers an additive feeling on the succession of units—is undermined, but not entirely erased, by the overlap between each unit and its immediate successor; this also subtracts from the impression of closure within each unit. Indeed, the mobility of model 1d units contributes not a little to the movement's organicism.

Example 5.22. Origins of model 1d units.

Example 5.23. Model 1d units.

The most disguised of the units in example 5.23 is unit 8, a Sturm und Drang passage within the second key area. In example 5.24, I read it as a I–V–I progression, the opening I being minor, its closing counterpart being in major, and the long dominant being prolonged by a German sixth chord. Harmonically, example 5.24 is plausible, but it is the rhetorically marked threefold repetition of the augmented sixth-to-dominant progression that contributes to the disguise. Note, also, that in the second half of unit 8, the treble arpeggiates up a minor seventh before beginning its descent to the tonic. The association with the opening of unit 1 (model 1c) is thus reinforced.

Example 5.24. Origins of model 1d, unit 8.

$$\text{I} \qquad \text{Ger6}^{\text{II}} \qquad \text{V} \qquad \text{I}$$

In an important sense, all of the units gathered under models 1a, 1b, 1c, and 1d do more or less the same harmonic—but not tonal—work. A certain degree of redundancy results, and this in turn contributes a feeling of circularity to the formal process. It is as if these 26 units, which comprise 196 out of a total 269 bars (72.86% of the movement) offer a consistent succession of small worlds. The process is additive and circular. The self-containment and potential autonomy of the building blocks counters the normative goal-oriented dynamic of the sonata form.

Models 2 and 3 express I–V and V–I progressions, respectively (see the abstracts in examples 5.25 and 5.28). These progressions are not syntactically defective; rather, they are notionally incomplete. Playing through the model 2 units displayed in example 5.26 immediately makes evident a progression from a local tonic to its dominant (units 10, 11, 29, 30, 37, 26), or from a local tonic to a nontonic "other" (units 9 and 28). Unit 10, which heads model 2 units, is a 4-bar antecedent phrase—a question that might have been answered by a 4-bar consequent. The "answer," however, is a transposition of this same unit from C major into its relative minor, A minor. Thus, unit 11 simultaneously embodies contradictory qualities of question and answer at different levels of structure. Units 29 and 30 replay this drama exactly, now in F major and D minor, respectively, while unit 37, initiator of the coda, is answered by a unit that belongs to model 3 (unit 38).

Example 5.25. Origins of model 2 units.

$$\text{I} \qquad \text{V} \qquad \text{I} \text{———} \text{V}$$

Other model 2 units are only tenuously related to the model. Unit 26, for example, whose abstract is given as example 5.27, is the striking passage at the end of the development that closes on a C-sharp major chord (where C-sharp functions as V of F-sharp minor); it marks the point of furthest remove. Although it is shown as a I–V progression, its beginning (bars 147–148) is less strongly articulated as a phrase-structural beginning and more a part of an already unfolding process. Nevertheless, it is possible to extract a I–V progression from it, the V prolonged by an augmented-sixth chord. Units 9 and 28 are I–V progressions only in a metaphorical sense; essentially, they both resist synopsis. Unit 9 begins in a stable A major with a bass arpeggiation that dissipates its dominant-seventh over 4 bars and then,

Example 5.26. Model 2 units.

Example 5.27. Origins of model 2, unit 26.

by means of chromatic voice leading, enharmonic substitution, and common-tone linkage, reaches the dominant-seventh of C major. Similarly, the transpositionally equivalent unit 28 moves from D major to the dominant of F major. When I say that these passages resist synopsis, I mean that they resist a prolongational explanation. Each step in the progression is necessary. It is as if the narrator stepped forward to announce the destination of the story, rather than letting it unfold according to its own principles. The seams of Beethoven's craft show in these moments; we are reminded of a speaking subject. (Note, incidentally, that evidence for narrativity in Beethoven is typically lodged in transitional sections, where the utterance is often prose-like, as in units 9 and 28, rather than stanzaic or poetic.)

The third and last of our models reverses the process in model 2, progressing from V (sometimes preceded by a predominant sonority) to I. The conceptual origins displayed in example 5.28 show a passing seventh over a dominant and a chromaticization of that motion. Stated so abstractly, the process sounds straightforward enough, but listening to the transpositionally equivalent units 16 and 35, for example (included in the display of model 3 units in example 5.29), suggests that the effect may sometimes be complex. An underlying V–I progression is hearable in retrospect, but because the individual chords sound one per bar, followed in each case by loud rests, the listener's ability to subsume the entire succession under a single prolongational span becomes difficult. Ratner refers to "a series of peremptory, disembodied chords, a play of cut against flow. These chords represent total disorientation."[18] This may be slightly overstated, but he is surely right to draw attention to their effect. Unit 23 features a normative predominant-dominant-tonic progression in A minor, which becomes the model for a sequence encompassing units 24 and 25. The latter two feature 2 and 3 bars of predominant activity, before closing on a B minor and an F-sharp minor chord, respectively.

To summarize: the first movement of op. 18, no. 3, is made from a number of simple two-voice progressions common in the eighteenth century and embodying the basic utterances of the tonal system. By our segmentation, there are essentially three of these models: I–V–I, I–V, and V–I. For the complete I–V–I progression, we identified four variants: model 1a with seven units, model 1b with six units, model 1c with 7 units, and model 1d with six units. For the open or I–V model 2, we identified eight units, while the closing but not closed V–I model 3 has six units. We have thus heard the entire first movement of op. 18, no. 3; there are no remainders. We have heard it, however, not in Beethoven's temporal or real-time order but in a new conceptual order.

If we refer back to example 5.15, we see the succession of models at a glance and some of the patterns formed by the 40 units. I have also indicated affinities with the sonata form in order to facilitate an assessment of the relationship between the paradigmatic process conveyed by repetition and the linear or syntagmatic process implicit in the sonata form's normative narrative. These data can be interpreted in different ways. For example, model 1c, the main alla breve material,

Example 5.28. Origins of model 3 units.

18. Ratner, *The Beethoven String Quartets*, 50.

Example 5.29. Model 3 units.

begins and ends the movement and also marks the onset of both the development and the recapitulation. It acts as a fulcrum; its sevenfold occurrence may even be read as gesturing toward rondo form. Unit 1a, the little bourrée tune, occurs only in clusters (5, 6, 7 and 19, 20, 21, 22). In this, it resembles unit 2, the opening out I–V progression. Unit 1b, the alla breve in stretto, is totally absent from the development section. Model 3, an expanded cadence, functions like 1c in that it occurs roughly equidistantly in the exposition, development, and recapitulation. On another level, one could argue that the essential procedure of the movement is that of variation since, in a deep sense, models 1a, 1b, 1c, and 1d are variants of the same basic harmonic-contrapuntal progression. This is not a theme and variations in the sense in which a profiled theme provides the basis for thematic, harmonic, modal, and figurative exploration. Rather, variation technique is used within the more evident sonata-form process. Obviously, then, the paradigmatic analysis can support several different narratives.

Melodic Discourse in Brahms' "Die Mainacht" (May Night), op. 43, no. 2

Although the monophonic version of "God Save the King" with which we introduced certain basic principles of paradigmatic analysis seems worlds removed from Brahms' "Die Mainacht," our whimsical four-part harmonization in the manner of Brahms (example 5.8) provided an indication of the challenges to such analysis brought on by enriched harmony. Brahms' magnificent 1866 song on a text by Ludwig Heinrich Christoph Hölty is so richly textured, laced with gorgeous harmonies, and endowed at the phrase level with a deep sense of organic growth that one may not think it a natural place to extend the kind of paradigmatic thinking that we have been exploring in this chapter. And in one sense, given the emphasis in the following (necessarily selective) analysis on the melodic fabric, the challenge of developing a comprehensive paradigmatic account remains. We can nonetheless invoke the spirit of paradigmatic analysis to illuminate Brahms' melodic impetus and the resultant organic growth of musical phrases. In what follows, the aim is not to exemplify the paradigmatic method—as in the earlier discussion of "God Save the King"—but to show Brahms in an engaged variation mode and to admire his ability to recast ideas imaginatively. Thinking in terms of precedents and subsequent transformations is a good way of conveying this aspect of the composer's technique.

Hölty's poem is an evocative nature portrait. Although the protagonist, in his reflective state, ultimately unveils a need for meaningful companionship, the path to expressing this need embraces an imaginary dialogue with nature's many gifts: basking in moonlight on grass, hearing a nightingale's song, envying the nightingale's marital bliss (Brahms did not set this stanza, the second of four that Hölty wrote), and admiring the play of doves. These are contrasted with the tears of one who remains lonely. The warm key of E-flat major, the slow arpeggio figuration, the modal interchanges, the carefully placed high points, and an overall quiet intensity of expression (triplet textures, pedal points, hidden melodies)—all of these combine to create a powerful setting.[19]

At the largest level, the message of "Die Mainacht" is delivered in three strophes, bars 1–14 (beginning in E-flat major, pausing on G-flat major, and ending on

19. See Walter Frisch, *Brahms and the Principle of Developing Variation* (Berkeley: University of California Press, 1982), 105–109, for a study of "Die Mainacht" as an exemplar of techniques of developing variation.

the dominant of E-flat minor), 15–32 (beginning in B major as the enharmonic equivalent of C-flat, tonicizing A-flat minor [or G-sharp], and returning to E-flat, first minor then major), and 33–51 (in E-flat major, with inflections of V, vi, iv, and most strikingly, flat-ii). Because these are roughly comparable in bar length—14, 18, and 19 bars, respectively—the strophic sense is immediately conveyed. At the same time, the song features significant processes of expansion and recomposition. It would be more accurate then to describe it as a *modified strophic* song. The point to bear in mind is that, for Brahms (as for Mozart), the strophic impulse is foundational, extending in range from relatively strict hymn-like settings and folk-song arrangements to relatively free songs and instrumental movements with a phraseology which repeats—but not always exactly.

Strophic periodicity is signified at the beginnings and endings of each of the three verses. At the outset, the pianist's 2-bar melody (example 5.30), one of the two main motifs in the song, is gratefully received by the singer and rendered vocally as "Wann der silberne Mond." Strophe 2 begins (in bar 15) with a transposed variant of this motif while strophe 3 (beginning in bar 33) returns to the sung opening of strophe 1. These three beginnings are thus identical on one level but collectively dynamic insofar as they describe a statement-departure-restatement trajectory.

Example 5.30. Opening motif of Brahms, "Die Mainacht."

Strophe endings are less straightforward and altogether more interesting. Strophe 1 ends in E-flat minor, the modal opposite of the E-flat major that began the song and a direct correlative of the change in sentiment from basking in nature to admitting sadness. Brahms distributes the elements of closure so as to create a wonderfully fluid ending which doubles in function as interlude (a pause for the singer to take a breath and for the listener to reflect just a little on the message of this unfolding tone poem) and as prelude to the next strophe. The singer's $\flat\hat{3}$–$\hat{2}$–$\hat{1}$ (bars 12–13) sounds over a dominant pedal, so the downbeat of bar 13 attains melodic closure but limited harmonic closure; the actual harmonic cadence comes a bar later (in the second half of bar 14). This displacement is possible in part because bars 13–14 replay 1–2, only now in a modal transformation and with a more decisive ending. In this way, the work of closing is achieved even as Brahms lets the piano announce a new beginning by using the familiar material of the song's inaugural motif.

Closure in strophe 2 is achieved in the wake of a melodramatic high point on *Träne* (tears; bars 29–30). The singer stops on scale-degree 5 (E-flat in bar 31), leaving the pianist to complete the utterance by domesticating the 6/4 into a conventional cadential group. The 6/4 chord in bar 31 is duly followed by a dominant-seventh in 32, complete with a 4/3 suspension, but the expected tonic resolution is withheld. Unlike the close at the end of strophe 1 (bars 12–14), this one has a heightened indexical quality, pointing irresistibly to the beginning of another strophe.

The last of our closings also functions globally for the song as a whole; not surprisingly, it is also the most elaborate of the three. The phrase containing the previous high point on *Träne* (27–31) is repeated (as 39–43) and is immediately superseded by a rhetorically more potent high point on the repeated word *heisser* in bar 45, an F-flat chord that functions as a Neapolitan in the key of E-flat major. And, as in strophe 1, but this time more deliberately, the singer's closing line descends to the tonic (bars 47–48), achieving both harmonic and melodic closure on the downbeat of bar 48. We are assured that this is indeed the global close. Now, the motif that opened the work rises from the piano part (bar 48) through two octaves, ending on a high G in the last bar. The effect of this twofold statement of the motif is itself twofold. First, the motif here sounds like an echo, a remembered song. Second, in traversing such a vast registral expanse in these closing 4 bars, the motif may be heard echoing the active (vocal) registers of the song. Since, however, it reaches a pitch that the voice never managed to attain (the singer got as far as F-flat in bars 21–22 and again in 45), this postlude may also be heard carrying on and concluding the singer's business by placing its destination in the beyond, a realm in which meaning is pure, direct, and secure because it lacks the worldliness of words. As always with Brahms, then, there is nothing perfunctory about the pianist's last word.

The fact that the B♭–E♭–F–G motif was heard at the beginning of the song, again in the middle, and finally at both the beginning and the end of the ending, fosters an association among beginnings, middles, and endings and suggests a circularity in the formal process. It would not be entirely accurate to describe the form of "Die Mainacht" as circular, however. More accurate would be to hear competing tendencies in Brahms' material. Strophic song normatively acquires its dynamic sense from the force of repetition, which is negotiated differently by different listeners and performers. Strophic song is ultimately a paradoxical experience, for the repetition of strophes confers a static quality insofar as it denies the possibility of change. Some listeners deal with this denial by adopting a teleological mindset and latching on to whatever narratives the song text makes possible. A modified strophic form, on the other hand, speaks to the complexity of strophic form by undercomplicating it, building into it a more obvious dynamic process. In "Die Mainacht," the high-point scheme allows the imposition of such a narrative curve: D-flat in strophe 1, first F-flat and then—more properly—E-flat in strophe 2, and a frontal F-flat in strophe 3.

I have strayed, of course, into the poetics of song by speculating on the meanings made possible through repetition and strophic organization. Without forcing the point, I hope nevertheless that some of this digression will have reinforced a point made earlier, namely, that there is a natural affinity between ordinary music analysis and so-called paradigmatic analysis insofar as both are concerned on some primal level with the repetition, variation, or affinity among units. Still, there is much more to discover about the song from a detailed study of its melodic content. Let us see how a more explicitly paradigmatic approach can illuminate the melodic discourse of "Die Mainacht."

Example 5.31 sets out the melodic content of the entire song in 20 segments (see the circled units), each belonging to one of two paradigms, A and B. Example 5.32

then rearranges the contents of 5.31 to make explicit some of the derivations and, in the process, to convey a sense of the relative distance between variants. Example 5.33 summarizes the two main generative ideas in two columns, A and B, making it possible to see at a glance the distribution of the song's units. One clarification is necessary: the mode of relating material in example 5.32 is internally referential. That is, the generating motifs are in the piece, not abstractions based on underlying contrapuntal models originating outside the work. (The contrast with the Beethoven analysis is noteworthy in this regard.) We are concerned entirely with relations between segments. To say this is not, of course, to deny that some notion of abstraction enters into the relating of segments. As always with these charts, the story told is implicit, so these supplementary remarks will be necessarily brief.

Example 5.31. Melodic content of "Die Mainacht" arranged paradigmatically.

From the outset, Brahms presents a melodic line that has two separate and fundamental segments. It is these that have determined our paradigms. The first, unit 1, the originator of paradigm A units, encompasses the first bar and a half of the vocal part, itself based on the pianist's humming in bars 1–2. This overall ascending melody, rising from the depths, so to speak, carries a sense of hope (as

Example 5.32. Motivic affiliation in "Die Mainacht."

(continued)

Deryck Cooke might say). Although the associated harmony makes it a closed unit, the ending on a poetic third (scale-degree 3) slightly undermines its sense of closure.

The second or oppositional segment, unit 2 (bars 4–5), the originator of paradigm B units, outlines a contrasting descending contour, carrying as well a sense of resolution. Just as the inaugural unit (1) of paradigm A went up (B♭–E♭–F) and then redoubled its efforts to reach its goal (E♭–F–G), so paradigm B's leading unit (2) goes down (B♭–A♭–G) before redoubling its efforts (B♭–G–E♭) to reach its goal. Each gesture is thus twofold, the second initiating the redoubling earlier than the first.

It could be argued on a yet more abstract level that paradigms A and B units are variants of each other, or that the initiator of paradigm B (unit 2) is a transformation of the initiator of paradigm A (unit 1). Both carry a sense of closure on their deepest levels, although the stepwise rise at the end of unit 1 complicates its sense of ending, just as the triadic descent at the end of unit 2 refuses the most conventionally satisfying mode of melodic closure. Their background unity, however, makes it possible to argue that the entire song springs from a single seed.

Example 5.32. continued

Indeed, this is a highly organic song, as I have remarked and as will be seen in the discussion that follows, and this view is supported by a remark of Brahms' concerning his way of composing. In a statement recorded by Georg Henschel, Brahms refers specifically to the opening of "Die Mainacht." According to him, having discovered this initial idea (unit 1 in 5.30), he could let the song sit for months before returning to it, the implication being that retrieving it was tantamount to retrieving its potential, which was already inscribed in the myriad variants that the original made possible:

Example 5.32. continued

There is no real creating without hard work. That which you would call invention, that is to say, a thought, an idea, is simply an inspiration from above, for which I am not responsible, which is no merit of mine. Yes, it is a present, a gift, which I ought even to despise until I have made it my own by right of hard work. And there need be no hurry about that, either. It is as with the seed-corn; it germinates unconsciously and in spite of ourselves. When I, for instance, have found the first phrase of a song, say [he cites the opening phrase of "Die Mainacht"], I might shut the book there and then go for a walk, do some other work, and perhaps not think of it again for months. Nothing, however, is lost. If afterward I approach the subject again, it is sure to have taken shape: I can now begin to really work it.[20]

And so, from the horse's own mouth, we have testimony that justifies the study of melodic progeny, organicism, and, implicitly, the paradigmatic method.

Let us continue with our analysis, referring to example 5.32 and starting with paradigm A units. The piano melody carries implicitly the rhythmically differentiated unit 1. Unit 3 is a transposition of 1, but what should have been an initial C is replaced by a repeated F. Unit 5, too, grows out of 1, but in a more complex way, as shown. It retains the rhythm and overall contour of units 1 and 3 but introduces a modal change (C-flat and D-flat replace C and D) to effect a tonicization of the third-related G-flat major. Unit 7 begins as a direct transposition of 1 but changes course in its last three notes and descends in the manner of paradigm B units. (At

20. George Henschel, *Personal Recollections of Johannes Brahms* (New York: AMS, 1978; orig. 1907), 111.

a more detailed level of analysis, we hear the combination of both paradigm A and B gestures in unit 7.) Unit 9 resembles 7, especially because of the near-identity of the rhythm and the initial leap, although the interval of a fourth in unit 7 is augmented to a fifth in unit 9. But there is no doubting the family resemblance. Unit 12, the approach to the first high point, retains the ascending manner of paradigm A but proceeds by step, in effect, filling in the initial fourth of unit 1, Bb–Eb. Units 14 and 16, which open the third strophe, are more or less identical to 1 and 3, while 18 is identical to 12. This completes the activity within paradigm A.

The degree of recomposition in paradigm B is a little more extensive but not so as to obscure the relations among segments. Unit 4 avoids a literal transposition of 2, as shown; in the process, it introduces a stepwise descent after the initial descent of a third. The next derivation suggests that, while reproducing the overall manner of units 2 and 1, unit 6 extends the durational and intervallic span of its predecessors. Unit 8 follows 1 quite closely, compressing the overall descent and incorporating the dotted rhythm introduced in unit 4. Unit 10 resembles 8 in terms of rhythm and the concluding descent; even the dramatic diminished-seventh in its second bar can be imagined as a continuation of the thirds initiated in unit 2. Unit 10 may also be heard as incorporating something of the manner of paradigm A, specifically, the stepwise ascent to the F-flat, which is inflected and transposed from the last three notes of unit 1.

Unit 11 fills in the gaps in unit 2 (in the manner of units 4 and 6) but introduces another gap of its own at the end. Unit 13 is based on unit 4, but incorporates a key pitch, B-flat, from unit 2. Units 15 and 17 are nearly identical to 2 and 4, but for tiny rhythmic changes. Unit 19, the fallout from the climactic unit 18, is derived from 13. Finally, unit 20 magnifies the processes in 19, extending the initial descending arpeggio and following that with a descending stepwise line that brings the melodic discourse to a full close.

Example 5.33 summarizes the affiliations of the units in "Die Mainacht." The basic duality of the song is evident in the two columns, A and B. The almost

Example 5.33. Summary of motivic affiliation in "Die Mainacht."

	Column A units	Column B units
	1	2
Strophe 1	3	4
	5	6
	7	8
	9	10
Strophe 2		11
	12	13
	14	15
Strophe 3	16	17
	18	19
		20

strict alternation between A units and B units is also noteworthy. Only twice is the pattern broken—once in the succession of units 10 and 11 (although the affiliation between unit 10 and paradigm A units should discourage us from making too much of this exception) and once at the very end of the song, where the closing quality of paradigm B units is reinforced by the juxtaposition of units 19 and 20.

Again, I do not claim that Brahms prepared analytical charts like the ones that I have been discussing and then composed "Die Mainacht" from them. The challenge of establishing the precise moments in which a composer conceived an idea and when he inscribed that idea—the challenge, in effect, of establishing a strict chronology of the compositional process, one that would record both the written and the unwritten texts that, together, resulted in the creation of the work—should discourage us from venturing in that direction. I claim only that the relations among the work's units—some clear and explicit, others less clear—speak to a fertile, ever-present instinct in Brahms to repeat and vary musical ideas and that a paradigmatic display of the outcome can be illuminating. While it is possible to recast the foregoing analysis into a more abstract framework that can lead to the discovery of the unique system of a work, this will take me too far afield. I will return to Brahms in a subsequent chapter to admire other aspects of this economy of relations in his work.

Conclusion

My aim in this chapter has been to introduce the paradigmatic method and to exemplify the workings of a paradigmatic impulse in different stylistic milieus. I began with "God Save the King" and explored questions of repetition, identity, sameness, and difference, as well as harmonic continuity and discontinuity. I then took up, in turn, discontinuity and form in a Mozart sonata movement, chronological versus logical form in a Chopin prelude, tonal models in a Beethoven quartet movement, and melodic discourse in a Brahms song. While I believe that these analyses have usefully served their purpose, I hasten to add that there is more to the paradigmatic method than what has been presented here. In particular—and reflecting some doubt on my part about their practical utility—I have overlooked some of the abstract aspects of the method, for despite the intellectual arguments that could be made in justification (including some made in these very pages), I have not succeeded in overcoming the desire to stay close to the hearable aspects of music. Thus, certain abstract or "on paper" relations that might be unveiled in the Brahms song were overlooked. Similarly, the idea that each work is a unique system and that a paradigmatic analysis, pursued to its logical end, can unveil the particular and unique system of a work has not been pursued here. For me, there is something radically contingent about the creation of tonal works, especially in historical periods when a common musical "language" is "spoken" by many. The idea that a unique system undergirds each of Chopin's preludes, or each of the movements of Beethoven's string quartets, or every one of Brahms' songs, states an uninspiring truth about artworks while chipping away at the communal origins of musical works. But I hope that the retreat from this kind of paper rigor has been compensated for by the redirecting of attention to the living sound.

I hope also to have shown that, the existence of different analytical plots notwithstanding, the dividing lines between the various approaches pursued in the first part of this book are not firm but often porous, not fixed but flexible. Professionalism encourages us to put our eggs in one basket, and the desire to be rigorous compels us to set limits. But even after we have satisfied these (institutionally motivated) intellectual desires, we remain starkly aware of what remains, of the partiality of our achievements, of gaps between an aspect of music that we claim to have illuminated by our specialized method and the more complex and larger totality of lived musical experience.

PART II

Analyses

CHAPTER $\overset{\circ}{\mathrm{S}}\mathrm{ix}$

Liszt, *Orpheus* (1853–1854)

Although the shadows cast by words and images lie at the core of Liszt's musical imagination, his will to illustration, translation, or even suggestion rarely trumped the will to musical sense making. For example, in rendering the Orpheus myth as a symphonic poem or, rather, in accommodating a representation of the myth in symphonic form, Liszt's way bears traces of the work's poetic origins, but never is the underlying musical logic incoherent or syntactically problematic. But what exactly is the nature of that logic, that formal succession of ideas that enacts the discourse we know as Liszt's *Orpheus*? It is here that a semiotic or paradigmatic approach can prove revealing. By strategically disinheriting a conventional formal template, a semiotic analysis forces us to contemplate freshly the logic of sounding forms in *Orpheus*. The idea is not to rid ourselves of any and all expectations—that would be impossible, of course. The idea, rather, is to be open-minded about the work's potential formal course. Accordingly, I will follow the lead of the previous chapter by first identifying the work's building blocks one after another. Later, I will comment on the discourse of form and meaning that this particular disposition of blocks makes possible.[1]

Building Blocks

Unit 1 (bars 1–7)

A lone G breaks the silence. There are too many implications here to make active speculation meaningful. We wait. We defer entirely to the composer's will. Then, the harp (our mythical hero) enters with an arpeggiation of an E-flat major chord.

---

1. In preparing this analysis, I found it convenient to consult a solo piano transcription of *Orpheus* made by Liszt's student Friedrich Spiro and apparently revised by the composer himself. The transcription was published in 1879. For details of orchestration, one should of course consult the full score. Students should note that the numbering of bars in the Eulenberg score published in 1950 is incorrect. Orpheus has a total of 225 bars, not 245 as in the Eulenberg score.

These sounds seem to emanate from another world. The harp chord rationalizes the repeated Gs: they are the third of the chord, a chord disposed in an unstable second inversion. But the functional impulse remains to be activated. Indeed, nothing is formed here. All is atmosphere and potentiality.

Unit 2 (bars 8–14)

The lone G sounds again, repeated from bars 1–3. This repetition invites speculation. Will the G be absorbed into an E-flat major chord as before, or will it find a new home? We wait, but with a more active expectancy. The chord that rationalizes G is now an A7, duly delivered by the harp. Now G functions as a dissonant seventh. Our head tone has gone from being relatively stable to being relatively unstable. What might its fate be? If the harp chords mean more to us than space-opening gestures, we will wonder whether they are related. Although linked by a common G (the only common pitch between the successive three-note and four-note chords), the distance traveled in tonal terms is considerable. The chords lie a tritone apart; in conventional terms, this is the furthest one can travel along the circle of fifths (assuming this to be the normative regulating construct even in the 1850s). Between the sound of this *diabolus in musica*, the otherworldly timbre of the harp, and the ominous knocking represented by the two Gs, we may well feel ourselves drawn into supernatural surroundings.

Unit 3 (bars 15–20)

With this third, fateful knock on the door, we are led to expect some direction, some clarity, though not necessarily closure. Conventional gestural rhetoric recommends three as an upper limit. The first knock is the inaugural term; it is given and must be accepted. The second reiterates the idea of the first; by refusing change, it suggests a pattern, but withholds confirmation of what the succession means. Finally, the third unveils the true meaning of the repetition; it confirms the intention and assures us that we did not mis-hear. (A fourth knock would risk redundancy and excess.) Clarity at last emerges in the form of a melodic idea. This will be the main theme led by the note G. We now understand that the protagonist was attempting to speak but kept getting interrupted. The theme is closed, descending to $\hat{1}$ and sporting a cadential progression from I6. A relatively short phrase (5 bars in length), its manner suggests an incremental or additive modus operandi. We also begin to make sense of the tonal logic: E-flat and A lie equidistant on either side of the main key (C); in effect, they enclose it. The main key is thus framed tritonally although the approach to it is somewhat oblique. A certain amount of insecurity underpins this initial expression of C major.

Unit 4 (bars 21–26)

Since the beginnings of the previous unit and this one share the same chord albeit in different positions (unit 3 opens with the C-seventh chord in 6/5 position, while unit 4 begins with the chord in 4/2 position), we might wonder whether this unit is going to be a consequent, a repetition, or some mixture of both. The thematic substance is similar, but unit 4 ends by tonicizing G as dominant, whereas 3 ended with an authentic cadence in C. Thus, the I–V relationship between units 3 and 4 offers a new, more conventional tonal premise to counterbalance the symmetrical E♭–A relationship expressed by units 1 and 2. The pairing of units 3 and 4 and the absence of fermatas over rests ushers in a more continuous mode of articulation, suggesting that the main business may have finally begun. We might say with Adorno that we are fully "conscious of the time [that *Orpheus*] consumes" so far because we recognize and hear more and thus are caught up in the unfolding rhetoric rather than observing it from a distance.[2]

Unit 5 (bars 27–31)

This is a repeat of unit 3, with a change in register (the melody migrates up) and slight but telling modifications of local harmony in the first 2 bars.

Unit 6 (bars 32–37)

This is a repeat of unit 4, with minor changes. Repetition of the 3–4 pair as 5–6 enhances the sense of a larger emerging periodicity.

Unit 7 (bars 38–41)

Alas, the sense of a larger periodicity is not sustained. If we thought that we were going to be treated to a dialectical symphonic argument, we now have to think again. On offer here is an ensemble of effects and images disposed in an accumulative logic. The new unit, marked *un poco marcato*, contains two little phrases, both expressing prominent neighbor-note motion in the bass (B–A–B in bars 38–39 and B–C–B in bars 40–41). The latter, more chromatic phrase will be put to considerable use as a continuation figure. Because these two motives melodically prolong G, one might hear a larger connection between unit 7 and units 1, 2, and 3. In units 1 and 2, the G was absorbed into a tritone-related pair of chords; in unit 3, G led the melody. Here in unit 7, G first stalls as a point of melodic focus and then gives a hint of what it could do chromatically if offered the opportunity.

Unit 8 (bars 41–44)

This is a repetition of unit 7, with which it overlaps. A small but striking change of harmony is introduced in the second half of bar 43 to prepare the new harmony at the beginning of unit 9. The rhythm of Liszt's rhetoric seems now to take on the character of briefer utterances. This affects the dynamic of the symphonic poem directly. In other contexts, we might predict development or transition; here, however, we settle for a simulation of those functions.

2. Theodor Adorno, *Essays on Music*, ed. Richard Leppert (Berkeley: University of California Press, 2002), 255.

Unit 9 (bars 44–47)

This is a transposition up a minor third of unit 7 from C major to E-flat major. Such direct elevation intensifies the dynamic, of course, but because the transposition is real rather than tonal, it undermines our sense of a synoptic progression. In any case, we sense that we are reaching for a more stable moment, although there is no way to predict the material contours of that moment. The compositional persona remains in charge.

Unit 10 (bars 47–54)

This unit begins as an exact repetition of unit 9 and then extends the chromatic idea sequentially, incorporating a quasi-canonical inflection of the texture (from bar 51) as it approaches a half-cadence in C (bars 53–54). This is the most decisive articulation since the conclusion of unit 6 in bar 37. In terms of an overall structural rhythm, units 7–10 display an acceleration, and this produces an intensifying effect. Note how the cadence in bars 53–54 literally harnesses the music back to C. We have apparently not heard the last expressions of will by the "characters" in units 7–10.

Unit 11 (bars 55–58)

This is the same as 7.

Unit 12 (bars 58–61)

This is the same as 8.

Unit 13 (bars 61–64)

This repeats the material in 9.

Unit 14 (bars 64–72)

This is the same as 10, with a modification of the chromatic extension to lead to a new, lyrical idea. The extensive sameness recognized here confirms the essential function of units 7–14 while pointing to a larger periodicity. Let us take stock. After the introductory, speech-mode gestures of units 1 and 2, the main theme enters in song mode as 3 and 4 and is repeated immediately as 5 and 6. Then, a stuttering new idea—promising song, but trapped in speech mode—leads the way as unit 7. The large-scale repetition of units 7–10 as 11–14 reinforces the additive mode of formal construction. It is possible to interpret a still larger grouping, but the atomistic phrase procedures seem to convey the essential character of Liszt's rhetoric.

Unit 15 (bars 72–78)

The beginning of this unit marks the biggest contrast we have heard so far. The material is new: an intensely lyrical idea, more continuous than anything we have heard up until now. Although parsed in 2-bar segments, a broader trajectory emerges from the gradual rise of the melody (G-sharp, C-sharp, and F-sharp on the downbeats of bars 72, 74, and 76, respectively) and the compelling joins between bars 73–74 and 75–76. Several factors combine to signify a new beginning in bar 72. First, there is a change of key from C major to E major (Liszt in fact inserts the new key signature); second, the lyrical idea is built initially on an E pedal lasting 6 bars, and although the effect of stasis is offset by a sinuous inner-voice chromatic progression, the ground as such does not shift, only the superstructure quivers; third, the English horn and clarinet timbres provide a new lead; and finally, the melody proceeds in a strategically unhurried manner, promising a longer period than anything we have heard so far. (Note that these qualities are not invariant markers of beginning as such; indeed, they could just as easily be put to use as markers of ending. The sense of bar 72 as beginning is thus partly contextual.)

Unit 16 (bars 78–82)

After reaching a peak on G-sharp (bar 78), the melody initiates a broad and deliberate move toward a cadence. In a hearing that is more retrospective than prospective, units 16 and 17 together combine to form a cadential group. (They are kept separate here because, as we will see, the latter unit occurs later in the piece without the former.)

Unit 17 (bars 82–84)

The expected cadential moment finally arrives. Laced with appoggiaturas, the melody, beginning on a high G-sharp (as in unit 16), eventually finishes on a low C-sharp. And the harmony effects a broad V–I progression not in E major as indicated in unit 15, but in the relative minor, C-sharp. This is by far the strongest cadential articulation we have experienced in the piece so far. The fact that it occurs away from the home key says absolutely nothing about the relationship between C major (the "first key area") and E major (the presumed "second key area"); indeed, Liszt's manner mimics classical rhetoric in accenting (what will turn out to be) a subsidiary key.

Unit 18 (bars 84–86)

Marked *dolce espressivo*, this new idea effects the manner of a conventional closing section; there is a sense of codetta, complete with an echo quality. And the high placement of the solo violin utterance further underlines the precious nature of the moment. Unit 18 confirms the previous cadence on C-sharp minor by means of an ingenious modal succession, whereby minor is followed by major and then minor again, the middle term acquiring (by default) the quality of a dominant.

Melodically, the unit incorporates a prominent neighbor-note motion (G♯–A–G♯) reminiscent of unit 7, thus gaining a further retrospective quality.

Unit 19 (bars 86–88)

This unit begins as an exact repeat of 18, but alters the modal succession (bar 88 should have been minor, not major). Together with a repeat of the neighbor-note figure in bar 87 and a melodic bass, the alteration lends mobility to the end of this unit, thus erasing its previous sense of closure.

Unit 20 (bars 89–92)

The second of the two cadential phrases that sealed off the lyrical melody (unit 17) is heard here in transposition as part of a cadence in F minor. Units 17 and 20 are thus equivalent, although they differ in minor textural details.

Unit 21 (bars 92–94)

The codetta figure familiar from unit 18 now underlines the shift from C-sharp minor to F minor. Thus, units 17–18 are also transpositionally equivalent to 20–21.

Unit 22 (bars 94–97)

This is a repetition of the codetta figure as before, with a little appendix to usher in the increasingly familiar cadential phrase heard in units 17 and 20. This unit is equivalent to 19, extending the parallelism in the succession from two to three units: 17–18–19 is repeated in transposition as 20–21–22. We may speak not of a recapitulation but of a large-scale repetition implying a postponement of final resolution. If we were taking stock of the formal profile, we would conclude that the composer's means include a circular trajectory and an attendant permutation of thematic ideas.

Unit 23 (bars 97–100)

The seams of Liszt's patchwork are evident in the less than felicitous move from bar 97 (end of unit 22) to 98 (beginning of unit 23). This melody is a variant of the cadential figure we first heard as unit 17, but where that unit went from V to I harmonically, this one prolongs V. The V is the V of E, the key with which this (ostensibly) middle section began, complete with a continuous lyrical melody. One reason, perhaps, that this unit does not reach I (E major) is that it is not the last but the penultimate cadential gesture; it must stay open if the following unit is to serve a real rather than redundant function.

Unit 24 (bars 100–102)

This is a repeat of unit 23, modified to attain closure.

Unit 25 (bars 102–108)

We've heard this material before, of course. It is the big lyrical melody (unit 15) that provided the first major contrast in the work and that served also as the first grounded idea to be worked out over a period of time. Again, but for minor changes in orchestration, units 25 and 15 are the same. If we were inclined to read this unit as a recapitulation of sorts, we would be inconvenienced by the fact that it is heard here in the same key as before. Restatement, not recapitulation, is what Liszt offers. Apparently, nothing in the earlier dynamic necessitated tonal adjustment.

Unit 26 (bars 108–112)

The large-scale reprise continues: unit 26 is equivalent to 16, but a change toward its end effects continuation not in C-sharp minor as before but in G-sharp minor in the following unit. Again, the local logic of Liszt's tonal planning is evident: G-sharp lies a third above E while C-sharp lies a third below it. The third above is major, the third below is minor. These relations recall the tonal nexus of the work's beginning, where C, the main key, is approached by E-flat and A7 chords. Here, however, both C-sharp minor and G-sharp minor are tonicized. This enhances their role in defining the tonal shape of a work whose modes of articulation have so far not invested considerably in the normal dynamics of large-scale tonal drama.

Unit 27 (bars 112–114)

This unit is the equivalent of 17 (as well as 20 and, less exactly, 23 and 24).

Unit 28 (bars 114–116)

This is the equivalent of 18.

Unit 29 (bars 116–119)

This is equivalent to 19.

Unit 30 (bars 119–122)

This is equivalent to 20.

Unit 31 (bars 123–124)

This is equivalent to 21.

Unit 32 (bars 125–128)

This is equivalent to unit 22.

Unit 33 (bars 128–130)

This is equivalent to unit 23 from a formal point of view, although the actual melodic intervals are reminiscent of 20. Since 23 was itself based on 20, the affinities among them are readily grasped. Unit 33 promises but finally withholds a cadence in E minor. This long series of equivalences captures a large-scale repeat in the music: units 15–24 are heard again as 25–33. A number of internal repetitions obscure this large-scale repeat, however, and contribute something of a circular rather than linear feel.

Unit 34 (bars 130–133)

This is equivalent to unit 7, minor changes in scoring notwithstanding.

Unit 35 (bars 133–136)

This is the equivalent of unit 8.

Unit 36 (bars 136–139)

This is equivalent to unit 9.

Unit 37 (bars 139–144)

This is the equivalent of unit 10, but instead of ending with a half-cadence in C as before, it flows directly into a return of the main theme (unit 3) in unit 38.

Unit 38 (bars 144–149)

This unit marks the triumphant return of the main theme. It is equivalent to unit 3 (and also 5).

Unit 39 (bars 150–155)

This is equivalent to unit 4 (and also 6).

Unit 40 (bars 156–163)

This unit reiterates the chromatic idea from the second half of unit 7 (bars 39–40). It may therefore be heard as a modified version of unit 7.

Unit 41 (bars 164–180)

This is mostly a repetition (with variants in scoring) of the previous unit.

Unit 42 (bars 180–186)

This is an unexpected recapitulation of the first two two-measure phrases of the lyrical melody first exposed as unit 15. "Recapitulation" is appropriate here, for the key is now B major, not E major as before. The place of this large-scale transposition in the tonal logic of the work as a whole is not immediately obvious, however. Also, the beginning of the unit on a second inversion chord (bar 180) undercuts its articulative strength. The briefest of allusions to the codetta theme first heard as unit 18 is made toward the end of this unit (bars 184–185), while an equally brief allusion to the chromatic portion of unit 7 may be heard in bars 185–186.

Unit 43 (bars 186–194)

The lyrical theme from unit 15 (bar 72) is heard for the first time in the tonic key, C major, but this version lacks the pedal grounding of its initial appearance. As before, it proceeds at first in 2-bar units (186–187 and 188–189); then follow three 1-bar units (191, 192, and 193) based on the second of the 2-bar ideas. Finally, 2 bars of dominant lead to another triumphant return of the main theme, this one marked *fff*.

Unit 44 (bars 195–197)

This is the equivalent of unit 3 (and 5 and, most recently, 38).

Unit 45 (bars 197–200)

The main theme continues (the equivalent of unit 4), harmonically enriched with a chromatic patch.

Unit 46 (bars 200–206)

Lower strings develop the chromatic idea from unit 7. The effect is anticipatory, even while incorporating a reference to the main theme in bars 204–206.

Unit 47 (bars 206–208)

The codetta theme (first heard in unit 18) is played at a slower tempo and enveloped in melodramatic string tremolo.

Unit 48 (bars 208–210)

This is a repeat of the previous unit.

Unit 49 (bars 210–214)

This is also a repeat of the preceding unit. The note values are now in augmentation, and only the initial part of the motif is harmonized; the rest is heard alone, as if to mark a transition or a final dissolution and the eventual approach of silence.

Unit 50 (bars 214–225)

The most striking and magical contrast in the movement, this unit features a series of chords beginning on C and ending on C, laid out as one per bar, and descending in register. They bear no immediately obvious relation to what has come before. On reflection, however, they may be heard as a gloss on the enigmatic opening of the work (units 1 and 2). There, the E-flat and A7 chords were posed as questions—not logical questions to be answered by what would follow, but rhetorical questions broaching existential matters, perhaps. Those two chords are contained in this series (bars 217 and 215, respectively), although in reverse order from their earlier appearance; also, the A chord is now a regular triad, not a seventh chord as before. Our instinct is to read the passage programmatically, to imagine it coming from or leading to another world. There is little directed motion from here until the end, only a succession of colors. In terms of tonal syntax, unit 50, by beginning and ending on C and by ending with a resounding V7–I progression in 221–222, places us where we want to be, without offering a normative prolongation of C. The succession of chords is thus not meaningless, even though it resists a synoptic, hierarchic explanation.

Form

With this first pass through Liszt's *Orpheus*, I have identified its units or building blocks on the basis of repetition and equivalence. Each unit is more or less clearly demarcated, although some units overlap, and while the basis of associating some may change if other criteria are invoked, the segmentation given here confirms the intuition that *Orpheus* is an assembly of fragments. If we now ask what to do with our 50 units, we can answer at two levels. The first, more general level suggests a mode of utterance that is more speech-like than song-like. (There is no dance here, or at least no conventional dance, unless one counts the unpatterned movements that Orpheus's playing solicits.) As a rule, when units follow one another as predominantly separate units, they suggest speech mode; when they are connected, they are more likely to be in song mode. The speech-mode orientation in *Orpheus* betrays its conception as a symphonic poem, with obligations that originate outside the narrow sphere of musical aesthetics. Another way to put this is to suggest that the illustrative, narrative, or representational impetus—whichever it is—confers on the music a more language-like character.

At a more detailed level, the foregoing exercise conveys the form of *Orpheus* with clarity. Aligning the 50 units according to the criteria of equivalence adumbrated in the verbal description yields the design in figure 6.1.

The main difficulty with this kind of representation is that, by placing individual units in one column or another (and avoiding duplications), it denies

Figure 6.1 Paradigmatic chart of all 50 units of Liszt's *Orpheus*.

1							
2	3						
	4						
	5						
	6	7					
		8					
		9					
		10					
		11					
		12					
		13					
		14	15	16	17	18	
						19	
					20	21	
						22	
				23	24		
			25	26	27	28	
						29	
					30	31	
						32	
				33			
		34					
		35					
		36					
		37					
	38						
	39	40					
		41	42				
			43				
	44						
	45	46				47	
						48	
						49	50

affiliations with other units. But this is only a problem if one reads the material in a given unit as an unhierarchized network of affiliations. In that case, rhythmic, periodic, harmonic, or other bases for affiliating units will be given free rein, and each given unit will probably belong to several columns at once. But the arrangement is not a problem if we take a pragmatic approach and adopt a decisive view of the identities of units. In other words, if we proceed on the assumption that each unit has a dominating characteristic, then it is that characteristic that will determine the kinds of equivalences deemed to be pertinent. The less hierarchic approach seems to promote a more complex view of the profile of each given unit, thus expanding the network of affiliations that is possible among units. It runs the risk, however, of treating musical dimensions as if they were equally or at least comparably pertinent and therefore of underplaying the (perceptual or conceptual) significance of certain features. Yet, I believe that there is often an intuitive sense of what the contextually dominant element is, not only by virtue of the internal arrangement of musical elements, but on the basis of what precedes or follows a given unit and its resemblance to more conventional constructs.

As we have seen in similar analyses, several stories can be told about the paradigmatic arrangement made above. One might be based on a simple statistical measure. Three ideas occur more frequently than others. The first is the material based on unit 7, the neighboring figure expressed in a haunting, implicative rhythm, which registers 15 times in figure 6.1. On this basis, we may pronounce it the dominant idea of the movement. The second idea is the codetta-like figure first heard as unit 18; this occurs 11 times. Third is the main theme, heard initially as unit 3, and subsequently 7 more times. This frequency of occurrence reflects the number of hits on our paradigmatic chart. Had we chosen a different segmentation, we might have had different results. Note, further, that the frequency of appearance is not perfectly matched to the number of bars of music. Material based on unit 7 occupies 80 bars, that based on 18 only 27 bars, and that based on 3 equals 39 bars. If we now consider the character of each of these ideas, we note that the units based on 7 have an open, implicative quality, serving as preparations, middles, transitions, or simply as neutral, unsettled music. They are fragmentary in character and thus possess a functional mobility. This is the material that Liszt uses most extensively. Units based on the main theme occur half as much. The theme is closed, of course, although in the segmentation given here, closure is present at the end of each unit, thus missing out on the question-and-answer sense of pairs of units. For example, the very first succession, units 3–4, may be read not as question followed by answer but as answer followed by question. That is, 3 closes with a tonic cadence while 4 modulates to the dominant. Had we taken the 3–4 succession as an indivisible unit, we would have read the main theme as open. But by splitting it into two, we have two closed units, although closure in the second is valid on a local level and undermined on a larger one. The third most frequently heard idea carries a sense of closure. Even though it occupies only 27 bars, its presentation is marked in other ways. Then also, if we add its occurrences to those of the main theme, we have a total of 66 bars, which brings the material with an overall closing tendency closer to the 80-bar mark attained by material with an open tendency.

In whatever way we choose to play with these figures, we will always be rewarded with a view of the functional tendencies of Liszt's material. And it is these tendencies that should form the basis of any association of form. Of course, the simple statistical measure will have to be supplemented by other considerations, one of which is placement. The main theme, for example, is introduced early in the movement (units 3–6), disappears for a long while, and then returns toward the end (38–39 and 44–45). The animating idea introduced in unit 7 enters after the main theme has completed its initial work. It dominates a sizable portion of the continuation of the beginning (units 7–14) before being superseded. It returns to do some prolonging work before the main theme returns (34–37) and stays toward the close of the work (units 40–41 and 46). If the main theme is roughly associated with beginning and end, the animating theme functions within the middle and the end. The codetta theme (introduced as unit 18) dominates the middle of the work (units 18–19, 21–22, 28–29, and 31–32), lending a strong sense of epilogue to the middle section. It returns toward the very end of the movement (units 47–49) to confer a similar sense of closure now—appropriately—upon the work's end.

The closing unit, 50, also invites different kinds of interpretation. The novelty of its chords places it immediately in a different column. By this reading, the ending is entirely without precedent or affiliation. But I have pointed to a sense of affiliation between unit 50, on the one hand, and units 1 and 2, on the other. By the lights of this alternative reading, unit 50 may be placed in the column containing units 1 and 2, so that the work ends where it began. This particular affiliation would be the loosest of all, and yet it is supportable from a gestural point of view. And since the key is C major, the home tonic, the expression of tonic harmony in unit 3 comes to mind, for that was the first composing out of what would turn out to be the main key. Again, these affiliations show that unit 50, despite its obvious novelty, is not entirely without precedent. In this case, our paradigmatic chart does not do justice to the web of connections.

The paradigmatic chart also sets units 15–33 apart as a self-contained section. Indeed, the lyrical theme introduced at unit 15 evinces a stability and well-formedness that are not found in the outer sections. Consider the mode of succession of units 15–24. Unit 15 begins the lyrical song, 16 prepares a broad cadence but denies the concluding syntax (this is only the first try), and 17 achieves the actual cadence. Unit 18 confirms what we have just heard, while 19 echoes that confirmation. Unit 19 meanwhile modifies its ending to engender another cadential attempt, albeit in a new key. Unit 20 makes that attempt, succeeds (in bars 91–92), and is followed again by the confirming units 21 and 22. Another shift in key leads to the third effort to close in unit 23. Its successor, 24, achieves the expected closure, but now dispenses with the codetta idea that followed the cadences at the end of units 17 and 20. This little drama across units 15–24 unfolds with a sense of assurance and little sense of dependency. The self-containment and relative stasis confer on these units the spirit of an oasis. The idea of repeating such an interlude could not have been predicted from earlier events, but this is precisely what Liszt does. Thus, units 15–24 are repeated more or less verbatim as 25–33. If the former provided temporary stability within a largely fragmented discourse, the latter confirm that which demonstrated no inner need for confirmation. Of course, we become aware of the repetition only gradually and only in retrospect, and so the sense of redundancy is considerably mediated. At 33, matters are not closed off as at 23–24 but kept open in order to resume what we will come to know as the process of recapitulation.

The view of form that emerges from a paradigmatic analysis recognizes repetition and return at several different levels, small and large. Some listeners will, however, remain dissatisfied with this more open view of form, preferring to hear *Orpheus* in reference to a standard form. Derek Watson, for example, writes, "'Orpheus' is akin to the classical slow-movement sonata without development."[3] Richard Kaplan repeats this assertion: "*Orpheus* has the 'sonata without development' form common in slow movements, the only development takes place in what [Charles] Rosen calls the 'secondary development section' following the first theme area in the recapitulation."[4]

Kaplan is determined to counter the image of a revolutionary Liszt who invented an original genre ("symphonic poem") that necessarily announces its difference from existing forms. His evidence for the relevance of a sonata-form model to *Orpheus* embraces external as well as internal factors. The fact that this symphonic poem, like others, began life as an overture (it prefaced a performance of Gluck's *Orfeo ed Euridice*) and the fact that Liszt's models for writing overtures included works by Beethoven and Mendelssohn that use sonata form (this latter fact, Kaplan says, is confirmed by Reicha and Czerny, both of whom taught Liszt) lead Kaplan to search for markers of sonata form. He finds an exposition with two key areas (C and E) and two corresponding theme groups in each area, no development, and a recapitulation in which theme Ib precedes Ia, IIa is recapitulated first in B major and then in C major, themes Ia and IIb follow (again) in C major, and then a closing idea and a coda round off the work.

The argument for a sonata-form interpretation is perhaps strongest in connection with the presence of two clearly articulated keys in the exposition and the return—not necessarily "recapitulation"—of the themes unveiled during the exposition. But in making a case for a sonata-form framework for *Orpheus*, Kaplan is forced to enter numerous qualifications or simply contradictory statements. For example, he says that "three-part organization is the most consistent and logical explanation of large-scale form in [*Faust* Symphony/1, *Prometheus*, *Les Preludes*, *Tasso*, and *Orpheus*]." But *Orpheus* lacks one of these three parts, the central development section. He finds "many of [Liszt's] usages . . . unconventional"; the

3. Derek Watson, *Liszt* (London: Dent, 1989), 267.
4. Richard Kaplan, "Sonata Form in the Orchestral Works of Liszt: The Revolutionary Reconsidered," *19th-Century Music* 8 (1984): 150.

introduction is "very brief"; the repetition of the big lyrical theme (Kaplan's theme II) is "non-standard"; the reordering of themes in the recapitulation is "subtle"; the "use of themes in dual roles" is "unusual"; there are "several departures from classical tradition" in the handling of tonality; and recapitulating the second theme follows an "unusual key scheme." These qualifications do not inspire confidence in the pertinence of a sonata-form model. Granted, Kaplan's study is of several symphonic poems plus the opening movement of the *Faust* Symphony, and it is possible that sonata form is more overtly manifested there than in *Orpheus*. Nevertheless, hearing *Orpheus* as a "single-movement sonata structure" is, in my view, deeply problematic.

Listeners are more likely to be guided by the musical ideas themselves and their conventional and contextual tendencies. The drama of *Orpheus* is an immediate one: ideas sport overt values; return and repetition guarantee their meaningfulness. Attending to this drama means attending to a less directed or less prescribed formal process; and the temporal feel is less linearly charged. Liszt marks time, looks backward, even sideways. Succession rather than progression conveys the pull of the form. Gathering these constituents into a purposeful exposition and recapitulation obscures the additive view of form that our paradigmatic analysis promotes.

An analysis altogether more satisfactory than Kaplan's is provided by Rainer Kleinertz.[5] Kleinertz's main interest is the possible influence of Liszt on Wagner, not from the oft-remarked harmonic point of view, but as revealed in formal procedures. Wagner himself had been completely taken with *Orpheus*, declaring it in 1856 to be "a totally unique masterwork of the highest perfection" and "one of the most beautiful, most perfect, indeed most incomparable tone poems," and still later (in 1875) as a "restrained orchestral piece...to which I have always accorded a special place of honor among Liszt's compositions."[6] Although Wagner appears to have been especially taken with Liszt's approach to form, especially his jettisoning of traditional form and replacing it with something new, Kleinertz's essay concretizes the earlier intuitions in the form of an analysis.

From the point of view of the analysis presented earlier, the main interest in Kleinertz's study stems from his interpretation of *Orpheus* as unfolding a set of formal units. His chart of the "overall form" contains 18 units (all of the principal boundaries of his units coincide with those of my units, but his segmentation takes in a larger hierarchic level than mine does). Noting (in direct contradiction to Kaplan) that "there is no resemblance to sonata form"[7] and that "*Orpheus* has no 'architectonic' form,"[8] he argues instead that "the whole piece seems to move slowly but surely and regularly along a chain of small units, sometimes identical,

5. Rainer Kleinertz, "Liszt, Wagner, and Unfolding Form: *Orpheus* and the Genesis of *Tristan und Isolde*," in *Franz Liszt and His World*, ed. Christopher H. Gibbs and Dana Gooley (Princeton, NJ: Princeton University Press, 2006), 231–254.
6. Quoted in Kleinertz, "Liszt, Wagner, and Unfolding Form," 234–240.
7. Kleinertz, "Liszt, Wagner, and Unfolding Form," 234.
8. Kleinertz, "Liszt, Wagner, and Unfolding Form," 237.

sometimes varied or slightly altered."[9] "Liszt's intention," he continues, "is not to create 'closed' formal sections, but to develop or 'unfold' small elements into greater units."[10] This dynamic conception of form is labeled *unfolding form*,[11] "a constant process, which leads toward the climax and finally fades away."[12] Kleinertz concludes that "the 'secret of form' in Liszt's *Orpheus* . . . is not 'closed forms' or a concrete 'form model', but rather a constant unfolding of small, 'open' elements into greater units."[13]

Kleinertz does not describe his approach as a paradigmatic analysis, but it is obvious that by privileging contextually determined repetitions and their associations and by aligning them in an effort to isolate a formal imperative, his approach is deeply compatible with a paradigmatic one. Although the object of analysis is ostensibly an unusual work, thus demanding explanation without the crutches of conventional form, I believe that the approach is equally revealing when applied to less "experimental" works. The reason is that the paradigmatic analyst is forced to confront the materials of a work directly, instead of thinking of them solely in terms of conformance to, or departures from, a conventional archetype.

Meaning

Because they originate in a verbal narrative or plot or are earmarked for illustrative work, symphonic poems have a twofold task: to make musical sense and to create the conditions that allow listeners so disposed to associate some musical features with "extramusical" ones. Both tasks subtend a belief about musical meaning. The first is based in the coherence of meanings made possible by musical language and syntax; the second is based on the prospect of translating that language or drawing analogies between it and formations in other dynamic systems.

Although *Orpheus* resists a reading as a continuously illustrative work, certain features encourage speculation about its illustrative potential. I mentioned some of these in my survey of its building blocks. The disposition of the opening harp chords and the lone G that announces them mimic the making of form out of formlessness; they identify a mythical figure, our musician/protagonist, and they convey a sense of expectancy. Even the tonal distance in these opening bars could be interpreted as signifying the remoteness of the world that Liszt seeks to conjure. The main theme, delivered by strings, carries a sense of the journey's beginning; we will follow the contours of a changing landscape through its coming transformations. The ominous neighbor-note idea, with its sly, chromatic supplement, is permanently marked as tendering a promise, pushing the narrative forward to some unspecified goal. The beautiful lyrical theme in E major announces a new

9. Kleinertz, "Liszt, Wagner, and Unfolding Form," 234.
10. Kleinertz, "Liszt, Wagner, and Unfolding Form," 235.
11. Kleinertz, "Liszt, Wagner, and Unfolding Form," 235.
12. Kleinertz, "Liszt, Wagner, and Unfolding Form," 240.
13. Kleinertz, "Liszt, Wagner, and Unfolding Form," 240.

character or, rather, a new incarnation of the previous character. Unfolding deliberately, complete in profile, and burdened with closure, it provides an extended tonal contrast that may well suggest the outdoors. The large-scale repetition of this passage signifies a desire on the protagonist's part to remain within this world, but the return of the main theme is harder to interpret as an element of plot. Because the associations are presumably fixed from the beginning and because verbal or dramatic plots do not typically retrace their steps in the way musical plots do, the fact of return forces the interpreter into a banal mode: hearing again, refusing to go forward, recreating a lost world. Finally, the concluding magic chords—"mysterious chords," in Kleinertz's description—may well signify Orpheus in the underworld. They connote distance as well as familiarity—familiarity stemming from their affiliation with the work's opening, with its floating chords marked "destination unknown." We are always wiser in retrospect.

Listeners who choose to ignore these connotations, or who reject them on account of their contingency, will not thereby find themselves bored, for everything from the thematic transformations through the formal accumulation of units is there to challenge them and guarantee an engaged listening. But if we ask, how do these competing perspectives promote a view of musical meaning? it becomes apparent that the interpretive task poses different sorts of challenges. It is in a sense easy to claim that the magic chords at the end of *Orpheus* signify something different or otherworldly, or that the big lyrical theme signifies a feminine world, or that the harp is associated with the heavens, or even that chromaticism engenders trouble, slyness, or instability. These sorts of readings may be supported by historical and systematic factors. They provide ready access to meaning, especially that of the associative or extrinsic variety. But they are not thereby lacking a dimension of intrinsic meaning, for the remoteness of the closing chords, for example, stems more fundamentally from the absence of the regular sorts of semitonal logic that we have heard throughout *Orpheus*. In other words—and recognizing the fragility of the distinction—intrinsic meaning is what makes extrinsic meaning possible. It is within the intrinsic realm that music's language is formed. Its meanings are therefore both structural and rhetorical at birth. They are, in that sense, prior to those of extrinsic associationism. They may signify multiply or neutrally, but their semantic fields are not infinite in the way that unanchored extrinsic meanings can be. If, therefore, we opt for intrinsic meanings, we are expressing an ideological bias about their priority, a priority that is not based entirely on origins but ultimately on the practical value of music making. This chapter has explored a mode of analysis that seeks to capture some of that value.

CHAPTER $\mathcal{S}$even

Brahms, Intermezzo in E Minor, op. 119, no. 2 (1893), and Symphony no. 1/ii (1872–1876)

How might we frame an analysis of music as discourse for works whose thematic surfaces are not overtly or topically differentiated, the boundaries of whose building blocks seem porous and fluid, and whose tendencies toward continuity override those toward discontinuity? Two works by Brahms will enable us to sketch some answers to these questions: the second of his op. 119 intermezzi and the second movement of the First Symphony. Unlike Liszt's *Orpheus*, whose building blocks are well demarcated, Brahms' piano piece has a contrapuntally dense texture and a subtle, continuous periodicity marked by a greater sense of through-composition. And in the symphonic movement, although utterances are often set apart temporally, the material is of a single origin and the overall manner is deeply organic. Dependency between adjacent units is marked. Nevertheless, each work must breathe and deliver its message in meaningful chunks; each is thus amenable to the kind of analysis that I have been developing. In addition to performing the basic tasks of isolating such chunks and commenting on their affiliations, I hope to shed light on Brahms' procedures in general, as well as on the specific strategies employed in these two works.

Intermezzo, op. 119, no. 2

At the largest level, op. 119, no. 2, displays an ABA' outer form (bars 1–35^2, 35^3–71^2, and 71^3–104, respectively). The A sections exploit and explore the speech mode through motivic repetition and transformation. The B section, by contrast, explores the song and dance modes—song mode in the form of compelling, singable trajectories and dance mode by means of unambiguous periodicity and an invitation to waltz. This distribution of modes of utterance suggests in the first instance that there will likely be many more units in the outer sections than in the middle section. If the protagonist is heard to "speak" in relatively short utterances in the A and A' sections, to stutter even, she sings in longer, continuous phrases in the B section.

A paradigmatic analysis conveys this division of labor by registering a striking difference in population of units: 22 in the A section, 19 in the A' section and a mere 8 in the B section.

Anyone who plays through this intermezzo will be struck by the constant presence of its main idea. A brief demonstration of the structural origins of this idea will be helpful in conveying the nature of Brahms' harmonically grounded counterpoint. At level *a* in example 7.1 is a simple closed progression in E minor, the sort that functions in a comparable background capacity in works by Corelli, Bach, Mozart, Beethoven, and Mendelssohn—in short, a familiar motivating progression for tonal expression. The progression may be decorated as shown at level *b*. Level *c* withholds the closing chord, transforming the basic idea into an incomplete utterance that can then be yoked to adjacent repetitions of itself. Level *d* shows how Brahms' opening enriches and personalizes the progression using temporal displacements between treble and bass. This, then, is the kind of thinking that lies behind the material of the work.

In preparing a reference text for analysis (example 7.2), I have essentialized the entire intermezzo as a two-voice stream in order to simplify matters. (A few irresistible harmonies are included in the middle section, however.) Example 7.2

Example 7.1. Origins of the main idea in Brahms, Intermezzo in E Minor, op. 119, no. 2.

Example 7.2. Units of structure in Brahms, op. 119, no. 2.

should thus be read as a kind of shorthand for the piece, a sketch whose indispensable supplement is the work itself. Units are marked by a broken vertical line and numbered at the top of each stave. Bar numbers are indicated beneath each stave.

Unit 1 (bar 1)

A tentative utterance progresses from tonic to dominant and exposes the main motif of the work. This idea will not only dominate the outer sections but will remain in our consciousness in the middle section as well. The intermezzo thus approaches the condition of a monothematic work. This building block is open, implying—indeed, demanding—immediate continuation.

Unit 2 (bars 1–2)

Overlapping with the preceding unit, this one is essentially a repetition, but the melodic gesture concludes differently—with an exclamation (B–D♯) that suggests a mini-crisis. Shall we turn around and start again, or go on—and if so, where?

Unit 3 (bars 2–3)

This is the same as unit 1. Brahms chose to start again.

Unit 4 (bars 3–7)

Beginning like 1 (and 3), this unit replaces D-sharp with D-natural on the downbeat of bar 5, hints at G major, but immediately veers off by means of a deceptive move (bass D–D-sharp) toward B major, the home key's major dominant. Arrival on B major recalls unit 2, but here the utterance is louder and rhetorically heightened.

Unit 5 (bars 7–9)

Lingering on the dominant, this unit extends the dominant of the dominant just triumphantly attained, but it effects a modal reorientation toward the minor. The main motive continues to lead here.

Unit 6 (bar 9)

This is the same as unit 1.

Unit 7 (bars 9–10)

This repeats the material from unit 2.

Unit 8 (bars 10–11)

This is the same as 1 (and 3 and 6).

Unit 9 (bars 11–12)

Five chromatic steps (B to E) provide a link to A minor from E minor. In this transitional unit, the E-minor triad is turned into major and, with an added seventh, functions as V7 of A minor to set up the next unit.

Unit 10 (bars 12–13)

Unit 1 (and its repetitions) is heard here in the key of the subdominant, A minor, with a slight rhythmic/textural differentiation featuring triplets.

Unit 11 (bars 13–14)

This is a repeat of unit 10.

Unit 12 (bars 15–17)

An idiomatic linear intervallic pattern in the form 8–5–8–5–8–5 (bars 15^2–17^1) is used to engineer a grand cadence in A minor's relative, C major. This is the broadest such cadence in the intermezzo so far.

Unit 13 (bars 17–18)

The main motive (unit 1) is heard in F minor over a local dominant (C) pedal. The effect is one of transience, reinforcing the ongoing variation process.

Unit 14 (bars 18–19)

This is transpositionally equivalent to unit 2, with slight changes in contrapuntal rendition.

Unit 15 (bars 19–20)

The C pedal of unit 13 is replaced by a B pedal, thus orienting us to E minor. It will emerge later that, within the A section, this unit marks a return to its opening material.

Unit 16 (bars 20–23)

Equivalent to the second half of unit 4, this unit culminates in a big cadence on B as V of the coming E minor.

Unit 17 (bars 23–24)

This resolution is not to a pure E minor but to one that is inflected by elements from its subdominant major.

Unit 18 (bars 25–27)

A synthesis of melodic elements from units 2 (the B–D♯ exclamation) and 5 reinforces the recapitulatory function of this material.

Unit 19 (bars 27–28)

Over a V pedal, a variant of the main motive announces the coming end by slowing things down.

Unit 20 (bars 28–29)

The main motive is heard in tonic with a more contrapuntally and rhythmically active bass.

Unit 21 (bars 29–30)

This unit begins as a near repetition of 18, oriented this time toward the relative major.

Unit 22 (bars 30–35)

This unit reaches for and attains a big cadence in the tonic, complete with chromatic and plagal coloring in bar 32. A suffix in bars 34–35 prepares the next major section of the piece. With hindsight, we can now rehear units 20–22 as rhetorically heightened, as the point of culmination of several significant processes stemming from the first bars of the intermezzo. The piece began with a strategic tentativeness and continued in this manner, only occasionally overcoming its shyness—but never for long. We have heard short phrases ending on the dominant, sudden cadential effusions without extensive preparation, a persistent presence of the main theme, shifts into other keys, and finally, an overt confirmation of motive and key but without dwelling on them. This discourse has known no regular periodicity. We may speak of prose rather than poetry, speech mode rather than song or dance mode, without, however, underplaying the poetic elements enshrined in prose or the singing impulses that underpin speech. And, given the predominance of a single motive, we may speak of an agent or narrator who embodies a subjectivity.

Unit 23 (bars 36–39)

Serene, settled, and in dance mode, the B section proceeds in clear four-measure phrases and with an unambiguous differentiation between melody and accompaniment (although the accompaniment, as often in Brahms, incorporates melodic motives). This combination of attributes creates a new atmosphere. The mode is major, sweeter, and less troubled, and the temporal profile is non-urgent, almost retrospective—pointing to an "other" world. The affective contrast, however, masks a significant element of continuity: the main motive from the A section leads here, too, only now it assumes a major-mode identity.

Unit 24 (bars 40–43)

Alternation between tonic and dominant chords (over tonic pedal) in the previous unit prepares this rewarding, harmonically more active unit. A tonicization of V in bar 42 is undercut by the A-natural in bar 43, which keeps the B7 chord functioning as dominant-seventh in E.

Unit 25 (bars 44–47)

This is the same as unit 23, only it is displaced up by an octave, with the melody doubled.

Unit 26 (bars 48–51)

This is the same as 24 but with one tiny but telling difference: the concluding B chord lacks the A-natural from bar 43, thus strengthening the sense of a tonicized dominant.

Unit 27 (bars 52–59)

A characteristically Brahmsian modal shift involving $\hat{5}$–$\flat\hat{6}$ in the bass initiates a strongly directed linear motion in the treble, providing the tonal contrast we normally associate with the beginning of the second reprise in a classical minuet form.

Unit 28 (bars 60–63)

This unit is a return of 23, but its first bar is modified to lead felicitously from the previous unit. Note the doubling of melody and the shift of register after 2 bars, as if to simultaneously recapitulate units 23 and 25.

Unit 29 (bars 64–67)

Although this unit begins as if it were going to be a repeat of 24 and 26, both of which ended on their dominants, continuation is modified to produce a cadence in the tonic and thus to round off the intermezzo's self-standing middle section.

Unit 30 (bars 68–71)

This unit comprises 4 bars of lingering on the main motive over a tonic pedal. There is a touch of poetry in this wistful, backward-looking gesture. The head motive slows down, and the melodic notes $\hat{6}$ and $\hat{5}$ in the major are prominent, preparing their transformation into the minor in the next unit. At the last minute (bar 71), G-natural replaces G-sharp to indicate a modal shift from the major of the B section to the minor of the A' section. Transitional function is accomplished by this last incorporation of G-natural, which recalls the join between the A and B sections (bars 33–35). The energy in the main motive is neutralized somewhat.

Unit 31 (bars 71–72)

This unit is the equivalent of unit 1. As typically happens in ternary structures like this, the reprise (starting with the upbeat to bar 72) reproduces the content of the first A section with slight modifications. My comments below will mainly acknowledge the parallels between the two sections.

Unit 32 (bars 72–73)

This is the same as unit 2.

Unit 33 (bars 73–74)

This is equivalent to unit 3.

Unit 34 (bars 74–75)

This unit proceeds as if recapitulating unit 9, but it curtails its upward chromatic melodic rise after only three steps.

Unit 35 (bars 75–76)

This is the proper equivalent of unit 9, differently harmonized, however.

Unit 36 (bars 76–77)

This unit is a rhythmic variant of unit 10. The process of rhythmic revision replaces the earlier triplets with eighths and sixteenths, bringing this material more in line with the original rhythm of the main theme. We may make an analogy between this process and the tonic appropriation of tonally "other" material during a sonata-form recapitulation.

Unit 37 (bars 77–78)

Equivalent to 11, this unit is also heard as an immediate repeat of 36.

Unit 38 (bars 79–81)

This is the equivalent of 12, with rhythmic variation.

Unit 39 (bars 81–82)

This unit is equivalent to 13.

Unit 40 (bars 82–83)

This is the equivalent of 14.

Unit 41 (bars 83–84)

This is equivalent to 15.

Unit 42 (bars 84–87)

This is the same as 16.

Unit 43 (bars 87–88)

This is the equivalent of 17.

Unit 44 (bars 89–91)

This is equivalent to 18.

Unit 45 (bars 91–92)

This is the equivalent of 19.

Unit 46 (bars 92–93)

This is the same as unit 20.

Unit 47 (bars 93–94)

This is equivalent to 21.

Unit 48 (bars 94–99)

This is the same as 22.

Unit 49 (bars 99–104)

For a moment, this might suggest the beginning of the B section, unit 23. In retrospect, it emerges as the end of the middle section, unit 30. A low E in the bass on the downbeat of the penultimate bar (103) makes all the difference to the sense of this as the ultimate closing gesture. Melodically, G-sharp prevails and, with that, the optimism of the major mode.

These internal parallelisms may now be displayed in a paradigmatic chart encompassing all 49 units of the intermezzo (example 7.3).

Example 7.3. Paradigmatic chart of the units in Brahms, op. 119, no. 2.

1	2										
3			4	5							
6	7										
8					9						
10											
11						12					
13	14										
15			16				17	18	19		
20											
21									22	23	24
										25	26	27
										28			29	30
31	32										
33				34							
				35							
36											
37					38						
39	40										
41			42				43	44	45		
46											
47									48				49

Form and Meaning

What kinds of insights into form and meaning are made possible by the foregoing analysis? At the largest level, the ABA' outer form or ternary structure is straight-forwardly reflected in example 7.3. Parallelism between units in the A and A' sections is conveyed directly. Beyond this larger and obvious level, the division into units brings other features into view. First is the sheer numerical superiority of the paradigmatic class headed by the main motive, unit 1. It is no secret that the inter-mezzo is based on a single main motive and that this circumstance might encourage us to hear the work as an instance of developing variation. The paradigmatic analysis confirms that 18 of the 49 units are replicas or near-replicas of the head motive. But this does not exhaust the motive's filiations and affiliations. Unit 2, too, might be heard as a variant of unit 1, so that its fivefold appearance in the work (units 2, 7, 14, 32, 40) may be added to the paradigmatic class of the main motive to make a total of 23 hits. Then, there is the middle section, whose opening unit (23), a major-mode version of the minor-mode unit 1, is heard twice more (25 and 28). If we add this to the collection, we now have 26 units, a little over half of the total units in the work.

The paradigmatic layout thus confirms what is readily heard, namely, the pre-dominance of a single motive, but it also enables a ready view of the strategies that determine the outer trace. For example, in the A section, "new" ideas appear gradually while the main idea remains as a constant but variable presence. Novelty is charted by the following succession: unit 2; then units 4–5; then 9; then 12; then 14; then 17–19; and finally 22. The degree of compositional control is noteworthy. A similar strategy is evident in the middle section, where 23, 25, and 28 serve as springboards that enable departures within the span of units encompassing this section (23–30).

A third feature conveyed in the paradigmatic analysis is the pacing of utterances. In the B section, for example, there are only 8 units, compared to 41 in the combined A sections. This conveys something of the difference in the kinds and qualities of the utterances. Much is "said" in the A and A' sections; there is a greater sense of articulation and rearticulation in these sections. The speech mode predominates. Fewer "words" are spoken in the B section, where the song mode dominates. As narration, the intermezzo advances a self-conscious telling in the A section, pauses to reflect and sing "innerly" in the B section, and returns to the mode of the A section in the A' section, incorporating a touch of reminiscence at the very end.

The paradigmatic analysis, in short, makes it possible to advance descriptive narratives that convey the character of the work. In principle, these narratives do not rely on information from outside the work, except for a generalized sense of convention and expectation drawn from the psychology of tonal expression. They are bearers, therefore, of something like purely musical meaning. Some listeners may choose to invest in other sorts of meaning, of course; the fact, for example, that this is a late work may engender speculation about late style: conciseness, minimalism, essence, subtlety, or economy as opposed to flamboyance, extravagance, determination, and explicitness. The title "Intermezzo" might suggest an in-betweenness or transience. I am less concerned with these sorts of meanings than with those that emerge from "purely" musical considerations. The kinds of meaning that ostensibly formalist exercises like the foregoing make possible have not, I feel, been sufficiently acknowledged as what they are: legitimate modes of meaning formation. They do not represent a retreat from the exploration of meaning. As I have tried to indicate, and as the following analysis of the slow movement of the First Symphony will further attest, formalist-derived meanings are enabling precisely because they bring us in touch with the naked musical elements as sites of possibility. Reticence about crass specification of verbal meaning is not an evasion, nor is it a deficit. On the contrary, it is a strategic attempt to enable a plurality of inference by postponing early foreclosure. Boundaries, not barriers, are what we need in order to stimulate inquiry into musical meaning. Indeed, not all such acts of inferring are appropriate for public consumption.

Brahms, First Symphony, second movement

One of the most pertinent features of the slow movement of Brahms' First Symphony is conveyed in Walter Frisch's description of its first 27 bars as "a splendid example of what Schoenberg was to call 'musical prose.'"[1] To speak of prose is to distinguish it notionally from poetry. Speech-like rather than verse-like, musical prose displays contours that are more freely ordered, phrases that do not evince a strict, regular, or predictable periodicity. Listeners are drawn into an evolving narrative. Verse-like construction, on the other hand, engenders a more conventional phrase discourse; symmetries are not hard to come by. The listener *contemplates* musical discourse that is cast in speech mode; in song or dance mode, by contrast, the listener *participates* (which does not mean that there isn't a contemplative element in the dance mode). The composer rules in the former regime; in the latter, both composer and listener share power.

Frisch develops his reading of musical prose by charting the progress of thematic groups and phrase structure. His analysis is implicitly semiotic; to make it explicit, we must return to the beginning and take repetition as our principal criterion for analysis and speak more neutrally of units or segments. The motivating questions for the analyst, then, are the classical ones: What are the building blocks? and how does the movement work as a succession of units?

To suggest some terms in which these questions about morphology and meaning might be answered, I will begin at the beginning and continue to the end, pausing to comment on each segment. As a general guideline, and in order to make a concession to conventional approaches to form, let us agree at the outset that the movement may be divided into four main sections: A (bars 1–27), B (bars 27–66), A' (bars 66–100), and coda (bars 100–end). Each section is in turn constituted by smaller segments or units, and these will form the focus of our analysis.

Segments are defined as small words, minimal syntactic units that serve as building blocks. They may be fragments (like unit 2, bars 3^1–4^2) or wholes (like unit 1, bars 1^1–2^3) when considered in isolation. They may be bordered by silences, or elided with adjacent units. Depending on the dynamics of its internal articulation, a segment may be known prospectively or retrospectively. A segment may be a melodic, harmonic, or rhythmic gesture—material with a distinct shape, usually repeated immediately to emphasize its relative autonomy. Segments, in short, emerge from particular contexts; indeed, alternative segmentation is often possible since different analysts privilege different dimensions. This sort of flexibility in specifying the makeup of segments or units may arouse suspicion that methodological rigor is being sacrificed. But the range of styles in the way that ideas are formed in Romantic music demands such flexibility.[2]

A Section (bars 1–27)

Unit 1 (bars 1^1–2^3)

A self-contained, closed progression, this opening 2-bar phrase will return variously as melody, as bass, and as affect. The material is partly hymn-like, thus carrying

1. Walter Frisch, *Brahms: The Four Symphonies* (New York: Schirmer, 1996), 52.
2. For this analysis, I found it convenient to work from a piano score of the movement made by Otto Singer and published in Leipzig by Peters in 1936.

a *religioso topos*, and partly warm in an archetypically Romantic, secular vein. The basic harmonic progression is I–V–I, the initial I prolonged through vi and IV. Crucial to the meaning of this phrase is the retention of the pitch G-sharp (3̂) in the melody. Although we hear the phrase as somewhat self-contained, we also understand that it remains in a suspended state; it remains incomplete. Conventionally, G-sharp's ultimate destination should be E (1̂). We carry this expectation forward. The difference in effect between the two framing tonic chords (with 3̂ in the top voice) reminds us of the role of context in shaping musical meanings. The 3̂ in bar 1 is a point of departure; the 3̂ in bar 2 is a point of arrival. A return to the point from which we embarked on our journey may suggest a turnaround—we have not gone anywhere yet, not realized our desire for closure. So, although the progression in unit 1 is closed, its framing moments carry a differential degree of stability in the work: the second 3̂ is weaker than the opening 3̂.

Unit 2 (bars 3¹–4²)

This 2-bar phrase "answers" the previous one directly. The sense of an answer is signaled by parallel phrase structure. But to gloss the succession of 2-bar phrases as question and answer is already to point to some of the complexities of analyzing musical meaning. These 2 bars differ from the preceding 2-bar unit insofar as they are oriented entirely to the dominant. Unit 1 progressed from I through V and back to I; this one prolongs V through a secondary-dominant prefix. To say that unit 2 answers 1, therefore, is too simple. Musical tendencies of question and answer are complexly distributed and more than a matter of succession. The close of unit 2 on the dominant tells us that this particular answer is, at best, provisional. The answer itself closes with a question, a pointer to more business ahead. Unit 2 is thus simultaneously answer (by virtue of phrase isomorphism and placement) and question (by virtue of tonal tendency).

A number of oppositions are introduced in this succession of units 1 and 2: diatonic versus chromatic, closed versus open, disjunct versus conjunct motion, major versus minor (conveyed most poignantly in the contrast between G-sharp in unit 1 and G-natural in unit 2), and active versus less active rates of harmonic change. The more we probe this juxtaposition, the more we realize that the overall procedure of units 1 and 2 is not a causal, responsorial 2 + 2 gesture, but something less directed, less urgent in its resultant cumulative profile. When we think of classical 4-bar phrases divided into 2 and 2, we think, at one extreme, of clearly demarcated subphrases, the second of which literally answers the first. But the degree to which the subphrases are independent or autonomous varies from situation to situation. Nor is this a feature that can always be determined abstractly; often, it is the force of context that underlines or undermines the autonomy of subunits. In Brahms' opening, the horns enter with a threefold repeated note, B (bar 2), to link the two phrases. These Bs function first as an echo of what has gone before, as unobtrusive harmonic filler that enhances the warmth of tonic harmony, and as elements embedded spatially in the middle of the sonority, not at its extremities, where they are likely to draw attention to themselves. The three Bs not only point backward, they point forward as well. They prepare unit 2 by what will emerge as an anacrusic, or extended upbeat, quality. Indeed, many subsequent units are headed by similar anacruses.

Unit 3 (bars 4³–6¹)

Even without the hindsight of the first movement, we are able to sense in this unit a quality of recall, a sense of distance, of novelty mediated by the familiar. The chromaticism of unit 2 is in evidence here too but, by dropping the bass voice, Brahms leaves us with the impression that something from the past is being awakened. Later, this unit, which is strongly affiliated with unit 2, will be heard variously as link, intensifier, and, at the end of the movement, as a previously amputated progression whose limbs are restored in the closing bars of the movement.

Units 4 (bars 6¹–6³), 5 (bars 6³–7³), 6 (bars 7³–9³)

Unlike units 1 and 2, which were demarcated as separate entities, unit 3 is interrupted by a new melodic gesture at the beginning of unit 4. Being overtaken in this manner may be figured in different ways. A new character steps in front to carry this discourse forward. S/he may be a previously silent member of the group who, however, has been keenly following everything that has gone on so far. Thinking of narrative in Brahms in terms of alternating narrators helps to underline the fact that the musical idea is often complex, comprising a thread woven from multiple voices in which now one, now another takes the lead.

Units 3, 4, 5, and 6 (and, as we will hear in a moment, 7 and 8) are fragmentary and thus stretch the normative sense of well-formedness attributed to units. But the thematic rhetoric here leaves little doubt that each of these sound terms carries a certain amount of autonomy. Unit 3 is a lead-in. Only after unit 4 has begun do we hear the 3–4 boundary. Unit 5 repeats the gesture of 4—intensifies it, even—and we fully expect unit 6 to outdo the two previous units in strength of gesture. This expectation is met not by merely repeating the 1-bar gestures of the previous units, but by extending the phrase to make a more expansive statement. Indeed, the bass line in bar 8 (A♯–B–E) is a relative of the melodic G♯–A–C♯ from bar 1. Here, as in the intermezzo we looked at earlier, the organic element in the musical fabric is underlined by incorporating melody into bass. When unit 6 ends on a V6 chord with a 7–6 suspension in the treble (bar 9), we understand that this is a temporary point of rest because it lacks the relative finality of bar 4.

Aficionados of motivic relationships in Brahms and admirers of the organic thrust of his themes will have their hands full tracing various motivic relationships throughout this movement: some are direct and obvious, others are obscure or disguised. This emphasis will not be the main one here, however, partly because motivic relationships almost never assume exclusive responsibility for the compositional dynamic in Brahms. The harmonic-contrapuntal impetus always precedes the thematic.

Units 7 (bars 9³–10³), 8 (bars 10³–11³), 9 (bars 11³–13²)

Brahms retains in unit 7 the decorated 7–6 suspension over V6 that ended unit 6; then, keeping the same melody notes (C♯–B), he alters the bass to create a 6–5 suspension over a I♮7 chord in unit 8. This chord functions first as a I♮7 and then prepares the next unit as V7/IV. The effect of units 7 and 8 is one of waiting, tarrying. Speech mode intrudes here precisely because there is no larger regulative periodicity. Brahms is in charge, revealing his calculations moment by moment, rather than leaving us to infer them from a constraining periodicity or phrase structure. The culmination of this waiting process is unit 9, which achieves a high point on the downbeat of bar 12 in the context of a 3 4–3 suspension. We know immediately that this is a turning point, perhaps the turning point of the opening section. We sense that closure is at hand.

Units 10 (bars 13²–16²), 11 (bars 16³–17²)

The falling fifths in treble (C♯–F♯, bar 13) and bass (C♯–F♯ followed by B–E, bars 14 and 15) are freighted with a sense of closure. Coming after the heightened expressivity of unit 9, they supply a release of tension. Not only are we more confident that a cadence is forthcoming, but we believe that it will be in the tonic. Brahms does not disappoint, but his way is not what we might have predicted exactly. A cadence duly arrives at the end of unit 10 and is immediately echoed as unit 11, but it is a half-cadence, not a full one; indeed, the falling fifths of unit 10 are followed by material imported from unit 2, complete with its cadence on to V and a hint of the tonic minor. (Some readers might wonder why I have not created a separate unit to take account of this reuse of unit 2 in unit 10. The answer is that the gesture in these 2 bars of unit 10 is so logically and organically derived from what precedes it that the "quotation" acquires an ornamental rather than structural value.)

Units 12 (bars 17³–19²), 13 (bars 19³–21²), 14 (bars 21³–23²)

If the beginning of unit 3 took us back in time, the beginning of unit 12 is even more deeply retrospective. The origin of this effect is partly timbral: the solo oboe emerges as a new timbre to remind us of past times, not so much the immediate past of this work but the very idea of pastness. One way of engendering this aura of pastness is to create a melody that mimics a consequent phrase but whose anteced-ent is suppressed; another way is to leave the entire unit suspended on a dominant, thus retaining its essential desire to go somewhere. Brahms has carefully crafted the extension of V harmony, beginning with V7 (bar 18) and ending with V (bar 19²), incorporating an inner-voice descending chromatic line within a harmonic progression enabled by neighboring motion.

Heard in the context of the unfolding narrative, unit 12 remains suspended: scale-degree 5̂, which initiated the three-note anacrusis in the melody, is the very note to which the melody returns; and, as we have noted, the harmony extends V.

Then, revoicing the lower parts of unit 13, Brahms enhances their essential identity. These units are the first two of a threefold gesture that culminates in a high
point on the downbeat of bar 22 (unit 14) with a high B. As mentioned earlier, this
moment of culmination also features a return of the melody from unit 1 as a bass
voice, providing a spectacular sense of textural fusion at a rhetorically superlative
moment.

Units 15 (bars 23^3–25^1), 16 (bars 25^2–27^2)

High points invariably bring on the end. The downbeat of bar 22 carries a promise of closure. Unit 15 reclaims the material of unit 2, but instead of advancing to
a half-close as in the comparable gesture in bar 12, it simply abandons the first
attempt at cadence and proceeds to a second, successful attempt (16). The means
are direct: Brahms brings back material we have heard twice previously (bars 3–4
and 15–16), withholds its continuation, and finally allows it. The anacruses that
shaped previous occurrences are present here too, though they now take the form
of a descending triad (bars 23 and 25). The long-awaited cadence in bars 26–27 is
engineered by this figure. Looking back, we now see how Brahms has led us gradually but inexorably to this point.

Figure 7.1 Paradigmatic arrangement of units 1–16 in Brahms' Symphony
No.1/ii.

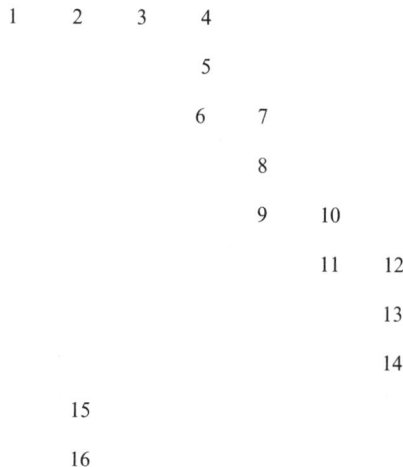

Let us review the A section from the point of view of paradigmatic affiliation
(figure 7.1). The strategy is immediately apparent. Narrating rather than associating seems to be the process. We begin with a sequence of four sufficiently differentiated ideas (units 1–4). Then, we dwell on the fourth one for a bit (5, 6), add a new
idea (7), which we play with for a while (8, 9). Yet another new idea is introduced
(10). Its tale—which, in this interpretation, embodies its essential identity—is
immediately repeated (11). The last of our new ideas follows (12) and is repeated

twice in progressively modified form (13 and 14). Finally, by way of conclusion, we return to an earlier idea, unit 2, for a twofold iteration (15 and 16). Overall, the process is incremental and gradual. Brahms' music unfolds in the manner of a speech discourse, complete with asymmetrical groupings and subtle periodicity. The idea of "musical prose" captures this process perfectly.

B Section (bars 27–66)

Unit 17 (bars 27^2–31^2)

If the A section featured musical prose in small segments, the B section may be said to begin with musical prose in larger chunks (units 17–22) before taking up small segments again in order to bring this contrasting section to a satisfying close. Unit 17 inscribes a I–V–I wave in E major. The melodic sweep enhances this progression, proceeding first as an arpeggiation from low B (bar 27) to high G-sharp (bar 28) and then stepwise to high B; thereafter, the melody returns from high to low. Those unable to switch off their intertextual antennae may well hear the slow movement of Beethoven's Fourth Symphony in the dotted-note accompaniment figure that enters on the upbeat to bar 29.

Unit 18 (bars 31^2–34^1)

Beginning as a modified repeat, this unit reaches a high G-sharp in its ascent phase. But there is a harmonic divergence here. The motion is not from I to V and back to I but from I (bar 31) through vi (bar 33) to its dominant at the start of the next unit.

Unit 19 (bars 34^1–39^1)

The G-sharp in the bass supports a dominant-functioning chord that eventually attains 5/3 position in bars 38–39. The motivic profile suggests a three-part grouping: first, bars 34 and 35, then 36^1–36^2 and 36^3–37^1, and finally 37^2–39^1 as an undivided unit. Taken together, they create the feeling of an arrival at a plateau.

Units 20 (bars 38^3–42^3), 21 (bars 42^3–47^1), 22 (bars 46^3–49^1)

The key signifier of the beginning of this unit is the solo oboe that intones a long G-sharp beginning at the end of bar 38 and continuing through the middle of 39. This way of announcing oneself becomes the modus operandi for the two subsequent units in this middle section, 21 and 22. In each, a long held note is marked for consciousness, eventually spiraling downward in the manner of a dissolution. An E-flat heads unit 21 while A-flat heads 22. The succession of head notes suggests a low-level imitative process, not the hard-core learned style that Brahms employed on other occasions. It is obvious that the periodic trajectories we have been following since unit 17 are longer than those in the A section. Combined with

imitation, this extension of temporal units is Brahms' way of meeting the normative need for contrast and development in this portion of the movement.

Units 23 (bars 49¹–50¹), 24 (bars 50¹–50³), 25 (bars 51¹–52¹), 26 (bars 52¹–53²)

Units 20, 21, and 22 were grouped together on account of their morphological similarities. What follows in the next four units is a cadential gesture that leads us to
expect a close in D-flat major, the enharmonic relative of C-sharp. Brahms makes
much of the gesture of announcing and then withholding a cadence. Thus, unit 23
prepares a cadence, but the onset of 24, while syntactically conjunct, dissolves the
desire for a cadence by replaying part of the melody that dominated units 20, 21,
and 22. Again, 25 repeats 23, evoking the same expectation, but 26 avoids the 6/4
of unit 24 and sequences up a step from 25, at the same time extending the unit
length. The cumulative effect is an intensification of the desire for cadence.

Unit 27 (bars 53²–55³)

We reach a new plateau with the arrival on a sforzando G-sharp at 53², the beginning of unit 27. The familiar sequence of features—a long note followed by a doodling descent—is soon overtaken by a fortissimo diminished-seventh chord (bar
55³), a chord that (again, in retrospect) marks the beginning of the next unit.

Units 28 (bars 55³–57¹), 29 (bars 57¹–57³), 30 (bars 58¹–59²)

The beginning of the end of the movement's middle section is signaled strongly
by the diminished-seventh chord at 55³. This is not a moment of culmination as
such; rather, it sounds a distant note and then gradually diminishes that distance.
It carries the aura of a high point by virtue of rhetoric, but it is achieved more by
assertion than by gradual accumulation. Indeed, it is the staged resolution in its
immediate aftermath that confirms the markedness of this moment.

   Units 28, 29, and 30 are thematic transformations of each other. Unit 30 is the
most intricate from a harmonic point of view. After 30, the need for a cadence
becomes increasingly urgent, and over the next six units, the obligation to close the
middle section is dramatized by means of Brahms' usual avoidance strategy.

Units 31 (bars 59²·⁵–60¹), 32 (bars 60¹·⁵–61¹), 33 (bars 61¹–61²), 34 (bars 61³–62¹), 35 (bars 62²–63¹)

Speech mode intrudes here as the units become notably shorter. Unit 31 ends
deceptively, while 32 avoids a proper cadence by dovetailing its ending with the
beginning of 33. Units 33 and 34 are materially identical but are positioned an
octave apart; the connection between them is seamless despite the timbral changes
associated with each group of four sixteenth-notes. And unit 35 is left to pick up
the pieces, echoing the contour of the last three notes of 34 in a durational augmentation that suggests exhaustion.

Unit 36 (bars 63¹–66³)

It remains for this unit to enact a final compensatory and decisive gesture in order to bring things to a close. Brahms retrieves his descending fifths from bars 14–15 and superimposes on them a broad-scaled, stepwise melody whose ending overlaps with the beginning of the return, the A' section. Something of the warmth of units 1–2 and especially 9–10 is incorporated into this final phrase of the B section.

∞

Figure 7.2 Paradigmatic arrangement of units 17–36 in Brahms' Symphony No.1/ii.

```
      17

   18    19    20
               21
               22    23
               24    25
               26
               27          28
                           29
                           30
                           31 (truncated)
                           32              33
                                           34
                                     35 (fragment)  36
```

We may now summarize the affiliations among the units of the B section (see figure 7.2). Immediately apparent are two features: first, but for units 19 and 36, each vertical column contains a minimum of two and a maximum of five elements. This indicates a strategy of use and immediate reuse of material, the extent of which exceeds what we heard in the A section. If the A section seemed linear in its overall tendency, the B section incorporates a significant circular tendency into its linear trajectory. Second, but for the succession 26–27, where we return to previous material, the overall tendency in this section is to move forward, adding new units and dwelling on them without going back. This, again, promotes a sense of narration. The process is additive and incremental, goal-directed and purposeful.

While the A and B sections share an overall incremental strategy, there are differences, the most telling being a sense of return in the A section (for example, units 15–16 belong with unit 2 in the same paradigmatic class), which is lacking in the B section. In other words, a sense of self-containment and closure in the A section is replaced by an openness and goal-directedness in the B section.

A' Section (bars 66–100)

The occasion for return in Brahms is often the occasion for recomposition. Among his gifts as a composer is the uncanny ability to render familiar or previously heard material in a guise that transforms, indeed transfigures, the original meaning and brings genuine delight. A return thus compels us to listen comparatively, to admire the composer's ingenuity in saying the same thing differently. The events in this reprise follow closely those of the A section, but there are a few significant differences, one of them residing in the realm of key allegiance. The A section was entirely in E major, with several cadences on (rather than in) the dominant. The B section took us to the submediant (C-sharp/D-flat minor/major) as the main alternative to the home key. The A' section will now restore I, but Brahms decides to enhance the sense of dominant by dwelling in rather than merely on the dominant. Accordingly, he reverses sonata-form procedure by presenting material in the dominant that was previously in the tonic. Thus, after recapitulating units 1 and 2 as 37 and 38, unit 11 as 39, and unit 3 as 40, all in E major, he offers a hearing of the passage spanning units 4–10 in the dominant, B major, in units 41–50. There is method in this modification, of course, deriving in part from the relative restraint in tonal exploration and in part from the remaining tonal work that will be accomplished by the upcoming coda.

If we compare the A and A' sections from the point of view of their material content, we can say that nothing new happens in the A' section. As listeners, our attention is focused as much on process and imaginative recasting as on the sensual value of the materials. This key fact, namely, that no unit in the reprise lacks ancestry within the movement, engenders fresh in-time attention to Brahms' craft. Here are the equivalent units:

37 = 1	46 = (based on) 9
38 = 2	47 = (based on) 10
39 = 11	48 = 10
40 = 3	49 = 47 = 10
41 = 4	50 = 48 = 10
42 = 5 (but 42 ends on a V7 chord,	51 = 12
not on a stable triad)	52 = 13
43 = 6 (transposed)	53 = 14
44 = 7 (transposed)	54 = 15
45 = 8 (transposed)	55 = 16

In figure 7.3 is a paradigmatic arrangement. The stacking of units 47–50 tells us that the passage of falling fifths from unit 10 is being expanded. There are, of course, changes of texture and scoring that are not conveyed in a paradigmatic layout, changes that in some cases inflect the expressive trajectory. One such example

Figure 7.3 Paradigmatic arrangement of units 37–55 in Brahms's Intermezzo in E minor, op. 119, no. 2.

```
37     38
        39 (truncated) 40     41
                              42
                        43     44
                              45     46     47
                                          48
                                          49
                                          50     51
                                                 52
                                                 53
        54
        55
```

is the recasting in unit 51 of the memorable oboe melody from unit 12. Its closing quality is enhanced by doubling and by the incorporation of a triplet figure in the accompaniment.

Coda (bars 100–end)

Units 56 (bars 100³–102²), 57 (bars 102³–104²)

The flattened-seventh degree of the scale is sometimes put to poignant, poetic use by Brahms.[3] The beginning of this coda (bar 100) provides a memorable example. In general, ♭7 announces the beginning of the end, signals a plagally inflected beginning, or reinforces the reciprocal functions of beginning and ending. In bar 11 of this movement, the appearance of D-natural (the seventh) over an E major chord intensified the progression to the subdominant and, with it, the first high point of the piece. Similarly, in the broadly expressive passage that leads the B

---

3. For an in-depth study of flat-$\hat{7}$, see Jason Stell, "The Flat-7th Scale Degree in Tonal Music" (Ph.D. diss., Princeton University, 2006).

section to the A' section, the appearance of flat-7 (D-natural in bar 64) intensi-fies the progression to the subdominant. Meanwhile, solo cello adds an epigram-matical quality to this moment, while the E pedal ensures the stasis that reeks of homecoming. Texturally, the music rises from a middle to a high register across 2 bars (101–102), then Brahms repeats the gesture (102–104) with the slightest of rhythmic decorations in unit 57.

Units 58 (bars 104³–105³), 59 (bars 106¹–106³), 60 (bars 107¹–107³), 61 (bars 108¹–108³), 62 (bars 109¹–111³)

One way of enhancing the retrospective glance of a coda is to return to earlier, familiar material and use it as the basis of a controlled fantasy, as if to signal dis-solution. Brahms retrieves the motive from bars 21–23 (unit 14, itself affiliated with the two preceding units and with the opening unit of the work by virtue of its G♯–A–C♯ bass motion) for use in units 58–62. The process features varied repeti-tion of 1-bar units in each of bars 105, 106, 107, 108, and 109, this last extended for another 2 bars. The 3-bar unit 62 functions as the culmination of the process, as a turning point, and as an adumbration of the return to the opening material. Indeed, while the last bar of unit 62 (111) is equivalent to the last bar of unit 1 (bar 2), the preceding bars of the two units are different.

Unit 63 (bars 112¹–114²)

Unit 2, with its prolonged dominant, returns here to continue this final phase, the ending of the ending, so to speak. Dark and lugubrious in bar 112, the material brightens on a major-mode 6/4 chord (bar 113), reversing the effect of the minor 6/4 coloration that we have come to associate with this material. Again, the long-term effectiveness of this modal transformation—a modal fulfillment, we might say—is hard to underestimate.

Unit 64 (bars 114¹–116¹)

Another plateau is reached with this resolution to tonic. As if imitating the begin-ning of the coda (bars 100–101), the melody descends through a flattened-seventh. We recognize the accompaniment's dotted figure from bar 28, where it announced the beginning of the B section. Here, it is incorporated into a reminiscence of past events. Brahms puts a little spoke in the wheel to enhance the desire for tonic: in bar 116, an E–A♯ tritone halts the serene, predictable descent and compels a relaunching of the momentum to close.

Unit 65 (bars 116³–118¹)

With this reuse of the chromatic material from unit 3, we infer that the protagonist will have to make his peace with this chromatic patch. The effect is one of intru-sion, as at the first appearance, but the presence of directed chromatic motion in the previous unit mutes the effects of quotation or intrusion. There is a sense that we have entered a dream world—only for a moment, of course.[4]

Unit 66 (bars 118¹–120²)

Only in retrospect are we able to interpret bar 118 as the beginning of this unit. This is because the link across the bar line in 117–118 is conjunct rather than disjunct. Here, we are treated to the same bass descent of fifths that we encountered in units 10 (C♯–F♯–B–E), 48, and 50 (G♯–C♯–F♯–B), bringing us once more to the tonic (bar 120). Something about the melody of this unit evokes a sense of pastness, the same sense that we associated with units like 3. Overall, the freight of retrospection introduced in unit 56 (bar 100) continues to hang here.

Unit 67 (bars 120²–122²)

This material is a repeat of 64, with slight modifications of texture and registral placement; it encounters the same tritonal crisis at the end of the unit.

Unit 68 (bars 122³–128)

One more intrusion of the chromatic segment finds its final destination in a clean E major chord, the goal of the movement. The final approach incorporates a strong plagal element (bars 123–124), not unlike the link between the B and A' sections. Five bars of uninflected E major provide the phenomenal substance for an ending, inviting us to deposit all existing tensions here and to think of heaven.

Figure 7.4 Paradigmatic arrangement of units 56–68 in Brahms' Symphony No.1/ii.

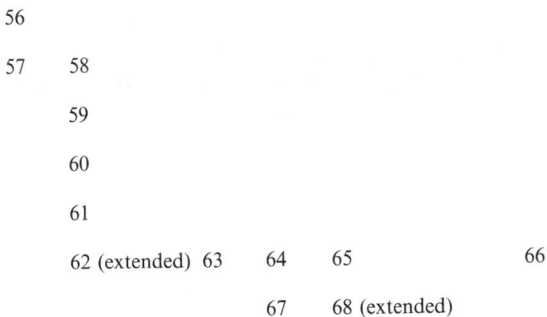

```
56

57    58

      59

      60

      61

62 (extended) 63   64   65                    66

              67   68 (extended)
```

4. The archetypical dimensions of "introspection, interiority [and] subjective inwardness," which Margaret Notley essentializes for Brahms' adagio movements, are awakened in moments like this in an andante. See Notley, "Late-Nineteenth-Century Chamber Music and the Cult of the Classical Adagio," *19th-Century Music* 23 (1999): 33–61.

A paradigmatic arrangement of the coda taken on its own would look like figure 7.4. Again, the stacking of the column with units 58–62 conveys the extensive use of repetition as the movement nears an end; this curbs the narrative tendency by withholding novelty. Indeed, the coda uses several prominent materials from earlier in the movement. Units 58–62, for example, are based on the first bar of the main material of the movement, unit 1. Unit 63 is equivalent to unit 2, while units 65 and 68 are equivalent to unit 3, the latter extended to close the movement. There is nothing new under the sun.

What, then, has the foregoing semiotic analysis shown? As always with analysis, a verbal summary is not always testimony to its benefits, for what I hope to have encouraged is hands-on engagement with Brahms' materials. Nevertheless, I can point out a few findings. I began by invoking Walter Frisch's remark that this movement is a supreme example of Brahmsian musical prose. The movement is indeed segmentable, not according to a fixed, rule-based phrase structure but on the basis of contextual (some might say ad hoc) criteria, that is, according to what Brahms wishes to express in the moment, from phrase to phrase and from section to section. I sought to characterize each bit of material according to its locally functional tendency and then to see what constructional work it is doing in the course of the movement. In some cases, the paradigmatic analysis simply confirms—or gives external representation to—long-held intuitions about musical structure. For example, the idea that closing sections feature extensive reiteration of previously heard material is conveyed by the affiliations among units 58–62. The narrative-like sense of the A section is conveyed by the number of "new ideas" that Brahms exposes there. The different pacing in utterance between the A and B sections—roughly, the prose-like nature of the A section against the initially verse-like nature of the contrasting B section, which, however, returns to prose from about unit 28 onward—is underwritten by the rhythm of units.

Enumerating these structural functions, however, does not adequately convey the sensual pleasure of analyzing a movement like this—playing through it at the piano, juxtaposing different units or segments, imagining a different ordering, writing out some passages on music paper, and listening to different recordings. In one sense, then, no grand statement is necessary because the process is multifaceted, multiply significant, and dedicated to doing. To have undertaken the journey is what ultimately matters; the report of sights seen and sounds heard signifies only imperfectly and incompletely.

CHAPTER Eight

Mahler, Symphony no. 9/i (1908–1909)

How might we formulate a semiotic interpretation of a large-scale work whose units, if reckoned in notes, measures, or even groups of measures, might easily run into the hundreds, thus obscuring the work's larger design? How, in other words, might we reasonably convey something of the paradigmatic construction of such a work without getting lost in minutiae? Is it possible to retain something of the spirit of the methodology applied to the 6-bar tune of "God Save the King" (chapter 5) in analyzing the 454 bars of the first movement of Mahler's Ninth? The following analysis will incorporate answers to these questions, drawing on a variety of criteria for segmentation. It will emerge—again—that a paradigmatic analysis does not sever all connections with more traditional approaches, whether they be concentrated on theme, harmony, voice leading, texture, rhythm, or periodicity. Rather, paradigmatic analysis repackages some of the insights produced in the course of a traditional analysis into a form that emphasizes the constructive role of repetition and its associated transformations.

Writing about Mahler's last works (as distinct from his late style), Adorno echoed a long-standing dichotomy in the historical discourse about music by separating "the directly musical qualities and their technical organization" from "the spirit of the music." To "understand music," he proclaimed, "is nothing other than to trace the interaction of the two."[1] The dichotomy works at a methodological level and has rhetorical consequences as well. It is ultimately problematic, however, because something of "the spirit of the music" surely influences analysis of its "directly musical qualities"; it is hard to believe that the spirit of the music can be grasped by listeners who possess no feeling whatsoever for the directly musical qualities, whether or not they are able to provide technical designations for such qualities. In practice, a number of challenges are presented by upholding spirit and technique as ideals, while at the same time seeking to convey the dynamics of their interaction. That is why, despite their obvious fragility, frequently invoked oppositions between structure and expression, autonomous and nonautonomous

---

1. Adorno, *Mahler*, 149.

structure, the musical and the extramusical, or even structuralism and hermeneutics have not been rendered totally irrelevant in contemporary musicological
discourse. The differences they promulgate lie at the very root of almost all theori-
zation of musical meaning.

The main intellectual labor in this book has been geared toward explicating the
directly musical qualities while letting the spirit of the music emerge from individual or even personal narratives drawn from these qualities. My reticence may
seem evasive, but is intended to be strategic. It is motivated in part by the recognition that the range of responses provoked by the spirit of the music is irreducibly
plural and unavoidably heterogeneous. Plurality and heterogeneity, however, speak
not to unconstrained speculation but—more pragmatically—to the nature of our
(metalinguistic and institutional) investments in critical practice. Nor do I mean
to imply that the directly musical qualities finally admit of homogeneous characterization. I believe, however, that the degree of divergence within the domain of
technical characterization is significantly narrower than the diversity within characterizations of spirit. This difference does not in itself carry a recommendation
about what is more meaningful to explore. Since, however, part of the burden of
this book has been to encourage (spiritual) adventures emanating from the observation of technical procedures, I will retain that stance in the analysis that follows.
"Directly musical qualities" will be constructed from the specific viewpoint of the
use of repetition.

Let us turn, then, to a work that is not exactly lacking in extensive analytical commentary.[2] Indeed, some analyses—such as that by Constantin Floros—are
implicitly paradigmatic. My own approach differs only to the extent that it is more
explicit in this regard. As before, I will follow a two-step analytical procedure.
First, I will identify the building blocks or units in the entire movement; second,
I will explore some of the affiliations among the building blocks. It is at this latter
stage—the stage of *dispositio*, we might say—that matters of discourse will come
to the fore.

Criteria for Segmentation

How does one break a relatively complex texture like that of the first movement of
Mahler's Ninth into manageable, meaningful units? At 454 bars, this is of course
a sizable movement—a far cry, indeed, from the 6 bars of "God Save the King"
with which I introduced the paradigmatic method in chapter 5, or the 104 bars

2. Henry-Louis de La Grange provides a useful synthesis of the major analytical studies of the Ninth
while offering his own original insights. See *Gustav Mahler: A New Life Cut Short (1907–1911)*
(Oxford: Oxford University Press, 2008), 1405–1452. See also Stephen Hefling, "The Ninth Symphony," in *The Mahler Companion*, ed. Donald Mitchell and Andrew Nicholson (Oxford: Oxford
University Press, 2002), 467–490. Dániel Bíro emphasizes timbre in the course of a holistic appreciation of the movement in "Plotting the Instrument: On the Changing Role of Timbre in Mahler's
Ninth Symphony and Webern's op. 21" (unpublished paper).

of Brahms' E Minor Intermezzo, op. 119, no. 2, which we studied in the previous chapter. In terms of gesture, Mahler's movement is perhaps closest to Liszt's *Orpheus*, but the building blocks there are set apart more distinctly than in Mahler. Yet the same general principles of segmentation apply. Units must be meaningful and morphologically distinct. Repetition may be exact or varied (with several stages in between). Where it involves tonal tendencies, voice-leading paradigms, or thematic identities, repetition must be understood with some flexibility in order to accommodate looser affiliations. For example, if two units begin in the same way, or indicate the same narrative intentions, and conclude in the same way (syntactically) without, however, following the same path to closure, they may be deemed equivalent on one level. This loosening of associative criteria is necessary in analyzing a fully freighted tonal language; it is also necessary in order to accommodate Mahler's intricate textures and to register their narrative tendency. As we will see, a number of units carry an intrinsic narrative disposition. Narration is often (though by no means always) melody-led and imbued with tendencies of beginning, continuing, or ending.

Related criteria for segmentation are contrast and discontinuity. *Contrast* may be expressed as the juxtaposition of dense and less dense textures, the alternation and superimposition of distinct tone colors or groups of such colors, opposing or distantly related tonal tendencies, or differentiated thematic gestures.[3] We typically encounter contrast from the left, that is, prospectively—as if we walked into it. Not all apparent gestures of discontinuity sustain the designation of contrast, however. When the collective elements of difference separating two adjacent units seem to outnumber or be more forcefully articulated than the collective elements of sameness, we are inclined to speak of *discontinuity*. Neither continuity nor discontinuity can be absolute, however.

In short, segmentation is guided by the tendency of the material: its proclivities and its conventional and natural associations. Listening from this point of view involves attending to the unfolding dynamic in an immediate sense even while recognizing associations with other moments. We listen forward, but we also entertain resonances that have us listening sideways and backward.

It should be noted that the boundaries separating adjacent units are not always as firm as our segmentation might sometimes imply. Processes within one unit may spill over into the next. Sometimes, newness is known only in retrospect. And the conflation of beginnings and endings, a procedure that goes back to the beginnings of tonal thinking, is often evident in Mahler. Units may be linked by a fluid transitional process whose exact beginning and ending may not be strongly marked. The boundaries indicated by bar numbers are therefore merely convenient signposts—provisional rather than definitive indicators of potential breaks. Listeners should not be denied the opportunity to hear past these boundaries if they so desire; indeed, such hearing past is well-nigh unavoidable during a regular audition

---

3. On contrast in Mahler, see Paul Whitworth, "Aspects of Mahler's Musical Style: An Analytical Study" (Ph.D. diss., Cornell University, 2002). On the composer's manipulation of tone color, see John Sheinbaum, "Timbre, Form and Fin-de-Siècle Refractions in Mahler's Symphonies" (Ph.D. diss., Cornell University, 2002).

of the work. I ask only that listeners accept the plausibility of these boundaries for the purposes of analysis.

Paradigmatic Analysis

I have divided the movement into 33 units. Let us make a first pass through the movement by describing their features and tendencies. Later, I will speculate on form and meaning. (From here on, the reader needs access to a full score of the movement in order to verify the description that follows.)

Unit 1 (bars 1–6³)

The feeling of emergence that we experience in these opening bars (see the piano score of these bars in example 8.1) will be transformed when first violins enter at the end of bar 6 with F-sharp followed by E, a $\hat{3}$–$\hat{2}$ melodic gesture that will be repeated immediately and, in due course, come to embody the narrative voice. The opening bars are fragmentary and timbrally distinct, and they lack an urgent or purposeful profile. It will emerge in retrospect that these bars constitute a metaphorical upbeat to the movement's beginning proper. Their purpose is to expose a number of key motifs: a syncopated figure or "halting rhythm" played by cellos and horns; a "tolling-bell figure" played by the harp (which includes a 025 trichord suggesting pentatonic affiliation); a "sad phrase" played by horns based on a $\hat{5}$–$\hat{6}$ melodic gesture ($\hat{5}$–$\hat{6}$ frames bars 3–4² and then is stated directly in bars 5⁴–6²); and a "rustling or palpitation" in the viola (which, although figured functionally as accompaniment, is nevertheless essential to the movement's discourse). The summary effect is atmospheric and descriptive; there is a sense that nothingness is being replaced.[4]

Example 8.1. Opening bars of Mahler's Ninth, first movement.

Unit 1 not only sets out the principal motives of the movement, it will return in a recomposed guise to begin the so-called development section (unit 10). It will also be heard at the climax of the movement (unit 24). Nothing in this initial presentation allows us to predict subsequent functions and transformations—nothing, perhaps, except the embryonic manner of the beginning, which suggests a subsequent

---

4. I have borrowed Deryck Cooke's descriptive phrases for unit 1 because they seem particularly apt. See Cooke, *Gustav Mahler: An Introduction to His Music* (London: Faber, 1980), 116–117.

presentation of more fully formed ideas. Significant, too, are the relative autonomy and separateness of the passage (bars 1–6 were crossed out of Mahler's autograph score at one point during the compositional process; they were later restored), its spatial rather than linear manner, and its fascinating and unhierarchic display of timbres in the manner of a *Klangfarbenmelodie*. If, in spite of the unit's spatial tendencies, one is able to attend to its overall tonal tendency, then pitch-class A will emerge as anchor, as a source of continuity throughout the passage.

Unit 2 (bars 6^4–17^5)

The main theme (or subject) is exposed here. (Example 8.2 quotes the melody.) The material is in song mode, unfolds in a leisurely manner, and carries an air of nostalgia. The unhurried aura comes in part from the grouping of motives: two notes and a rest, two notes and a rest, threefold articulation of two notes and a rest, fivefold articulation of four notes followed by a rest, three notes and a rest, the same three notes and a rest, and finally an expansive gesture in which seven notes are offered in 13 attack points. The melody seems to go over the same ground even as it gradually and subtly breaks out of its initial mold.

Example 8.2. Main theme of Mahler's Ninth, first movement, bars 7–16.

While unit 1 was grounded on an A, unit 2 rationalizes the tonal tendency in that A as the dominant of D. Cutting through the polyphonic mix in unit 2 is a $\hat{3}$–$\hat{2}$ melodic gesture that will dominate the movement. The sound term $\hat{3}$–$\hat{2}$ is a promise, of course, because it is syntactically incomplete. This is not a uniquely Mahlerian rendition; $\hat{3}$–$\hat{2}$ bears over a century of conventional use, most famously in the first movement of Beethoven's *Les Adieux* Sonata, op. 81a, and in "Der Abschied" from Mahler's own *Das Lied von der Erde*. In this unit, $\hat{3}$–$\hat{2}$ appears first as a beginning; then, in bars 14–18 (the ending of the unit), it appears in the context of an ending.

The once-upon-a-time quality conveyed by the string melody and its horn associates suggests a movement of epic proportions. Among other things, the ostinato bass in bars 9–13 underlines the largeness of the canvas. Significant, too, is the muting of leading-tone influence such that the harmonic ambience, pandiatonic rather than plainly diatonic, acquires an accommodating feel rather than a charged profile. Among other features, $\hat{6}$ is incorporated into the tonic chord; some sonorities contain unresolved appoggiaturas while others suggest a conflation of tonic and dominant functions. Unit 2 ends incompletely. The dialogue between second violins (carrying the main melody) and horns (singing a countermelody in bars 14–17) is dominated by gestures promising closure. The listener carries forward an expectation for eventual fulfillment.

Unit 3 (bars 17⁶–28)

The main theme is sounded again, but the rhetoric and the harmonic goal are modified. First violins lead in an upper register—an octave above the beginning of the previous unit. By beginning as if to say the same thing again, the violins intensify the rhetoric and underline the sense of archaism intrinsic to unit 2. This unit concludes with a $\hat{3}$–$\hat{2}$–$\hat{1}$ melodic progression (bars 24–25), and is followed by the same sort of echoes that ended the previous unit (bars 14–17). Here, the echoes take on a charged quality as their mode is transformed from major to minor; $\hat{3}$–$\hat{2}$ in minor being a half-step carries a more poignant affect than the whole-step $\hat{3}$–$\hat{2}$ in major.

Taking stock: we began with a self-contained prelude (unit 1) that seemed to stand outside the narrative frame. Then, the main theme emerged to indicate the movement's beginning proper and to announce its narrative intentions (unit 2). We noted that this is not as emphatic a statement as we might imagine for a purposeful symphonic opening; the manner is indulgent, the idea unfolds at its own glacial pace. Finally, unit 3 offered a varied repetition of the previous unit, reaching a proper cadence, and ending with the same sort of transitional material that ended the previous unit. Affectively contrasting, this transitional material promises something ominous.

Unit 4 (bars 29–47)

Here, we encounter the most striking contrast so far in the movement. The mode switches decisively from major to minor, the predominant diatonicism (perhaps even a hint of the folksiness) is replaced by a chromatic network in which, among other configurations, the augmented triad appears frequently (A–C♯–F in bars 29–30, 36, and 38, and D–B♭–F♯ in bar 37); melodic narration is busier, more agitated, and seemingly troubled; and the constraining register for the melody covers a massive three octaves at least. This heightening of the rhetoric produces the first high point of the movement in bar 39—a point of culmination rather than a tensional high point demanding immediate resolution (it sits on D, the tonic). This statistical climax is the result of combined activity in the domains of texture, dynamics, range, and register.

The high point in bar 39 is followed by another process of intensification. Bars 44–47 feature a decisive drive to a cadence. Mahler employs a charged, linear, and goal-oriented procedure for what is the biggest cadence in the movement so far. Where units 1–3 seemed reticent about employing leading-tone action (except in the transition between units), unit 4 exploits the intrinsic dependency of chromatic affiliation. Notice the trumpet fanfare (bars 44–46) that intensifies the affect while bringing thematic potential to this ending. Unit 4 literally discharges into the next unit.

Taking stock again: unit 1 is spatially oriented, offering a mosaic of motifs in a non-urgent temporal profile. Units 2 and 3 begin the narrative process, pointing to a future that is yet to be realized. Unit 4 stimulates the ordinary language of the work by cooking up the first climax and introducing darker affections; and unit 5, as we will see, continues from where the 2–3 pair left off, introducing a new level of narration that, however, is soon truncated. Mahlerian narrative as displayed in these first five units is based on networks of activity in which leading ideas and processes vie for attention. While it is of course possible to extract a *Hauptstimme*, claims for melodic priority are made by different instrumental parts. What we are dealing with, then, are "degrees of narrativity" (as Vera Micznik calls them).[5] For example, the simple act of melodic telling in units 2 and 3 is transformed into a more communal activity in unit 4. Unit 1, likewise, effected the manner of a constellation, a communality by default rather than by design. (I'm talking not about the composer's intentions but about the tendency of the musical material.) There is, as always in Mahler, a surplus, an excess of content over that which is needed to establish a narrative line.

Unit 5 (bars 46⁶–54²)

This appearance of the main theme incorporates motifs from the prelude (unit 1), including the palpitating sextuplet figure introduced in bar 5 by the violas and entrusted now to double basses and bassoons, and the "sad phrase" announced by the horns in bars 4–5, which is now given to the trumpets (bars 49–50). The music makes a deceptive close in bars 53–54 by means of a V–♭vi motion, thus opening up the flat side of the tonal spectrum. We recall the juxtaposition of D major and minor in units 3–4 and project the thought that similar dualities will carry a fair amount of the movement's dynamic.

The aftermath of the cadence in bars 53–54 carries a strong sense of codetta at first, but a new melodic idea in a different tonal environment (bars 57 onward, in B-flat major) confers a sense of beginning rather than ending. This conflation of functions is partly why I have located the beginning of unit 6 in bar 54; the join between units 5 and 6 is porous.

Unit 6 (bars 54³–63³)

Although some of the motivic elements on display here have been adumbrated in previous units, the overriding tendency is that of dream or recall—as if a lost song (sung by second violins and flutes) were filtering through. The moment has the character of a parenthesis, a tributary to the narrative. This feature will emerge even more forcefully when oboes and violins barge in at bar 63 to resume the main narration. We may suspect that a certain amount of tonal business is being transacted here (the key of B-flat lies a third away from D), but we are not yet in a position to know for sure. The ending of this unit illustrates Mahler's penchant for problematizing conventional syntax: what begins as a 6/4-induced cadential gesture in B-flat (bars 62–63) is abandoned or cut short. We may with some confidence speak of an interruption or even a disjunction between units 6 and 7. (Ana-

---

5. Vera Micznik, "Music and Narrative Revisited: Degrees of Narrativity in Mahler," *Journal of the Royal Musical Association* 126 (2001): 193–249.

lysts inclined to find continuity will, of course, succeed: the pitch B-flat provides a link between the two units.)

Unit 7 (bars 64–79)

This begins as another version of the main theme, featuring the promise or "farewell" motif, 3̂–2̂. Continuation is modified, however, to lead to extended closure. From bar 71 onward, a network of closing gestures within diatonic polyphony generates expectations for something new. We may well feel that the work of the main theme (as heard in units 2, 3, 5, and now 7) is nearly done and that something new needs to happen to counter the pervasive sense of stasis. The neat juxtaposition of major and minor in bars 77 and 78, respectively, sums up the modal history of the movement so far without, however, giving the impression that unit 7 is capable of resolving all of the tensions accumulated.

Unit 8 (bars 80–91)

This unit starts on, rather than in, B-flat. Among other previously heard motifs, it incorporates the movement's main contrasting material, the chromatic idea first introduced as unit 4, where it was grounded on D. Here, the ground shifts to B-flat, but the melodic pitches remain the same—a use of pitch invariance that is not common in Mahler. A strong dominant sense in 86–87 conveys the imminence of closure. All of the signs are that we will close in B-flat, a key that has made only sporadic appearance so far (most notably in unit 6), but this expectation is not fulfilled. What seems pertinent here, and is entirely in keeping with Mahler's metamusical impulses, is not the tonicization of a specific scale degree but a more primal desire for some sort of cadential articulation. Mosaic-like motivic construction thus combines with cadential suggestiveness to mark this unit as an on-its-way gesture.

Unit 9 (bars 92–107)

The closing gesture introduced at the end of the previous unit is intensified with this marked off-beat passage (example 8.3), which will return at subsequent moments of intensification. Reinforced by a cymbal crash and underpinned by a circle-of-fifths progression (example 8.4), the unit prepares a cadence in B-flat. At bar 98, a subdominant-functioning chord further signals closure, but once again normative continuation is withheld. In other words, while the spirit of intensification is kept up, the conventional supporting syntax is denied. Eventually, material marked *allegro* (bar 102) rushes the unit to a dramatic conclusion in bar 107. This moment is marked for consciousness by its 6/3 harmony on B-flat. It is something of a transgressive gesture, for in place of the longed-for stable cadential close, Mahler supplies an unstable ending. Indeed, the 6/3 chord points, among other things, to a possible E-flat cadence (see the hypothetical progression in example 8.5). An upbeat rather than a downbeat, a precadential harmony rather than a cadential close, this moment reeks of abandonment. Mahler writes in a double bar at 107 to

Example 8.3. "Intensifying phrase," Mahler's Ninth, first movement, bars 92–95.

Example 8.4. Model for "intensifying phrase" quoted in example 8.3.

becomes

Example 8.5. Hypothetical continuation of bars 105–106 of Mahler's Ninth, first movement.

mark off a major segment of the work. Were this not also the end of the exposition, the strategic violence of refusing forward drive would be less intense.

Taking stock: the alternation between the main theme (in D major) and the subsidiary theme (in D minor) establishes a large-scale structural rhythm that leads the listener to imagine a work of large proportions. So far, the mosaic-like circulation of motifs together with the absence of purposeful tonal exploration have combined to undermine any expectations we might entertain for clear sonata-form articulation. The movement in fact forges its own path to understanding. We finish the exposition with the summary understanding that a diatonic, nostalgic idea (the main theme), repeated in varied form, alternates with a "tormented" (Cooke's word) chromatic idea, which retains some pitch invariance in repetition while adapting to new tonal situations. We are also haunted by a third, subsidiary element, the B-flat major theme (unit 6), which opened the door to the otherworldly. A paradigmatic arrangement of the units would look like figure 8.1.

Figure 8.1 Paradigmatic arrangement of units 1–9 in Mahler's Ninth Symphony, first movement

1	2	
3	4	
5	6	
7	8	9

The arrangement confirms that things are weighted toward the main theme (a fourfold occurrence, units 2, 3, 5, and 7) and that the contrasting theme makes a twofold appearance (units 4 and 8). Of course, there is more to the formal process than this external disposition of materials. For example, a teleological process embodied in the 2–3–5–7 sequence contributes an accumulative sense, but this is not readily observable from a simple paradigmatic arrangement. Similarly, affiliations between the relatively autonomous opening unit (1) and subsequent units (perhaps most notably, units 8 and 9) may not be readily inferred. The experience of form in Mahler is often a complex business, depending as much on what is *not* said as on what is said and how it is said. To take Mahler on his own is to risk an impoverished experience. Even in a work like the first movement of the Ninth, where intertextual resonance is less about thematic or topical affiliation, an internally directed hearing will still have to contend with various dialogues. For example, without a horizon of expectations shaped by sonata form, rondo form, and theme and variations, one might miss some of the subtle aspects of the form. These categories are not erased in Mahler; rather, they are placed under threat of erasure, by which I mean that they are simultaneously present and absent, visible but mute. Mahler demands of his listeners the cultivation of a dialogic imagination.

Unit 10 (bars 108–129³)

Immediately noticeable in this unit is the activation of the speech mode. Motivic development often takes this form since it in effect foregrounds the working mode, the self-conscious and ongoing manipulation of musical figures without the constraint of regular periodicity. The unit is marked at the beginning by a strong motivic association with the opening of the work: the syncopated figure leads off (bars 108–110), followed by the tolling-bell motif in bars 111–112 and in the following. Soon, other elements join in this loose recomposition of unit 1. Manipulation, not presentation, is the purpose here. From the sparseness of texture, we infer that several of the motifs seem to have traveled a considerable expressive distance. The working mode gives way to a codetta sense around bar 117, where a new figure in oboes, English horn, violas, and cellos conveys the gestural sense of closure without, however, supplying the right syntax. This sense of closing will persist throughout units 10 and 11 before being transformed into an anticipatory feeling at the start of unit 12 (bar 136). In a sense, units 10, 11, and 12 constitute a giant recomposition of unit 1, thus setting up expectation for a sequence of events reminiscent of units 1–9.

Unit 11 (bars 129⁴–135³)

The brevity of unit 11 matches the brevity of its earlier appearance in unit 6, where it functioned almost like a recall of a forgotten melody—meandering and not particularly strongly profiled. Here, its retroactive, veiled qualities are retained, alongside the deeply affecting sighing of flutes and horns—all of this accompanied by the tolling-bell figure in the harp.

Unit 12 (bars 135⁴–147)

A pedal point on D inflected at first by minor-mode harmonies and then by major underlies a tremolo-laden passage led by a gradually unfolding chromatic scale. All of this suggests some kind of thematic or tonal arrival. On display here is the composer's ordinary language, not his poetic language. The purpose is to make good on the legacy of the first 10 units of the movement. Listeners attached to conventional formal schemes will claim that we have begun the formal process of development, but the brief statement in unit 11 may well undermine this sense because it is functionally more presentational than developmental. The overtly anticipatory unit 12 in turn suggests retransition rather than transition, though this would be premature given where we have reached in the formal narrative. The fact, however, that it sits on a "tonic" pedal introduces an element of incongruity. Endowing materials with mixed functional profiles is typical of Mahler.

Unit 13 (bars 148–160¹)

This warm and nostalgic variant of the main theme appears in one of its most stable forms: harmonies alternate between tonic and dominant, and the phrase structure is a square 4 + 4 followed by a 5-bar phrase overlapping with the next unit. Is the process of development over already with this appearance of the main theme? Unit 13 has something of the quality of an oasis. Note the influence of context on meaning. In previous appearances, and despite the aura of pastness that surrounded this material, the main theme had always signified presence. Here, in the context of a developmental process that evokes more of a devastated landscape than determined (Brahmsian) exploration, the main theme acquires the character of a dream, of recall.

Unit 14 (bars 160–195)

The working mode activated in unit 10, which was suspended in unit 13, is reactivated here using the closing gestures from unit 10. Unexpectedly, the main theme appears again in its most recent stable form (bar 166), but it is now in E-flat major, not D, and is soon to be superseded by busywork. Some of the motivic material seems new (the pitch material played by the basses at 174 is an example, though not the accompanying rhythm), while some of it is familiar. The unit as a whole is tonally unstable in spite of the flirtation with G major from bar 182 on. Proceedings intensify from bar 174 onward. Previously heard motives are laboriously incorporated in a full contrapuntal texture, and this working mode—a struggle of sorts—continues through the rest of the unit, reaching something of a local turning point at the beginning of the next unit.

Unit 15 (bars 196–210)

As in its previous appearance, this off-beat, syncopated passage, underpinned by bass motion in fifths, signals intensification, culminating this time in the first high point of the development (bar 202). Again, the bass note is D, and so the high point is produced not by the tension of tonal distance but by activity in the secondary parameters of texture and dynamics. In the aftermath of the high point, sixteenth-note figures derived from the movement's contrasting idea (heard also in unit 10, bars 121–24) are incorporated into the accompaniment, preparing its melodic appearance in the next unit.

Unit 16 (bars 211–246[1])

The affectively charged material that functions as the main contrasting material in the movement appears once again. When it was first heard (unit 4), it sported a D minor home. Later, it appeared with the same pitches over a B-flat pedal (unit 8). On this third occasion, pitch invariance is maintained, and the B-flat pedal of the second occurrence is used, but the modal orientation is now minor, not major.

This material signals only the beginning of a unit whose purpose is to advance the working-through process. It does so not, as before, by juxtaposing different themes in a mosaic-like configuration, but by milking a single theme for expressive consequence. Throughout this unit, string-based timbres predominate and lines are often doubled. (The string-based sound provides a foretaste of the finale, while also recalling the finale of Mahler's Third Symphony.) In its immediate context, the materials signal an act of cadencing on a grand scale. The approach in bar 215 is not followed through, however; nor does the local high point at 221 discharge into a cadence. Finally, at 228, the syntax for a cadence on B-flat is presented in the first two eighth-notes, but nothing of the durational or rhetorical requirements for such a cadence accompanies the moment. The goal, it turns out, is none other than the tonic of the movement, and this cadence occurs at 235–236, although the momentum shoots past this moment and incorporates a series of reminiscences or postcadential reflection.

Although key relationships are explored from time to time in this movement (as Christopher Lewis has shown),[6] the overall drama does not depend fundamentally on purposeful exploration of alternative tonal centers. The tonic—be it in a major or minor guise—is never far away; indeed, in a fundamental sense, and despite the presence of third-related passages in B-flat major and B major, the

---

6. Christopher Lewis, *Tonal Coherence in Mahler's Ninth Symphony* (Ann Arbor, MI: UMI Press, 1984).

movement, we might say, never really leaves the home key. It concentrates its labor on thematic, textural, and phrase-structural manipulation.

Unit 17 (bars 245⁴–266)

The tremolo passage from unit 12 returns to announce a coming thematic stability. A constellation of motifs (including the $\hat{3}$–$\hat{2}$ gesture, the augmented triad, and the chromatic descent) accompanies this announcement.

Unit 18 (bars 266⁴–279²)

The main theme is given melodramatic inflection in the form of a solo violin utterance (bars 269–270). Solo timbre sometimes signals an end, an epilogue perhaps; sometimes the effect is particularly poignant. This overall sense of transcendence is conveyed here even as other motifs circulate within this typical Mahlerian constellation.

Unit 19 (bars 279²–284)

Previously associated with moments of intensification, this syncopated passage appears without the full conditions for intensification. This is because the preceding unit was stable and assumed a presentational function. (A continuing or developmental function would have provided a more natural or conventional preparation.) Only in its last 2 bars (277–278) was a token attempt made to render the beginning of the next unit nondiscontinuous. In one sense, then, this intensifying unit functions at a larger level, not a local one. It harks back to its sister passages and reminds us that, despite the sweet return of the main theme in bar 269, the business of development is not yet finished. In retrospect, we might interpret unit 18 as an interpolation.

Unit 20 (bars 284⁴–295¹)

An ascending, mostly chromatic bass line in the previous unit (E♮–F♮–A♭–A♮–A♯) discharges into the initial B major of this one. Horn and trumpet fanfares activate the thematic dimension, as does the sad phrase from the opening bars of the work, now in a decidedly jubilant mood (bar 286).

Unit 21 (bars 295²–298)

We single out this 4-bar phrase as a separate unit because we recognize it from previous occurrences. In context, however, it is part of a broad sweep begun in unit 20 that will reach a climax in unit 24. Part of what is compositionally striking about this moment is that a gesture that seemed marked in its three previous occurrences (units 11, 15, 19) now appears unmarked as it does its most decisive work. Here, it is absorbed into the flow, neutralized by name, so to speak, so that we as listeners can attend to the production processes.

Unit 22 (bars 298⁴–308)

Retrieving the key and material from unit 20 and resuming the process begun there, this unit advances the rising dynamic trajectory. It reaches the dominant of A-flat major in 304, declines the opportunity to cadence, and then charges on to another statement of the intensifying phrase. The sense of an approaching high point is especially strong at the end of this unit, contributed by the emphatic dec-lamation at the beginning of bar 304, the deliberate slowing down in bar 307, and high-placed Cs played by violins and clarinets in the same bar.

Unit 23 (bars 308²–320)

With its beginning in medias res (harmonically as well as rhythmically), this intensifying phrase takes over the narrative and prepares a cadence in B major. Mahler's expressive marking is *Pesante (Höchste Kraft)*. If any of the thematic agents encountered so far are capable of engendering a crisis, it is almost certainly this one. In this fourth and, for now, final appearance, an F♯–C tritone underlines its structural instability (bar 308, second beat, treble and bass notes). Melodically, the F-sharp in bar 308 is approached from the C below, while in the bass, C appears enharmonically as B-sharp (a member of the dominant of the supertonic). The C in turn leads to C-sharp (the supertonic, bar 309) and then to F-sharp (the domi-nant, bar 310). Seven bars later (bar 314), the collapse comes with an overwhelm-ing conflation of falling gestures, crashing percussion playing *mit höchster Gewalt* (with the greatest force), an unyielding C–F♯ tritone anchoring the sonority, the syncopated rhythm from the very beginning of the work, and dynamics at *fff* fol-lowed by diminuendo. We have had high points before, but none of them matches this one in sheer intensity.

Unit 24 (bars 320⁴–346)

While the idea of a coming high point was conveyed prospectively and unequivo-cally in preceding units, only in retrospect do we understand the climactic moment as, in effect, a recomposition of unit 1. The syncopated rhythm in bars 314–315 was the rhythm that began the work—quietly, without fanfare, almost unnoticed, as if in the womb. It was this same rhythm that announced the beginning of the movement's working mode after more than 100 bars (unit 10, bar 108). In unit 23, it signifies collapse; indeed, the cumulative effect of bars 313–314 is a neutralizing of tonal sense, a crossing over into the realm of nonmusic within the limits of tonal expression. The syncopated rhythm also carries a promise of recovery, and it is out of the ruins engendered by the huge climax that thematic flashbacks emerge in unit 24. In addition to the syncopated rhythm, the tolling-bell motif plays a promi-nent role here, appearing as an ostinato in every bar between 319 and the end of the unit (bar 346). Then, there are the authentically realized brass fanfares that punctuate what Mahler himself describes as a funeral march (*Wie ein schwerer Kondukt*). A sense of desolation pervades this passage as the 3̂–2̂ narrating motif from unit 2 provides the material basis for procession.

Figure 8.2 Paradigmatic arrangement of units 10–24 in Mahler's Ninth Symphony, first movement.

10	11	12	13			
			14	15	16	
		17	18	19		20
			21			22
			23/1			
23/2						
24						

The paradigmatic story of development may be inferred from figure 8.2.[7] Again, the means of representation are limited because the numerous complex affinities among the units have been sacrificed for simplified, gross distinctions based on similarity and difference. Nevertheless, one feature emerges with particular force: the succession of "differences" from unit 10 through 16 (broken only by 14, which "repeats" 13), producing the second longest of such chains in the work. (The longest chain is 7, 8, 9, 10, 11, 12, 13, but the fact that the 7–9 portion belongs to the exposition while the 10–13 portion belongs to the development undermines the sense of consistent novelty.) If the succession of new ideas is a mark of musical narrative, then this portion of the work may be said to exemplify the most sustained narration. The mode is prose-like rather than verse-like. Indeed, the contrast to the exposition—where a single, dominant idea led the proceedings—is striking. We will see later that the recapitulation proceeds more like the exposition than the development.

Unit 25 (bars 346³–356)

The nostalgic main theme returns in a settled manner. After the intervening crisis (or even crises), most listeners will assign greater weight to this return from the point of view of its cathartic function than to the "little returns" in units 3, 5, 7, 13, and 14. It is not that a desire for D major has been satisfied, nor that the nostalgic main theme has left us hankering for more of it. It is simply that the gesture of problematization that reached its acme in unit 24 has prepared us psychologically for the reassurance of thematic return.

How does one listen to a recapitulation under a paradigmatic regime? The question may not be as trivial as it might sound at first. It arises because repetition denies material novelty (or grants it in a limited way), concentrating its novelty in

---

7. Unit 23 is divided into two because the parts are affiliated with different materials. It is, however, retained as a single unit because its overall gesture seems continuous and undivided.

the temporal and experiential realms. Temporal novelty in turn denies material sameness. But unmitigated difference is psychologically threatening, for without a sense of return, without some anchoring in the familiar, music simply loses its ontological essence. Mahler understood this keenly, following in the spirit of his classical predecessors. But, like Brahms before him, recapitulation for Mahler was always a direct stimulus to eloquence, artistic inflection, and creativity. We never say the same thing twice. To do so would be to lie. Hearing a recapitulation, then, means attending to sameness in difference or, rather, difference in sameness. While our scheme of paradigmatic equivalence glosses over numerous details, it nevertheless orients us to gross levels of sameness that in turn facilitate individual acts of willed differentiation.

Unit 26 (bars 356⁴–365²)

Unit 25 is repeated (making the 25–26 succession the equivalent of the earlier 2–3), beginning in a higher register and with the first violins in the lead. The period ends with a deceptive cadence on B-flat as flattened-sixth (bars 364–365), thus leaving things open. The drive to the cadence incorporates a rising chromatic melody (bars 363–365) reminiscent of bars 44–46, but the cadence is deceptive rather than authentic.

Unit 27 (bars 365²–372²)

The pattern of bass notes suggests that we hear this unit as an expanded parenthesis, a dominant prolongation. Beginning on B-flat, the music shifts down through A to G-sharp (bar 370) and then back up to A as V of D. The themes are layered. A version of the main theme occurs in the violas and cellos, while a subsidiary theme from bar 54 (cellos) is now elevated to the top of the melodic texture. The last 2 bars of this unit (371–372) derive from unit 7 (bars 69–70). In short, if unit 26 offered a sense of tonic, unit 27 prolongs that tonic through chromatic neighbors around its dominant.

   An aspect of the production process that this unit reveals is Mahler's attitude toward recapitulation. In certain contexts, reprise is conceived not as a return to the first statement of a particular theme but as a return to the paradigm represented by that theme. In other words, a recapitulation might recall the developmental version of a theme, not its expositional version, or it may recall an unprecedented but readily recognizable version. In this way, the movement's closing section incorporates references to the entire substance of what has transpired. This is Mahlerian organicism at its most compelling.

Unit 28 (bars 372²–376²)

The bass note A serves as a link between units 27 and 28, finding resolution to D in the third bar of this unit. The thematic field being recapitulated is the tormented idea first heard as unit 4. This lasts only 4 bars, however, before it is interrupted by a spectacular parenthesis. Meanwhile, the brasses recall the fanfare material.

Unit 29 (bars 376³–391)

This passage seems at first discontinuous with what precedes it. It offers perhaps the single most salient contrast in the entire movement. Marked *misterioso*, it wears its otherness on its sleeve. This is chamber rather than orchestral music. The instruments effect the improvised manner of a cadenza. The passage as a whole thus acquires the quality of a prolonged upbeat. But signification here is also inflected by the formality of imitation—the flute theme at 383 is passed on to the lowest strings at 386. The sense that the material is pursuing its own course, unconstrained by external, formal imperatives, intensifies the parenthetical aura of the unit. In the absence of periodic regulation, the mode of utterance comes across as speech-like, not song-like.

Unit 30 (bars 391–398)

The recapitulation of the tormented theme begun in unit 28 and interrupted by 29 is resumed here, with the head of the theme played by cellos and basses. The basic intent here is to achieve a significant punctuation, and so the unit rises to a modest climax at 396–397 on D as V of G, but G as I never materializes. Again, the thematic substance is richly allusive. The cadenza material from the preceding unit, especially the chain of sixteenth-notes, continues into this unit. The broad and warm string gestures that seemed to make a meal of cadential prospect back in unit 16 (marked *Leiden schaftlich*) feature here too. Finally, bar 396 resembles the climactic moment at bar 39 in the exposition, a resemblance that is all the more pertinent because the earlier climax occurred as part of the first appearance of the tormented theme (unit 4).

Unit 31 (bars 398–406)

Although the D-major sonority that begins this unit was prepared as V, it is now heard as I. This is another of Mahler's innovations: syntactic revisionism achieved through nonsyntactic means, in this case by sheer assertion. The unit features a prolongation of D as tonic; its thematic manner, dominated by a recall of frag-ments, continues to reinforce an emerging suspicion that we are in a period of home-going. The cadenza-like parenthetical episode in unit 29 already marked one extreme in the conventional articulation of a sense of global closure by allow-ing a small group of soloists to be lost in their own worlds. It is as if the composer wished to suggest what was possible within his otherwise controlled "world"—the symphony. The return of the orchestra in unit 30 signaled a return to normality and the business of closing. This unit in turn reinforces the retrospective qual-ity engendered by closing; it features the fanfare motif played by horns (398ff.), cadenza-like material in the upper strings and upper winds, and the augmented triads of the tormented idea in the strings at 403–405 (Mahler writes A–C♯–F♮ over a D-minor sonority; F-natural is then enharmonically reinterpreted as E-sharp to lead to F-sharp, the third of the D-major triad at the start of the next unit). Overall, then, this unit features an unstable tonic prolongation, first major then minor—unstable because, while the underlying syntax is there, the rhetorical manner is too fragmentary to provide a firm sense of a concluding tonic.

Unit 32 (bars 406³–433)

The movement seems fated to end in chamber-music mode! A change of tempo, a reduction in orchestral forces, and a turning up of the expressivity dial all combine to suggest closing, dying, finishing. A single horn intones the syncopated idea that we have associated with moments of intensification (bar 408²), and this is succeeded by fanfares and sighs. Between 406 and 414, the harmony remains on D; then, it shifts for 2 bars on to its subdominant, a moment that also (conventionally) signifies closure, before getting lost again in a mini–flute cadenza (bars 419–433). An E-flat major chord frames this particular excursion (419–432), and although it may be read as a Neapolitan chord in the home key, hearing it as such would be challenging in view of the way we come into it. The retention of a single voice during the closing process is a technique that Mahler will use spectacularly in the closing moments of the opening movement of his Tenth Symphony.

Unit 33 (bars 434–454)

The main theme returns for the last time. This is the stable, foursquare version—or so it begins, before it is liquidated to convey absolute finality. The most spectacular feature of this unit is the choreographing of closure through a sustained promise that the melodic tendency enshrined in the $\hat{3}$–$\hat{2}$ motion will eventually find its $\hat{1}$. Mahler had previously played with this tendency, perhaps most notably in "Der Abschied" of *Das Lied von der Erde*. Elsewhere, the procedure of hinting at, delaying, and then attaining closure is imaginatively realized. The $\hat{3}$–$\hat{2}$ promise is kept alive by a fourfold reiteration by solo violin (bars 434, 436, 437, 438), modified by clarinet to effect partial closure (bars 438–439, 439–440, but note that $\hat{1}$ does not appear), delayed by horns (bars 440–441, 441–442), and, as with the clarinet gesture, partially resolved by horns (443–444, and twice more until the end). Closure is partial because, against the conventional V–I gesture, $\hat{9}$–$\hat{5}$ replaces $\hat{2}$–$\hat{1}$. And although the substitution carries the feel of a fall and therefore of some sense of resolution, it also introduces a melodic gap that is less able to cement full closure.

It is the oboes' turn to take a shot at the melodic problem. They begin with $\hat{3}$–$\hat{2}$ within a single bar (444), then $\hat{3}$–$\hat{2}$ across a bar line with longer note values (446³–447²), and finally $\hat{3}$–$\hat{2}$ spread over 6 bars ($\hat{2}$ occupies 5 of those bars). And just when the listener is resigned to accepting a syntactically incomplete gesture as a notional ending, the long-awaited $\hat{1}$ finally arrives in the penultimate bar of the movement (453), cut off after a quarter-note in all instruments except clarinet, harp, and high-lying cellos. The $\hat{3}$–$\hat{2}$–$\hat{1}$ gesture for which we have been waiting since the beginning of the movement finally arrives. But, as often with Mahler, the attainment of $\hat{1}$ is problematized by two elements of discontinuity, one timbral, the other registral. A conventional close might have had the oboe reach the longed-for $\hat{1}$ on D, a major second above middle C in bar 453. But D arrives in two higher octaves simultaneously, played by flute, harp, pizzicato strings, and cellos. And, as if to emphasize the discontinuity, the oboes extend their D into the articulation of 1̂ by the other instruments on the downbeat of bar 453, thus creating a momentary dissonance and encouraging a hearing that accepts 2̂ as final. Of course, the higher-placed Ds (in violins and violas) and longer-lasting ones (in flutes and cellos) dwarf the oboes' E, so the ultimate hierarchy privileges 1̂ as the final resting place. It is hard to imagine a more creative construction of an equivocal ending.

Listeners who have not forgotten the material of the movement's opening unit may be struck by how it is compressed in the last two units. At the beginning, a syntactic element in the form of a dominant prolongation provided the background for a free play of timbres and a mosaic-like exhibition of motives. Only when the narration proper began in the second violin in unit 2 did the various strands coalesce into a single voice. In these last bars, much is done to deny the integrity of simple melodic closure; indeed, it may even be that not until we experience the silence that follows the weakly articulated Ds in bars 453–454 are we assured that a certain contrapuntal norm has been satisfied.

Form

By way of summary, and again recognizing the limitation of this mode of representation, we may sketch the larger shape of the movement as in figure 8.3.

Several potential narratives are enshrined in this paradigmatic chart. And this is an important property of such charts, for although they are not free of interpretive bias, they ideally reveal conditions of possibility for individual interpretation. To frame the matter this way is to emphasize the willed factor in listening. This is not to suggest that modes of interpretation are qualitatively equal. For example, some may disagree about the placement of boundaries for several of the units isolated in the foregoing analysis. Indeed, in a complex work like the first movement of Mahler's Ninth, giving a single label—as opposed to a multitude of labels in a network formation—may seem to do violence to thematic interconnectedness and the numerous allusions that constitute its thematic fabric. The issue is not easily resolved, however, because segmentation resists cadence-based classical rules. To say that the movement is one continuous whole, however, while literally true on some level, overlooks the variations in intensity of the work's discourse. It seems prudent, then, to steer a middle course—to accept the idea of segmentation as being unavoidable in analysis and to approach the sense units with flexible criteria. What has been attempted here is a species of labeling that recognizes the potential autonomy of individual segments that might make possible a series of associations. In the end, paradigmatic analysis does not tell you *what* a work means; rather, it makes possible individual tellings of *how* it means. Those who do not mind doing the work will not protest this prospect; those who prefer to be fed a meaning may well find the approach frustrating.

The most literal narrative sanctioned by the paradigmatic approach may be rehearsed concisely as follows. Preludial material (1) gives way to a main theme (2), which is immediately repeated (3) and brought into direct confrontation with

Figure 8.3 Paradigmatic arrangement of all 33 units of Mahler's Ninth Symphony, first movement

```
    1        2

        3        4

        5              6

        7        8           9

 10                    11          12

        13             14    15

             16                    17

        18             19          20

                       21          22

                       23/1

 23/2

 24      25

        26             27

             28                              29

             30

             31        32

        33
```

a contrasting theme (4). The main theme is heard again (5) followed by a subsidiary theme (6). The main theme appears again (7) and now heads a procession that includes the contrasting theme (8) and a new idea that functions as an intensifier (9). The preludial idea returns in a new guise (10), followed by the first subsidiary theme (11) and yet another new idea (12)—all in the manner of development or working through. The main theme is heard again (13), followed by the exposition's subsidiary and intensifying themes (14, 15), the contrasting idea (16), and the second subsidiary theme (17). Again, the main theme is heard (18), followed, finally, by its most prolonged absence. Starting with the intensifying theme (19), the narrative is forwarded by materials that seem distinct from the main theme (20, 21, 22, 23/1). Units 23/2 and 24 merge into each other as the preludial material returns in a rhetorically heightened form (24). This also marks the turning point in the movement's dynamic trajectory. The rest is recall, rhyme, flashback, and the introspection that accompanies reflection, following closely the events in the first part (25, 26, 27, 28, 29, 30, 31, 32, 33), while incorporating an extended parenthesis in the form of a cadenza (29).

This relatively neutral account notes an incremental process, acknowledges the effect of grounding the movement in one thematic area (2, 3, 5, 7, 13, 18, 25, 26, 33), and demonstrates the effect of contrast bordering on polarity (4, 8, 16, 28, 30, 31). But a third body of material, the syncopated figure that serves an intensifying purpose throughout the movement, lays claim to being among the primary and most familiar materials (units 9, 15, 19, 21, 23/1, 32). If the diffuseness associated with development leads us to temper the neat paradigmatic layout, this is as it should be, of course. Form, after all, is a complex measure; it is, according to Dahlhaus, "the sum of the associations between all the elements in a composition."[8]

We may also interpret the movement's form with explicit reference to the sonata-form model (as invoked by Floros, Andraschke, Hefling, and others).[9] In this understanding, the exposition consists of units 1–9, the development units 10–24, and the recapitulation units 25–33. Immediately obvious is the fact that the main theme occupies the center of the work as a kind of phenomenological home. Things happen in and around it, and it serves throughout as a kind of fulcrum. The phenomenal substance of the movement is weighted toward this theme, whose $\hat{3}$–$\hat{2}$ melodic gesture essentializes it and provides the lead role in the narrative's unfolding. In the exposition, the main theme occurs four times, it appears twice in the development and three more times in the recapitulation. The surprising feature here is the occurrence not once but twice of this main theme in the tonic key during the so-called development section—a section that signifies the absence of the home key *in principle*. This suggests a modification of the strategy for enacting a tonal drama that is associated with an earlier generation of composers. The persistence of the main theme has also led some to hear this movement as an instantiation of rondo form, the main evidence being drawn from the alternation of the main theme and "other" material. The paradigmatic chart supports both sonata-form and rondo readings.

Like the main theme, the principal contrasting material first heard as unit 4 and then as unit 8 returns in the course of the development and the recapitulation; it also gives birth to stretches of music. Its function as opposition rather than as mere contrast or difference is most salient in the exposition, where 3–4 and 7–8 embody this opposition. Nowhere else in the movement are the two themes brought into such direct confrontation. This promising sonata gesture is undermined by the fact that the oppositional stance is not a product of tonal desire; indeed, the dispersal of motifs in a kind of network claims a significant part of the movement's teleology.

The exposition contains two other ideas. One is a compound idea that begins with a codetta-like sense and then exposes a new melodic idea (unit 6); it is affiliated with a number of passages in the development (including the explicitly developmental passage in unit 14); it also returns once in the recapitulation (unit 27). The other idea is one I have mentioned frequently in the foregoing analysis: the syncopated figure underpinned by a circle-of-fifths progression that functions as

8. Dahlhaus, *Between Romanticism and Modernism*, 47.
9. See the discussion in Hefling, "The Ninth Symphony."

an intensifier at important junctures. Its first occurrence is at the end of the exposition (9). Then, as often happens in Beethoven, an idea introduced almost casually or offhandedly at the end of the exposition becomes an important agent in the exploratory business of development. Mahler uses this idea four times in the course of the development, making it the most significant invariant material of the development. This is perhaps not surprising since the unit displays an intrinsic "developmental" property. It is worth stressing that, unlike the main and contrasting themes, this syncopated idea lacks presentational force; rather, it is an accessory, an intensifier.

One factor that underlines the movement's coherence concerns the role of unit 1, a kind of source unit whose components return in increasingly expanded forms as units 10 and 23/2–24. Unit 1 exposes the movement's key ideas in the manner of a table of contents. Unit 10 fulfills a climactic function while also initiating a new set of procedures, specifically, the deliberate manipulation of previously held (musical) ideas. Finally, unit 23/2 marks the biggest high point of the movement. The trajectory mapped out by the succession of units 1–10–23/2–24 is essentially organic. Unlike the main theme, which in a sense refuses to march forward, or perhaps accepts that imperative reluctantly, the syncopated rhythm that opens the work is marked by a restless desire to go somewhere (different).

The paradigmatic chart is also able to convey exceptions at a glance. Columns that contain only one item are home to unduplicated units. There is only one such element in this movement: the *misterioso* cadenza (unit 29) in the recapitulation, which does not occur anywhere else. This is not to say that the analyst cannot trace motivic or other connections between unit 29 and others; the augmented triad at bar 378[4], for example, is strongly associated with the tormented material we first encountered as unit 4; indeed, this material will return at the start of the next unit in bar 391. It is rather to convey the relative uniqueness of the unit in its overall profile. Within the development space, four units seem materially and gesturally distinct from others in the movement. They are 12 and 17 and to a lesser extent 20 and 22. Units 12 and 17 are preparatory, tremolo-laden passages, complete with rising chromaticism that intrinsically signals transition or sets up an expectation for a coming announcement or even revelation. Although they incorporate the brass fanfare from unit 4 (bars 44–45), units 20 and 22 feature a marked heroic statement in B major that, alongside the syncopated intensifying passage (units 19, 21, 23), prepares the movement's climax (unit 23).

Also evident in the paradigmatic chart is the nature of community among themes. The prelude and main theme are associated right at the outset (1–2); they are also allied at the start of the recapitulation (24–25) but *not* in the development section. The main theme and the contrasting idea are strongly associated throughout the exposition, but not as strongly in the development or recapitulation; they find other associations and affinities.

It is also possible to sense a shift in thematic prioritization. Units 6 and 9 appeared in a subsidiary role in the exposition. During the development unit, 6 assumed a greater role, while unit 9 took on even greater functional significance. In the recapitulation, they returned to their earlier (subsidiary) role (as 27 and 32), making room for the 3–4 pair to conclude the movement.

There is a sense in which all approaches to form, traditional or modern, rely either implicitly or explicitly on paradigmatic criteria. This is because each approach relies on repetition as a guide to the construction of identity and association. Differences arise in the choice of constituent parameters and in the limits of construing two units as the same or as different. One possible disadvantage in taking such an open and flexible view of form is that it sanctions a kind of flabby pluralism which, at its worst, accepts any and all characterizations. The main advantage, however, is a recognition of the genuine complexity of musical form and its constituent tendencies. When we find ourselves using simple formal labels to represent complex formal processes, or winning arguments about whether this movement is a theme and variations, or a rondo, or in sonata form, we should keep in mind how much such labels hide and what violence they do to the phenomena we seek to characterize.

Meaning

The ideal meaning of the first movement of Mahler's Ninth is the sum total of all of the interactions among its constituent elements—a potentially infinite set of meanings. Although there exists a relatively stable score, implied (and actual) performances, and historically conditioned performing traditions, there are also numerous contingent meanings that are produced in the course of individual interpretation and analysis. Acts of meaning construction would therefore seek a rapprochement between the stable and the unstable, the fixed and the contingent, the unchanging and the changing. In effect, they would represent the outcome of a series of dialogues between the two. Refusing the input of tradition, convention, and style amounts to denying the contexts of birth and afterlife of the composition, contexts that shape but do not necessarily determine the specific contours of the trace that is the composition. At the same time, without an individual appropria-tion of the work, without a "performance" by the analyst, and without the specula-tive acts engendered by such possession, the work remains inaccessible; analysis ceases to convey what I hear and becomes a redundant report on what someone else hears.

Of the many approaches to musical meaning, two in particular seem to domi-nate contemporary debate. The first, which might be dubbed *intrinsic*, derives from a close reading of the elements of the work as they relate to each other and as they enact certain conventions. Analysis focuses on parameters like counterpoint, harmony, hypermeter, voice leading, and periodicity, and it teases out meaning directly from the profiles of their internal articulations and interactions. One way to organize the mass of data produced by such analysis is to adopt an umbrella category like "closure." As we will see, the first movement of Mahler's Ninth pro-vides many instances of closure as meaningful gesture. ("Intrinsic" is affiliated with formalist, structuralist, and theory-based approaches.)

The second approach to meaning construction is the *extrinsic*; it derives from sources that appear to lie outside the work, narrowly defined. These sources may be conceptualized as baggage that the interpreter brings to the act of interpretation. For example, biographical knowledge centering on the making of the Ninth Symphony during Mahler's last period may influence a particular reading. Symbolic associationism, such as the interpretation of the syncopated rhythm heard in the opening 2 bars as a faltering heartbeat, would be entertained. The idea here is to match a biographical circumstance to a musical configuration, to construct (ad hoc) alliances that assure us that musical works do not stand apart from the social world. In this way, the apparently psychological deficit that arises for certain interpreters if music is not read in terms of other constructions is reduced. ("Extrinsic" is institutionally affiliated with hermeneutic, aesthetic, extramusical, historical, or musicological approaches.)

As noted in chapter 1, however, the intrinsic-extrinsic dichotomy is problematic. Access to intrinsic meanings can never escape the mediation of extrinsic structures. Ostensibly extrinsic meanings, on the other hand, may represent a historical, cultural, or symbolic sedimentation that may once have been figured as intrinsic. Still, the dichotomy is retained to provide broad orientation, not to limit or—worse—discourage certain kinds of inquiry. While my own inclination is to the intrinsic pole of meaning construction, I am nevertheless conscious of what it excludes.

Pursuing the idea of meaning deriving from closure, let us return to the last two units of the movement (32 and 33) to observe three salient features of ending. That the end is nigh is immediately indicated by the sounding of a solo horn. Out of the ruins following collapse, a voice emerges—half-articulate, almost dreaming, and in a reflective mood. These are conventional signs of closure. "Conventional" means that they are partly extrinsic, shared by other works that subscribe to the premises of this musical language. But, by 1908, such signs had become naturalized; they had crossed over into the realm of the intrinsic. Those of Mahler's listeners brought up on Beethoven, Schumann, Mendelssohn, Verdi, and Smetana, plus Mahler's own earlier works, including—and especially—the song cycles, would have appreciated these modes of signifying an ending.

Another striking closing gesture is the flute passage at 419—another cadenza, perhaps—which comes in the wake of earlier turbulence and the subsequent flashbacks indicating recapitulation. An egotistical tendency possessed by all instruments manifests itself here but is not exactly given free rein. Many listeners would interpret this brief moment of excess as a sign of ending—emptying out, desolation, aloneness. Finally, harmonic modesty in the form of V–I gestures is figured as closing in principle. More vitally, the $\hat{3}$–$\hat{2}$ melodic tendency, with more than a century of regular usage behind it, further supports the inference of impending closure.

Or, consider the passage first heard as unit 9, which I described as an intensifying unit. Its underlying fifths suggest process, a middle preparing an ending. Were Mahler to exploit the most normative tendency of this unit, it would likely lead to a tonic resolution (see the hypothetical completion in example 8.5). But observe where unit 9 and its paradigmatic equivalents lead. First, the succession of units 9–10 engenders a feeling of postponed closure. Unit 10 begins with V as an open unit, then continues and ends with the same tendency. In the case of units 15–16, intensification does lead to resolution; or rather, resolution involves a unit marked by instability. Therefore, while the sense of that particular succession (15–16) is of tension followed by release, the latter is not the pristine, diatonic world of the main theme but the more troubled, restless, and highly charged world of the subsidiary theme. In the successions of units 19–20 and 21–22, closure is attained, but an element of incongruity is set up in the case of 19–20 because the key prepared is E-flat major (bars 281–283) while the key attained lies a third lower, B major (bar 285). Although B major is reached by means of a chromatic bass line, it is, as it were, approached by the "wrong" dominant. This is immediately corrected, however, in the case of units 21–22, where the intensifying phrase leads to closure in its own key. Given the proximity of the occurrences, units 19–22 represent a large moment of intensification, a turning point. In other words, the local tension-resolution gestures I have been describing are agents in a larger tension-creating move within the macro form.

The most dramatic use of this intensifying phrase is embodied in the succession of units 23–24, which parallel 9–10 in syntactic profile but differ fundamentally from a rhetorical point of view. Unit 23/1 is the third occurrence of the phrase within a dramatically accelerating passage, the culmination of a stretto effect produced by the rhythm of the phrase's temporal placement. This last then discharges into the movement's climax, units 23/2–24, which, as we have noted, replay the syncopated rhythm from the opening of the work. There is no more dramatic moment in the movement.

The intensifying phrase seems spent. Not surprisingly, it appears only once more in the movement, completely expressively transformed (unit 32). The great stroke in this ending lies in the conjunction of units 32–33. The cadence-promising unit 32 finally finds resolution on the stable main theme of the movement. Perhaps this is the destination that has been implied from the beginning, from the first hearing of unit 9. If so, the listener has had to wait a very long time for the phrase to find its true destination—as ending, as ultimate fulfillment, perhaps as death.

Listeners who base their understanding of the form of the movement on the trajectory mapped out by this intensifying phrase will conclude that this is one of Mahler's most organic compositions. True, the phrase works in conjunction with other material, so the organicism is not confined to one set of processes. Indeed, the large-scale dynamic curve that the phrase creates is partly reinforced and partly undermined by concurrent processes. Reinforcement comes, for example, from the expanding role of the prelude (units 1, 10, and 24). On the other hand, the recurrences of the main theme lack a patent dynamic profile. The theme seems to sit in one place; it returns again and again as if to assure us of its inviolability. Meaning in Mahler is at its most palpable when dimensional processes produce this kind of conflict in the overall balance of dimensional tendencies. By focusing on the production processes, paradigmatic analysis facilitates the construction of such meanings.

Narrative

Mahlerian narrative is melody-led. The leading of melody takes a number of forms, ranging from a simple tune with accompaniment to a more complex texture in which a *Hauptstimme* migrates from one part of the orchestra to another. "Melody" itself is not necessarily a salient tune but a more diffuse presence that is understood as embodying the essential line or idea within a given passage. Melody-led narration occurs on several levels, from the local to the global. What such tellings amount to may be divined differently and put to different uses. At the most immediate level, narrative points to the present in an active way; it shows the way forward. Its meaning is hard to translate satisfactorily out of musical language, but it can be described in terms of pace and material or rhetorical style (which includes degrees of emphasis, repetition, and redundancy and a resultant retrospective or prospective quality).

Mahlerian narrative typically occurs on more than one level, for the leading of melody cannot in general be understood without reference to other dimensional activities. Since it would be tedious to describe all of the facets of narrative in Mahler, let me simply mention a few salient features.

The melody played by first violins as the main theme starting in bar 7 (quoted in example 8.1) is in song mode, although its little motivic increments, by eschewing the long lines found elsewhere, suggest the halting quality of speech mode. Notice that the horns are in dialogue with the strings and thus effect a complementary song mode. Coming after a spatially oriented (as distinct from a temporally oriented) introduction which had no urgent melodic claims (bars 1–6), this song signifies a beginning proper. An important feature of narrative phrases is how they end—whether they conclude firmly by closing off a period or remain open and thus elicit a desire for continuation.

How might we describe the narrative progress of this melody? An opening idea, $\hat{3}$–$\hat{2}$, with a closing or downward tendency, is repeated. It continues with the same rhythmic idea (incorporating an eighth-note) but changes direction and heads up. This idea, too, is repeated in intensified form, incorporating an appoggiatura, B-natural. The pitch B takes on a life of its own, acquiring its own upbeat. This gesture is repeated. These two little phrases mark the tensest moments in the arc generated by the melody so far. Resolution is called for. Next comes an expansive phrase, marked *espressivo* by Mahler, which fulfills the expectations produced so far, engendering a high point or superlative moment. This culminating phrase ends where the narration began with a $\hat{5}$–$\hat{4}$–$\hat{3}$–$\hat{2}$ pattern, the last two scale degrees literally reclaiming the openness of the melody's point of departure. Whether one hears a half-cadence, or the shadow of a half-cadence, or a circular motion, or an abandoned process, it is clear that the process of the phrase is kept open. We hear $\hat{3}$–$\hat{2}$ again, even though it now carries the sense of an echo, as if we had begun a codetta, and it is then repeated in slightly modified form. The entire phrase carries a powerfully unified sense, leaving no doubt about which voice is the leading one. We could complicate the foregoing description by pointing to the motivic interplay (among horns, clarinets, bassoons, and English horn) that animates this more primal string melody. However, these only contribute a sense of narration as a more communal affair; they do not undermine the fact of narration in the first place.

First violins literally take over in bar 18 as the tellers of the tale. We know that the tale is the same but also that the teller is new. Novelty comes from the change of register, beginning roughly an octave higher than where the previous period began. The new teller will not merely repeat the previous telling; she must establish her own style of saying the same thing. The use of embellishments facilitates this personalization of the narrator's role. But the pacing of motivic exposition is kept the same. Perhaps this phrase will be more expressive on account of its being a repeat. Its most dramatic feature is the $\hat{3}$–$\hat{2}$–$\hat{1}$ close (bars 24–25), which fulfills the promise made in the previous phrase. Fulfillment is tinged with equivocation, however. A structural dissonance at the phrase level arises as we move into an adjacent higher register. Registral imbalance will need to be resolved eventually. After the attainment of $\hat{1}$ (bar 25), the promissory $\hat{3}$–$\hat{2}$ motive is kept alive, undermining any sense of security brought on by this close. The $\hat{3}$–$\hat{2}$ in the major is replaced by $\hat{3}$–$\hat{2}$ in the minor to signal a new thematic impulse. What unit 3 tells is mostly the same as what was told in unit 2, but the difference lies in the fact that unit 3 resolves some of the cadential tension exhibited in the previous unit while introducing its own new tensions. In this way, the process of the music is kept open and alive. Parallel periods do not merely balance one another; antecedents and consequents may provide answers on one level, but new questions often arise when old ones are being laid to rest. The direct pairing of units 2 and 3 draws us into this comparative exercise.

∞

This blow-by-blow description could be extended to cover the entire movement, of course, but there is no need to pursue it further because the essential approach is, I believe, sufficiently clear. I embarked on it in connection with units 2 and 3 in order to illustrate the nature of melody-led narration in Mahler. Narrative and meaning are implicated in paradigmatic understanding, and it has been my purpose here to suggest ways in which the movement might be appreciated in these terms. Of course, other scholars have studied this movement from various points of view; indeed, some have shed light on the very dimensions that have been my main focus here, but none has employed a specifically paradigmatic approach. It is my hope that the paradigmatic approach pursued here has provided another path to the construction of musical meaning, one that complements rather than replaces existing approaches.

CHAPTER Nine

Beethoven, String Quartet, op. 130/i (1825–1826), and Stravinsky, *Symphonies of Wind Instruments* (1920)

If, as I have shown, musical discourse is essentially a discourse of repetition and, given that all phenomena we normally designate as "music" feature repetition at various levels (including the repetition of silence as encountered in the limit work, John Cage's 4'33"), how might we distinguish acts of repetition that are necessary to structural articulation from those that function rhetorically within a given work? Where shall we draw the line between the necessary and the contingent? And how might this distinction facilitate a comparative analysis of individual composers' "styles"? In this concluding analytical chapter, we will examine two works that may serve as bookends to the project attempted here: the first movement of Beethoven's Quartet in B-flat Major, op. 130 (which dates from 1825–1826), and Stravinsky's *Symphonies of Wind Instruments* (composed in the summer of 1920). The juxtaposition of Beethoven with Stravinsky may seem shocking at first, but the juxtaposition of *late* Beethoven with Stravinsky should not be all that shocking in view of the acknowledged radical elements (manifest especially in temporal and material discontinuity) in the former composer, which then become part of the latter's ordinary language—or so some conventional accounts have it. Then also, for some listeners, repetition is foregrounded in both composers; it manifests an excess. Approaching their work with a similar methodology should thus prove instructive. It should reveal not only some of the basic ways in which Beethoven's strategies differ from Stravinsky's, but also set into relief their differences from Liszt, Brahms, and Mahler. As in previous chapters, I will comment on the building blocks of each work separately and then conclude with remarks of a directly comparative nature.

Beethoven, String Quartet, op. 130/i

We might approach this movement with a generalized set of (willed) expectations drawn from observable routines in the late works as a set. The most obvious of these is that the movement will be in, or will enact a dialogue with, sonata form. But the expectations associated with sonata form are rather complex, for surely Beethoven's understanding of the form was an evolving one, not a fixed or immutable one. Analysis errs when it fails to hypostatize such understanding, when, relying on a scheme fixed on paper, it fails to distinguish Beethoven's putative understanding of sonata form in, say, 1800 from his understanding in 1823. To the extent that an invariant impulse was ever enshrined in the form, it resides in part in an initial feeling for a stylized contrast of key (and, to a lesser extent, thematic material), which is then reconciled in an equally stylized set of complementary moves. From here to the specifics of op. 130 is a long way, however. In what follows, I will retain sonata-form options on a distant horizon—as place markers, perhaps—while concentrating on the movement's materials and associated procedures.

As a point of reference for the analysis, examples 9.1–9.15 provide a sketch of the main materials of the movement broken into 15 sections and comprising a total of 79 units, including subdivisions of units. These are mostly melodic ideas,

Example 9.1. Units 1–11 of Beethoven, String Quartet in B-flat Major, op. 130, first movement.

and they are aligned in order to demonstrate their affiliations. Although several additional units produced by nesting, recomposition, or motivic expansion could be incorporated, the segmentation undertaken here should be adequate for a first pass through the movement.

Exposition

Units 1 (bars 1–2²) and 2 (bars 2²–4²)

The movement opens with a complementary pair of units. The first unit begins as a unison passage and is transformed after the fourth note into a full-voiced chorale, ending as a question mark (on V). The second answers the first directly, retaining the four-part harmonization and finishing with a perfect cadence, albeit of the "feminine" rather than "masculine" variety. This pairing of units is both closed and open. Within the harmonic and phrase-gestural domain, the succession is closed and balanced; within the registral domain, however, it remains open because unit 2 lies in a higher register. Posing a question in a lower register and answering it in a higher one introduces an incongruity or imbalance that provokes registral manipulation later in the movement. Note also that the contrast between unharmonized (opening of unit 1) and harmonized (unit 2) textures evokes a parallel contrast in modes of utterance. Something of the speech mode may be inferred from the forced oneness of unison utterance; the ensuing hymn brings on communal song.

Units 2a (bars 4³–5²), 2b (bars 5³–7¹)

Using the gesture at the end of unit 2 as a point of departure, unit 2a moves the melodic line up and 2b takes it to F through E-natural, thus tonicizing the dominant. There is something speech-like about these small utterances, all of them set apart by rests, as if enacting an and-then succession.

Units 3 (bars 7²–9¹), 3a (bars 9²–11¹), 3b (bars 10²–11¹), 3c (bars 11²–13¹)

From bar 7 onward, a new idea is presented in imitation, almost like a ricercar. Voices enter and are absorbed into the ruling texture in an orderly way until we arrive at a cadence on—rather than in—the dominant (bar 14). When first heard, units 1–3 (bars 1–14) seem to function like a slow introduction. We will see later, however, that their function is somewhat more complex. For one thing, the "slow introduction" is repeated when the exposition is heard a second time. Then also, the material returns elsewhere in the movement, suggesting that what we are hearing here is part of a larger whole. Indeed, Ratner suggests that, if we assemble all of the slow material (bars 1–14, 20–24, 93–95, 98–100, 101–104, 213–220, and 220–222), the result is an aria in two-reprise form. It is as if Beethoven cut up a compact aria and fed the parts into a larger movement to create two interlocking

284 ∾ PART II *Analyses*

key-area forms.[1] (Edward Cone relates an anecdote about Stravinsky composing the fugue from his *Orpheus* in just this cut-and-paste manner.)[2]

Paradigmatic succession in bars 1–14 reveals a straightforward linear approach in which an initial idea (unit 1) is followed by a complementary idea (unit 2). The latter is then dwelled upon for a while (units 2a and 2b), before yielding to another new idea (unit 3), which is in turn elaborated (units 3a, 3b, 3c). The design is illustrated in figure 9.1.

Figure 9.1 Paradigmatic arrangement of units 1–3c in Beethoven's String Quartet in B–flat major, op. 130, first movement.

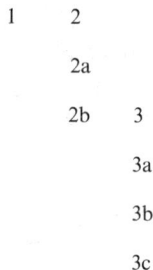

1	2	
	2a	
	2b	3
		3a
		3b
		3c

If we overlook the suffixes, then the essential motion of the units is a 1–2–3 succession—a linear progression with no sense of return. If we include the suffixes, we notice that elements of the second and third units are immediately reused. If we consider the fact, however, that unit 2 is closely based on unit 1, departing only at its end to make a perfect cadence, then we see that the slow introduction is essentially binary in its gesture, the first 7 bars based on one idea, the next 7 based on a different one. The prospects of segmenting these bars differently serve as an indication of the fluid nature of tonal form and material and might discourage us from fixing our segments too categorically.

Units 4 (bars 15²–16), 5 (bars 17²–18)

A change of tempo from *adagio ma non troppo* to *allegro* brings contrasting material. Unit 4 is layered, featuring a virtuosic, descending sixteenth-note figure (first violin) against a rising-fourth fanfare motive. (I quote the fanfare motive but not the sixteenth-note figure in example 9.1.) Although the two seem equally functional in this initial appearance, the fanfare will later be endowed with a more significant thematic function while the sixteenth-note concerto figure will retain its role as embroidery.

1. Ratner, *The Beethoven String Quartets*, 217.
2. "Here, you see, I cut off the fugue with a pair of scissors. . . . I introduced this short harp phrase, like two bars of an accompaniment. Then the horns go on with their fugue as if nothing had happened. I repeat it at regular intervals, here and here again. . . . You can eliminate these harp-solo interruptions, paste the parts of the fugue together and it will be one whole piece." (Quoted in Edward T. Cone, "Stravinsky: The Progress of a Method," in *Perspectives on Schoenberg and Stravinsky*, ed. Cone and Benjamin Boretz [New York: Norton, 1972], 164.)

Although units 4 and 5 occur as a pair, they are open; they begin a sequential pattern that implies continuation. In classic rhetoric, a third occurrence of the fanfare motive would be transformed to bring this particular process to a close and to initiate another. But there is no third occurrence to speak of; instead, unit 5 is extended to close on the dominant, thus creating a half-cadence similar to the one that closed the slow introduction (end of unit 3).

Units 6 (bars 20^3–22^2), 7 (bars 22^3–24^2)

It sounds as if we are back to the slow introduction (Beethoven marks "Tempo 1" in the score at bar 20), only we are now in V rather than in I. At this point, we might begin to revise our sense of the emerging form. Oriented toward F as V—unit 7 sits entirely on an F pedal—the 6–7 pair of units reproduces the material of the 1–2 pair, but at a different tonal level. The presentation of the 6–7 pair is however modified to incorporate stretto in unit 6 and a distinct expansion of register in unit 7 (first violin).

Units 8 (bars 25^2–27^1), 9 (bars 27^2–31^1)

We hear the fanfare motive and its brilliant-style accompaniment as in units 4–5, but in keeping with the dominant-key allegiance established in units 6 and 7, units 8 and 9 now sound in V. Like unit 5, unit 9 extends its temporal domain while shifting the tonal orientation of the phrase.

Units 10 (bars 31^2–32), 11 (bars 33^2–37^1)

The fanfare motif is sung by the bass voice in the tonic, B-flat (unit 10), and is immediately repeated sequentially up a second (as in units 4 and 5). Then, with a kind of teleological vengeance, it is extended and modified to culminate decisively in a cadence at bars 36–37. This is the first perfect cadence in the tonic since the beginning of the allegro. With hindsight, we can see that the fanfare motive from bars 15–16 held within itself the potential for bass motion. This potential is realized in unit 11.

When dealing with complex textures like that of op. 130, where one often has to reduce textures in order to pinpoint the essential motion, it is well to state the obvious: discriminatory choices have to be made by the analyst regarding the location of a *Hauptstimme*. The sense of fulfillment represented in the bass voice in unit 11 bears witness to such choosing.

Let us now pause to take stock of the activity within the first key area (bars 1–38, units 1–11, figure 9.2). A clear hierarchy emerges in the concentrations of activity within the thematic fields. The paradigm containing the fanfare motif leads (units 4, 5, 8, 9, 10, 11), followed by the imitative passage (units 3, 3a, 3b, 3c), then the cadential motif (units 2, 2a, 2b, 7), and finally the inaugurating motif (units 1 and 6). This particular scale of importance comes strictly from the relatively abstract perspective of our mode of paradigmatic representation; it says nothing about the temporal extent of individual units nor their rhetorical manner.

Figure 9.2 Paradigmatic arrangement of units 1–11 in Beethoven's String Quartet in B–flat major, op. 130, first movement.

1	2		
	2a		
	2b	3	
		3a	
		3b	
		3c	4
			5
6	7		8
			9
			10
			11

An obvious limitation of this paradigmatic presentation is that it underplays larger aspects of voice leading. For example, the first 7 bars (units 1, 2, 2a, 2b) are held together by an ascending line in the treble: B♭–C–D–E♮–F or a $\hat{1}$–$\hat{2}$–$\hat{3}$–$\sharp\hat{4}$–$\hat{5}$ ascent. This across-the-units line does not, however, appear at this level of paradigmatic parsing. While this is not an inherent limitation of paradigmatic analysis as such (my discussion of Beethoven's op. 18, no. 3, in chapter 5 managed to draw on simple voice-leading models in the construction of units), it points nevertheless to the method's bias in favor of small-scale units. In general, rather than assume the

Example 9.2. Units 12–16c of Beethoven, String Quartet in B-flat Major, op. 130, first movement.

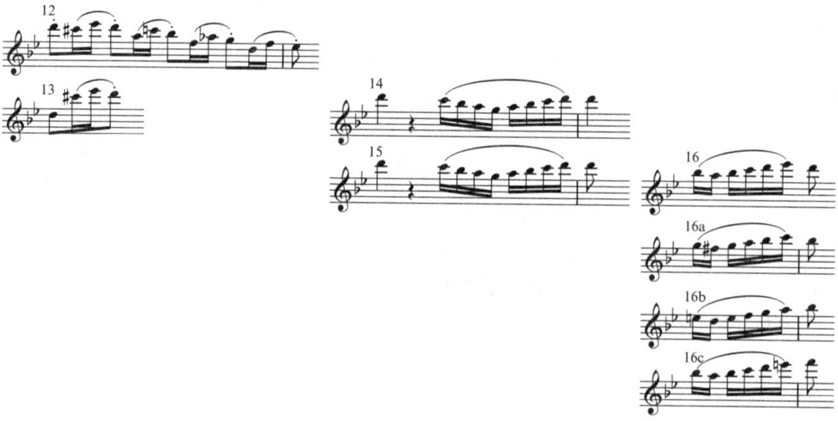

a priori pertinence of a particular mode of paradigmatic parsing, it is better to let context suggest what might be significant.

Units 12 (bars 37–39¹), 13 (bars 39¹–41¹)

With its origins in unit 3 (specifically bar 8, where, however, it carried a different affect), unit 12 serves as confirmation of the cadence on B-flat that we have just heard. Scherzo-like in design, units 12 and 13 differ from the brilliant, concerto-style material combined with fanfare that immediately preceded them. Each is 2 bars long, closing into the next unit. The 2-bar length restores a sense of periodicity, which was obscured in the course of units 8–11. From here on, Beethoven will utilize a systematic change of design in the drive to the next key area.

Units 14 (bars 41–42¹), 15 (bars 42–43¹)

Underpinned by an elided I–V–I progression, these two identical units provide further confirmation of B-flat.

Units 16 (bars 43¹–43³), 16a (bars 43³–44¹), 16b (bars 44¹–44³), 16c (bars 44³–45¹)

Incorporating hints of the relative minor and the dominant, these motivically identical units seem to indicate the start of a move away from home, a transition.

Example 9.3. Units 17–20 of Beethoven, String Quartet in B-flat Major, op. 130, first movement.

Units 17 (bars 45–47¹), 18 (bars 47–49¹)

"Not yet," says unit 17, whose falling and rising arpeggios index yet another kind of design. The note E-flat (bar 45) at first cancels the E-natural of the preceding unit (bar 44), but the latter returns on the last eighth-note of the unit (bar 46). Such chromatic ambivalence usually demands extra attention from listeners, for it exposes a thought process, a discourse. Unit 18 is a near-literal repeat of unit 17, but it eschews the E-natural of the previous unit and so weighs in on the B-flat major rather than F major side of the tonal contest.

Unit 19 (bars 49–51¹)

Shaped melodically by a rising contour followed by a falling one, this unit features yet another change of (rhythmic) design. The E-natural is predominant here, suggesting that the transition (presumably to F major) has finally begun in earnest.

Unit 20 (bars 51–53)

This unit marks yet another change in design—an ascending chromatic line punctuated by rests. It effects the manner of speech and seems to promise nothing except whatever we can infer in retrospect. The chromatic ascent stops rather than ends on a held D-flat (bar 53), and although the span is a minor sixth, which interval will initiate the melody of the second key (bar 55), the relation is not articulated with special rhetorical force.

Example 9.4. Units 21–24 of Beethoven, String Quartet in B-flat Major, op. 130, first movement.

Unit 21 (bars 53–55)

The emergence of a new character in the bass makes us wonder whether this 2-bar cello passage is a prefix to the approaching hymn-like second theme, or whether it is already part of the theme. That it arpeggiates a G-flat-major triad downward prepares the color and tonality of the new key. The transition signaled F as the new (conventionally expected) center, but at the moment of truth, ♭VI, not V, is the preferred destination.

Units 22 (bars 55–57³), 23 (bars 57⁴–59¹), 24 (bars 59–63)

Built on a pedal, this alla breve material embodies the alternative tonal premise of the movement. Contrasts of key, design, and affect are normative, but the specific key chosen is not. Unit 23 is a variant of 21 and prepares 24. Unit 24 in turn begins by restating the material from 22 in a higher register, then extends the musical thought past the 2.5-bar limit set previously.

Units 25 (bars 63–64, 26 (bars 64⁴–66³), 27 (66⁴–71)

Unit 25 may well be heard as a part of 24 since, in one sense, it completes its melodic gesture, but the accompanying harmonies—oriented toward V rather than I in G-flat—and especially the new design reflected locally in a sequential relation between bars 63 and 64 suggest that unit 25 should be regarded as a separate entity. Unit 26 features yet another change in design. Employing sixteenth-notes as the energizing agent, it outlines a harmonic progression that confirms our new, temporary tonic, G-flat, in effect making a cadence at bars 65⁴–66¹. Unit 27 functions similarly, but the cadential gesture is grander, beginning with an

Example 9.5. Units 25–27 of Beethoven, String Quartet in B-flat Major, op. 130, first movement.

inflection toward vi (67^1) and then, incorporating a circle of fifths, progressing to G-flat as local I. Listeners may well begin to suspect that we're in for a period of cadential reiteration.

The rampant changes of topic and design that we have encountered so far in the movement promote a feeling of discontinuity in the narrative. Listen again to the beginnings of units 12, 14, 16, 17, 19, 20, 21, 22, 25, and 26, and you will notice that no two units are identical in rhythmic design. Inferring discontinuity, however, rests on a definition. Often in late Beethoven, subsurface voice leading provides the rationale for the breaks or fissures that we experience on the surface. Because the subsurface can elude those who are not alert to that level of compositional activity, continuity may be overlooked. On the other hand, the construction of subsurface continuity through voice-leading analysis may lead some analysts to deny or understate the pertinence of the immediately hearable aspects of a work. In general, one learns to hear larger trajectories and the transformation of strict counterpoint into free composition, but one does not need to learn to hear changes of design. In any case, only by attending to more than one level of structural unfolding can we properly appreciate the peculiarities of Beethoven's discourse.

Example 9.6. Units 28–32 of Beethoven, String Quartet in B-flat Major, op. 130, first movement.

Units 28 (bars 70⁴–73¹), 29 (bars 73–77¹), 30 (bars 77–87), 31 (bars 87–90¹)

The confirming function is played out in earnest across the span of these four units. Unit 28 uses a 5/6 progression in the lower voices against the brilliant first violin figuration to provide material confirmation of the new key. In unit 29, the first violin sings a new tune in quarter-notes that carries a wrapping-up sense. The tune is taken up by the cello in unit 30, expanded and exaggerated rhetorically. The composer's voice now occupies an increasingly high register (bars 80 and after), and the resulting declamation may be figured if not as shouting then at least as emphasizing the functionality of the moment. The functionality in question is the attainment of the second key. Eventually, the point of greatest culmination is reached in unit 31, which combines half-notes (reminiscent of unit 22, the beginning of the second key) with sixteenth-notes (from unit 4, the beginning of the allegro) in a grand cadential gesture worthy of Mendelssohn.

Unit 32 (bars 90–93)

While the celebratory song of cadential confirmation (unit 31) reinforced the syntactic function of closing the second key area, this unison passage in speech mode embodies a change in narrative orientation. The unanimity of group recitation in this unit replaces the many-in-one-ness of the four-part harmony from the previous unit. We are led at a more deliberate pace and in a didactic manner to a new beginning—the formal repeat of the beginning of the movement. Indeed, the A♭–B♮ term that ends this unit also begins unit 1. If we thought that unit 1 was a slow introduction to the movement, we will be forced to rethink that supposition as we hear it again. One would not normally introduce a set of proceedings twice.

Taking stock, the paradigmatic pattern in figure 9.3 emerges for the exposition as a whole. What kind of story does this display make possible? There are altogether 15 columns, meaning that there are 15 distinct spheres of material influence. This alone suggests an accretion of differentiated ideas. As we might expect, there is no overall return; rather, the overall motion is forward. While this forward sense is not surprising from a tonal point of view, it is significant from a thematic perspective. If, for the sake of comparison and in order to hint at what might be unique in op. 130, we were to compare this movement to the opening movement of op. 18, no. 3 (discussed in chapter 5), we will notice that, whereas the earlier movement goes over the same ground, proceeding in a more or less circular motion even while meeting the external obligations of sonata form, this one proceeds additively even as it pauses and dwells on certain kinds of material. Linearity in op. 18, no. 3/i, is subsumed under a reigning circular impulse, while op. 130 moves inexorably forward, conquering new territory in the process.

Development

Beethoven begins the development in the same key in which he ended the exposition, namely, ♭VI. This will be a short development—35 bars only, less than half the length of the preceding exposition.

Figure 9.3 Paradigmatic arrangement of units 1–32 in Beethoven's String Quartet in B–flat major, op. 130, first movement.

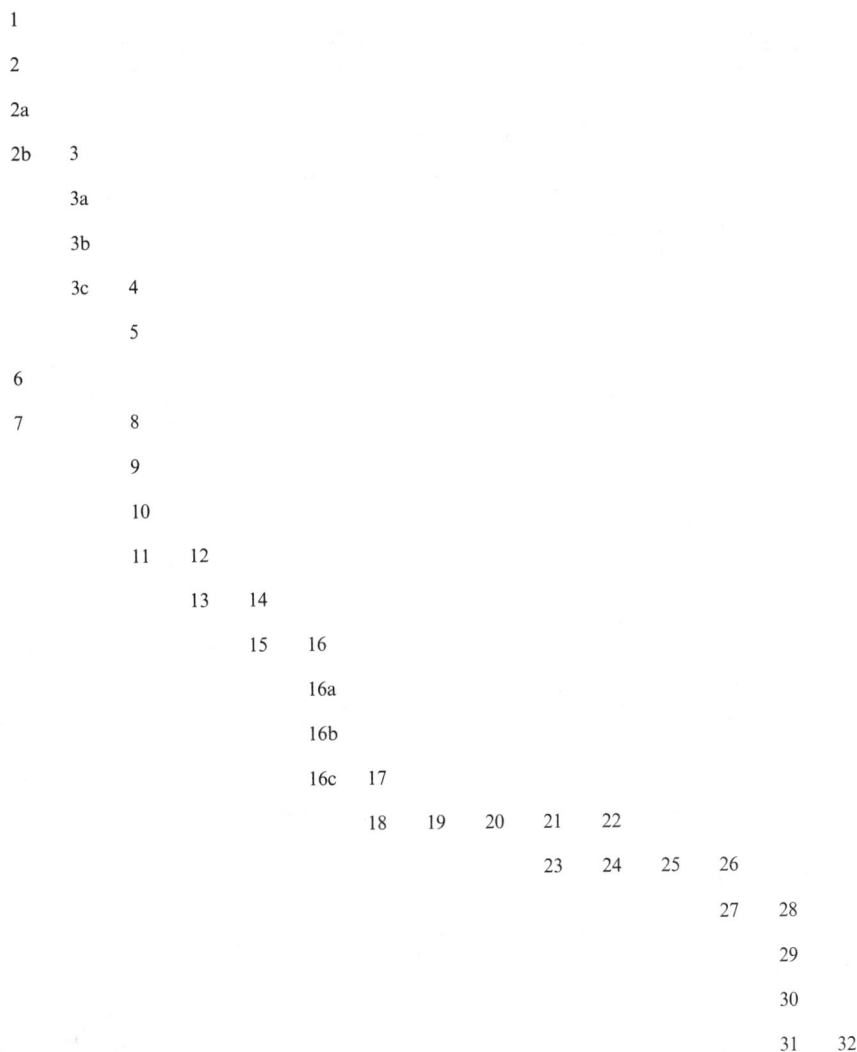

1

2

2a

2b   3

      3a

      3b

      3c   4

            5

6

7   8

            9

            10

            11   12

                  13   14

                        15   16

                              16a

                              16b

                              16c   17

                                     18   19   20   21   22

                                                 23   24   25   26

                                                             27   28

                                                                   29

                                                                   30

                                                                   31   32

Units 33 (bars 93⁴–95¹), 34 (bars 96²–97²), 35 (bars 97³–100¹), 36 (bars 100²–101²)

We begin with a set of fragments. Unit 33 presents material from earlier in the movement, not the unharmonized motto heard as unit 1, but the harmonized (stretto) version heard as unit 6. Unit 34 effects an enharmonic change (from G-flat major to F-sharp major) using the head of the fanfare/brilliant-style material first heard in unit 4. This affective and material contrast is repeated a major third down in ♭VI of F-sharp/G-flat major. That is, unit 35 is equivalent to 33 just as 36 is equivalent to

Example 9.7. Units 33–37 of Beethoven, String Quartet in B-flat Major, op. 130, first movement.

34. Often in Beethoven, the freezing of thematic novelty is a way of marking other processes for consciousness. In this case, the key scheme sports a rather radical progression of major thirds: B-flat for the first key area, G-flat for the second and for the start of the development, and now E[double-flat] or, enharmonically, D. The progression is "radical" in the sense that it eschews the hierarchy of tonic-dominant polarity for a more "democratic" and symmetrical set of major third relations. Each of these four units is framed by silence, and although I have pointed to a thematic parallelism in the pairing of 33–34 against 35–36, the overall effect of their disposition is a strategic aloofness, a refusal to connect. The question posed in unit 33 is not answered by unit 34; rather, 34 goes about its own business, proposing its own idea in hopes of getting a response. Similarly, the question posed by unit 35 is not answered by unit 36. Of course, tonal continuity between 33–34 and 35–36 mediates the rejection of these opportunities for dialogue, but it is worth registering the mosaic-like construction and the rereading of familiar tonal gestures—moves that we have encountered in Mahler and will encounter again in Stravinsky.

Unit 37 (bars 101³–104¹)

Not for the first time in this movement, Beethoven extracts a cadential figure from the end of one unit—unit 35—and uses it to begin a subsequent one (37). In this case, the figure in question is repeated several times as if revving up the developmental engine. Our attention is arrested; we hold our breaths for something new.

Units 38 (bars 106–109), 38a (bars 110–115), 38b (bars116–122), 38c (bars 123–129), 38d (bars 130–132¹)

The main thematic substance of the development is a new, lyrical tune that begins with an octave exclamation and then winds down in a complementary stepwise gesture. The tune is first sung by the cello (bars 106ff.) to an accompaniment comprising three previously heard motives: the long-short figure isolated in unit 37, an incipit of the brilliant-style sixteenth-note figure that originated in unit 4, and its companion fanfare figure. The ethos in these measures is unhurried—a lyrical oasis, perhaps. Again, Beethoven's freezing of thematic accretion allows the listener

Example 9.8. Units 38–38d of Beethoven, String Quartet in B-flat Major, op. 130, first movement.

to contemplate other elements of the discourse, in this case the key scheme, which begins with D major in unit 38, G major in units 38a and 38b, and C minor in 38c, and finally, disrupting the pattern that has aligned key and theme, 38d rereads the C minor melody within a ii–V–I progression in B-flat major. The attainment of B-flat signals the beginning of the recapitulation.

What a brief and relatively stable development! And what a contrast it presents to the active exposition, with its numerous and regular changes in design. We may be tempted to look for an explanation. And yet, any reason we offer will almost by definition be a lie. To say, for example, that the brevity of the development compensates for the extended exposition is to say something singularly unilluminating. No, there are no firm causalities in artistic production (that would only produce critical casualties), no inevitabilities. There is only the artistic product in its magnificent contingency. If we, burdened with various neuroses, feel a need to offer an explanation rooted in causes and effects, no one can of course stop us.

Recapitulation

As always, we are immediately forced into comparative mode as we pass through the recapitulation. To the extent that there exists a normative recapitulation function, it is to bring the nontonic material that was heard in the second part of the exposition—the "dissonant" material—into the orbit of the home key. By dwelling phenomenally on the tonic, the recapitulation meets the desire engendered by the development—whose normative function is to ensure the absence of the tonic within its space—to effect a stylized reconciliation of materials previously associated with the tonic and nontonic spheres.

Again, this normative scenario exists on a distant horizon for Beethoven. Let us recall the main developments so far. The work began with a slow introduction that was repeated in the exposition (not like op. 59, no. 3, where the repeat of the opening movement *excludes* the slow introduction). The first key area did not work organically or consistently with one idea but celebrated heterogeneity in design; it revealed a surplus of design features, we might say. The transition to the second key was ambivalent, first pointing to the dominant key, but then denying it as a destination; eventually, the music simply slid into ♭VI as the alternative tonal premise. The ♭VI was amply confirmed in the rest of the exposition by changes of design and by cadential articulation. The development began with fragments of material from early in the movement, but instead of working these out in the manner of a proper *Durchführung*, it settled into a relaxed hurdy-gurdy tune that was taken through different keys in a kind of solar arrangement, leading without dramatic or prolonged retransition to the recapitulation.

It is in the recapitulation that we encounter some of the most far-reaching changes, not so much in the treatment of material but in the ordering of units and in the key scheme. The first part seems to continue the development process by bypassing the tonic, B-flat, and reserving the greater rhetorical strength for the cadence on the subdominant, E-flat major (bar 145).[3] Drawing selectively on earlier material, the music then corrects itself and heads for a new key. Beethoven chooses D-flat major for the second key material, thus providing a symmetrical balance to the situation in the exposition (D-flat and G-flat lie a third on either side of B-flat, although the lower third is major in contrast to the upper third). But recapitulating material in D-flat is not enough; being a nontonic degree, it lacks the resolving capacity of the tonic. Beethoven accordingly replays most of the second key material in the home key, B-flat, to compensate for the additional "dissonances" incurred in the first part of the recapitulation. Finally, a coda rounds things off by returning to and recomposing the thematic material associated with the opening units of the movement. Some of these recompositions involve large-scale thematic and voice-leading connections that are only minimally reflected in a paradigmatic analysis. The details may be set out as in example 9.9.

Unit 39 (bars 132–134¹)

This is the same as 4.

Unit 40 (bars 134²–136³)

This is the same as 5.

Unit 41 (bars 136⁴–139¹)

Unit 41 is an extension of 40, whose short-short-long motif it develops. This unit will return in the coda.

---

3. Daniel Chua provides a vivid description of this and other moments in op. 130 in *The "Galitzin" Quartets of Beethoven* (Princeton, NJ: Princeton University Press, 1995), 201–225.

Example 9.9. Units 39–43 of Beethoven, String Quartet in B-flat Major, op. 130, first movement.

Example 9.10. Units 44–52a of Beethoven, String Quartet in B-flat Major, op. 130, first movement.

Unit 42 (bars 139²–141²)

This is the same as 10. The ascending perfect fourth that heads the fanfare motive is replaced by a descending diminished fourth. This unusual interval supports an augmented triad (bar 140) and carries greater instability than might seem warranted at this point in the form. A sense of digression is in the air.

Unit 43 (141²–145¹)

This is the same as 11. The operative descending interval becomes a diminished fifth (bars 43⁴–44¹), further intensifying the instability of the moment and suggesting a secondary development. The motion culminates in a grand cadence in E-flat major (a fifth below the tonic).

Unit 44 (bars 145²–146¹)

This is the same as 14. This unit confirms the cadence on E-flat, while waiting to launch another move.

Unit 45 (bars 146–148¹)

This is the same as 15.

Unit 46 (bars 147–148¹)

This unit further confirms the cadence in E-flat major, using the thematic material from unit 12 (itself originating in unit 3, bar 8).

Unit 47 (bars 148–149¹)

This is the same as 14. This unit continues the cadential and confirmatory role of the preceding four units by using thematic material from units 44 and 45, now changed from major to minor.

Unit 48 (bars 149–150¹)

Unit 48, which is the equivalent of 15, is also an immediate repeat of 47.

Unit 49 (bars 150–150³)

This parallels unit 16.

Unit 49a (bars 150³–151¹)

This is the same as 16a. The bass voice is now in treble. The E-flat minor chord facilitates a move to D-flat major, the goal of this portion of the piece, which will be confirmed in bar 162 (unit 57).

Unit 50 (bars 151–152[1])

Unit 50 is equivalent to 14, but is now in D-flat major. From here until the end of unit 59, the recapitulation reproduces the exact content of the exposition, omitting only the 2 bars of unit 19.

> Unit 51 (bars 152–153[1]) = 15
> Unit 52 (bars 153–153[3]) = 16
> Unit 52a (bars 153[3]–154[1]) = 16a

Example 9.11. Units 53–55 of Beethoven, String Quartet in B-flat Major, op. 130, first movement.

> Unit 53 (bars 154–156[1]) = 17
> Unit 54 (bars 156–158[1]) = 18
> Unit 55 (bars 158–160[3]) = 20

Example 9.12. Units 56–63 of Beethoven, String Quartet in B-flat Major, op. 130, first movement.

> Unit 56 (bars 160[4]–162) = 21
> Unit 57 (bars 162–163[3]) = 22
> Unit 58 (bars 163[4]–166) = 23
> Unit 59 (bars 166–172) = 24

Unit 60 (bars 172[3]–174)

The descending arpeggio figure that led directly to the second theme in the exposition (unit 21) is used again as a link between the D-flat major area within the recapitulation and the B-flat major area. The join is in bar 172, where the F-major triad serves a double function as V of vi in D-flat and as V of F.

The following set of equivalences shows that the second phase of the recapitulation, whose purpose is to transform previously "dissonant" material into consonance by offering it in the home key, follows the exact order of the exposition's material.

Unit 61 (bars 174–178) = 22
Unit 62 (bars 175⁴–178) = 23
Unit 63 (bars 178–182¹) = 24

Example 9.13. Units 64–66 of Beethoven, String Quartet in B-flat Major, op. 130, first movement.

Unit 64 (bars 182–183³) = 25
Unit 65 (bars 183⁴–185³) = 26
Unit 66 (bars 185⁴–190²) = 27

Example 9.14. Units 67–71 of Beethoven, String Quartet in B-flat Major, op. 130, first movement.

Unit 67 (bars 189⁴–192¹) = 28
Unit 68 (bars 192–195) = 29
Unit 69 (bars 196–206¹) = 30
Unit 70 (bars 206–209¹) = 31
Unit 71 (bars 209–213³) = 32

Coda

The last two units of the recapitulation, 70 and 71, both recall and transform their earlier functions. Unit 70, the equivalent of unit 31, provides the grandest rhetorical elaboration of B-flat, while its successor, 71, the equivalent of 32, adopts a speech mode in preparing to go somewhere. In the exposition, unit 32 led to a repeat of the exposition; here, it leads to yet another beginning, this one the beginning of the end—the coda. And it does so by taking up for the last time the material that opened the movement.

The following set of equivalences shows that the coda is essentially a recomposition of the opening of the movement (units 1–5). The only missing material is unit 3, the passage of imitative counterpoint, some of whose content has already appeared in units 12–13 and 46.

Example 9.15. Units 72–79 of Beethoven, String Quartet in B-flat Major, op. 130, first movement.

Unit 72 (bars 213^4–215^2) = 1
Unit 73 (bars 215^3–217^2) = 2
Unit 73a (bars 217^3–218) = 2a

Unit 73b (bars 218^4–219^3) = 2a
Unit 73c (bars 219^4–220) = 2a
Unit 73d (bars 220^4–221^2) = 2a
Unit 73e (bars 221^3–222^1) = 2a
Unit 74 (bars 218^2–219^3) = 4
Unit 75 (bars 220^2–221^2) = 5
Unit 76 (bars 222–223) = 4
Unit 77 (bars 223–229^1) = 41
Unit 78 (bars 229^2–231^1) = 4
Unit 79 (bars 231–234) = 4

The paradigmatic representation of the coda in figure 9.4 shows immediately the stacking of the two middle columns and the isolation of unit 77. (Unit 72, by the way, is not as isolated as the diagram suggests, since it and its successor, 73, are essentially the same material, the former open, the latter closed.) Again, the pattern is what we might expect in a closing section, namely, extensive use of contiguous as well as noncontiguous repetition. No other sequence of units shows this much contiguous repetition.

Figure 9.4 Paradigmatic arrangement of units 72–79 in Beethoven's String Quartet in B–flat major, op. 130, first movement.

72	73		
	73a	74	
	73b		
	73c	75	
	73d		
	73e	76	77
		78	
		79	

The main interest in this economy of recomposition is a polyphonic rendition of earlier material in a manner reminiscent of Bach and foreshadowing Stravinsky. The units marked 73a, 73b, 73c, and 73d are based on a single idea. Recall that, very early in the movement, the closing gesture of one unit (2) was isolated and used to propel the music to a new destination (2a, 2b). A similar procedure is used here. Unit 73a echoes the closing gesture of 73, 73c does the same for 73b, and 73e takes over 73d. Note, however, that the upper line of this sequence of units unfolds chromatically despite the interruptions: B♭ (bars 214–218)–B♮ (bar 219)–C (bar 220)–C♯ (bar 221)–D (bar 222). This intensifies the goal-oriented quality of the passage. The culmination of this chromatic motion is in unit 77 (itself based on unit 41). Unit 77 carries the process forward, reaching the expressive climax of the coda (bars 222–223) before discharging into a diatonic cadence (227–229). In the remaining units, 78 and 79, bass answers treble's fanfare motive call. While unit 78 remains open (the E-flat in bar 230 is left hanging), unit 79 takes the line to the tonic in bar 233.

The interpenetration of tempi, the play of register, and the juxtaposing of distinctly profiled material collectively endow this coda with a synthesizing function. For some listeners, therefore, the tensions raised in the course of the movement are nicely resolved on this final page. Unit 77 emerges as especially important in this process of synthesis because, despite its allegro tempo, it subtends an adagio sentiment. Put another way, it gestures toward song while being in speech mode, the latter evident in the effort to speak words again and again. Song returns in units 78 and 79.

For other listeners, however, the reification of contrasting materials does not produce synthesis; rather, it upholds the contrasts. One tiny voice-leading event at the very end of the work may support the view that things are not necessarily nicely resolved: the first violin's E♭–A tritone in bar 232 is not resolved linearly in the following bar but absorbed into the dominant-seventh chord. The high melodic E-flat is a dissonant seventh that does not resolve to an adjacent D; rather, it is, as it were, taken down two octaves to beat 2 of bar 233 (second violin) from where it is led to an adjacent D. The movement finishes with a lingering sense of an unresolved seventh.

These comments about the first movement of op. 130 aimed to identify the building blocks, note the material affinities among them, and describe their roles in the movement. The emphasis on building blocks may obscure the larger trajectories that some analysts would prefer to see and hear, but I have argued that working at this level can be revealing. Perhaps the larger trajectories can take care of themselves; or perhaps they are our own invention.

Regarding necessary and contingent repetition, the distinction is at once unavoidable and problematic. Necessary repetition defines structure, perhaps even ontology; we would not want to leave home without it. But reducing away the repetitions, transformations, equivalences, and samenesses on account of their ostensible redundancy amounts to setting aside the peculiar rhetoric that defines a work; such an act leaves us with an empty shell, with only the potential for content. Necessary repetition captures a trivial but indispensable quality, namely, the motivating forces that make a work possible; contingent repetition conveys a nontrivial but dispensable quality, namely, the very lifeblood of a work, the traces left by acts of composing out. Both are needed. There is no necessary repetition without its contingencies; at the same time, contingent repetition is grounded in certain necessities. Paradigmatic analysis, in turn, embodies this paradox by asserting both the trivial and the nontrivial. By investing in the literalism or iconicity of repetition, by encouraging the analyst's pretense of a naïve stance, it embodies the innocence of a child's view. On the other hand, by displaying patterns that may be interpreted semiotically as style or strategy, it broaches the mature world of symbolic and indexical meaning; it leads us to a series of cores and shows us why music matters.

Stravinsky, *Symphonies of Wind Instruments*

Stravinsky's early masterpiece from 1920, the *Symphonies of Wind Instruments*, has elicited considerable commentary from a vast range of critics. It is said to be aloof, cold, and dry and famously marked by discontinuity. How time passes, how the individual blocks of material relate to each other, and whether coherence is finally achieved are questions that have engaged writers.

In one sense, *Symphonies* obviously lies beyond the boundaries defined by Romantic music. Stravinsky's early language, with its Russian roots, its rhythmic vitality, its greater investment in succession than in functional progression, and its tendency toward moment form all seem to be worlds removed from the organic interconnectedness of the musical languages of Liszt, Brahms, and Mahler. And yet, from a semiotic point of view, there are, as we will see, important points of similarity between this extreme work of 1920 and the more normative products of the 1800s. The claim seems counterintuitive. Hyper-Romantic expression as encountered in Brahms or Mahler seems quite distant from the dry, detached blocks that are assembled into a kind of montage in Stravinsky. If there are procedural parallelisms, they must be on a superficial level; differences, it might be said, are more pertinent.

My purpose here is to unveil aspects of the structure of *Symphonies* following the classic semiological method of first identifying the building blocks—or units or segments—and then speculating on how they succeed each other. In the course of constructing this structure, I will suggest ways in which Stravinsky's language and procedure differ from as well as resemble the languages of Beethoven, Mahler, Liszt, and Brahms. In other words, I offer here a stylistic finding as an accessory within a structural analysis.

Segmenting *Symphonies* is easy. (I'm using the revised 1947 version for this analysis.) This is in part because Stravinsky himself has done it for us. Material is packaged as a series of differentiated or maximally contrasted blocks, sometimes separated by silences, other times marked by textural breaks. Onsets of new blocks are rarely obscure, even when there is a clear motivic connection or overlap between adjacent units. There is a stop-and-start quality to the work that elicits reciprocal acts of enumeration from the analyst. The process is in part additive, and Stravinsky's metrical succession conveys this immediately. The first 7 bars, for example, are 2/8, 3/8, 2/8, 3/8, 2/8, 3/8, and 3/4.

While segmentation is thus easy to perform, it nevertheless gives rise to the questions: What is the status of individual blocks? Are they autonomous, or are they burdened with tendency and implication? Let us make a first pass through the work, noting the basic units and a few of their salient features.

Unit 1 (bars 1–7²)

A distinctive "bell motive"[4] opens the work: high Ds lying two octaves above middle C are played by clarinets and flutes and repeated, incorporating falling thirds

---

4. Here and elsewhere in the following analysis, I borrow Eric Walter White's "invented titles" for some of the materials in *Symphonies*. See his *Stravinsky: The Composer and His Works* (Berkeley: University of California Press, 1966), 291–298.

that evoke nature, perhaps, and they are subjected to "unnatural" melodic embellishment. The harmony embodies presence only; it enacts no desire.

Unit 2 (bars 7^3–11^2)

Stravinsky uses a distinctly constituted and memorably scored sonority as motive. The chord is repeated, but the speaker appears to be overcome by a stutter. Although the chord is literally sounded five times, we might group these into a threefold utterance as a long-short, long-short, long pattern, where the shorts fall off the longs like immediate echoes. The material gives rise to no real expectations. It lacks melodic tendency and is therefore quite different from unit 1, which, while static in terms of an overall progression, nevertheless displayed an incipient linear tendency in the form of cadence-simulating falling thirds. The fullness of the scoring, including the filling in of the middle registers by brasses, produces a further contrast between units 2 and 1.

Unit 3 (bars 11^3–$13^{0.5}$)

The close harmony suggests that this might be part of a chorale. We accept the authenticity of the dissonant harmonies within this particular composer's idiolect. The melody, too, is hymn-like, but the relative brevity of the unit suggests that this might be no more than a fragment. The sense of chorale is only emergent; the music has a way to go before it can display the full identity of the chorale *topos*.

Unit 4 (bars $13^{0.5}$–13^3)

The sonority from unit 2 (the chord) interrupts, as if to say that it had not quite finished its utterance when the hymn broke in at the end of bar 11. There is only one sounding of the chord on this occasion.

Unit 5 (bars 14–18^2)

This unit is a near-exact repeat of unit 1. (The first and last bars of unit 1 are suppressed.) The return of the bell motive marks the emerging form for attention. So far, we have experienced a clearly differentiated succession of ideas, some juxtaposed with no obvious interdependency. Of course, we can begin to connect things on paper if we so desire. For example, the sequence of melodic pitches in the chorale melody, E-flat, G, A-flat, E-flat (bars 11–12), could be extended to the following F (bar 13), so that units 3 and 4 may be heard as connected on one level. And because units 2 and 4 feature the same chord, they may be heard as one unit, with unit 3 read as an interpolation. It is as if unit 1 delayed sounding its final member. The emerging "metamusical" impulse is, of course, central to Stravinsky's aesthetic.

Individual units, of course, might be segmented further. Unit 1, for example, might be divided in two (bars 1–3 and 4–7), the second part being an embellishment and continuation of the first. Or it might be heard in three little segments comprising a statement (bars 1–3), a truncated restatement (bars 4–5^1), and a suffix (bars 5^2–7^2). Although significant, these internal repetitions have not influenced the segmentation adopted here. Instead, I have adopted something like a one-idea-per-segment philosophy, irrespective of the actual length. For example, the chorale that concludes *Symphonies* will be represented as one segment, even though it goes on for over 60 bars. Obviously, it can be segmented further, but the consistency of the chorale topical area together with its marked differentiation from the material of previous units justify leaving it as one large block. (There are also a few units whose contents are so obviously synthesized from previously distinct materials that separation into their constituent elements is not always productive.) The asymmetry in phrase structure that results from adopting this flexible approach may seem to underplay the strict regularities associated with Stravinsky's manner, but they convey an important distinction between regularities that lie at or close to the pulse level and irregularities that stem from grouping.

Unit 6 (bars 18^2–22^1)

This seemingly new material is timbrally affiliated with the hymn in unit 3; it may also be heard as an extension of the bell motive in units 1 and 5.

Unit 7 (bars 22^2–24^2)

This is an exact repeat of unit 2.

Unit 8 (bars 24^3–26^2)

This repeats the chorale from unit 3, adding two extra beats in the process.

Unit 9 (bars 26^3–27^3)

This is essentially the chordal gesture from units 2 and 4. There are slight differences in intervallic makeup, but these may be ignored at this descriptive level because the presentations are so alike and so strongly contrasted with the surrounding material.

Unit 10 (bars 28^1–29^3)

If we privilege timbre, then this unit may be aligned with unit 6 and, to a lesser extent, with its associates, 3 and 8. But the high register and the juxtaposition with the chord motive bring the bell motive of units 1 and 5 into view as well.

Taking stock: within the limits of a relatively literal reading of identity, the paradigmatic order of the first 29 bars of *Symphonies* may be given as shown in figure 9.5. If, however, we wish to recognize the deeper parallels between units 6 and 5 (and 1) and among 10, 8, and 3, we could rewrite this order (figure 9.6) to show that unit 6 extends the melodic impetus begun in 5, and that, although 10 functions in the most immediate sense as a bridge between 9 and 11, its timbre, melodic profile, and character call the chorale in 8 and 3 to mind.

Figure 9.5 Paradigmatic arrangement of units 1–10 in Stravinsky's *Symphonies of Wind Instruments*

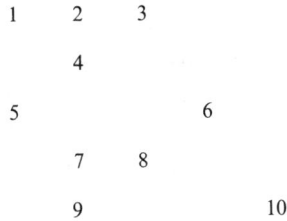

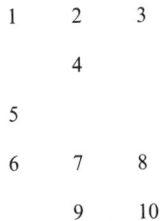

```
           1     2    3

                 4

     5                      6

                 7    8

                 9                10
```

Figure 9.6 Alternative paradigmatic arrangement of units 1–10 in Stravinsky's *Symphonies of Wind Instruments*

```
              1     2    3

                    4

        5

        6     7    8

              9    10
```

The first arrangement (figure 9.5) shows an incremental process centered on the paradigm containing units 2, 4, 7, and 9; on a second tier are the pairs of units 1 and 5, and 3 and 8. Units 6 and 10 are "outsiders" whose task is to introduce new content in order to rejuvenate the narrative. The second arrangement (figure 9.6) conveys a more evenly spread process in which the first three blocks are each repeated twice, three times, and twice, respectively. The process of repetition is interesting in its unpredictability. First to be repeated is not unit 1 but 2 (as 4); then 1 is repeated as 5; then the 1–2–3 sequence reappears as 6–7–8; finally, the 7–8 pair is repeated as 9–10. While repetition as such may serve to anchor a process, an unpredictable pattern of repetition may produce anxiety or (extra)narrative interest. Later, we will see that subsequent repetitions of these units do not necessarily follow the order of their earlier appearances. Thus, the form acquires a quality of permutation.

Unit 11 (bars 30–39)

The onset of this unit marks perhaps the strongest contrast so far. This may seem surprising in view of the overlap of pitch (D-flat) and register between the end of unit 10 and the beginning of unit 11. The sense of contrast emerges over the period of the melody; the longer we hear this Russian melody with its popular flavor, the more we understand that something significantly new is being offered. The relentless diatonicism of the extended flute melody is a further element of contrast. (It also recalls melodies from *Rite of Spring*, *Firebird*, and *Petrushka*, among other works.) The sparse accompaniment also announces a further textural difference.

Unit 12 (bars 40–46)

A second Russian popular melody is sung by solo bassoon in a relatively high tessitura (again, the opening of *Rite of Spring* comes to mind). The pitch resource is limited to three notes, the first three of the minor scale. Although timbral and tonal contrasts at the onset of unit 12 (bar 40) confirm its separateness from 11, there is a topical continuity between the two units. Later, when the melodies are recapitulated in a different order, we will be able to confirm this segmentation.

Unit 13 (bars 47–52²)

The bell motive returns a half-step down from where we last heard it. (Hearing this long-term semitonal relation between D-natural and D-flat will be a challenge for most listeners not looking at a score, so I will decline the invitation to invest in large-scale semitone relations.)

Unit 14 (bars 52³–54)

The chorale is played by oboes and English horn and echoed by clarinets. The separation of the two groups may encourage a hearing of this as two separate, adjacent units (52³–54¹ and 54²–54³), but the topical constancy is strong enough to override the disjunction in orchestration.

Unit 15 (bars 52³–70)

This longer, more heterogeneous unit recalls and develops several ideas heard earlier even while introducing new ones. The chorale is played by trombones, the bell motive by clarinets and later oboes, while second oboes, English horn, and bassoon collectively explore the second of the Russian folk melodies from unit 12 in bars 65–70. At the same time, new scherzo-like material is played by trumpets. While the unit as a whole presents a synthesis of sorts under the sign of a single tempo, the overall result may be said to be new.

Unit 16 (bars 71–87)

Eric White calls this "pastorale" presumably on account of its "winding, serpentine" quality of movement. The doodling and wind timbres recall the Russian melodies from units 11 and 12. Here, the performance is led by flute and followed at close quarters by clarinet.

Unit 17 (bars 88–104)

This is a repeat of the pastorale from the previous unit, beginning this time with clarinets and joined by flute. One difference from unit 16 is a series of playful interferences or interjections by oboes and English horn (bars 100–102), which will take on greater significance later.

Unit 18 (bars 105–122)

We hear the pastorale for the third time, with scherzo-like interjection as before (bars 112–114). These last four units (15, 16, 17, and 18) develop and augment familiar material not by worrying individual motifs to their limits (or to death) but by flashing images of the familiar in new contexts.

Unit 19 (bars 122²–125¹)

This short, contrasting unit may well be heard as a suffix (to unit 18) or as a transition (between 18 and 20). (The character of a suffix is retrospective while that of a link is prospective, so the distinction is nontrivial. Stravinsky manages to evoke both functions simultaneously.) Three melodic lines with an overall descending contour unfold simultaneously in English horn and bassoons. The English horn melody may be affiliated affectively with a chorale, but its pentatonic material and disjunct intervals evoke a folk register. The first bassoon's stepwise manner is in keeping with a chorale, while the second bassoon incorporates a large leap (within framing stepwise progressions; bar 124) that tweaks the sense of chorale.

Unit 20 (bars 125–129²)

The bell motive returns.

Unit 21 (bars 129²–132)

The chorale from unit 3 overlaps with the bell motive. We hear two strains of the hymn (bars 129²–130 and 131–132), the first in a fuller texture in which oboes, bassoons, trumpets, and trombone join forces, the second in a reduced texture featuring horns and tuba. The chorale topic gains in authenticity by virtue of the "pure" brass choir.

Unit 22 (bars 133–134)

Solo instruments retrieve the English horn idea from unit 19 and give it a new presentation: the first bassoon partly doubles the cor anglais while the second freely counterpoints the fourths-dominated melody.

   Although there are points of contact between endings and beginnings, the succession of units 19, 20, 21, 22 suggests a juxtaposition of self-contained units rather than any kind of organic or causal process. There are, to be sure, motivic links (as between 19 and 22), but these do not cancel the more pertinent feeling of an unmotivated succession of blocks of distinctly constituted material.

Unit 23 (bars 135–169)

This is a repeat of the pastorale from units 16, 17, and 18 with minor changes.

Unit 24 (bars 169²–172¹)

Unit 19 is repeated here.

Unit 25 (bars 172²–174)

The bell motive sounds again but in a truncated form.

Unit 26 (bars 175–181)

The second of the Russian popular melodies (unit 12) is heard here in a different transposition—a half-step down. The more palpable and immediate effect is of interrupting the bell motive. This particular juxtaposition of materials has not been heard previously.

Unit 27 (bars 182–186)

The bell motive is continued from unit 25.

Unit 28 (bars 186–188)

This recalls unit 19 and underlines the growing importance of its material.

Unit 29 (bars 189–196¹)

The first of the Russian popular melodies—the five-note, 6-bar version—appears here, spread over 7 bars and overlapping with the following unit.

Unit 30 (bars 195³–200)

Although gesturally new, this material is actually drawn from unit 22. Its catchy, jazzy feel and the brevity of its initial appearance lead us to suspect that it will be heard again. We may even speculate that it will be brought back at strategic moments to do some dynamic or motivating work.

Units 31 (bars 201–203), 32 (bars 204–205)

Another change of tempo ushers in two bits of material. The first, unit 31, is the beginning of what will turn out to be the main chorale (harmonized by big chords) that dominates the closing section of *Symphonies*. A single chord is extended over 3 bars and is given melodic profile in the form of a neighbor-note progression. The second is the chorale first presented as unit 3 and heard many times subsequently. Hearing the two in juxtaposition confirms their close relation. Most notable is the occurrence of the pitches D and C in each opening and the complementary sense of opening and closing in units 31 and 32, respectively.

Unit 33 (bars 206–207)

This is a segment of the jazzy material from 30, now in slower tempo and endowed with an aura of premonition. .

Unit 34 (bars 208–212)

This new material, with its explicit scherzo character, recalls unit 15 and the interjections in 17 and 18. Here, we have a sense that it is, as it were, pointing beyond itself.

Unit 35 (bars 213–216)

The jazzy material extends over 4 bars.

∾

For some time now, we have been hearing familiar materials in the manner of cinematic flashbacks. Their order reveals no consistency, their individual lengths vary, but their topical identities are preserved. This is Stravinsky's formal strategy, which I will now render in a paradigmatic chart (figure 9.7).

Figure 9.7 Paradigmatic arrangement of units 1–35 in Stravinsky's *Symphonies of Wind Instruments*

1	2	3						
	4							
5			6					
	7	8						
	9			10	11	12		
13		14					15	16
								17
								18	19
20		21						22
							23	24
25					26			
27							28	
				29				30
	31							
	32						33	34
							35	

The bell motive and chorale serve as anchors; they occur periodically throughout the movement. Although they are subject to recomposition, they mostly preserve their essential form. That is, they change, but not in a developmental way. The contrasting pastorale introduced in unit 16 and repeated as 17 and 18, given a suffix in 19, also returns (23, 24, 28). While the portion of the movement dominated by these materials provides contrast, it is notable that the bell motive and chorale are not banished from their domain. The most dramatic reorientation in the form will be registered as an absence: the bell motive makes its last appearance as unit 27. After this, it cedes power to the chorale which, in an expanded form, dominates the ending of the work. Absence and presence in paradigmatic representation are often equally telling.

Unit 36 (bars 217–270)

A "wild dance" deriving from the scherzo material is given full air time here. Its opening melody has been adumbrated but within different expressive milieus: in the little wind link of unit 6 and in the jazzy material of unit 30. This unit is longer than most in part because of the consistency of the scherzo expression. There are, however, reminiscences of other ideas (in bars 258ff., for example, the melody resembles the two Russian folk melodies). All of this wildness concludes with shapes of savage simplicity: a five-finger, white-note figure, going up and down in the bass (bars 267–269).

Unit 37 (bars 271–274)

The head of the closing chorale appears in a second premonition. (The first was in bar 201.) On reflection—as distinct from immediately apprehending relations—the chord introduced at the beginning of the work (unit 2) and repeated (without melodic content, so to speak) is shown to be a foreshadowing of that which begins the closing chorale (example 9.16). The two recent premonitions (unit 31 and this one, 37) encourage long-range associations with units 2, 4, 7, and 9. Significant is the fact that earlier appearances of this form of the chord disappeared after unit 9, although they were figured as potential rather than actualizations.

Example 9.16. Comparison of chords in bars 7–8 and 271 of Stravinsky, *Symphonies of Wind Instruments*

Unit 38 (bars 275–310)

The jazzy material is finally developed at some length through a variety of expressive contexts. These include a swing sound, a scherzo sound, and a pastorale sound. The resulting topical mixture confers on unit 38 something of the synthetic character of unit 15.

Unit 39 (bars 311–371)

The closing chorale is now thoroughly fused with the adumbrated version first heard near the beginning of *Symphonies* (unit 3). This, too, is a long unit, but it is more stable from a topical point of view than other long units in this work. Within this larger level of stability, however, there occurs an intense development of small ideas. Among the factors that enhance the interiority of these closing moments of the work are the religious connotations set in motion by the chorale, an attendant speech mode in melodic expression, and the gentle striving for a (final) resting place.

The closing chorale is the most organic part of the entire work. Stravinsky's expression is concentrated, intense, and internally directed. Subtly positioned breath marks allow us to sing effectively throughout this extended moment of religious expression. At bar 335, we seem to begin a second stanza of the chorale, but at 345, Stravinsky turns the intensity up a notch by altering the harmonization of the initial melodic D. And at 363, the entire group of worshippers and musicians is heard at its most affecting—wailing quietly but intensely, bringing the work to a close on a complex sonority resting on a low C.

It is well known that this closing chorale was composed before the rest of *Symphonies* and that it was offered to *La Revue musicale* as a memorial to Debussy. It is not therefore surprising to encounter a consistency, stability of expression, and seamlessness in the flow of its musical ideas that discourage further segmentation. What is remarkable is how this preexisting trace is incorporated into *Symphonies* in the manner of an outcome. Stephen Walsh has studied the genesis of the work in detail and has left us a vivid account that attributes an element of caprice and a possible strategic incoherence. The work was composed "back to front" and may be better conceptualized as a "metawork":

> [The score was] compiled . . . back to front. . . . Nothing could be farther from the popular conception of musical composition as a process of starting with a tune, contrasting it with other tunes, developing them, repeating them, coming to a climax, then finishing. Stravinsky had been messing around with these ideas for the best part of a year with no clear idea what sort of work they would make. Now, having been forced to write a two-and-a-half-minute ending, he surveys his sketchbooks, pastes ideas together, inserts other ideas, adds inserts to inserts, then assembles the whole thing in an order and an architecture which seem to bear not the slightest relation to a coherent or organic plan. No wonder the resulting work is in formal terms one of the most radical even he had ever written. It might seem surprising that it hangs together at all.[5]

5. Stephen Walsh, *Stravinsky: A Creative Spring: Russia and France 1882–1934* (Berkeley: University of California Press, 1999), 317.

Figure 9.8 Paradigmatic arrangement of units 36–39 in Stravinsky's *Symphonies of Wind Instruments*

36   37   38

39

Completing our stock taking, we may show the last four units as in figure 9.8. This shows a linear unfolding broken only by the return of the big chorale at the end. As far as the overall form, then, Stravinsky goes from juxtaposing blocks of differentiated materials to suspending an extended chorale as the point of culmination. Some will hear something of a synthesis in the closing chorale while others will imagine that the discontinuities and stark juxtapositions of earlier moments have been absorbed in the continuous and serene chorale utterances.

Beethoven and Stravinsky

The juxtaposition of a late Beethoven string quartet movement (composed in 1825–1826) with an ensemble piece for only wind instruments by Stravinsky (composed a century later) was meant to reinforce the (purely pragmatic) chronological limits set for the analytical approaches explored in this book. One can cite a number of external factors to justify this juxtaposition. For example, among the things that Stravinsky admired in Beethoven was his rhythmic language. He singled out certain passages from the quartets in which rhythmic manipulation seemed especially marked and praised the German composer for his rhythmic vision. (Not surprisingly, there is an affinity between the passages Stravinsky admired in Beethoven and some of his own procedures.) Then also, one of the features of late Beethoven that has been noted by critics since Bekker and Riezler is discontinuity and its constitutive contrasts. These qualities are also held to be emblematic of Stravinsky. So, let us follow the impulse to compare the two composers directly by using some of the analytical criteria explored in previous chapters. The binary casting will of necessity undercomplicate certain aspects of both composers' work, but it may also help to highlight others.

Beethoven and Stravinsky are both concerned with repetition. By this, I do not simply mean that their compositions use repetition or even do so extensively. I have noted that repetition is the very lifeblood of tonal expression. But there is a difference between coming to terms with repetition as a necessary process and foregrounding repetition in a discourse. Repetition in both composers performs not only a (necessary) structural function but a rhetorical function as well. It is as if the medium ("function") and the message ("rhetoric") reinforce each other through imaginative and extensive uses of repetition. Repetition occurs in all musical dimensions, of course, but rhythmic and motivic/melodic repetition seem especially salient in both composers. (I would say that chordal repetition is salient in Stravinsky but not harmonic repetition, which is more salient in Beethoven.) Since the paradigmatic method attends first and foremost to traces of repetition, it may prove to be especially illuminating when applied to both composers. And because they thus respond at a methodological level to a similar analytical impulse, their strategies may be united at a deep level. Stravinsky repeats (something in) Beethoven.

The material progression of ideas in the works of the two composers displays significant contrasts, however. In Stravinsky—and here, *Symphonies* should stand as paradigmatic—units are detached, and materials are often sharply differentiated. This is why Pieter van den Toorn speaks of "blocks" in this (and other) works, while Jonathan Kramer identifies a series of moments, "entities [that are] self-contained to the extent that they appear static in context."[6] The ready morphology of Stravinsky's units is not unheard of in Beethoven, but even in a work marked by contrasts like the first movement of op. 130, the predominant disposition of adjacent units is not one of detachment but of dependency. Stravinsky's units seem detached because they seem lifeless, inorganic, without implication and without "intention" (the latter would be Adorno's characterization). Beethoven's units, by contrast, are burdened with tendency, implication, and dependency. In Stravinsky, connection is apprehended in retrospect, rarely in prospect, except in the banal sense in which one expects events to follow each other in any musical discourse. The characterization of Stravinsky's form as mosaic-like recognizes the containment and autonomy of his building blocks. While we can speak with some confidence of unfinished business in Beethoven by isolating the normative syntactical procedures that demand a certain kind of completion (a cadence, a voice-leading idiom, a diminution, or a phrase complement), Stravinsky's business at local levels frequently denies the teleological trajectory. Stravinsky's materials speak in an emphatic present tense; Beethoven's rhetoric, too, is geared toward the present, but the building blocks are charged with a future tense. And while Beethoven's units can be summarized by reducing them to a contrapuntal essence, Stravinsky's units for the most part resist such acts of reduction. Model and music are apparently identical in Stravinsky, whereas Beethoven's models are abstractions from the music. Schenker indeed once went out of his way to demonstrate the incoherence of Stravinsky's diminutions, thus in effect showing not that there are no (contrapuntal) models but that they are malformed. The technical aspect of Schenker's argument is less controversial than the aesthetic and moral judgment placed on Stravinsky's resistance to convention.[7]

6. Pieter van den Toorn, *The Music of Stravinsky* (New Haven, CT: Yale University Press, 1983), 232; Jonathan Kramer, *The Time of Music: New Meanings, New Temporalities, New Listening Strategies* (New York: Schirmer Books, 1988), 224.

7. Heinrich Schenker, *Das Meisterwerk in der Musik*, vol. 2 (Munich: Drei Masken, 1926), 37–40. Just about everything I've said in this paragraph about Stravinsky would seem to go against the grain of American theory-based analysis of the composer, which has labored to show elements of long-range thinking in his work. Allen Forte, for example, includes voice-leading graphs in *Contemporary Tone-Structures* (New York: Teachers College, Columbia University, 1955); Felix Salzer followed a similar approach in *Structural Hearing*; Adele Katz did the same in *Challenge to Musical Tradition: A New Concept of Tonality* (New York: Knopf, 1945); and Joseph N. Straus, "A Principle of Voice Leading in the Music of Stravinsky," *Music Theory Spectrum* 4 (1982): 106–124, claimed that an implication-realization model was at work in Stravinsky, the implications based on the completion of certain tetrachordal set-classes. Even Edward Cone, discussing an aspect of Stravinsky's

If the ontology of units is as I have described it, then form in Stravinsky takes on an additive quality. Succession replaces causal connection, and the distinction between "mere" succession and a regulated progression based on a governing construct is blurred. In Beethoven's op. 130, for example, the question raised by the first 2 bars demands an answer. That answer will be constrained by the 2-bar length—which it is obliged to accept, or whose rejection it is obliged to justify either immediately or eventually—and by the combined melodic and harmonic progression, which registers incompletion. These causalities are possible because of a shared language, a common practice. When, however, an aesthetic arises whose motivating factors include commentary on convention or simple denial of its principal prescriptions, the props for listening become inferable only from an individual context. We cede all authority to the composer.

Additive construction and the relative autonomy of units undermine the sense of music as narrative as distinct from music as order or event succession. Narration in Stravinsky often comes not from the music itself but from its contexts and associations. The moving dance images in *Petrushka*, for example, allow us to infer a plot as well as a sense of narration; stripped of dance, however, the burden of narration falls entirely on the movement of *topoi*. Alternatively, subsequent soundings of the chord first heard in bar 7 of *Symphonies* deliver a sense of return and progress. But is there a subject that enacts the narrative? If there is a subject in Stravinsky, it is a split one. The *Hauptstimme* is often plural. Even in moments where the texture features a clear melody and its accompaniment (as in the flute and clarinet exchanges beginning in bar 71 of *Symphonies*), that which ostensibly accompanies has strong claims to perceptual priority. Thus, a treble-bass polarity is placed under the possibility of erasure—present but at the same time undermined. The tendency in Stravinsky is toward an equalization of parts. (A potential historical point emanating from this distinction concerns the difference between Stravinsky and Schoenberg. Stravinsky does not merely assert—verbally or precompositionally—this tendency toward overturning the conventional treble-bass hierarchy. Schoenberg the theoretician, on the other hand, had much to say about some of these elements of radicalism although the practical evidence in his scores often leaves the polarity intact. Stravinsky, in this reading, was a far more radical composer.)

---

method, draws an analogy between the composer's technique of "stratification" and Bach's polyphonic melody, where strands of melody are begun, suspended, and eventually brought to a satisfactory conclusion. I do not doubt that score analyses can produce such connections in Stravinsky, but there is a critical difference between Bach's polyphonic melody (or, for that matter, Beethoven's) and Stravinsky. The former operates within specified conventional constraints, so that the syntactic governors are well understood or readily inferred from their contexts. Stravinsky's constraints in *Symphonies* (and elsewhere), by contrast, cannot be inferred or predicted; they must simply be accepted. Indeed, part of the creativity at work in Stravinsky stems from his taking the license to complete or not to complete something that is open (in conventional language). In Beethoven, there is a *contract* between composer and listener; in Stravinsky, there is no a priori contract. Alternatively, we might say that the Stravinskian contract consists precisely in denying the existence of an a priori contract.

On the matter of representation, we might say that paradigmatic representation is more faithful to Stravinsky's material than it is to Beethoven's. The autonomy asserted by discrete numbers (1, 2, 3, etc.) captures the presumed autonomy of Stravinsky's units more meaningfully than it does Beethoven's. For example, if we recall the disposition of units in the opening of the two works studied in this chapter as 1, 2, 2a, 2b, 3, 3a, 3b, 3c for op. 130 and as 1, 2, 3, 4 for bars 1–7 of *Symphonies*, we would say that missing from the representation of Beethoven are the linear connections that would convey the dependency of adjacent units, including the stepwise melodic line $\hat{1}$–$\hat{2}$–$\hat{3}$–$\hat{4}$–$\hat{5}$ that holds the progression as a whole together. Units 2a and 2b in the quartet are in a literal sense caused by unit 2, or at least made possible by it. In the Stravinsky, by contrast, and local melodic connections notwithstanding, the sense of causation and dependency is less pertinent, so that the representation in numbers fairly conveys what is going on.

These presumed oppositions between Beethoven and Stravinsky are presented starkly in order to dramatize difference and encourage debate. It would be foolish to claim, however, that all of Beethoven can be reduced to the organic while all of Stravinsky is inorganic, or that Stravinsky is always easier to segment than Beethoven, or that hierarchic structuring is never elusive in Beethoven. Neither style system is, in the end, reducible to such simple categories. There is discontinuity aplenty in Beethoven, material is sometimes organized in blocks, and certain units succeed each other with a logic that is not always obviously causal. In Stravinsky, on the other hand, a local organicism is often at work, producing diminutions like passing notes and especially neighbor-notes (or clusters of neighboring notes) as well as conventional cadential gestures that often attract an ironic reading. Adjacent units may depend on each other, too. So the truth in the differences between the two composers lies in between. For a more nuanced understanding, we will need to embrace the interstitial wholeheartedly.

Music as discourse is probably indifferent to aesthetic choices. The degree of meaningfulness may vary from context to context, and the dramatization of that discourse may assume different forms, but the very *possibility* of reading a discourse from the ensemble of happenings that is designated as a work always exists. An aesthetic based on the intentional violation of convention, for example, is just as amenable to a discourse reading as one marked by the creative enactment of such convention. Perhaps, in the end, the two approaches are indistinguishable. Perhaps, the idea that Stravinsky stands as a (poetic) repetition of Beethoven is not as outlandish as it might have seemed at first. Our task as analysts, in any case, is not primarily to propagate such opinions (although historical understanding through music analysis remains an attractive option) but to make possible the kinds of technical exploration that enable a reconstruction of the parameters that animate each discourse.

Epilogue

At the close of these adventures in music analysis, it is tempting to try and put everything together in a Procrustean bed, sum up the project neatly as if there were no rough edges, no deviant parameters, no remainders, no imponderables. Yet music, as we have seen, is an unwieldy animal; it signifies in divergent and complex ways. Its meanings are constructed from a wide range of premises and perspectives. The number and variety of technical approaches to analysis together with the diversity of ideological leanings should discourage us from attempting a quick, facile, or premature synthesis. Nevertheless, to stop without concluding, even when the point of the conclusion is to restate the inconclusiveness of the project, would be to display bad manners. So, let me briefly rehearse what I set out to do in this book and why, and then mention some of the implications of what I have done.

I set out to provide insight into how (Romantic) music works as discourse—the nature of the material and the kinds of strategies available for shaping it. The aim was to provide performers, listeners, and analysts with a pretext for playing in and with (the elements of) musical compositions in order to deepen their appreciation and understanding. The institutional umbrella for this activity is musical analysis, and it is under this rubric that we conventionally place the collective actions of getting inside a musical composition in order to identify its elements and to observe the dynamics of their interactions. There is, of course, nothing new about the curiosity that such actions betray; every analyst from Schenker and Tovey to Dahlhaus, Ratner, and Adorno has been motivated by a desire to figure things out.

But which paths to understanding do we choose? How do we turn concept into practice? What concrete steps allow us to establish or at least postulate an ontology for a given composition? What is an appropriate methodology for analysis? It is here that we encounter striking differences in belief and approach. In this book, I proceeded from the assumption that (Romantic) music works as a kind of language that can be "spoken" (competently or otherwise), that music making is a meaningful activity (for the participants first and foremost, but also for observers), that the art of musical composition or *poiesis* is akin to discoursing in sound, and that it is the purpose of analysis to convey aspects of that discoursing by drawing on a range of appropriate techniques. Since the ability to create presupposes a prior ability to speak the relevant language, knowledge of the basic conventions of organizing sound (as music) is indispensable. To ignore conventions, to turn a blind eye to the grammatical constraints and stylistic opportunities available to an individual composer, is to overlook the very ecology that made the work possible. Indeed, a poor grasp of conventions can lead either to an underappreciation of individual creativity or to an overvaluing of a particular achievement.

Reconstructing this ecology can be a formidable challenge, however, since it is liable to involve us in long and arduous investigation (some of it biographical, some of it social, some of it historical, and some of it musical). Attempting such reconstructions here would probably have doubled the size of this project without bringing proportional rewards in the form of conceptual clarity. So, I chose instead to draw on a number of existing studies.

In the first part of the book, I began by rehearsing some of the ways in which music is or is not like language (chapter 1). My 10 propositions on this topic were designed with an interrogative and provocative purpose, not as laws or—worse—commandments, but as propositions or hypotheses. Each of them is, of course, subject to further interrogation; indeed, writings by, among others, Nattiez, Adorno, Schenker, Ratner, and Jankélévitch speak directly or indirectly to issues raised by thinking of music as language and to exploring the nature of musical meaning.

In chapters 2 and 3, I provided six criteria for capturing some of the salient aspects of Romantic music. Again, my chosen criteria were designed to capture certain conventions as prerequisites for insightful analysis—the functioning of *topoi* or subjects of musical discourse; beginnings, middles, and endings; the use of high points; periodicity, discontinuity, and parentheses; the exploration of registers or modes of utterance, including speech mode, dance mode, and song mode; and the cultivation of a narrative thread. Without claiming that each criterion is pertinent to every musical situation, it is nevertheless hard to imagine *any* listening to Romantic music that is not shaped on some level by one or more of these factors.

Chapter 4 took us further into the heart of the musical language, demanding what we might as well call an insider's perspective. Musical insiders are those individuals and communities who compose and/or perform music; they may also include others whose perspectives as listeners and analysts are shaped fundamentally by these experiences. While certain features of Romantic music—like topics or even high points—can, as it were, be identified by "outsiders," speculation about the harmonic, contrapuntal, or phrase-structural foundations of a given composition often have to come from the inside, from direct engagement with the musical code itself. It is precisely this kind of engagement that has produced some of the most sophisticated and influential views of musical structure (such as that of Schenker). The generative approach to understanding which I adopted in the fourth chapter invited participation in the dance of meaning production not through detached observation and the subsequent spinning of (verbal) tales but by direct participation through acts of hypothesizing compositional origins. I suggested that this kind of activity is akin to "speaking" music as a language. Indeed, although logically obvious, the procedure of postulating a simplified or normative construct in order to set into relief a composer's choices can be of profound significance. The normative and conventional are reconstructed as background, as foil, as ecology, as a nexus of possibility; the composer's choices emerge against this background of possibility, highlighting paths not taken and sounding a series of might-have-beens.

My final theoretical task (chapter 5) was to isolate what many believe to be the most indigenous feature of music, namely, its use of repetition, and to see what insights flow from focusing on it. Tonal expression is unimaginable without repetition, but repetition takes many forms and encompasses different levels of structure. In chapter 5, I followed the lead of semiological analysts (Ruwet, Nattiez, and Lidov, among others) in exploring a range of repetitions from simple pitch retention through thematic transformation to harmonic reinterpretation. Rather than place the emphasis on abstract method, however, the analyses in this chapter were offered under specific rubrics stemming from intuited qualities that could be made explicit in paradigmatic analyses: logical form versus chronological in Chopin, discontinuity and additive construction in Mozart, and developing variation in Brahms. Jankélévitch's claim that "music's regime par excellence" is one of "continuous mutation" manifesting in "variation and metamorphosis" reinforces the central justification for the paradigmatic method.[1]

With the theoretical part of my project completed in chapter 5, I turned to a number of close readings of works by Liszt, Brahms, Mahler, Beethoven, and Stravinsky (chapters 6–9). Although each analysis was framed as a semiological study of units and their patterns of succession, our concerns, adumbrated in earlier analyses, were broader, embracing issues of formal strategy and narrative. The case studies were designed not as systematic applications of method but as flexible explorations of musical articulation and the kinds of (formal and associative) meanings that are possible to discover. Analysis must always make discovery possible; if it seems closed, if it provides answers rather than further questions, it betrays its most potent attribute.

The implications of the book's analyses may be drawn according to individual interest. I have already hinted at a number of them in the course of specific analyses of such features as beginnings, middles, and endings in Mendelssohn; discontinuity in Stravinsky; logical form in Chopin; and tonal modeling in Beethoven. Exploring modes of utterance by contrasting speech mode with song mode, for example, may stimulate further speculation about the "linguistic" nature of music while making possible a deeper exploration of its temporal dimensions (including periodicity). A focus on closure likewise encourages further speculation about the dynamics that shape individual compositions into meaningful discourses.

Attention to high points similarly conveys immediately perceptible aspects of a work, while narrative trajectories may be experienced by isolating a migratory "voice" from beginning to end—a voice that may sometimes (choose to) remain silent according to the rhetorical needs of the moment. Again, the fact that these features were discussed in isolation does not mean that they are experienced that

---

1. Jankélévitch, *Music and the Ineffable*, 93.

way. On the contrary, they are all connected if not in actuality then very definitely potentially. For example, high points are typical harbingers of closure; in other contexts, they may signify specific moments within the narrative trajectory. The musical experience tends, in principle, toward holism; the analytical procedure, on the contrary, entails a (provisional) dismantling of that whole—it tends toward isolation. Ideally, an analysis should unveil the conditions of possibility for a musical experience. Although it may serve to rationalize aspects of that experience, analysis can never accurately report the full dimensions of that experience. Recognizing the intended partiality of analytical application may thus help us to evaluate analytical outcomes more reasonably than expecting analysts to work miracles.

In order to begin to capture the work of the imagination as expressed in Romantic music, we need to get close to it. We need to enter into those real as well as imaginative spaces and temporalities that allow us to inspect a work's elements at close quarters. We enter these spaces, however, not with the (mistaken) belief that the object of analysis is a tabula rasa, but with the knowledge that it is freighted with the routines, mannerisms, and meanings of a "spoken" (musical) language. We enter these places armed with a feeling for precedent and possibility and free of the delusion that we are about to recount the way in which a specific artwork actually came into being. The power of analysis lies precisely in this open-ended pursuit of understanding through empathy, speculation, and play.

This view of analysis is, I believe, akin to what Adorno had in mind when he enjoined us to pursue the "truth content" (*Wahrheitsgehalt*) of musical composition. It resonates with Schenker's search for (the truth of) the composer's vision in the unfolding of the *Urlinie* and in the various transformations of the contrapuntal shapes of strict counterpoint into free composition. It is implicit in the qualities that Ratner sought to capture with his notion of topics or subjects to be incorporated into a musical discourse; topics lead us on a path to the discovery of truth in musical style, a discovery that may in turn illuminate the historical or even sociological aspects of a work. And it shares the idealization that led Nattiez to arrange his Molino-inspired tripartition (consisting of a poeitic pole, a neutral level, and an esthesic pole) into a mechanism for uniting the (indispensable and complementary) perspectives of listeners, the production processes, and the work itself as an unmediated trace. This view of analysis may even—and strangely at first—be affiliated with Jankélévitch's relentless protestations of the suitability of various categories for music: form, expressivity, development, communicability, and translatability. Of course, the material expression of this unifying ideology—if that is what it is—will sooner or later produce differences; these theories cannot ultimately be collapsed into one another. Their shared motivating impulse remains the same, however: curiosity about the inner workings of our art. In the end, it is not the analytical trace that matters most; the trace, in any case, yields too much to the imperatives of capital accumulation. If, as Anthony Pople imagines, "meaning is a journey rather than a destination,"[2] then edification will come from doing, from undertaking the journey. The materiality of analytical proceeding serves as its own reward.

2. Anthony Pople, "Preface," in *Theory, Analysis and Meaning in Music*, ed. Pople (Cambridge: Cambridge University Press, 1994), xi.

BIBLIOGRAPHY

Abbate, Carolyn. *Unsung Voices: Opera and Musical Narrative in the Nineteenth Century*. Princeton, NJ: Princeton University Press, 1991.

——. "Music—Drastic or Gnostic?" *Critical Inquiry* 30 (2004): 505–536.

Adorno, Theodor. *Mahler: A Musical Physiognomy*, trans. Edmund Jephcott. Chicago: University of Chicago Press, 1992.

——. "Music and Language: A Fragment," in *Quasi una Fantasia: Essays on Modern Music*, trans. Rodney Livingstone. London: Verso, 1992, 1–6.

——. *Beethoven: The Philosophy of Music*, trans. Edmund Jephcott, ed. Rolf Tiedemann. Stanford, CA: Stanford University Press, 1998.

——. *Essays on Music*, ed. Richard Leppert. Berkeley: University of California Press, 2002.

——. "Schubert (1928)," trans. Jonathan Dunsby and Beate Perrey. *19th-Century Music* 24 (2005): 3–14.

Agawu, Kofi. "Structural Highpoints in Schumann's *Dichterliebe*." *Music Analysis* 3 (1984): 159–180.

——. "Tonal Strategy in the First Movement of Mahler's Tenth Symphony." *19th-Century Music* 9 (1986): 222–233.

——. "Concepts of Closure and Chopin's op. 28." *Music Theory Spectrum* 9 (1987): 1–17.

——. "Stravinsky's *Mass* and Stravinsky Analysis." *Music Theory Spectrum* 11 (1989): 139–163.

——. *Playing with Signs: A Semiotic Interpretation of Classic Music*. Princeton, NJ: Princeton University Press, 1991.

——. "Haydn's Tonal Models: The First Movement of the Piano Sonata in E-flat Major, Hob. XVI:52," in *Convention in Eighteenth- and Nineteenth-Century Music: Essays in Honor of Leonard G. Ratner*, ed. Wye J. Allanbrook, Janet M. Levy, and William P. Mahrt. Stuyvesant, NY: Pendragon, 1992, 3–22.

——. "Does Music Theory Need Musicology?" *Current Musicology* 53 (1993): 89–98.

——. "Prolonged Counterpoint in Mahler," in *Mahler Studies*, ed. Stephen Hefling. Cambridge: Cambridge University Press, 1997, 217–247.

——. "The Challenge of Semiotics," in *Rethinking Music*, ed. Nicholas Cook and Mark Everist. Oxford: Oxford University Press, 1999, 138–160.

——. *Representing African Music: Postcolonial Notes, Queries, Positions*. New York: Routledge, 2003.

——. "How We Got Out of Analysis and How to Get Back In Again." *Music Analysis* 23 (2004): 267–286.

Agmon, Eytan. "The Bridges That Never Were: Schenker on the Contrapuntal Origin of the Triad and the Seventh Chord." *Music Theory Online* 3 (1997). http://www.societymusictheory.org/mto

Albrechtsberger, Johann Georg. *Gründliche Anweisung zur Composition*. Leipzig: Johann Immanuel Breitkopf, 1790.

Allanbrook, Wye J. *Rhythmic Gesture in Mozart: Le nozze di Figaro and Don Giovanni.* Chicago: University of Chicago Press, 1983.

——. "Two Threads through the Labyrinth: Topic and Process in the First Movements of K. 332 and K. 333," in *Convention in Eighteenth- and Nineteenth-Century Music: Essays in Honor of Leonard G. Ratner*, ed. Wye J. Allanbrook, Janet M. Levy, and William P. Mahrt. Stuyvesant, NY: Pendragon, 1992, 125–171.

——. "K331, First Movement: Once More, with Feeling," in *Communication in Eighteenth-Century Music*, ed. Danuta Mirka and Kofi Agawu. Cambridge: Cambridge University Press, 2008.

Almen, Byron, and Edward Pearsall, eds. *Approaches to Meaning in Music.* Bloomington: Indiana University Press, 2006.

Andriessen, Louis, and Elmer Schönberger. *Apollonian Clockwork: On Stravinsky*, trans. Jeff Hamburg. Oxford: Oxford University Press, 1989.

Ayrey, Craig. "Review of *Playing with Signs* by K. Agawu." *Times Higher Education Supplement* 3 (May 1991): 7.

——. "Debussy's Significant Connections: Metaphor and Metonymy in Analytical Method," in *Theory, Analysis and Meaning in Music*, ed. Anthony Pople. Cambridge: Cambridge University Press, 1994, 127–151.

——. "Universe of Particulars: Subotnik, Deconstruction, and Chopin." *Music Analysis* 17 (1998): 339–381.

Barry, Barbara. "In Beethoven's Clockshop: Discontinuity in the Opus 18 Quartets." *Musical Quarterly* 88 (2005): 320–337.

Barthes, Roland. *Elements of Semiology*, trans. Annette Lavers and Colin Smith. New York: Hill and Wang, 1967.

——. *Mythologies*, trans. Annette Lavers. New York: Hill and Wang, 1972.

Becker, Judith, and Alton Becker. "A Grammar of the Musical Genre Srepegan." *Journal of Music Theory* 24 (1979): 1–43.

Bekker, Paul. *Beethoven.* Berlin and Leipzig: Schuster and Loeffler, 1911.

Bellerman, Heinrich. *Der Contrapunct; Oder Anleitung zur Stimmführung in der musikalischen Composition.* Berlin: Julius Springer, 1862.

Bent, Ian D., ed. *Music Analysis in the Nineteenth Century.* 2 vols. Cambridge: Cambridge University Press, 1994.

Bent, Ian, and Anthony Pople. "Analysis." *The New Grove Dictionary of Music and Musicians*, 2nd ed. London: Macmillan, 2001.

Benveniste, Émile. "The Semiology of Language," in *Semiotics: An Introductory Reader*, ed. Robert E. Innis. London: Hutchinson, 1986, 228–246.

Berger, Karol. "The Form of Chopin's Ballade, op. 23." *19th-Century Music* 20 (1996): 46–71.

Bernhard, Christoph. *Ausführlicher Bericht vom Gebrauche der Con- und Dissonantien, Tractatus compositionis augmentatus in Die Kompositionslehre Heinrich Schützens in der Fassung seines Schülers Christoh Bernhard*, ed. J. Müller-Blattau, 2d ed. Kassel: Bärenreiter, 1963. English translation by W. Hilse, "The Treatises of Christoph Bernhard." *Music Forum* 3 (1973): 1–196.

Berry, David Carson. *A Topical Guide to Schenkerian Literature: An Annotated Bibliography with Indices.* Hillsdale, NY: Pendragon, 2004.

Biró, Dániel Péter. "Plotting the Instrument: On the Changing Role of Timbre in Mahler's Ninth Symphony and Webern's op. 21." Unpublished paper.

Boilès, Charles L. "Tepehua Thought-Song: A Case of Semantic Signalling." *Ethnomusicology* 11 (1967): 267–292.

Bonds, Mark Evan. *Wordless Discourse: Musical Form and the Metaphor of the Oration.* Cambridge, MA: Harvard University Press, 1991.

Boretz, Benjamin. "Metavariations, Part 4: Analytic Fallout." *Perspectives of New Music* 11 (1973): 156–203.

Brahms, Johannes. *Symphonien: Klavier zu 2 Handen.* Leipzig: Peters, 1936.

Brown, Matthew. "Tonality and Form in Debussy's Prelude à L'Après-midi d'un faune." *Music Theory Spectrum* 15 (1993): 127–143.

———. *Explaining Tonality: Schenkerian Theory and Beyond.* Rochester, NY: University of Rochester Press, 2006.

Bukofzer, Manfred. *Music in the Baroque Era, from Monteverdi to Bach.* New York: Norton, 1947.

Bülow, Hans von. Preface to C. P. E Bach, *Sechs Klavier-Sonaten.* Leipzig: Peters, 1862, 3–5.

Burmeister, Joachim. *Musica Poetica [Musical Poetics],* trans. Benito V. Rivera. New Haven, CT: Yale University Press, 1993.

Burnham, Scott. *Beethoven Hero.* Princeton, NJ: Princeton University Press, 1995.

Caplin, William E. *Classical Form: A Theory of Formal Functions for the Instrumental Music of Haydn, Mozart and Beethoven.* Oxford: Oxford University Press, 2000.

———. "The Classical Cadence: Conceptions and Misconceptions." *Journal of the American Musicological Society* 57 (2004): 51–117.

———. "On the Relation of Musical *Topoi* to Formal Function." *Eighteenth-Century Music* 2 (2005): 113–124.

Chafe, Wallace. *Discourse, Consciousness, and Time: The Flow and Displacement of Conscious Experience in Speaking and Writing.* Chicago: University of Chicago Press, 1994.

Chua, Daniel. *The "Galitzin" Quartets of Beethoven.* Princeton, NJ: Princeton University Press, 1995.

———. *Absolute Music and the Construction of Meaning.* Cambridge: Cambridge University Press, 1999.

Clarke, Eric F. *Ways of Listening: An Ecological Approach to the Perception of Musical Meaning.* Oxford: Oxford University Press, 2005.

Cohn, Richard, and Douglas Dempster. "Hierarchical Unity, Plural Unities: Toward a Reconciliation," in *Disciplining Music: Musicology and Its Canons,* ed. Katherine Bergeron and Philip Bohlman. Chicago: University of Chicago Press, 1992, 156–181.

Cone, Edward T. "Words into Music," in *Sound and Poetry,* ed. Northrop Frye. New York: Columbia University Press, 1957, 3–15.

———. *Musical Form and Musical Performance.* New York: Norton, 1968.

———. "Stravinsky: The Progress of a Method," in *Perspectives on Schoenberg and Stravinsky,* ed. Edward T. Cone and Benjamin Boretz. New York: Norton, 1972, 155–164.

Cook, Nicholas. "Review Essay: Putting the Meaning Back into Music; or, Semiotics Revisited." *Music Theory Spectrum* 18 (1996): 106–123.

———. *Analysing Musical Multimedia.* Oxford: Oxford University Press, 2001.

Cook, Nicholas, and Mark Everist. *Rethinking Music.* Oxford: Oxford University Press, 1999.

Cooke, Deryck. *The Language of Music.* Oxford: Oxford University Press, 1959.

———. *Gustav Mahler: An Introduction to His Music.* London: Faber, 1980.

Cross, Ian. "Music and Biocultural Evolution," in *The Cultural Study of Music: A Critical Introduction,* ed. Martin Clayton, Trevor Herbert, and Richard Middleton. New York: Routledge, 2003, 19–30.

Cumming, Naomi. *The Sonic Self: Musical Subjectivity and Signification.* Bloomington: Indiana University Press, 2000.

Czerny, Carl. "Harmonic Groundwork of Beethoven's Sonata [no. 21 in C] op. 53 ('Waldstein')," excerpted in *Music Analysis in the Nineteenth Century,* vol. 2: *Hermeneutic Approaches,* ed. Ian D. Bent. Cambridge: Cambridge University Press, 1994, 188–196.

Dahlhaus, Carl. *Between Romanticism and Modernism,* trans. Mary Whittall. Berkeley: University of California Press, 1980.

324 ∾ *Bibliography*

Dahlhaus, Carl. "Fragments of a Musical Hermeneutics," trans. Karen Painter. *Current Musicology* 50 (1991): 5–20.

Dale, Catherine. "Schoenberg's Concept of Variation Form: A Paradigmatic Analysis of *Litanei* from the Second String Quartet, op. 10." *Journal of the Royal Musical Association* 118 (1993): 94–120.

Danuser, Hermann. *Gustav Mahler: Das Lied von der Erde.* Munich: Fink, 1986.

Derrida, Jacques. *Of Grammatology.* Translated by Gayatri Chakravorty Spivak. Baltimore: Johns Hopkins University Press, 1974. Original 1967.

Dickensheets, Janice. "Nineteenth-Century Topical Analysis: A Lexicon of Romantic *Topoi.*" *Pendragon Review* 2 (2003): 5–19.

Dougherty, William. "The Quest for Interpretants: Towards a Peircean Paradigm for Musical Semiotics." *Semiotica* 99 (1994): 163–184.

Dressler, Gallus. *Praecepta Musicae Poeticae.* In *Geschichts-Blätter für Stadt und Land Magdeburg* 49–50, ed. Bernhard Engleke (1916, original 1563), 214–249.

Dreyfus, Laurence. *Bach and the Patterns of Invention.* Cambridge, MA: Harvard University Press, 1996.

Dunsby, Jonathan. "A Hitch Hiker's Guide to Semiotic Music Analysis." *Music Analysis* 1 (1982): 237–238.

Dunsby, Jonathan, and John Stopford. "The Case for a Schenkerian Semiotic." *Music Theory Spectrum* 3 (1981): 49–53.

Dunsby, Jonathan, and Arnold Whittall. *Music Analysis in Theory and Practice.* London: Faber, 1988.

Eco, Umberto. "The Poetics of the Open Work," in Eco, *The Role of the Reader: Explorations in the Semiotics of Texts.* Bloomington: Indiana University Press, 1979, 47–66.

Eitan, Zohar. *Highpoints: A Study of Melodic Peaks.* Philadelphia: University of Pennsylvania Press, 1997.

Everett, Daniel L. "Cultural Constraints on Grammar and Cognition in Piraha: Another Look at the Design Features of Human Language." *Current Anthropology* 46 (2005): 621–646.

Fabian, Johannes. *Out of Our Minds: Reason and Madness in the Exploration of Central Africa.* Berkeley: University of California Press, 2000.

Feil, Arnold. "Two Analyses ['Im Dorfe' from *Winterreise* and Moment Musical in F Minor, op. 94, no. 3 (D. 780)]." in *Schubert: Critical and Analytical Studies,* ed. Walter Frisch. Lincoln: University of Nebraska Press, 1986, 104–125.

Feld, Steven, and Aaron Fox. "Music and Language." *Annual Review of Anthropology* 23 (1994): 25–53.

Floros, Constantin. *Gustav Mahler: The Symphonies,* trans. Vernon Wicker. Portland, OR: Amadeus, 1993.

Forte, Allen. *Contemporary Tone-Structures.* New York: Teachers College, Columbia University, 1955.

———. "Middleground Motives in the Adagietto of Mahler's Fifth Symphony." *19th-Century Music* 8 (1984): 153–163.

Forte, Allen, and Steven Gilbert. *Introduction to Schenkerian Analysis.* New York: Norton 1982.

Frisch, Walter. *Brahms and the Principle of Developing Variation.* Berkeley: University of California Press, 1982.

———. *Brahms: The Four Symphonies.* New York: Schirmer, 1996.

Fux, Johann Joseph. *Gradus ad parnassum.* Vienna: Johann Peter van Ghelen, 1725. Translated by Alfred Mann as *The Study of Counterpoint from Johann Joseph Fux's "Gradus ad Parnassum."* New York: Norton, 1965.

Garda, Michela. *L'estetica musicale del Novecento: Tendenze e problemi*. Rome: Carocci, 2007.

Grabócz, Márta. *Morphologie des oeuvres pour piano de Liszt: Influence du programme sur l'évolution des formes instrumentales*, 2nd ed. Paris: Kimé, 1996.

———. "Semiological Terminology in Musical Analysis," in *Musical Semiotics in Growth*, ed. Eero Tarasti. Bloomington: Indiana University Press, 1996, 195–218.

———. "'Topos et dramaturgie': Analyse des signifiés et de la strategie dans deux movements symphoniques de B. Bartok." *Degrés* 109–110 (2002): j1–j18.

———. "Stylistic Evolution in Mozart's Symphonic Slow Movements: The Discursive-Passionate Schema." *Intégral* 20 (2006): 105–129.

Hanslick, Eduard. *Vom Musikalisch-Schönen [On the Musically Beautiful]*, trans. Martin Cooper, excerpted in *Music in European Thought 1851–1912*, ed. Bojan Bujíc. Cambridge: Cambridge University Press, 1988, 12–39.

Hasty, Christopher. "Segmentation and Process in Post-Tonal Music." *Music Theory Spectrum* 3 (1981): 54–73.

———. *Meter as Rhythm*. New York: Oxford University Press, 1997.

Hatten, Robert. *Musical Meaning in Beethoven: Markedness, Correlation, and Interpretation*. Bloomington: Indiana University Press, 1994.

———. *Interpreting Musical Gestures, Topics, and Tropes: Mozart, Beethoven, Schubert*. Bloomington: Indiana University Press, 2004.

Hefling, Stephen E. "The Ninth Symphony," in *The Mahler Companion*, ed. Donald Mitchell and Andrew Nicholson. Oxford: Oxford University Press, 2002, 467–490.

Henrotte, Gayle A. "Music as Language: A Semiotic Paradigm?" in *Semiotics 1984*, ed. John Deely. Lanham, MD: University Press of America, 1985, 163–170.

Henschel, George. *Personal Recollections of Johannes Brahms: Some of His Letters to and Pages from a Journal Kept by George Henschel*. New York: AMS, 1978.

Hepokoski, James, and Warren Darcy. *Elements of Sonata Theory: Norms, Types, and Deformations in the Late-Eighteenth-Century Sonata*. Oxford: Oxford University Press, 2006.

Hoeckner, Berthold. *Programming the Absolute: Nineteenth-Century German Music and the Hermeneutics of the Moment*. Princeton, NJ: Princeton University Press, 1978.

Horton, Julian. "Review of *Bruckner Studies*, ed. Paul Hawkshaw and Timothy Jackson." *Music Analysis* 18 (1999): 155–170.

———. "Bruckner's Symphonies and Sonata Deformation Theory." *Journal of the Society for Musicology in Ireland* 1 (2005–2006): 5–17.

Hughes, David W. "Deep Structure and Surface Structure in Javanese Music: A Grammar of Gendhing Lampah." *Ethnomusicology* 32(1) (1988): 23–74.

Huron, David. "Review of *Highpoints: A Study of Melodic Peaks* by Zohar Eitan." *Music Perception* 16(2) (1999): 257–264.

Ivanovitch, Roman. "Mozart and the Environment of Variation." Ph.D. diss., Yale University, 2004.

Jackson, Roland. "*Leitmotive* and Form in the *Tristan* Prelude." *Music Review* 36 (1975): 42–53.

Jakobson, Roman. "Language in Relation to Other Communication Systems," in Jakobson, *Selected Writings*, vol. 2. The Hague: Mouton, 1971, 697–708.

Jankélévitch, Vladimir. *Music and the Ineffable [La Musique et l'Ineffable]*, trans. Carolyn Abbate. Princeton, NJ: Princeton University Press, 2003.

Johns, Keith T. *The Symphonic Poems of Franz Liszt*, rev. ed. Stuyvesant, NY: Pendragon, 1996.

Jonas, Oswald. *Introduction to the Theory of Heinrich Schenker: The Nature of the Musical Work of Art*, trans. and ed. John Rothgeb. New York: Longman, 1982 (orig. 1934).

Kaplan, Richard. "Sonata Form in the Orchestral Works of Liszt: The Revolutionary Reconsidered." *19th-Century Music* 8 (1984): 142–152.

Katz, Adele. *Challenge to Musical Tradition: A New Concept of Tonality.* New York: Knopf, 1945.

Keiler, Alan. "The Syntax of Prolongation: Part 1," in *Theory Only* 3 (1977): 3–27.

———. "Bernstein's 'The Unanswered Question' and the Problem of Musical Competence." *Musical Quarterly* 64 (1978): 195–222.

Klein, Michael L. *Intertextuality in Western Art Music.* Bloomington: Indiana University Press, 2005.

Kleinertz, Rainer. "Liszt, Wagner, and Unfolding Form: *Orpheus* and the Genesis of *Tristan und Isolde*," in *Franz Liszt and His World*, ed. Christopher H. Gibbs and Dana Gooley. Princeton, NJ: Princeton University Press, 2006, 231–254.

Koch, Heinrich Christoph. *Versuch einer Anleitung zur Composition*, vols. 2 and 3. Leipzig: Böhme, 1787 and 1793.

Kramer, Jonathan D. *The Time of Music: New Meanings, New Temporalities, New Listening Strategies.* New York: Schirmer, 1988.

Kramer, Lawrence. *Music and Poetry: The Nineteenth Century and After.* Berkeley: University of California Press, 1984.

———. *Music as Cultural Practice.* Berkeley: University of California Press, 1990.

Krebs, Harald. "The Unifying Function of Neighboring Motion in Stravinsky's *Sacre du Printemps*." *Indiana Theory Review* 8 (1987): 3–13.

Krumhansl, Carol. "Topic in Music: An Empirical Study of Memorability, Openness, and Emotion in Mozart's String Quintet in C Major and Beethoven's String Quartet in A Minor." *Music Perception* 16 (1998): 119–132.

La Grange, Henry-Louis de. *Gustav Mahler: A New Life Cut Short (1907-1911).* Oxford: Oxford University Press, 2008.

Larson, Steve. "A Tonal Model of an Atonal Piece: Schoenberg's opus 15, number 2." *Perspectives of New Music* 25 (1987): 418–433.

Leichtentritt, Hugo. *Musical Form.* Cambridge, MA: Harvard University Press, 1951 (orig. 1911).

Lendvai, Erno. *Bela Bartók: An Analysis of His Music.* London: Kahn & Averill, 1971.

Lerdahl, Fred, and Ray Jackendoff. *A Generative Theory of Tonal Music.* Cambridge, MA: MIT Press, 1983.

Lester, Joel. "J. S. Bach Teaches Us How to Compose: Four Pattern Prelude of the *Well-Tempered Clavier*." *College Music Symposium* 38 (1998): 33–46.

Lewin, David. *Musical Form and Transformation: Four Analytic Essays.* New Haven, CT: Yale University Press, 1993.

———. "Music Theory, Phenomenology, and Modes of Perception," in Lewin, *Studies in Music with Text.* Oxford: Oxford University Press, 2006, 53–108.

Lewis, Christopher Orlo. *Tonal Coherence in Mahler's Ninth Symphony.* Ann Arbor: UMI Press, 1984.

Lidov, David. *On Musical Phrase.* Montreal: Faculty of Music, University of Montreal, 1975.

———. "Nattiez's Semiotics of Music." *Canadian Journal of Research in Semiotics* 5 (1977): 13–54.

———. "Mind and Body in Music." *Semiotica* 66 (1987): 69–97.

———. "The Lamento di Tristano," in *Models of Music Analysis: Music before 1600*, ed. Mark Everist. Oxford: Blackwell, 1992, 66–92.

———. *Elements of Semiotics.* New York: St. Martin's Press, 1999.

———. *Is Language a Music? Writings on Musical Form and Signification.* Bloomington: Indiana University Press, 2005.

Lowe, Melanie. *Pleasure and Meaning in the Classical Symphony*. Bloomington: Indiana University Press, 2007.

Marx, A. B. *Die Lehre von der musikalischen Komposition, praktisch-theoretisch*. Leipzig: Breitkopf & Härtel, 1837–1847.

Mattheson, Johann. *Der vollkommene Capellmeister*, trans. Ernest Harriss. Ann Arbor, MI: UMI Research Press, 1981 (orig. 1739).

Maus, Fred Everett. "Narratology, Narrativity," in *The New Grove Dictionary of Music and Musicians*, 2nd ed. London: Macmillan, 2001.

McClary, Susan. *Conventional Wisdom: The Content of Musical Form*. Berkeley: University of California Press, 2001.

McCreless, Patrick. "Syntagmatics and Paradigmatics: Some Implications for the Analysis of Chromaticism in Tonal Music." *Music Theory Spectrum* 13 (1991): 147–178.

———. "Music and Rhetoric," in *The Cambridge History of Western Music Theory*, ed. Thomas Christensen. Cambridge: Cambridge University Press, 2002, 847–879.

———. "Anatomy of a Gesture: From Davidovsky to Chopin and Back," in *Approaches to Meaning in Music*, ed. Byron Almen and Edward Pearsall. Bloomington: Indiana University Press, 2006, 11–40.

McDonald, Matthew. "Silent Narration: Elements of Narrative in Ives's The Unanswered Question." *19th-Century Music* 27 (2004): 263–286.

McKay, Nicholas Peter. "On Topics Today." *Zeitschrift der Gesellschaft für Musiktheorie* 4 (2007). http://www.gmth.de/zeitschrift/artikel/0124/0124.html. Accessed August 12, 2008.

Metzer, David. *Quotation and Cultural Meaning in Twentieth-Century Music*. Cambridge: Cambridge University Press, 2003.

Meyer, Leonard B. *Explaining Music: Essays and Explorations*. Chicago: University of Chicago Press, 1973.

———. "Exploiting Limits: Creation, Archetypes and Style Change." *Daedalus* (1980): 177–205.

———. *Style and Music: Theory, History, and Ideology*. Philadelphia: University of Pennsylvania Press, 1989.

Micznik, Vera. "Music and Narrative Revisited: Degrees of Narrativity in Mahler." *Journal of the Royal Musical Association* 126 (2001): 193–249.

Mitchell, Donald. *Gustav Mahler*, vol. 3: *Songs and Symphonies of Life and Death*. London: Faber and Faber, 1985.

Molino, Jean. "Musical Fact and the Semiology of Music," trans. J. A. Underwood. *Music Analysis* 9 (1990): 104–156.

Monelle, Raymond. *Linguistics and Semiotics in Music*. Chur, Switzerland: Harwood, 1992.

———. *The Sense of Music: Semiotic Essays*. Princeton, NJ: Princeton University Press, 2000.

———. *The Musical Topic: Hunt, Military and Pastoral*. Bloomington: Indiana University Press, 2006.

Monson, Ingrid. *Saying Something: Jazz Improvisation and Interaction*. Chicago: University of Chicago Press, 1996.

Morgan, Robert P. "Schenker and the Theoretical Tradition." *College Music Symposium* 18 (1978): 72–96.

———. "Coda as Culmination: The First Movement of the 'Eroica' Symphony," in *Music Theory and the Exploration of the Past*, ed. Christopher Hatch and David W. Bernstein. Chicago: University of Chicago Press, 1993, 357–376.

Morgan, Robert P. "Circular Form in the Tristan Prelude." *Journal of the American Musicological Society* 53 (2000): 69–103.

———. "The Concept of Unity and Musical Analysis." *Music Analysis* 22 (2003): 7–50.

Muns, George. "Climax in Music." Ph.D. diss., University of North Carolina, 1955.

Narmour, Eugene. *The Analysis and Cognition of Basic Melodic Structures: The Implication-Realization Model*. Chicago: University of Chicago Press, 1990.

Nattiez, Jean-Jacques. "Varèse's 'Density 21.5': A Study in Semiological Analysis," trans. Anna Barry. *Music Analysis* 1 (1982): 243–340.

———. *Music and Discourse: Toward a Semiology of Music*, trans. Carolyn Abbate. Princeton, NJ: Princeton University Press, 1990.

Neubauer, John. *The Emancipation of Music from Language: Departure from Mimesis in Eighteenth-Century Aesthetics*. New Haven, CT: Yale University Press, 1986.

Newcomb, Anthony. "Schumann and Late Eighteenth-Century Narrative Strategies." *19th-Century Music* 11 (1987): 164–174.

Notley, Margaret. "Late-Nineteenth-Century Chamber Music and the Cult of the Classical Adagio." *19th-Century Music* 23 (1999): 33–61.

Oster, Ernst. "The Dramatic Character of the Egmont Overture," in *Aspects of Schenkerian Theory*, ed. David Beach. New Haven, CT: Yale University Press, 1983, 209–222.

Oxford English Dictionary, 3rd ed. Oxford: Oxford University Press, 2007.

Perrey, Beate Julia. *Schumann's Dichterliebe and Early Romantic Poetics: Fragmentation of Desire*. Cambridge: Cambridge University Press, 2003.

Pople, Anthony, ed. *Theory, Analysis and Meaning in Music*. Cambridge: Cambridge University Press, 1994.

Powers, Harold. "Language Models and Music Analysis." *Ethnomusicology* 24 (1980): 1–60.

———. "Reading Mozart's Music: Text and Topic, Sense and Syntax." *Current Musicology* 57 (1995): 5–44.

Puffett, Derrick. "Bruckner's Way: The Adagio of the Ninth Symphony." *Music Analysis* 18 (1999): 5–100.

Ratner, Leonard G. *Music: The Listener's Art*, 2nd ed. New York: McGraw-Hill, 1966.

———. *Classic Music: Expression, Form, and Style*. New York: Schirmer, 1980.

———. "Topical Content in Mozart's Keyboard Sonatas." *Early Music* 19 (1991): 615–619.

———. *Romantic Music: Sound and Syntax*. New York: Schirmer, 1992.

———. *The Beethoven String Quartets: Compositional Strategies and Rhetoric*. Stanford, CA: Stanford Bookstore, 1995.

Ratz, Erwin. *Einführung in die musikalische Formenlehre*, 3rd ed. Vienna: Universal, 1973.

Reed, John. *The Schubert Song Companion*. Manchester: Manchester University Press, 1985.

Rehding, Alex. "Liszt's Musical Monuments." *19th-Century Music* 26 (2002): 52–72.

Réti, Rudolph. *The Thematic Process in Music*. New York: Macmillan, 1951.

Reynolds, Christopher. *Motives for Allusion: Context and Content in Nineteenth-Century Music*. Cambridge, MA: Harvard University Press, 2003.

Richards, Paul. "The Emotions at War: Atrocity as Piacular Rite in Sierra Leone," in *Public Emotions*, ed. Perri 6, Susannah Radstone, Corrine Squire, and Amal Treacher. London: Palgrave Macmillan, 2006, 62–84.

Richter, Ernst Friedrich. *Lehrbuch des einfachen und doppelten Kontrapunkts*. Leipzig: Breitkopf & Härtel, 1872.

Riemann, Hugo. *Vereinfachter Harmonielehre; oder, Die Lehre von den tonalen Funktionen der Akkorde*. London: Augener, 1895.

Riezler, Walter. *Beethoven*. Translated by G. D. H. Pidcock. New York: Vienna House, 1938.

Rosand, Ellen. "The Descending Tetrachord: An Emblem of Lament." *Musical Quarterly* 65 (1979): 346–359.

Rosen, Charles. *The Classical Style: Haydn, Mozart, Beethoven*. New York: Norton, 1972.

Rothstein, William. *Phrase Rhythm in Tonal Music*. New York: Schirmer, 1989.

———. "Transformations of Cadential Formulae in Music by Corelli and His Successors," in *Studies from the Third International Schenker Symposium*, ed. Allen Cadwallader. Hildersheim, Germany: Olms, 2006, 245–278.

Rowell, Lewis. "The Creation of Audible Time," in *The Study of Time*, vol. 4, ed. J. T. Fraser, N. Lawrence, and D. Park. New York: Springer, 1981, 198–210.

Ruwet, Nicolas. "Théorie et méthodes dans les etudes musicales: Quelques remarques rétrospectives et préliminaires." *Music en jeu* 17 (1975): 11–36.

———. "Methods of Analysis in Musicology," trans. Mark Everist. *Music Analysis* 6 (1987): 11–36.

Salzer, Felix. *Structural Hearing: Tonal Coherence in Music*. 2 vols. New York: Dover, 1952.

Salzer, Felix, and Carl Schachter. *Counterpoint in Composition: The Study of Voice Leading*. New York: Columbia University Press, 1989.

Samson, Jim. *Music in Transition: A Study of Tonal Expansion and Atonality 1900–1920*. London: Dent, 1977.

———. "Extended Forms: Ballades, Scherzos and Fantasies," in *The Cambridge Companion to Chopin*, ed. Samson. Cambridge: Cambridge University Press, 1992, 101–123.

———. *Virtuosity and the Musical Work: The Transcendental Studies of Liszt*. Cambridge: Cambridge University Press, 2007.

Samuels, Robert. "Music as Text: Mahler, Schumann and Issues in Analysis," in *Theory, Analysis and Meaning in Music*, ed. Anthony Pople. Cambridge: Cambridge University Press, 1994, 152–163.

———. *Mahler's Sixth Symphony: A Study in Musical Semiotics*. Cambridge: Cambridge University Press, 1995.

Saussure, Ferdinand de. *Course in General Linguistics*, ed. C. Bally and A. Sechehaye. New York: McGraw-Hill, 1966 (original 1915).

Schenker, Heinrich. *Das Meisterwerk in der Musik*, vol. 2. Munich: Drei Masken, 1926.

———. *Five Graphic Music Analyses*, ed. Felix Salzer. New York: Dover, 1969.

———. *Free Composition*, trans. Ernst Oster. New York: Longman, 1979.

———. *Counterpoint: A Translation of Kontrapunkt*, trans. John Rothgeb and Jürgen Thym. New York: Schirmer, 1987.

———. *Der Tonwille: Pamphlets in Witness of the Immutable Laws of Music*, vol. 1, ed. William Drabkin, trans. Ian Bent et al. Oxford: Oxford University Press, 2004.

Schoenberg, Arnold. *Fundamentals of Musical Composition*. New York: St. Martin's Press, 1967.

Sechter, Simon. "Analysis of the Finale of Mozart's Symphony no. [41] in C [K551('Jupiter')]," excerpted in *Music Analysis in the Nineteenth Century*, vol. 1: *Fugue, Form and Style*, ed. Ian D. Bent. Cambridge: Cambridge University Press, 1994, 82–96.

Sheinbaum, John J. "Timbre, Form and Fin-de-Siècle Refractions in Mahler's Symphonies." Ph.D. diss., Cornell University, 2002.

Silbiger, Alexander. " 'Il chitarrino le suonerò': Commedia dell'arte in Mozart's Piano Sonata K. 332." Paper presented at the annual meeting of the Mozart Society of America, Kansas City, November 5, 1999.

Sisman, Elaine R. "Brahms' Slow Movements: Reinventing the Closed Forms," in *Brahms Studies*, ed. George Bozarth. Oxford: Oxford University Press, 1990, 79–103.

———. *Haydn and the Classical Variation*. Cambridge, MA: Harvard University Press, 1993.

———. *Mozart: The "Jupiter" Symphony*. Cambridge: Cambridge University Press, 1993.

———. "Genre, Gesture and Meaning in Mozart's 'Prague' Symphony," in *Mozart Studies*, vol. 2, ed. Cliff Eisen. Oxford: Oxford University Press, 1997, 27–84.

Smith, Peter H. *Expressive Forms in Brahms' Instrumental Music: Structure and Meaning in His "Werther" Quartet*. Bloomington: Indiana University Press, 2005.

Spitzer, John. "Grammar of Improvised Ornamentation: Jean Rousseau's Viol Treatise of 1687." *Journal of Music Theory* 33 (1989): 299–332.

Spitzer, Michael. *Metaphor and Musical Thought*. Chicago: University of Chicago Press, 2004.

Stell, Jason T. "The Flat-7th Scale Degree in Tonal Music." Ph.D. diss., Princeton University, 2006.

Straus, Joseph N. "A Principle of Voice Leading in the Music of Stravinsky." *Music Theory Spectrum* 4 (1982): 106–124.

Tarasti, Eero. *A Theory of Musical Semiotics*. Bloomington: Indiana University Press, 1994.

———. *Signs of Music: A Guide to Musical Semiotics*. Berlin: de Gruyter, 2002.

Tarasti, Eero, ed. *Musical Semiotics in Growth*. Bloomington: Indiana University Press, 1996.

———. *Musical Semiotics Revisited*. Helsinki: International Semiotics Institute, 2003.

Temperley, David. "Communicative Pressure and the Evolution of Musical Styles." *Music Perception* 21 (2004): 313–337.

Tovey, Donald Francis. *A Musician Talks, vol. 2: Musical Textures*. Oxford: Oxford University Press, 1941.

———. *Essays and Lectures on Music*. Oxford: Oxford University Press, 1949.

Urban, Greg. "Ritual Wailing in Amerindian Brazil." *American Anthropologist* 90 (1988): 385–400.

Vaccaro, Jean-Michel. "Proposition d'un analyse pour une polyphonie vocale dux vie siècle." *Revue de musicology* 61 (1975): 35–58.

van den Toorn, Pieter. *The Music of Stravinsky*. New Haven, CT: Yale University Press, 1983.

Wallace, Robin. "Background and Expression in the First Movement of Beethoven's op. 132." *Journal of Musicology* 7 (1989): 3–20.

Walsh, Stephen. *Stravinsky: A Creative Spring: Russia and France, 1882–1934*. Berkeley: University of California Press, 1999.

Watson, Derek. *Liszt*. London: Dent, 1989.

White, Eric Walter. *Stravinsky: The Composer and His Works*. Berkeley: University of California Press, 1966.

Whittall, Arnold. *Romantic Music: A Concise Survey from Schubert to Sibelius*. London: Thames and Hudson, 1987.

———. *Musical Composition in the Twentieth Century*. Oxford: Oxford University Press, 2000.

Whitworth, Paul John. "Aspects of Mahler's Musical Style: An Analytical Study." Ph.D. diss., Cornell University, 2002.

Williamson, John. "Mahler, Hermeneutics and Analysis." *Music Analysis* 10 (1991): 357–373.

———. *Music of Hans Pfitzner*. Oxford: Clarendon, 1992.

———. "Dissonance and Middleground Prolongations in Mahler's Later Music," in *Mahler Studies*, ed. Stephen E. Hefling. Cambridge: Cambridge University Press, 1997, 248–270.

Wilson, Paul. "Concepts of Prolongation and Bartók's opus 20." *Music Theory Spectrum* 6 (1984): 79–89.

Wintle, Christopher. "Corelli's Tonal Models: The Trio Sonata op. 3, no. 1," in *Nuovissimi Studi Corelliani: Atti del Terzo Congresso Internazionale Fusignano, 1980*, ed. S. Durante and P. Petrobelli. Florence, Italy: Olschki, 1982, 29–69.

Wintle, Christopher, ed. "Hans Keller (1919–1985): A Memorial Symposium." *Music Analysis* 5 (1986): 343–440.

Wood, Patrick. "Paganini's Classical Concerti." Unpublished paper.

Zbikowski, Lawrence M. *Conceptualizing Music: Cognitive Structure, Theory, and Analysis*. New York: Oxford University Press, 2002.

———. "Musical Communication in the Eighteenth Century," in *Communication in Eighteenth-Century Music*, ed. Danuta Mirka and Kofi Agawu. Cambridge: Cambridge University Press, 2008, 283–309.

INDEX

Abbate, Carolyn, 18, 94, 103
Adorno, Theodor
  on Mahler's last works, 253–254
  on music and language, 18–19
  on narrative in Mahler, 102–103
  on Stravinsky's materials, 313
  on time in music, 213
  on tonality in Beethoven, 185
  on truth content, 320
African music, 16–17
Allanbrook, Wye Jamison, 42n.3
analysis
  criteria for, 41–107
  as mode of doing, 161–162
  nature of, 5–7, 9–12, 319–320
Andriessen, Louis, and Elmer
    Schönberger, 49
aria, 98, 283
Aristotle, 51, 53
Asafyev, 7, 46
authenticity, 27
autonomy, 3–4, 314
Ayrey, Craig, 51, 165, 166, 174

Bach, Carl Philipp Emmanuel, 26–27
Bach, Johann Sebastian, 6, 25, 300, 313n.7
  "Goldberg," Variations, 146
  Invention No. 1 in C major BWV 772,
    128, 129
  Minuet II from Suite No. 1 in G major
    BWV 1007, 144–148
  Prelude in C major from *The Well-*
    Tempered Clavier Bk. 1, 112, 115,
    148–153
  Prelude in C-sharp minor from *The*
    Well-Tempered Clavier Bk. 1, 117
background vs. foreground, 11, 111, 113
Barthes, Roland, 15, 18

Bartók, Béla, 3, 49
  "Improvisations for Piano," op. 20,
    no. 1, 90–93
  "Music for Strings, Percussion and
    Celesta," 71
Becker, Judith and Alton, 16
Beethoven, 4, 6, 7, 8, 17, 54, 93, 224,
    274, 276
  Piano Sonata in C major op. 53
    ("Waldstein"), first movement,
    127–128
  Piano Sonata in E-flat major op. 81a
    ("Les Adieux"), 257
  String Quartet in D major, op. 18, no.
    3, first movement, 184–198, 290
  String Quartet in F major, op. 59,
    no. 1, first movement, 97
  String Quartet in F major, op. 59,
    no. 1, third movement, 97–98
  String Quartet in B-flat major, op. 130,
    first movement, 12, 281–301
  String Quartet in B-flat major, op. 130,
    third movement, 99–101
  String Quartet in A minor, op. 132, first
    movement, 94–95
  String Quartet in A minor, op. 132,
    fourth movement, 101
  Symphony No. 3 ("Eroica"), 115
  Symphony No. 3 ("Eroica"), slow
    movement, 42
  Symphony No. 4, second movement,
    245
  Symphony No. 5, first movement, 25,
    103–104
  Symphony No. 5, finale, 52
  See also late Beethoven
Beethoven and Stravinsky compared,
    312–315